# The Meeting of Anni Adams

## *The Butterfly of Luxembourg*

# The Meeting of Anni Adams

## *The Butterfly of Luxembourg*

Lonnie D. Story

ACW Press
Eugene, Oregon 97405

**The Meeting of Anni Adams**


Cover Illustration by Matthew Jeffrey Adams
Cover Design by Alpha Advertising
Interior Design by Pine Hill Graphics

Packaged by ACW Press
85334 Lorane Hwy
Eugene, Oregon 97405
www.acwpress.com


Library of Congress Cataloging-in-Publication Data
*(Provided by Cassidy Cataloguing Services, Inc.)*
Story, Lonnie D.

The meeting of Anni Adams : the butterfly of Luxembourg / Lonnie D. Story. -- 1st ed. -- Eugene, Ore. : ACW Press, 2004.

p. ; cm.

ISBN: 1-932124-26-8

1. Adams, Anni. 2. Luxembourg Americans--Biography. 3. World War, 1939-1945--Women. 4. World War, 1939-1945--Personal narratives. 5. Luxembourg--History--German occupation, 1940-1944--Personal narratives. 6. Women immigrants--United States--Biography. I. Title.

E184.L88 S76 2004

304.8/73/04935--dc22 0403



**Printed in the United States of America.**

# Dedication

This book is dedicated to all of the men and women who fought and died during the dark years of World War II. To those brave men at Normandy and Bastogne. To the Sailors at sea and the Airmen who plied the skies. To those men, women and children who were family members at home in some other part of the world waiting, praying and hoping. To those that made sacrifices some have never heard tales of; such as the people that were a little less glamourous in the media but a major part of what brought justice to an evil empire of Axis Governments. Those are the men, women and children who suffered under the rule of German Armed Forces, the Nazi Regime and the Third Reich. Those that suffered indescribable grief, hardship and heartache as an occupied people in Europe. Likewise, those people that suffered in the Pacific at the hands of the Japanese. The people who suffered the thrust of the world's war machines rolling, marching and bombing their own back yards, homes and places of work. To the War Brides of World War II and all other wars. The American War Brides that left their homes and families behind to bring new strength and life to a nation that appreciates them. To their husbands who brought back a little magic and happiness from their hard fought battles.

To those who serve and have served. To the men, women and children displaced by all wars. Those that went so far as to give their own lives protecting their families, friends or compatriots against tyranny and brutality as innocent people. Those that worked day and night in work camps or other areas of forced labor away from their families and home. To the people of Luxembourg, France, Belgium, the Netherlands, Czechoslovakia, Poland and even Germany. To those that lived and those that died as witnesses to the firebrands of hell and evil incarnate in the hearts, minds and bodies of some terrible examples of humankind. To the brave at heart, all young and old, male and female that shed tears, joys, sorrows and laughter during a time when the world went "crazy". God forbid that such an apocalyptical thing occur again that the people of the earth should so challenge one another to the point of potential annihilation of all human creatures on this planet. It probably will. It is predicted by some, many. It is a curse of man that the past repeats itself and we are doomed if we, as those who have a choice, don't raise our voices as one and pray that God saves us all.

# CONTENTS

AUTHOR'S ACKNOWLEDGMENT .................... 9
ANNI'S ACKNOWLEDGMENT.................... 11
INTRODUCTION: The Butterfly of Luxembourg (Part I) .. 13

***I. FROM A "PEACEFUL" BEGINNING TO WAR CRIES ....... 15***

a. Born on a Day Dedicated to Peace .................... 17
b. A Comfortable Cocoon .................... 21
c. School friends, dreams and wishes .................... 25
d. The Butterfly spreads her wings and Flies .................... 45
e. If I dance, I dance .................... 53
f. Two fortresses for the future .................... 59
g. A glorious homeland .................... 69
h. An Iron Eagle flies over its own shadow.................... 75

***II. JOYS AND SORROWS IN THE DARK YEARS .............. 83***

a. Passover all over again, two days before Pentecost, No Less ... 85
b. Journey from home, the Butterfly's forced Flight .......... 95
c. Seclusion in a hideaway from the Storm .............. 113
d. Returning home .................... 133
e. What have they done to our Homeland? .............. 143
f. Learning the Way of the Iron Eagle.................... 157
g. Prelude to a Four Year War Song.................... 185
h. Strawberry fields aren't Forever.................... 189
i. Surviving in the Dark.................... 193
j. The "Oatmeal" Farm.................... 213
l. Freed for leaving and Finding Home .................... 227

***III. SHE'S ONE IN A MILLION; THE WAR BRIDE ERA........ 235***

a. Margot's Birthday and Three American GI's .............. 237
b. "Who is Charlie".................... 245
k. Charles Adams and the "Breakthrough Fourth" .......... 251
c. Translation Dictionary Dating Game .................... 257

d. The Aftermath of War, Courage and a Proposal .......... 263
e. Two Weddings; An Unusual Honeymoon and Love Letters .. 273
f. Love Letters from Charlie ........................................ 281
g. An American War Bride: The Adventure Begins .......... 287

***IV. COMING OF HER OWN IN AMERICA .................... 299***

a. For Better or Worse ........................................ 301
b. To Have and to Hold ........................................ 307
c. In Sickness and in Health ................................. 317
d. To Love, Honour and Cherish ............................ 329
e. They Met Anni ................................................ 337
f. Conclusion: The Butterfly of Luxembourg (Part II) ....... 351

# Author's Acknowledgments

First and foremost to my God, my Lord and Savior, Jesus Christ. To my mother, Mildred C. Prine for praying me through and being God's gift to me rather than the other way around. I love you, Mom; you are the greatest creature of faith I have ever witnessed. You are a true Proverbs 31 woman. To Papa, Frank Prine, my stepfather, for all the strength and standing beside me and behind me in all my ups and downs. To my brother Lamar, who went to be with the Lord August 19, 2003 in the middle of writing this book at the young age of forty-two years old. You kept your promise and spoke to Jesus for me. To my sister Linda, for teaching me to read and write when I was only three years old and inspiring me to fight people much bigger than me if I wanted to survive and for your dreams for me. To my brother-in-law Tuan, the most patient man I have ever known in life, you are a man of steel. To my son Shane, my whole heart and my life—my greatest award from God—who said "Dad, you just got to find your niche in life," when I started this adventure. Son, you are the greatest and more than I deserve, all my love. To my father, Capt. John O. Story, who told me "son, if a man can imagine it, it can be done." Thanks, Daddy, for showing me it is O.K. to be a dreamer and developing an unending imagination.

To Dr. Philip Jacowitz and Beverly Terry at ERAU, two of the kindest and truest friends a man could ask for; you believed in me when I didn't even believe in myself. God bless you richly. My half-sister Kathy and my good friend June, thank you for your continued prayers, faith, and love. To all my family, the Crumptons of Macon, Georgia and the Taylors of Jacksonville, Florida. To my attorney, Former Chief Judge Gayle S. Graziano, who knew the truth and delivered me from an unjust persecution. Also Gayle's staff, Wanda Nelson (a true praying and caring woman) and Cindy, for dancing at the victory. To Mr. Ed Roddy at Sunshine State Community Bank for showing me compassion on one of the darkest days of my life.

To my niece/adoptive sister, Rikki Laura, my nephews Christopher, Phillip, Shannon, Jonathan, and Joshua. To Shelley at WAPN, for being an inspiration and never permitting me to have a pity party over nine years of friendship. To all theee people and the numbers I cannot count or call upon by name. I thank you all for praying, believing, supporting, encouraging, and just being what Christ would have you be, good to others as you would have them be to you. Especially to all the readers of this work: Turn to the one true God for hope; He won't let you down. Just remember, it may be finished but it is never done. You will figure it out if you look to the Cross. To all the friends, family, and employees at ACW Press and FaithWorks, may God guide you, lead you and direct you in your every endeavor.

My humblest gratitude is not sufficient for expression. I am a blessed man, and I want every single person reading this to KNOW that they are no different than I. What God has done for me, He can and will most certainly do for you. To Anni my closest friend, what can I say? You inspired me, encouraged me, gave me a new life—we have had one heck of a wild ride. You are an amazing woman. I will always say I love you and God bless long after the ink is dry on the pages. I wrote about you and yet I cannot describe you in the words of my heart. Bless you.

God speed,
*Lonnie*

# Anni's Acknowledgment

To my son George, his wife, Jeannie, my grandsons Matthew J. and Brian Adams, and Claire. My step-granddaughter Nicole, for always being there for me. My brother Chuck and his wife Mimi. My sister Elfie, thanks for your help. My cousin Rene, niece Cindy and family. My nephew Kevin and his family. My nephew Rich Adams, sister-in-law Jeanny, sister-in-law Helen and their families. Thank you.

My family in Luxembourg: my cousin Margot, my cousin Josy, Elise and Henri with their children Marco and Guy. Their families as well. To Georgette Flammang, *merci*. The publisher Robert Stephan-Gollo and the entire Ministry of Culture, *villmols, merci.*

Monsignor E. Trench of South Hampton, whose therapy helped me get back to God. T.C. Jewell and members of the bereavement group were a great help. Thank you to my many friends in Arizona, especially the friends at Trilogy. To Gregg and Sally Schindel in Preston, AZ. My Florida friend Jean M. My neighbors, Diane and Tricia in the flower shop. My many friends in the Radiology Department at Bert Fish Hospital, New Smyrna Beach, Florida, where I am a volunteer. To the Long Island Ladies group of New Smyrna, my florist friends Dick and Lois Remis of Schenectady, NY. My many friends at FTD, Dick and Sally Schooler. My TeleFlora florist friends and Suzy at Flowerdale in Huntington, NY, whose friendship I will always treasure. My friends at Merl-Norman in New Smryna Beach, Florida. Dave and Company, thank you. All my friends at the Brannon Center in N.S. Beach Florida, thanks.

Sharon Gillmore, golf pro at Turnbull Bay Golf Course. Michelle, my former boss. Alan Contessa, my special friend on Long Island. Barbara and Christian Molsen of Germany and Cathy and Fred from Long Island, thanks. All these people and many others have had a place in my heart. My sincerest thanks to all and may God bless you all. Thank you to my friends at the Bible get together, Mary and Mary Lou. You all helped me believe what I could be and all that I am. To my God in whom I trust, show me the stairway I have to climb, Lord. For my sake, God, teach me to take one day at a time.

To my dear friend, Lonnie: My heartfelt thanks for writing this biography just the way I lived it. May this book be the beginning of many more such ventures, for you are truly a blessed man with a great and compassionate gift for writing. You most surely have made the rest of my life a most memorable one, and it will allow you to give others hope and faith in God. The same God who has been so good to me during my entire life.

With love and thanks,
*Anni*

# Introduction: The Butterfly of Luxembourg (Part I)

Nature and science teach us that a butterfly cannot reenter its cocoon once it has developed, once it has freed itself to life on the wind and vineyards. I tend to disagree with that unfortunate observation and terminal inequity because I have found a creature that does that very thing. While the cocoon—brown, dark brown, or even black in color—depicts an outward personification of unattractiveness, it is the inner containment that explains its need, purpose and existence. Why shouldn't we look at such an object and examine the beauty on the outside shell? The shiny, glossy appearance of the smooth object. Its impregnable fortress-like strength and resolve to protect what lies inside. The lackluster shell does such a marvelous job of harboring a very precious cargo.

It was in mid-March, 2003 that I encountered this extraordinary creature with its unique and incredibly curious ability. It was a fairly ordinary day on my round of errands that I stopped at Six Sisters Flower Shop in New Smyrna Beach, Florida to pick up some flowers for my sister. By happenstance, Tricia, the owner and operator, wasn't in and a stranger was manning the shop. At this most unforeseeable moment, I met Anni (pronounced *AH-nee*) Adams, and a life-impacting change occured. While that may sound somewhat dramatic, it is nevertheless the truth. You see, Anni Adams is indeed a unique person. She is the butterfly that can reenter the cocoon. Why do I say that? Well, you would have to meet Anni Adams to understand, and that is the very purpose of recording this remarkable woman in writing.

If you are fortunate enough to see her outside that protective bearing, or if you are trustworthy enough to peek inside, you will find the most inexplicable character, representing a way of life that contradicts all that most of us would ever consider. If you see her outside the shell or receive that cherished opportunity to peek inside, you will discover a butterfly such as no person has ever perceived. You will find a wingspan that is enormous in width and height, built and developed from the harsh pulls of the gravity of living. You will find a strong, resilient body, perfected for survival. At the head of such a phenomenal creature you will find the encasement of a mind that has become a storage machine, a history of moods, emotions, joyous feelings and hardships, with purpose and determination. The purest form of honesty that you will ever have the pleasure of knowing resides therein.

While you are about to ask yourself, "Just what is it besides all that, which makes this person so unusual or unique?," imagine the wings. Unusually oversized, beautifully ornate wings carry this creature. They extend beyond the norm because of all the very necessities of life. On these wings are paintings of suffering, laughter, anguish, sorrow and hope. These wings, if you see them, are the most entrancing kaleidoscopes of rainbow colors on a palette that depict every episode, adventure, tragedy and success of a woman born into an untimely world, thrust into adversity and survival at its purest form. You will see a rainbow of colors that reflect a multitude of experiences most of us could not imagine. The life of one woman that was born and lived, and lived as life gave it to her. Stubborn, strong, innocent, determined, gentle, kind and most of all, resilient.

As you read this account of her life, my deepest hope and desire is that you will see a strand of character in Anni Adams that few, very few, possess. The wings described will be explored color by color, collection and incorporation. I hope you will see the way in which this "butterfly" was forced from its cocoon on May 10, 1940. A world was going to war in her own backyard. On a black morning two days before the celebration of Pentecost, in the darkness of night and in a world torn in two by the inhumanities of war, she was thrust, at fourteen years of age, into sixty-three years of flight on the winds of life.

Anni took an unusual approach for any person or butterfly. Rather than flying her own course or setting out for her own destination, she rode the wind with her wings spread. If the wind blew hard, she drifted to the lighter side. If the winds were gentle, she flew to new heights. She never sought any particular nectar; she had an inborn knowledge that this flight itself was the nectar that sustained her. A grating epitaph was forged in her mind, her father's most unforgettable statement, "Anni, learn." The foundation of that simple instruction was her key to survival. Not only did she "make it," she learned, and she learned more than most of us could imagine. This is Anni's story. The Butterfly of Luxembourg.

# Part I

# From a "Peaceful" Beginning to War Cries

# Born on a Day Dedicated to Peace

*WHEREAS the 11th of November 1918, marked the cessation of the most destructive, sanguinary, and far reaching war in human annals and the resumption by the people of the United States of peaceful relations with other nations, which we hope may never again be severed, and*

*WHEREAS it is fitting that the recurring anniversary of this date should be commemorated with thanksgiving and prayer and exercises designed to perpetuate peace through good will and mutual understanding between nations; and*

*WHEREAS the legislatures of twenty-seven of our States have already declared November 11 to be a legal holiday: Therefore be it Resolved by the Senate (the House of Representatives concurring), That the President of the United States is requested to issue a proclamation calling upon the officials to display the flag of the United States on all Government buildings on November 11 and inviting the people of the United States to observe the day in schools and churches, or other suitable places, with appropriate ceremonies of friendly relations with all other peoples.*

An Act (52 Stat. 351; 5 U. S. Code, Sec. 87a) approved May 13, 1938, and the 11th of November in each year a legal holiday—a day to be dedicated to the cause of world peace and to be hereafter celebrated and known as "Armistice Day."

*On Armistice Day, November 11, 1918, the German armies had marched homeward in good order. "They fought well," said Marshall Ferdinand Foch, Generalissimo of the Allies, speaking in soldierly mood: "let them keep their weapons." But he demanded that the French frontier should henceforth be the Rhine. Germany might be disarmed, she might become prey to internal feuds, but all this would pass in ten years or in twenty. The indestructible might "of all the German tribes" would rise once more and the unquenched fires of warrior Prussia glow and burn again. But the Rhine, the broad, deep, swift-flowing, Rhine once held and fortified by the French Army, would be a barrier and a shield behind which France could dwell and breathe for generations. Very different were the sentiments and views of the English-speaking world, without whose aid France must have succumbed. The territorial provisions of the Treaty of Versailles left Germany practically intact. When Marshall Foch heard of the signing of the Peace Treaty of Versailles he observed with singular accuracy: "This is not Peace. It is an Armistice for twenty years."*

The Second World War by Winston S. Churchill and the editors of LIFE; Golden Press, New York, Copyright 1960; ppg. 13.

On November 11, 1926, in the Neuman residence at approximately 11:00 P.M., an hour before the night-breaking of a new day, a baby girl was pulled forth from her mother's womb into a world with a future as uncertain as the child herself, and on Armistice Day, no less.

Anny Jeanne Neuman (her true and given name prior to it being changed by the German occupying forces) came to breathe her first breath of "free air" in the home of her father, Albert Jakob Neuman (Albert Jacques Neuman, again the Nazi propagandized influence), and her mother, Margaretha Bost Neuman (Real name: Marguerite Bost Neuman (anything sounding French was changed) at Rue Ancion 17, Esch-Sur-Alzette (pronounced *Esh-Zur- Al Zeh*), Luxembourg.

Anni was born on a day dedicated to the hope of all mankind, or at least so intended by the rulers of the time. It was their hope that the end of the world's first war should be celebrated with a dream of a world made civilized—hope that the world could learn from its worst widespread disaster to date and be determined to maintain peace. A hope and compromise had been forged at Versailles and there was a collective sigh of relief in 1918. However, it was eight years of supposed enduring freedom and abstinence of conflict to this special day of a memorial to a father, who prayed for a son, and a mother who survived her first child's birth with the help of a midwife in their small factory-subsidized home. In the greatest irony of all, this little baby girl would grow another thirteen years to be torn from this very hometown three days prior to the celebration of **"The United States of America's Act 52 granted May 13, 1938, approving the November 11th Armistice Day Resolution."** It would be May 10, 1940 when she would be ripped from her comfort, torn from her peace, deprived of her happiness and forced into a world gone bizarre through terror, fear and disbelief. It was irony of the worst kind. The world's seventh largest exporter of iron, her home and country of Luxembourg, would fall into the hands of an Iron Eagle's talons, soon to be known as "The Third Reich."

It was 1926, the year Stalin established control over the Soviet Republic Union (USSR); Gertrude Ederle swam the English Channel in 14 hours, 31 minutes; it was twelve days before Adolf Hitler would recite his infamous "Speech at Essen" maligning and blaming Germany's problems upon Jews and Mother Russia. It was one month before the December publication of ***Mein Kampf*** by A. Hitler spewing the following text: "I used to think it an ill-deserved stroke of bad luck that I had arrived too late on this terrestrial globe, and I felt sad at the idea that my life would have to run its course along peaceful and orderly lines." If only that had been the case. While Hitler, at a critical thirty-seven years of age, mused his grave-song over an untimely birth, he set a course to rise like the proverbial Phoenix from the ashes. Meanwhile, a "larva" of sorts had developed and squirmed in its cocoon. Adolf Hitler had formed a plan for the future of Germany from his obsession to change and make his ideal conformations of "his" country and rule it himself. While he invited and ignored the costs of blood, body and sacrifices, a "pupa" had taken form and readied to break forth in the village of Esch-Sur-Alzette, Luxembourg.

While evil was incarnating from city to city throughout Deutschland, innocence was balancing the scale as a simple little baby girl was birthed into a small country caught in a world filled with hypocrisies, fantasies, dreams, politics, hunger and gluttony. Where one happened to be at the moment the clock ticked in "time eternal" on planet Earth determined what part pertained to whom. It was a time of unknowns, a time of "who would be and who wouldn't, what would occur and what vanquished, what dream became ethereally real, what hope became disaster, what lust became lost and what love became life." That was the year Anni Neuman was born and it was just the beginning of a divine plan to create color in a gray-black, dreary and dark world. She wasn't alone. God had others throughout His creation, but for this time and place, she possessed the yet unformed wings for a palette in testimony to how one survives by grace and grit.

For Albert and Marguerite Neuman, this was the time of culmination. A time that represented and reiterated their love for one another. Albert was a twenty-seven-year-old locksmith and lathe operator at the Arbed Iron Industrial Company and his lovely Marguerite, a twenty-three-year-old homemaker, wife, mother, and laborer wherever her feet stood. All this was overseen by the paternal grandmother, Deddy, Anni's great-grandmother. The three adults had now been encouraged, excited and influenced (willingly and unwillingly) by the little pudgy child which had burst forth into their world and circumstances. All this had taken place in company housing, apartments rented to the workers of Arbed, part of the "benefit" package for Albert's labors.

A cradle was placed at the foot of a chair, better yet, a foot was placed upon a cradle, as Deddy rocked away the hours and days during the first months of Anni's baby-life. Sustained by goat's milk, Anni grew daily, to the pleasure and pride of her parents. Their greatest joy came from the simple fact that their firstborn child was healthy, living and thriving. Deddy would lullaby the baby as she fastened her handiwork in her lap, passing the days in thought, consternation and prognostication of the evening with her grandson, his wife and this pink little package on the tip of her toes. It was a hard and heavy-tasked life for all except Anni, but it wasn't a waste; it was a pleasure, laughter and curiosity. The Neuman family was growing and a new generation was wrapped warmly in a wooden box set on rockers, with the cargo inside insulated against the breath of death, old man cold. Winter had come, but the apartment was a home and the home was warmed with love.

# A Comfortable Cocoon

***"Anni, dance for Papa, show him how you can dance!"***

It didn't take long for Anni to grow from Deddy's feet to find her own. Although cow's milk was something the child just could not digest (and though it was a pain and inconvenience to the family) goat's milk nurtured baby Anni into a healthy and happy, energetic child. Grandmother, or whoever was at call, would have to take the coins to the store up the road or to the house a few streets away and purchase the tin pail of goat's milk for the baby. For Papa, it was a worthy investment. Though he wanted a boy, this girl was the twinkle in his eye and the rolling in his heart. She would be a project of sorts for him. She would be strong, tough, educated and equal to, if not better than, the boys Albert trained in gymnastics. He was not going to let her "being a girl" deprive him from having his very own protege child.

If cows are lethargic upon the grazing field, it is fair that the milk of bucking, skipping and tromping goats was the source of liquid-life to this baby girl. She was by no means representative of the cattle on any hill; she was already showing signs that she was just as rambunctious as any kid goat and ready to stomp off on a full run. Of course, she would fall headlong and headfirst to the ground or whatever happened to be in her direction but that slowed her none. By age fifteen months, at least two months ahead of schedule, little Anni was already on her feet and near flights of fancy, to the detriment and energetic demise of the adults in the house. Quick and sharp, she sprang up, away and maneuvered around faster than their eyes could tell their hands to grab her. Spunky was an understatement. The child had excessive energy and a sure foot, even if she appeared a little bow-legged and wobbly. She was a lot to handle and getting a handle was always the challenge. Whether inside the home, out to the street or in a field of tall grass, Anni was movement. She embodied the perpetual-motion clock that has yet to be invented. From fumbling footsteps to feats of fancy and on to flight of foot, she rose as the butterfly that danced on the ground, the floor, the seashore and the wind as well.

At eighteen months, Anni was already doing her own little stomp, spin, hop and giggle, to the encouragement of Deddy and to the entertainment of Papa when he came home from his long day at the Iron Mill. Albert Neuman worked the factory life for a while as a locksmith and lathe operator, but he was a gymnast at heart and a very good teacher of the art. Albert also knew when one possessed the talent and skills the sport required. He did not hold back his delight when Deddy would tell young baby Anni to dance for Papa and she would, with great delight upon her cherried face. Her laughs and giggles would fill the house as she stomped her own little jig with her tiny, well-found feet and sturdy legs. Deddy, Mama and Papa would laugh and clap at her antics. She didn't feel like a fool, she wasn't being made sport of, she was genuinely being nurtured to be a free spirit, daring in a moment and learning to exercise mind and body as God intended.

By age two, Anni was a whirlwind of "where did she go," continuing her challenge of wills with the adults. She was everywhere and into everything. If curiosity did kill the cat, pittance to the cat because Anni had more lives than a thousand of them. Her curiosity could not be squelched and her speed of hand and foot matched the mind to a near dangerous level. All this, of course, was of great use to Papa because his baby girl was a natural for gymnastics. The sport demanded the very nature Anni possessed. It was a match made by heaven. Anni the dancing baby and Papa the gymnastics professor. By age three Anni was already an integral part in the local town gymnastics team with young children and young adults much her senior.

At the most inconvenient time for stubborn, strong-willed, "pain-in-the-neck" Anni came a new challenge. On July 20, 1929, the minor child and firstborn son to Anni's parents arrived. He would be dubbed Albert Neuman after his father. Competition had unwelcomed its way into Anni's near three-year reign as the child master of the home. Anni, with all her energy and assertiveness, was not one to play with dolls. However, she didn't resent this new "Albert." Instead, she took great curiosity in him because for the little child she was, she had not seen a baby so close and now a part of the family. It was intriguing at the least but at most, and more important, it was education and Anni thrived on education.

At age three, Anni was the top of the human pyramid and the focal point of pictures, applause and attention. The gymnastics team was not only well-choreographed, but well-trained and entertaining to the local community. They had grown under the masterful hands of her father, Albert, to become a team of top performers at carnivals, festivals and competitions leading beyond Luxembourg to France and Germany. All the while, Anni was its youngest member but no less an artist and performer. As she entered into her fourth year of life, she had begun summer trips to the south of France to stay for a month or so with her aunt. During the remaining days of those early years she passed weekdays and some Saturdays playing "beat the clock," hastily putting her shoes on before Papa's arrival at 2:00 P.M. Then it was off to the gym for classes.

These days continued forward, each with its own special touch of grace, curiosity, work and intermittent frustrations. In the simple home at Rue Ancion 17, the Neuman family grew. The sun would rise and set. The snows would come and melt. The stars would shine at times and the rains would bring flowers and vegetables into the large garden outside. The small house with the stable attached to it and an outside toilet was surrounded by a hedgerow of guardian plum trees and currants, both black and red. Inside was the cocoon that protected the close-knit family from the weather outside. They enjoyed the privacy and security of an unarmed fortress with Papa in full charge and command. Young Albert continued to grow, as well did Anni, and he became a little play partner for her Before long Anni had turned age six, and it was time to start school. Time had not stood still, just as it never has nor will, and a new era in this little girl's life was to begin with new demands, rewards, tests and explorations.

# School Friends, Dreams and Wishes

The year 1932 was coming to a close and 1933 was only months away. It was in no wise a year uneventful. There were both highlights and lowering of lights. For the year, Werner Karl Heisenberg had won the Nobel Prize in Physics for his scholarly work and professorship at the Leipzig University in Germany. John Galsworthy was presented with the Nobel Prize in Literature for his distinguished art of narration in the highest level for his writing of *The Forsyte Saga*, the novel based upon the chronicles of a well-to-do family torn by conflict between propriety and passions. It was a story of enormous proportions of social turmoil in class boundaries, reflecting upon the weak sides of the characters in contrast to their unbreakably strong convictions. It was, upon hindsight, an adequate synopsis of the time and times both fore and aft of the literary "ship" traveling upon the truth of humankind and the state of the world.

The United States was in the midst of its Great Depression, brought forth some three years prior by the stock market collapse. By now, the trickles of gross failures in the economy, as a whole, had developed into a torrential flood upon the plains of the countryside and throughout the rural areas, drowning the American farmer with disaster. Poverty was at its all-time worst in the history of the young nation, and hope seemed distant eternal at best.

It was of biblical crisis, a time when a true neighbor with two cloaks literally shared one with the neighbor owning an extra pair of shoes. Together, the country would survive. Not because of strength of the government or government programs but because the instinct, will and necessity of survival was thrust onto the shoulders of the average American and the decision was: There wasn't a choice. Some tried and survived. Some died trying and some died because basic needs could not be met. Sadness and sorrow were easily found in the struggle of it all, but as is customary to mankind, some rose to new heights and others celebrated personal victories. Success stories continued to grow from the gloomy grounds and there were still chances, here and there, for a barn dance, a new song or a holiday to humbly celebrate.

It was in this year that the great American composer, John Phillip Sousa, passed away. He had become a child prodigy at the age of six years old. His father had enlisted him into the United States Marine Corps for his best benefit at the ripe young age of thirteen years old. Master Sousa served his country and no less than five presidents during his lifetime while making a life's sacrifice to music. There were innumerable orchestrations, symphonic presentations, field drills with marching bands and the list goes on to this day attesting to his substantial contribution to the music world and worldly betterment through the joys of music. He was a true master and Master Sousa literally died doing what he loved best. At age seventy-seven, John Phillip Sousa slumped to the floor in front of the lit stage of music artisans brought together for his guidance. He was felled by time and at a time when he was yet to provide one more great presentation to an awaiting audience that would never hear the last and final performance of the composer and maestro. The practice session ended on a sad note, but the works of the musical genius went forward with his spirit and continues in flight today upon a cacophony of notes in melodies by the numbers.

In this era, a sensation was sweeping the United States and Europe. The song "Mimi" was at the top of the charts and America's new favored French singer, Mssr. Maurice Chavalier, was soothing the romantic hearts of all by his velvet voice (Anni would later meet him personally in a Paris train station in the far distant future, among many other renowned persons throughout her life). Songs such as "All of Me," "Brother can you Spare a Dime," "Night and Day," "Masquerade" and "Paradise" were riding the airwaves to entertain, enlighten, and provide respite and hope to the audiences of radio, phonograph, big bands and human songbirds.

All the while, a new era was beginning in the small town of "Esch" in Luxembourg, in the heart of Europe and in the simple home of the Neuman family. It was time for Little Albert (affectionately now known as "Bubby") and Anni to shift from homebodies to students. In Luxembourg, formal education starts early, the earlier the better. It is a European tradition of sorts and was a standard as old as "kindergarten" or "Children's Garden."

Indeed, it is a place where the children are somewhat "planted" in their assigned seats and rows and then nurtured to grow in mind. Because Anni did not turn six until November, she had to start her educational journey at a simple stone and mortar storefront. She would trek the six blocks daily with her living baby doll, the young three-year-old brother, Albert. "Anni, take your brother's hand and do not let go for any reason. Walk straight to school, don't talk to anyone and do not stop along the way. Bubby, you take sister's hand and do not let go, do as she says and stay with her until you come home." These were the strict instructions of their mother on the first morning and every morning to follow for the continuing year as the two grew together in age, education, love, affection and a budding bond that would last a lifetime.

As the days and weeks passed, it turned to months and the school year would soon end in May, 1933. It was now time for Anni to move up to the "big" school a mile away from home. The time together with Bubby walking to school, sharing the same classroom, returning home and even having him placed in her charge at home fostered Anni's deep love for Bubby. They filled their days with laughter and play. Anni didn't care for dolls like most girls her age and she really didn't need one anyway. In fact, the only doll Anni did possess was a unique doll for its time, a negro doll. It was a favorite, and something that would influence her in all remaining years of her life, that there is no room for prejudice. You judge the product of the person, not the appearance.

Anni not only mothered young Albert, but she became something of a brooding hen over him. She had a strong maternal instinct and this instinct would be suctioned for all it was worth in the dark years of war that lay in the future none too distant. Anni would have to be as wise as her grandmother, strong as her mother, smart as her father and as innocent as her brother. She became a puzzle completed from the best attributes of each member of the family. Thus, she grew in her uniqueness even though she had no working knowledge of it. For her it was something natural and that was the way that it came.

The time had come for Anni to rise earlier, 7:00 A.M. to be exact, at the rousing of her mother's hands to drearily shuffle to the table with eyes still blurred by sleep. There, young Bubby would already be seated with bread in his hand and jam on his face and fingers. She would sit in her chair next to him and Mama would put the plate in front her, "Hurry Anni, eat and get yourself and Bubby to school, it's getting late" she would exclaim into Anni's ear and over her shoulder. This scene would play out morning after morning and there was no count to the times of it. It was natural, part of her life and she liked it. Anni had a lust for education that would cause her to dangle her feet at the table, drink her coffee, as Bubby did, and eat her bread and jam while the anticipation of learning brought her from sleepiness to fidgety excitement.

It is now November, 1933 and the winter is starting to make its announcement of "weather in charge." Anni pulls on her high-top leather shoes, boots of sort, with a few inches of cover above the ankle, leather bound with hardened soles. The toes of the shoes curl upward as if bent permanently from the wear and weather they were made to breach. In the corner of the dark mid-room of the two-bedroom home, young Albert pries on his own shoes of the same sort upon his tender young feet. They rise and brace themselves for the early morning cold just outside the door that barriers them from the warmth of glowing embers in the wood stove and fireplace with its ashen-piled remnants representing the source of survival against all mother nature has at her disposal.

The two young children join hands and approach the door to the street outside and burst out the invisible wall with exhilaration as the wind rushes down the street. They propel themselves in the predestined trek that will take them hand-in-hand to kindergarten for Bubby. Anni then makes her roundabout of solo travel in the opposite direction down the ever-long Victor Hugo Street, past the cemetery, toward the school she attends. She braces herself against the weather until she reaches the forebodingly large concrete, stone and marble school nearly a mile from home and in passing to the place where the nuns will be coming soon for first class.

The children are anxious to scuttle and scurry all about and she is unable to control her energy. She is ready to shovel her way through the crowded passageway at the large double-door entrance of the mighty fortress. The three-story sarcophagus of living bones sits waiting to be breathed to life with a fleshly world of knowledge. She bounds up the marble stairs to the second floor where the girls turn left and the boys turn right, each down the long corridors of formal education, social interaction and development. By the time the nuns have come and gone and the priest, his holy father (name long forgotten), has shared his weekly advice, the morning begins to wane. The nuns have started the day with discipline, discipleship and repetitious, traditional occupations. All the while the sun has warmed the air outside and the ground has melted from cold, hard apparent death to springing life.

The lunch bell sounds with a second's late notice to the internal clock in Anni's mind and body. At the trumpeting sound she is already on her feet, aiming for the way out and toward her precious Bubby and home for lunch, the largest and most important meal of the day. She bounds down the wide marble steps through the gaping mouth of the giant's hold and into the sunlight of the winter's day. She traverses the mile's journey and arrives at the kindergarten just a matter of blocks from home. With her charge in hand, she heads to the doorway of the warm abode on Rue Ancione where mother and grandmother await. Inside, the aroma of a cooked meal waters her mouth, warms her soul and enlivens her spirit. "Bubby, there's nothing to eat, nobody is here!" she teases. Poor Bubby looks up at Sis and says, "Anni, I smell the food, I am hungry, don't be mean." They both laugh and begin to shed their outer garments of winter wear and shoes. It is time to let their socks dry out and enjoy the next hour at home before the remainder of the day at school and gorge their appetites with the contents of the large-bellied pot on the stove.

Mama has been busy while her children were away feeding their minds and imagination. She has exercised her own creative ability at home. The large pot on the stove has simmered to a thickened stew of fresh cabbage, potatoes, carrots, onions and chunks of pork with salt. A large loaf of bread is set at the table within easy reach of each bowl. As Grandma ladles out the stew to the two starving children, they laugh some more and grab a fistful each of bread. "Children!" Grandma reproves, "Say your prayers or you will have water for lunch tomorrow!" Both baby Albert and Sissy Anni bow heads and recite the teachings of the nuns. Bless the food, bless the family, bless us all and thank the Lord.

They feast upon the meal before them and another round of filled bowls is needed within minutes. There isn't much talk at the table, since it is Papa's rule that quiet is the conformity of appreciation for meals served. But, he is at work and some innocuous conversation occurs between Anni, Grandmother and Mother. Bubby chimes in with his latest song learned at kindergarten. The Neuman home is filled to bursting with faith, hope, love and joy.

After downing a bowl of cool applesauce, the children ready themselves for the remaining hours of the day at their respective schools. With the pungent taste of cinnamon still in their mouths, they don their soggy shoes and heavy coats to leave. "Anni, take Bubby's hand! Bubby, hold on to Sissy and don't let go!" Mama states this remarkable repetition on a daily basis so that it remains ingrained in their minds that they should be responsible for one another and most of all, stay as close together as brother and sister can be.

As they scurry past the door and out onto the sidewalk, Anni picks up speed to the unfair challenge of little Albert's feet. She is hustling and hurrying to return to the place where learning is living and learning is life. Poor Bubby can hardly keep two steps to her one, but he tries and falters behind, still clinging to her hand. "Anni! slow down, I'm trying to keep up with you, Mama says I can' let go." Anni slows her pace enough to keep young Albert in tow but her body is electrified with the thrill of the afternoons' learning. Soon enough, bubby is at the stone house kindergarten blocks from home. Then the race is on. Anni forges on another mile to the large, looming building in the opposite direction with the comforting knowledge that the nuns are gone and the balance of the day will be spent with her favorites—language, math, gymnastics and history. The best part of learning is the untold stories to young minds and the repetitions of old and ancient recitals brought forth from the wellspring of the elderly.

Knowledge is brought forth and handed down from books, yes, but books set to ink and paper from minds and memories of those having lived before this day and brought to life over and over again from years, decades and centuries past. The wonder of it all is that to Anni, it all applies to today, and when she wakes each day hence, it will apply again throughout every year to come.

Seven-year-old Anni is growing fast in a slow world of deep-rooted European tradition. December rolls in on the whirls of snowflakes as flighty and flitting as the butterfly in spring or the bumblebee on wings. This morning is special. Today, the sun is rising upon a blinding white snow outside the windows, and after a fast-paced breakfast, Anni does her duty by getting young Albert to school and herself on the path to a day of full anticipation.

Anni loves the physical. If it is climbing, jumping, running, dancing, the beat goes forward with her imagination and heart's desire. The girl loves life and lives for motion. Inaction is just too melancholy for her.

Everything has to be at an energized level that is beyond the norm for most adults or children. Of course, Papa would have it no other way. His protege is a powerhouse of energy and entertainment to herself and to those that behold her. Today is a skating field trip. This puts Anni in throes of exhilaration that words cannot describe. Her class will be checking out ice-skates and hiking through the ankle-deep snow to the frozen pond on the iron company's property.

They head out from the school, past the factories and into the open field that leads to the pine-encircled water hole with its massive crust of ice keeping its charge of the waters below and yet providing a protective barrier to the interlopers above. And interlope they do, by the dozens. The children don their skates and scramble to the surface of flight, fantasy and speeding, inherent danger. This is where children belong, challenging mother nature. It is a place where a child becomes all alone in the crowd, exploring what they are made of and what risks they are willing to take to be happy and satisfied with themselves. Anni is satisfied and then some. She laces her skates tight and hits the icy surface with a charge of adrenaline, excitement and joy. When it comes to the physical, fear doesn't even enter her thoughts. Papa would be proud because this is the way he raised her—this was his intention and purpose all along.

After two hours on the ice, without noticing the temperature due to the wealth of exertion, the children all are cackled in by the teachers. It is time to return to the school, then home for lunch. Each child disengages the razor-sharp utensils of wonderland from their feet, their magic shoes, and returns to the sturdy, practical leather and lacings of worn footwear that protect their tender feet from the seasons. Line upon line of children with adult guides wind their way back to the schoolhouse with skates slung over their shoulders.

The mile trek having been accomplished amongst taunts, laughter, teasing and chastisement from the teachers, the group bounds into the school to store their goods of freedom and brace themselves for the remainder of the day. All too soon the field trip has ended and there remains a half day of disciplined learning at the hard seat of a wooden desk. The good news is that it is time to head home for lunch. The laughter and freedom of the field trip will carry them into the rest of the week and make school life bearable.

Now that the skating equipment has been stowed away and the children returned to their winter dress, the teachers release them homeward by unison of command and each child rushes through the doors and outbound on their stomach-driven desire to open the door of "home" and smell something (anything) that represents food and eating to satisfy the adventures and the soul. Anni speedily makes her heart-wrenching way past home to gather Bubby from kindergarten and practically drags him back to the house where they once again take their respective seats at the table for a feast. To make the day more spectacular already special memory, Mama has made omelettes for the two darlings—fluffy folded eggs, puffed and steaming with cheese, ham and potatoes.

Childhood isn't so bad here; in fact, life is pretty good. It is good because family and friends make it that way. Reality, truth and perception all have their place, but for the children, it is the best that can be offered and it is better than the adults could imagine. The children take the simple, even hard, things and make them into their own life of joy. Only good memories last. If something isn't fun or joyous, it is thrown out and forgotten in the shadow of happiness.

By early April, 1934, things aren't as happy anymore. Young Anni is advised that she is to prepare for departure from the family home. She should pack immediately for a journey to a children's home north of here for nearly four months. "Why?" Well, no one will give her a straight answer. In fact, the questions are almost regarded as an offense and handled accordingly. Anni is not permitted to question this matter nor the circumstances which have propelled her into an unhappy hiatus from her home and family life, and especially her baby-doll brother, Bubby. "Why all the secrets, whisperings and this casting me away?" Anni asks herself. "What did I do? Did I do something wrong? Is something bad happening to Mama and Papa? Shouldn't I be here? Don't they need me for whatever it is?" But the questions won't get answered. She is placed on a train and sent away to the children's home for reasons unknown.

Early that April morning, Anni travels to the suburbs of Luxembourg City. Here she takes residence in an inconspicuous home for children who need temporary placement for one reason or the other. The wonderful care and concern of the Arbed Iron Company has assisted once again through one of its numerous programs to aid its workers and employees.

Four months pass and Anni continues her education in this foreign environment. True to her character, she has adapted once again to the change and challenge as if it were a whisper of wind on the cheek. She sweeps her hair back with her hands and pulls a brush through her tangled hair in front of the mirror. It is morning and word has been passed along to her that her father will be arriving within the hour. She is finally on her way home again, never forsaken by her family, only shrouded from a mystery that will later prove to be nothing more than old-fashioned propriety—an example of human nature and the inability of the age to share the dark secrets of the marvelous light of life and how it begins. The sweet truth hidden in a requiem of silence.

Papa arrives and Anni is again alive with bubbling joy. She hugs her father with great thankfulness just to behold his handsome figure. He is an arresting wall against the fears of an unknown world. She is ready to return her spirited life to the quiet comfort of his protection. However, there are still mysteries of silence from her father that Anni cannot decipher with all her skills at their working best. They sit side by side on the sparsely cushioned seat for the two-hour train ride home. Time after time, Papa glances or even gazes at his young girl child. He starts to speak and stops.

He turns his attention to the distance, although Anni feels it as as close as his strong arm next to her. He feels closer than ever to his lovely oldest child and daughter but he cannot bring the words to mouth. He is too troubled too express the reason behind all this goings on. An even greater surprise is coming closer by the passing of minutes which seem like hours. He must tell her but he cannot and does not, the train slides to a bumpy halt at the station and the opportunity is lost. But they are home now and let it be as it may be.

Upon arrival at the Neuman residence, she and Papa open the door into a world befitting *Alice in Wonderland*. The house is still the same. The walls are all in place, the furniture in order, the smell of food from the kitchen floods the house. The floors are worn as ever by the repetitious, short-footed journeys within. Suddenly, however, without the barest of warning, an alarm sounds from within the candlelit home and Anni knows the basis of the mystery. It is the cry of an innocent baby, enlightening Anni's ever so young and tender heart.

The Neuman family has a new member—that was what the whole silly secret was about. For four months, Anni sweltered in curiosity and torment of imagination, only to find that there was a new baby brother in the house. Her baby-doll and endearing playmate, Albert, had a younger brother to watch over and Anni had an addition to her duties, a double load. On April 30, 1934, with leaves, flowers and feathers on birds being renewed or made anew, with life springing forth from the cool ground to the warming sun, a child had been born in Esch, once again.

Charles "Charly" (later Chuck) Neuman, came forth from a comfortable womb into a world ever growing in adversity, unlike the times of his older sister and brother. This child would face dangers beyond comprehension in a very short span of time, envisioned in a way that could only be seen through his child's eyes. The older children were no less warned or surprised, but at the least, they had been given maturity by time and instructions from adults about survival.

Over the next two years the world continued to spin on its axis and the Moon and the Sun took their daily turns possessing the skyline over planet Earth. As the planetary revolutions repeated inexhaustibly, mankind was in no mood for repetition, or at least not for the present time. New things were continually coming forth in the world at large and news was always a few steps away from the door, at the foot of the sidewalk or over the neighbor's hedge. It all came as close as the daily paper, the radio broadcast or the scuttlebutt at a political cocktail party.

The year 1935 offered escapes from the reality of a horrific economic depression squalling over the United States like a hurricane in slow motion. For a few cents, one could dive into a Saturday matinee and relax in the air-conditioned hideaway of the theater and see the latest big hit. *Mutiny on the Bounty* was the highest grossing film of the year at an unbelievable $4.5 million in revenues, with macho, young American girls' heartthrob, Clark Gable filling the screen along with Charles Laughton.

The Plymouth Motor Company introduced its first of a kind automobile touting its ability to carry seven passengers in comfort and luxury. It was the Convertible Coupe, with a rumble seat, dressed out and ostentatious with its brass headlights, rich wood-grained interior and ivory knobs for all the interior controls and handles. It was a fastback, anticipating the future of sporting vehicles, and would later earn its reputation as a "rumble seat" car for more risque reasons. It was reasonably affordable at the showroom price of approximately $700.

Big band music was taking the world by storm on radio, dance floors, living rooms and honky-tonks as well as ballroom parlors. Swing had reached full swing in an era that would last another ten years. A young black artist by the name of Louis Armstrong would be at the helm, challenging his audience with high-strung, full-speed, swirling jazz never heard before nor since.

On the dark side of the world, Germany had succumbed to the full puppetry and control of Adolf Hitler. His command was unchallengeable.

He was still marking his course for the destiny of his black heart's desire. With the grin of a hyena, Adolf had reinstated the conscript of males for military service. He did this in direct violation of his, and his predecessor's, treaties with leading nations. He ordered and orchestrated the rapid development of a war machine with all its tools through army, air force and navy at a dizzying, round-the-clock pace.

As the year 1935 ebbed out with the tide, 1936 rolled in on its heels and flooded the world with a frantic new pace of industry, politics, worldwide uneasiness and trepidation. Hitler had proposed a remarkably absurd twenty-five-year peace plan with Britain, France, Belgium and Italy. The offer was actually being considered by the morally-mused, fantasy-eyed offerees. The diversion of the loftily-placed, street-level hoodlum (in control of his own country) went unheeded to because of his anesthesia-like methods. He gorged his appetite and took control, through military might of the peaceful Rhineland without so much as a wince from the rest of the world. In great irony, the world Olympics were held in Germany that same year in celebration of fair and equitable competition under the rules of good sportsmanship.

Evil became more apparent as Adolf Hitler refused to recognize the accomplishments of the world's gold medalist runner, the American, Jesse Owens. It was a total affront common to the bigoted prejudiced, perverted ideals of the Iron Eagle. Albert Neuman was there to shake Jesse's hand and congratulate him. On a better note, across the Atlantic Ocean, the New York Yankees had taken the first place title of the American League in major league baseball and launched forward to take the World Series title by a victory of 4-2. The movie *Swing Time* starring Fred Astaire and Ginger Rogers took the cinema by storm and ruled the year at a time when Hollywood was churning out "feel-good" movies for the depression. As a finale, the year's Oscar for Best Song went to "The Way You Look Tonight" as sung by Astaire in the movie while sitting at the piano and crooning to his darling Ginger.

In the same year, on a playground outside the large schoolhouse in Esch-Sur-Alzette, Luxembourg, Anni Adams is swinging as high as she can, reaching her toes to touch the sun. Summer has faded and given way to a new season and a new school year. As she reaches for the clouds, she becomes disinterested and slowly drags the seat back to earth. Stepping from the sandy pit, she comes across Lulu. The two third-grade students exchange awkward introductions and soon fall into the chatter and banter that launches the best formations of friendships. Anni has found a new friend and this friend is very special indeed.

Lulu was of the Theves family and her father was an engineer at the factory. Although they shared a common interest in the employment of their respective fathers, Lulu's father was a quite wealthy man and thus owned a beautifully appointed home and property.

Over the months of September through December, 1936, the friendship of Anni and Lulu developed and became an almost inseparable relationship. The girls thoroughly enjoyed one another's company. There was always plenty to do, laugh, and explore, and as an added bonus for Anni, Lulu had a brother, older by four years. He was as handsome as the strongest tree in the forest. Those were days of laughter, daring, secrets, make-believe, dreams and wishes. Next to Anni's adventures in Marseille, these were times of exposure to luxury, wealth and higher class she had never anticipated. She took it all in stride and paid no attention to the distinctions of elitism, rather she chose to be herself and that was plenty fun for young Lulu Theves. When the fun had ended for the day, after the evening had waned, the Theves family maid would take both Lulu and Anni by tramway to the closest stop by Anni's home porch. It was a wonderful time. The amazement dazzles and sparkles in Anni's eyes today with the fond memories of that place.

Each visit after school was special as she arrived past the iron gates into the wide open arms of the fence around the property. It was a fairytale land of close-kempt landscaping like a government park or public garden. The home was the size of any French *villa le largess* and Lulu's own personal room with its toys, dolls and the rocking horse made it complete. The two would play for hours, have coffee and cakes at four o'clock and spend another hour in starry realms until the call to return home came for Anni.

Every visit was exceptional, each unique, and yet there was always the pony. Long before Anni would actually sit astride a horse for her first true equestrian experience, she rode the rocking horse in Lulu's playroom. The brown, quarter-sized, wooden race horse was a work of art. The saddle of true leather, the hooves firmly planted on rockers that exceeded limitation, a bridle of strong, taut brown leather. A mane of genuine blond braid. Anni would mount the horse as if it were the truest of beasts. In a matter of seconds she would have the animal in full gallop, rocking forward and backward until it tilted on each end. She had no fear, only laughter and joy.

The Theves' maid would arouse from her work at the noise upstairs and bound up the stairs to open the door and chant her fair warning: "You girls are going to get yourselves in great danger! You rock that horse enough to throw yourself out the window and I will never be fast enough to get outside and catch you! Now, cease the silliness and foolish behavior! Ride the pony, that is fine, but if you send yourself in flight I am not responsible and you can tell your parents so!" Anni and Lulu would giggle and muffle their laughs but they knew they were treading a fine line and it would be wise to tone things down some. Thus, they do.

As these days pass, Anni finds herself at home on the late evenings after her visits with Lulu or the times when she has been required to be home for the evening. She spends the time studying and learning the art of knitting. It is a talent that will benefit her in later years not only as occupation for thoughtful reflection, but for necessity and hard-earned income for survival. She studies by the dim light of a small electric bulb and Papa sits beside her, correcting her math, showing her the correct answers and teaching her again and again until she remembers it better than she realizes. Anni is growing fast, and the times are starting to catch up with her level of speed.

By the end of December and the beginning of the new year, 1937, the happy childhood days of play at Lulu's and family life again turned to emotional challenges of will and spirit for Anni. As the Neuman family sat at the dinner table late Friday evening of the last week of December, the school holidays over, the news was delivered over Anni's already intrusive and persistent cough. "Anny, I want you to pack tonight and be ready in the morning, Pop is taking you to the train station for Coq-Sur-Mer [pronounced *Cohk-Zur-Mare*]."

"No, Mama, I don't want to go, it is freezing cold there and they make us go to the ocean everyday! Please, I don't want to go, I will be fine here. Besides, you need me with Bubby and Chuck, please?"

"Anni!" Papa places his fingertips just under the edge of the table with his thumbs on top as if he were going to flip the table with all its contents up and over. (This was something he seldom threatened—only when there was too much noise at the table and no one dared doubt that he would really do it.) "Anni, you must go. Your lungs are filled with the soot and ashes, if you stay you will only get worse, come down with pneumonia or worse, then you will be good for no one. Besides, the change will do you good and it is a good opportunity to learn and practice your French and math." The decision had already been made and it was final. Anni would go once again to Belgium to escape the industrial hazards of her hometown life.

The world seemed to be in a race to manufacture iron and steel for the revolution of building skyscrapers, ships and war machines, as well as automobiles and other major industrial needs of the day. Germany was in second place to the United States, each with a different agenda and purpose, contrasting their respective goals. The United States was trying to build a bigger nation through work programs designed to deliver the people from economic disaster, trying to build a stronger future. Constructing buildings and bridges created jobs and improved the economy slowly. Iron and steel were excellent exports to other countries as well. However, for Germany, steel and iron were for the grinding and growling war machine of Adolf Hitler being built under the newly appointed Chief of Economy, Hermann Goering. It was Goering's belief that the reactivation and buildup of a massive military—naval, air and land—would surge lifeblood into the weak German economy. Hitler loved it because it justified the "battering ram" he needed to beat down the doors of his neighbors.

Luxembourg was ranked seventh worldwide, but it didn't appear that way at home in Esch and nearby Differdange where the Arbed factory employed nearly every able-bodied male in the surrounding cities and small hamlets. France had the limestone needed for flux in the iron mills; Belgium and the Rhine had the fir trees—for the coke, or charcoal, for the heating of the *bosh*, the large bin where the new iron ore is "boiled" and reduced to iron. All of Europe seemed to have a need and lust for iron and steel and it was the perfect place to find the basic elements needed.

Across France, Italy, Belgium, Luxembourg and Germany, steel and iron factories ruled the skyline. The railways were jammed with traffic between the countries and within. In Luxembourg, where over head some of the richest deposits were mined, iron ore corridors were built through the hillsides and down into the towns, passing over small-town streets and the rooftops of the storefronts. The ore could be heard rumbling and tumbling day and night through the giant, enclosed troughs as large as a wooden bridge at a small river crossing.

Through the months of October and November, the cooler air became heavier, and cloud cover kept the roiling, billowing plumes of acrid smoke and residue low over the ceilings just above the housetops and tree lines. Because of the burn-off from the metallurgic concoctions, nearly all Luxembourgers were subject to lung illnesses, especially the elderly and young children. Young Anni was no exception. The black soot and ash not only covered the houses, streets and barns, it settled in the delicate tissues of the lungs of all who breathed the winter air. For some it was not so bad, for others it was best to stay indoors or leave for the few remaining months of cold weather to visit friends, family or some other safe haven.

For this family, Anni was the one most susceptible because of her being out-of-doors the most, with young Albert a close second. However, Anni was the only one that could be afforded to be missed and removed to safer environs by the elder Albert and his wife. Thus it was, Anni would go again to Coq-Sur-Mer for the coming months as she had done for the past three years. Once there, she would brave the freezing cold weather daily, dark, dreary and miserably homesick, not to mention lonely.

The place she would stay was supported by the benevolent Arbed company and companies like them for the health and well-being of their employees' families. Anni faced daily treks in the hard, cold, biting wind to the ocean as one of nearly eighty school-age children, not counting their chaperones. The program featured exercises of physical nature and breathing exercises to clean, purify and increase capacity of the lungs, encouraging revitalization of the respiratory system and the body as a whole. School continued and Anni shared her quarters within a building of four rooms of approximately equal size. Each room housed twenty children of the same condition and similar age, all overseen by a room matron to insure peace, stability and discipline.

After three months of exile, young Anni was finally relieved of her health's obligatory sojourn and could return to the warmth of home at Esch. The cool of spring was approaching, bringing fresh air once again. Anni would take a bus home. There she would be properly greeted with great welcome by her two siblings' laughter because that is what children do. Her mother's glowing smile, because mothers cherish their growing daughters in the deepest, silent parts of the heart, and a very, very proud Papa because his girl was strong, smart and independent.

Not only was Anni strong, smart and independent, she had traveled over the past several years and had become knowledgeable about four countries: France, Germany, Belgium and her own home of Luxembourg. She was fluent in three languages and had traveled hundreds of miles in all directions with family, strangers and even sometimes alone. She was knowledgeable far beyond her years, mature, developed mentally and physically, and she was not even close to puberty yet. She was a ten-year-old girl with a world of experience and learning both from extreme highs and lows, hardships and joys unspeakable. She was stretching her wings beyond the width of the breeze beneath her.

As if spring were some kind of reward for her sufferings, the season had burst through the windows of the Neuman home the day after Anni's arrival back to her soft and comforting bed. Life was large, bold and exciting again. Bubby was gathering his marbles in the living room floor and calling for Anni to stop being sleepy-lazy and come play. Mama was in the kitchen, as she had always seemed to be and Grandma had gone shopping at the market for fresh vegetables. Papa had already left earlier this morning. It was Saturday. School would be here again, come Monday, for the remaining two months. But today was the first day home, a weekend, and a time to let her clean, clear lungs challenge her muscles and sinewy body to breakpoint race of endurance through play, exploration and imagination of magical proportions.

Young Albert and Anni hastily put down a brief breakfast and rush out the door, running through the streets to the field where Papa stood with the football (soccer) team at the school grounds. There the two troubadours climb the fences, have sword fights, wrestle, run, chase, hide and scream with laughter as if it were the first day of a festival and fair. At midday, the two follow Papa home for the biggest meal of the day. As soon as they approach the door, still closed, the aroma of something enticing and mouth-watering bays at their nostrils. The threesome were starved for food and family fellowship. At the Neuman home at 17 Rue Ancione, once again life is good. Grandma has "tons" of berries and plums in baskets from neighbors and the market for canning, Mama has a feast set for the table and little Chuck is all giggles on the floor with his toys.

The family fills their bellies with all that Mama can carry to the table and all that two hungry young boys, one girl, a father and two matrons can dispose of gratefully. Whether it is graceful is of another consideration. Nevertheless, it is wonderful and happy to say the least.

Once done with eating, Anni helps clear the table with the older women, the boys tromp away to play and Papa sits upon his chair and relaxes with his pipe. He slowly and meticulously packs in the tobacco to fit just right for the best smoke, then lights the magnificent, sculpted and yet simple pipe. There, he puffs upon the red-glowing embers in the bowl, relaxes his eyes and then his body. Swirls of smoke slip from his lips as he exhales and the room soon fills with the sweet aroma of the tobacco. More importantly, the room fills with the sweet aroma of the comfort of a real man being at home and holding guard over his family. A symbol of serene, silent security but without question, it existed because that was the way he was, silent but sincerely present.

Eventually Papa rises from his settlement of respite and returns to the field for the final of the afternoon. Outside, he passes little Bubby and Sissy as they play hopscotch. Papa pauses for a moment and glares upon the children as if not wishing to be noticed but enjoying their antics. With such an audience, caution is thrown to the wind. Little Albert recognizes he has an audience and breaks into his favorite flights of imagination. For the moment, little Albert is a clown. Not just any clown, he is a circus clown, the real thing. He spins, bows, dances, tickles, chuckles, juggles and does "fall prats." Anything for a laugh, and thus this Albert would be for the rest of his life. He would always be the clown, during hard times and those of good to come, there he would be, ready to make one smile, no, make one laugh.

Past nightfall and long after the final meal of the day, the basement has already been arranged and put in order. Papa has his last smoke of tobacco. Mother and Grandmother hold late-night vigil over the boiling copper pot of plums dredged with thick clumps of crystalline sugar being turned into jam for preserving in the canning jars. Little "Charly" would long since passed out in his crib while Anni and Albert finalize their exhausted and yawning laughs. Saturday was over. However, day two of the weekend was yet to come and it was as close as the closing of the eyes to sleep, dream, wish and awake to a cool morning dew awash on the windows.

Sunday morning arrives with the crow of a rooster outside the house and two "mother hens" inside. It is time to get up, says one, and time to go to church says the other. It is a faithful duty that is not neglected nor disregarded and certainly not disrespected. Of course, while all make the march to the call of a Catholic cathedral, Papa remains home. Tomorrow morning will be his day of duty before God and thus he will rest on this day given by the Lord for such purpose. There is no guilt or shame in it. It is fitting and proper.

In a matter of a few hours, the family has once again filled the house with the orchestrated individualism and community that only a family can accomplish. Mama and Grandma are dutifully returning to the basement after all have been fed and there they will stand guard once again over the foot-high stove, cooking jelly from sweet ingredients. Since that is there intention, Papa decides to do an extra part to insure he has participated properly. "Anni, grab the baskets, we are going to get some blackberries up in the hills."

The words do not have to be spoken twice. Anni is about to slip, hit her head or fall trying to get the baskets and get to the door with Papa. This is one of her most favorite of all things she can imagine. At least when it comes to being with Papa. Just the two of them alone on the trails that head up the hillsides and into the woods, brushes and brambles. They reach the outskirts of the town while Anni incessantly chatters to a silent, nodding, smiling Papa. The love is undeniable. It is clearly spoken between the two without a word. She is still his firstborn "son" and he is her guardian angel of steel. They walk along the paths and aroung the bushes, looking for berries on their afternoon journey which will turn hours into minutes and pass all too soon. But the memories will last longer than the lifetime of them both because anyone tomorrow could make such a thing happen, even if it were just a spark of desire to do something simple with someone you love.

As they traipse through the calf-high lush green grass up to the bushes, the wetness of the deeper grass soils their shoes. They pay no attention and ignore Papa's pantlegs and Anni's bare legs, dirtied by the adventure as nature paints upon them from foot to knee. While they methodically move about in random directions Anni calls out to Papa, "Papa, can I eat this one?" She has picked a beautiful, unusually large ripe berry. "Sure, honey, if you wish, but, wouldn't it be grand in appearance atop all the other berries that it has out-performed and grown?" he says, smiling at his young daughter. "Yes, Papa, and everyone will be amazed at the size of this one, won't they?" "Yes, Anni, I do believe they will, and I don't think they will believe you found it!" he says teasingly.

As they venture further up the hillside, they encounter the pathway of the overhead trams that haul the iron ore in buckets from the mountainside caverns to the transport post at the foot of the hills. They are an amazing sight. They look like miniature Eiffel Towers with criss-crossed bars and piers reaching a point some thirty feet from the ground with a protruding arm holding a cable and pulleys.

"Papa, do the buckets ever fall?" Anni asks with trepidation. She has obviously been intimidated by the rumblings and bumpy travels of the heavy loads making their way blindly downhill without a soul in sight to direct their journey. "Not often, honey, they do sometimes but it is very rare," he assures her. "Why don't they fall, passing like that and always going back and forth so much?" she inquires more from fear than interest. "Well, Anni, it is like the math that we study all the time," he prods her mind. "What do you mean, Papa, I don't understand?" Just what he is waiting for, she has taken the bait. "It is like this, the men who designed that trolley system and helped build it, they had to do lots and lots of math like you are learning. If they do their math right, they can calculate the probability, or odds, of it failing and make adjustments to make sure the system works long and without accidents. Now, do you see why math is so important?" he asks.

"I guess so, but what does math have to do with the buckets, the towers and the cable?" she digs deeper. "Anni, everything is based upon a mathematical equation. It takes the numbers involving the length of the tramway and the height, weight and what it carries. Math is the only way to know how much energy it will take to move it, to hold it together and make it work. Most of all, math is what makes sure that those buckets don't fall on our heads and squash our berries," he laughs.

She is starting to understand. Papa is a very smart man and he is right about math. It really is important. Especially if she wants to get back down the hillside with her beloved father and home with their toppling payload of treasures. She is still learning, he is still teaching and there isn't going to be an ending.

# The Butterfly Spreads Her Wings and Flies

In the year 1937, Clinton Joseph Davisson and George Paget Thomson shared equally the Nobel Prize in Physics. House Resolution 6906 was debated in the United States Seventy-Fifth Congress regarding Taxation of Marihuana [(sic) according to the spelling as introduced to the House of Congress] and IBM reached an astounding thirty-one million dollars in net earnings after introducing its IBM Type 805, a scoring machine based on the examinee using a "fill in the bubble" score card for reading by the machine.

In this soft summer morning of July, outside the windows of the humble Neuman home there is the clear and distinct sound of a rooster sounding roll call. With a wide-breasted chest and belting lungs he announces the rising of the sun as if royalty were entering the township. Meanwhile, inside this same quaint, modest home, there is a "mother hen" of sorts announcing a most auspicious occasion as her feet shuffle to and fro upon the floors of the parlor, kitchen and bedroom. She hasn't said a word but there she is, making it known clear as a cloudless sky that it is time, past time, for Anni to rise and prepare for the annual summer vacation with Aunt Anne (pronounced *Ah-Nee*). The mother hen is Anni's maternal grandmother, Giedy (pronounced *Giddy*).

While the name, by American standards, would incite ideation of gleefulness and cheer, this is a woman as sincere and solemn as a willow tree. She is consistently and uniquely identifiable by her all-black attire no matter the weather or occasion. Once Protestant, now she is devoutly Catholic. She has made a sincere, unwavering commitment to a life of staunch propriety and servitude to her God through strength, wisdom, silence and leadership by handwork. She is the quintessential matriarch of the family.

Anni has waited impatiently, almost without containment, for the past three days, yet, as is so often the case, she stayed up late as if it were Christmas Eve; No this is bigger than Christmas Eve; Yet, here is the morn after she stayed up so late with visions, fantasies and anticipation coursing through her mind, body and spirit. It is the first day of a six-week vacation in Marseille, France. More particularly, L'Estaque, a subdivision of the grand Marseille city. The French city with a heartbeat and pulse akin to a thriving seaport city on the Mediterranean—particularly on the "Golfe Du Lion" (the lion's gulf). And that it is, the place where Spanish bastards of the sea meet smoke-piped Frenchmen, interrupted by burly Italian ship men, sailors and "wonder-bouts." If that isn't enough color, excitement and danger, Casablanca lies only miles away and within easy reach of the port.

Marseille was and is the belly of the oily mix of French culture and international sea trade for the mere pleasures of lust and love. Money means only that you will have another day here in this haven of runaway criminals, good-hearted souls, happy people and a city of lights and nightlife. Bustling in the dark of night and yet serene and solemn by the day. Here is the city with the citadel of the most ostentatious Catholic church, Notre Dame De La Garde (Our guardian Lady) on the hilltop overlooking the city and bay. In the distance are the twin islands and penetrating the very midst of the distance is the fortress, the formidable and daunting, daring, night-howling Chateau D'If, where the Count of Monte Cristo himself made his daring escape and became a true legend in history. Just as Marseille, so is the pair that are now preparing for their departure from Esch Sur Alzette, Luxembourg on this early July morn: Giedy with her solemn face and dress and Anni with her butterfly wings stretching, bristling gently in the testing air of imagination and the spirit of a girl-child aching for flight into smiles, laughter and sights beyond fairytale belief.

After a toast breakfast, after kisses of departure to Papa and Mother, with feigned sadness, an excited Anni (and now wide-eyed and wide awake), takes the hand of Giedy for the one-mile trek to the train station.

Each carries a suitcase, Giedy with her briefcase and lunch basket solidly stocked for the hours in the confines of the train ride and Anni with her mother's brown cardboard and leather suitcase lacking fullness but blessed with treasures prepared for the dance. They walk steadily, leaving before sunrise to reach the station by the break of day and the first departure scheduled for 7 A.M. The beginnings of a journey through the dividing line of Western France on a crash course to the south and into the welcoming, always awake, home of Aunt Anne, where laughter reigns supreme and sorrow is a word without place or position.

Their passages purchased and the boarding having taken place, Anni and Grandma sit silently at rest in their seats on the train as it shudders and rocks back and forth by inches in preparation to start its charge into the iron groove—pre-designed and custom-made for this recurring trek. This trip is particularly special. Anni will be turning eleven in November, just four short months ahead. But already she is rising from the dark of her cocoon, and light is brilliantly reflecting around her and upon her. Her colors are taking striking lines and variable shades etched by the deepest of heartfelt desires and dreams as only a girl of this age can imagine. She is soon to be eleven and feeling ready, strong and resilient enough to be better than those prissy older girls. Anni isn't one to wait. She has no resentment toward the older girls in her hometown; only, she knows the quiet confidence in her being that her father has instilled, she is stronger than average and experiencing more of what life has to offer.

Slowly, the train begins to move, rolling at first with a pull and tug at the passengers in its care and then the ground and surroundings seem to move as the transport machine advances on the course for the day. But it isn't the pictures outside the windows that are moving, we are moving forward and we are on our way. We are on our way to Marseille! Anni's spirit leaps inside her small-framed chest with excitement, "We're on our way, finally."

The main engine pulls the trail of traveling cars as if it were the drunken sailor at the lead of a conga line made up of sheet metal, steel and glass. It goes happily dancing, speeding, winding and weaving its way along a thin iron course into the hillsides, fields, hamlets and cities of the French countryside. The ride itself is all a part of this magnificent adventure. The potpourri of aromas that flow through the windows and down the aisles are as versatile as billowing clouds before a spring rain. The smell of fresh bread wafts through; the scent of forest trees and the damp, decaying leaves on the ground abound and flourish. Each nuance to the sense of smell is teased and left with a new flavor in its place. The smell of fresh-cut hay in the fields, the brief smell of the burnt fuel from the engine, clean crisp air that has rushed down a mountainside through the passenger cars as if a giant hand had fanned over it while it passed by.

The sounds of the rumbling track beneath and the undulating humming of the machine mesmerize the senses of the ears, mind and imagination. The slow, steady beat, sway and vibration of traveling, being in motion, plays upon the body as the strings of an old-fashioned upright bass. This is traveling and this is something that Anni will enjoy, cherish and make a part of her way of life long into the future from this day. Some get tired from traveling, some even dread it, but for Anni it is exhilarating and even more, it is in her blood. She yearns for it, hastens to it and embraces it for all its ups and downs but most of all the education it doles out by the bucket load. Again, she is making her father happy, "Learn, Anni, learn."

The train has picked up speed by Thionville and barrels into Metz for a brief debarkation and loading. Again the same scenario flashes along the set course as the hollow, stern metal and glass airplane without wings flies along the countryside through Nancy (pronounced *Nahn-See*), through Dijon and the preceding fields where cows are seen grazing and lumbering along their casual day. On to Lyon (pronounced *Lee-Ohn*), where the miles pass by, and through terraced hills and vineyards overflowing with dark, rich, plump grapes await like maidens for a September wedding down to Orange and slowing to a final, peaceful coast into the welcome station of the infamous Marseille. Over the long hours of trekking Giedy has sat securely by Anni's side, silently watching the child with wonderment and silent curiosity.

She has been there all the while as a rock and a fortress, while Anni explored the beauty and intrigue of the passage, at times peeking her head out the open window peering forward and back of the line. Inside Anni has shared a lunch of cheese and salami on cold rolls with Giedy and they doused the meal with a cup of wine and water. But now, it is the beginning of the vacation festival and it belongs to her personally. Anni has arrived in Marseille and Aunt Anne is here to greet them with a beaming smile, radiating enchantment and laughing with invisible angels all around. Sorrow has no place here and sadness is not permitted. This is "joyland" and Anni has the world to herself to explore as she pleases.

From the station, Anni, Giedy and Aunt Anne make their way by taxi to the electric trolley cars (tramways) that dice through the major seaport city following along the infamous coastal waterway. Stone walls are to the right, staunchly guarding the buildings a mere foot or two behind; the road is in between, and the fall of God's own rock garden rolled up from the saltwater bay lies to the left and below. It as an ancient city with ancient history and all the trappings of modern-day inventions and conveniences. It is history from the beginning of the world overlaid with all the newness that has been introduced from internal intellect and foreign gifts. It is almost like a great-grandfather with a new watch. The perfect blend of old and new without either winning or losing, neither giving or taking. Here time is shared and savored.

The tram is an engineering crossbreed with typical train doorways but the shelled body of a bus. Instead of tires, it has the rail axles of a train and follows the four-inch iron tracks set approximately a meter apart. Two "buses" buckled together make up a tram. Anni, Aunt Anne and Giedy are on their way to Aunt Anne's apartment in L'Estaque and the evening is waning upon the coast. While Giedy appears tired from the travel, Anni is bursting with reserve energy.

Since age three, Anni has been coming to this city of spectacular sights and events (expected and unexpected, alike); nightlife is extraordinaire and day-life is the likes of which dreams are made, fit for a "child" no matter how old. From five to ninety-five years old, youth pierces the soul of all who are here breathing immortality.

With faithful religiosity, the three Femmes of France make their historic, romantic and obligatory stop at the street vendors stationed at midpoint to Aunt Anne's apartment along the bay. This is the place where memories hang heavy in a deep and thick fog of lust for the exuberance of life. It is an exciting place that causes the heart to pound, the mind to spin and the ears to tickle with music and laughter. The eyes cannot consume the visions fast enough, they dart all about and dance upon the sky, winds, water and faces of the spellbound travelers. The color of the azure sea is set behind the near-blinding multifaceted rainbow of the gypsies' encampment. The gypsies come out of their wood-paneled wagons and canvas tents to entice and entertain. Their flavorful clothing is splashed with entwined cloth of colors no one had, nor even now could envision as existing on the earth.

The gypsies bewitch the crowd with their castanets and sonnets. Behind Anni are the two-wheeled street vendors with food from the gods; alive and living in the forefront of an earthen canvas made with chalky white hillsides, limestone cliffs, heavily clustered tall pines, secretly mixing the sweet pine aroma into the full-bodied sea air. The smell of *pomme frites* (pronounced *Pohm-Fritz*) permeates the air in the between. And it is for this very reason, amongst this blinding clash of throbbing human wildlife, that the threesome have stopped to cherish the joys of beginning a memorial vacation for all times. In this fairytale moment they dole out their handful of small coins for a bag of *pomme frites*.

The original, real and true French fries. Not like the American fries or the infamous English "chip," these are paper-thin rings of potato that have been fried in an instant and served just as quickly with no condiments: hot, delicious and a taste that one would understand the difference only from having been there and gorged on the delight (*viva la difference*). It is all that the mouth can handle for fullness of flavor without any other enhancement or spice. Of course, here in Marseille, the exception is that *pomme frites* are served with hearty portions of *moules* (mussels: pronounced *mools*), as fresh as this morning, when they were plucked from the Mediterranean Sea.

The hillsides are painted with gray stone buildings; encampments of houses and apartments, each with its red tile roof brightening (as if more could be done) an already spectacular summer days' picture of Southern France. The clouds overhead entrance Anni as she ponders each one and wonders which are most like the image of a creature here on earth or a structure matching the outline. Here is "the black-sheep child of France," Marseille, a place that is nearly a country in its own right. The ambling rock walls fortify the brief yard of every home and terrace the community to secure individual and community treasure troves against the weather; the walls brood over the beings and property held in their charge with comforting arms of solace and strength made over the ages and hardened by time.

Anni's adventurous spirit is piqued to a new level and as the others are waiting for their *pomme frites* to be ready, she starts across the street, bedazzled by the gypsies and their wares of magic. Suddenly, her dreamy flight is broken by the stern shout of Aunt Anne, "Anni! Get back over here! I have told you. The gypsies will steal you! They will take you and hide you away and I will never see you again!" Anni is suddenly brought out of her flight and perched on hard, cold truth.

Some things, no matter how beautiful or enticing and innocent in appearance, are deceptive and far from safe. This is a place where only the "already dead" dare wander from the safe zones. With all its beauty and life-luster, danger does abound. It is a perilous place for an innocent and curious ten-year-old girl. It is safe for such a girl with Aunt Anne and her tough spine and spit; and the fact that she is backed by Giedy, old maybe, but she is a force no average man would dare challenge if he were sober, especially not with God on her side.

Now, after having teased their appetites and satisfied their palates for the moment, they send their spirits into a warm comfort. They have tasted a piece of time and joy especially designed for entombment in the "fondest memories corner" of their minds. The three Femmes of France complete the balance of their journey by arriving at Aunt Anne's apartment. Upon stepping from the tram, the trio face a bar squarely in front of them. This is where Aunt Anne lives with her beloved husband, Augustine. However, Augustine, a richly dark black man from Martinique, is not here. He is a chef onboard a cruise liner, appropriately so from this vagabonds' seaport. He and Anne are lovemates for certain and have a hunger for making the most of all they face each moment and every day. So, Uncle Augustine is absent from this party but not forgotten. In his stead, Mony (Uncle) Lazare will be here soon to see his coveted *La Petite* (the little one).

The ladies forge ahead by the bar on the first floor and up the steps leading to the third floor where Aunt Anne and Uncle Augustine have their humble apartment, simple but busy with extravagant charm as one would expect in the highest chateau mixed with a pirate's guest room. As they climb the steps their arrival garners the attention of the bar's patrons. The locals know La Petite also, and it is another excuse or reason to take the party upstairs in a welcome festival and feast with wine and song. So begins the adventure into Anni's wonderland. Not only have her surroundings changed, but her name is different; She is La Petite and she is a young child queen of the court, entertaining all of Marseille and L'Estaque with her unbridled imagination. Colors are plenteously abounding upon her uncapped wings and thus it goes as they grow.

# If I Dance, I Dance

***"Quand je bois du vin rosee—je dance, je dance—et voila encore du vin rosee—on dance et dance" (When I drink pink wine—I dance, I dance—and so more pink wine—one dances and dances).***

Yes, the welcome mat has been laid out and the arrival celebration happened long ago, as it seems, in the night. The early morning cool gives way to the formidable sun as it rises from below the horizon in the east. CoCo (pronounced *Ko-Coh*), the foot-tall parakeet of flamboyant colours, announces the presence of a new day. It is hardly 6:00 A.M. but CoCo is proclaiming with all his screeches, screams and hollers that everyone should be as much awake as he. Even more so, because no one has had as much wine and yet he is the earliest riser.

CoCo is a taskmaster and demands attention, performance and adoration from his fans. He will not permit a stranger to draw his attention without great humility and recognition, and should it be tried, he will immediately provide a "silent treatment" to dispose the observer to acquiesced boredom. CoCo only does things as he pleases and expects generosity from all that are at his attendance. He is a twenty-five-year-old parakeet with a very big ego and a very bad attitude, of course, until he gets his wine. He is the royal parakeet deserving of homage as L'Estaque's only nonhuman balladeer and one of the best sources of nightlife entertainment.

This mid-July morning, L'Estaque has been taken by quiet storm. However, it is yet to be announced to the inhabitants that there is a singing parakeet, a staunch grandma, a flittering Aunt and La Petite in town and they will soon match up with Mony Lazare; then the dance will begin in full and last through the weeks to come.

It is nearing 7:00 A.M. and as Giedy rises to shuffle across the tile floors in her slippers toward the kitchen, Aunt Anne has closed the door in an exit to the daily market below to buy fresh fruit, vegetables and meat for the day's feast. This scene will be repeated over and over throughout this entire adventure and Anni will find no moment of it to be the same or redundant. Contrarily, it is her own fairyland, fairytale adventure minute by minute and her imagination causes her heart to soar, her spirit to fly and her wings to stretch wide and hard to grasp the winds of change and let the day splash color upon color upon the ever-growing pallette.

"What shall we do today?" The knock at the door has come and Anni has answered it as quickly as a cat to a mouse. She already has a good guess who it is, and it is indeed Mony Lazare. "*Ou' voulez-vous allez-soleil?*" (Where do you want to go, sunshine?) The words come again as she stands there barefooted upon the cool tile with the sea breeze starting to flow in from behind her, flowing through the open French doors on the terrace and rustling past the long strands of closely bunched beads.

The beaded doorway is enough to keep out the unwelcome and invite the smells and sounds of life into this little part of the world. The beads, however, reflect every part of the world with their cataclysmic clash of colors: reds, blacks, pink, orange, jade, purple, white, mother of pearl and on until there must be more than a hundred different shades. Like the gypsies below, the colored beads represent the exotic, the fantastic and the exuberance of lust for life. The breeze caresses La Petite's gentle gown and the nape of her neck and reminds her that there is an ocean nearby. She is ready to take it by storm, cartwheels, dance and dare the waters with her strength at swimming; her father has trained her well as a junior gymnast.

For as long as she can remember, she has been an entertainer without even knowing it was called performing. For Anni, it was working with her father, the professor of gymnastics and troupe manager for the gymnastics team performing all over Luxembourg and Germany. All the while, Papa made sure that Anni was a part of the team and he made special effort to keep her in the center of it all, humbly without her complete understanding or knowledge of how important it would be to her life in later years.

The man in front of her, filling the doorway, is beautiful. He is middle-aged, strong and handsome. He evinces a great sense of security, yet he is gentle. Not gentle as of weakness but gentle as in that which makes a gentleman. He is her date for the weeks to come and he does not lack a sense of adventure. What La Petite wants, she gets! Uncle Lazare loves his La Petite and he knows that she adores him. It is a match of a man with his wish for a daughter such as this and the imagination of a girl of ten that her fatherly guardian has arrived to escort her where children dare not go, into the depths of danger, excitement and adventure that can only be played out in her girl-child's mind. "To the beach!" she replies, "I want to go to the beach," without even bothering to try and contain her excitement.

Without so much as a yes or no from Uncle Lazare, Anni has already fled away to change into her clothes with bathing suit beneath. It will be an afternoon of fish and chips at the seaside street market and a full day of swimming in the water, imagining she is fleeing the Chateau d'If with the Count of Monte Cristo.

She charges the beach and breaks into a dance to celebrate her escape and arrival into a land of her own making of mind and living daydreams. She wildly plays upon the sand, spinning, dancing and turning cartwheel after cartwheel all to amuse herself and cause Uncle Lazare to break into full and happy laughter at her antics. She is an entertainer and Lazare is indeed entertained by the little gymnast and her never ebbing energy. Today the sun shines for her and she is warmed and reddened by it. Before the vacation is over, she will be tan, filled with new ideas and refreshed. But, for now, it is the first day of many, and today she has absorbed the warm embrace of sun and sky.

She has taken charge of the beach, breathed in the fresh salt-air and various aromas from the fresh fish, the pine and salt-air mix, the variety of foods being prepared along the roadways and in the cafes. She has taken Uncle Lazare by the hand and with it, his heart has been led into the world of a child and once again he himself is one. It is for this very inexplicable reason that he cherishes these moments with his La Petite.

The sun and the day have begun to wane away into the evening and with it a cooler breeze takes over in its place. The day is all but passed and yet oh so very far from over. It is not so much the end of anything. Rather, it is just an informal transition into the next stage and the coming hours of more fun and excitement. Only the scenery will change. All else remains the same. Everyone is filled with happiness, contentment and laughter. As stated before, sorrow has no place here and would not find a perch or veil to pierce. Sadness is forbidden.

Back at Aunt Anne's apartment the air has already filled with the excitement in anticipation of the evening's festivities. Aunt Anne is busying herself with preparations for the evening meal to celebrate a non-particular holiday, yet a greater event, vacation with family and friends. As her cooking permeates the apartment, Giedy quietly idles, absorbed in her faith and thoughts. Anni and Uncle Lazare arrive to the inviting charm of the little apartment and Anni is sent to the shower to remove some of the salt and sand from her small frame before dinner. She refreshes herself in the cool, clear water and it soothes the warmth of her flesh as the sun-drenched skin drinks in the relief and revitalizing force of the clean water.

Uncle Lazare busies himself by laughing and teasing Aunt Anne about anything that will make her smile. At moments, if one glances in a split second, a smile may even be seen on the face of Giedy as she holds back the laughter she feels welling up inside. She is the matriarch and loves her granddaughter as much as any doting grandmother could.

From the terrace there is the call of the balladeer with a screeching demand to be brought into the parlor as part of the games. He is not one to be ignored. Also, it is time for his rosé wine. CoCo has his own special little glass which is now fetched by the wet-headed little girl and brought to him. At the same time, Anni brings the cage in from the balcony, which is bountifully adorned with flowers.

Upon seeing Anni, CoCo is clearly ready to chat. He doesn't talk to strangers, but once again, La Petite's charm opens even the mind and voice of the multicolored singing, drinking bird. He is as much a sailor in a seaport as any below. Although his sea was on the air and not upon the water and that was long ago for him, he is now in the benevolent care of Aunt Anne and his exploits, although confined in body, are flying free in his mind. As Anni sets the cage inside the parlor, CoCo begins his well-pitched voicing, announcing the evening's entertainment, "*Quand je bois du vin rosee—je dance, je dance—et voila encore du vin rosee—on dance et dance.*" His little stemmed glass, perfectly fit for his fist-foot to hoist while balanced on one leg, invites the pouring of the liquid cheer which fills his appetite for triple sec, a strong drink for a strong bird. Anni begins to giggle, as does the rest of the room even as tipsy friends from the bar below enter the small show. Once again, the butterfly is letting her wings stretch and she spreads them to the wide space about her as she closes her eyes and slowly begins to spin, pirouette and waltz upon the tiles as if in a gilded ballroom of the King's palace. Uncle Lazare waltzes over to her and they clasp hands and gently sway to the songbird's silly song.

Laughter continues to grow throughout the room as does the aroma of Aunt Anne's wonderful gourmet cooking, and this is no understatement. She is in fact a cook extraordinaire, and such is her employment. The wine and aperitifs begin to flow into clinking glasses and the little gypsies' palace becomes thick with joy, fresh air and flights of fantasy on the night air beneath the sparkling stars and heavens outside the window and beyond. Before the night, or early morn, has closed the festivities, this gaggle of fun-purveyors will have danced, sung songs, told jokes and fallen to antics of which new jokes will be told. Even Giedy will join the singing and have a glass of wine or two, maybe three. Through it all, the walls are the only physical boundaries for the butterfly and they are barely noticed. She flies upon the song, drifts upon the lilting voices, absorbs the sensitive souls around her with innocent trust and enjoyment. Her thin white dress flies our from her waist and clings to her in a twirl of flight on foot. She will dance gently and wile herself with vivid, artistic, impromptu dance that only a child can comprehend.

One minute she is a ballerina, another moment a gypsy and then the princess of her own unnamed kingdom. The butterfly is showing the first glimpses of the beauty of her wings, breathtakingly beautiful even though far from complete. This is the finest art an eye may behold, as delicate as the flakes of a Parisian pastry. Tender and young, yet as unfathomable as it may be, the groundwork for an even greater picture has been laid.

# Two Fortresses for the Future

It is a new morning and only a few days have passed since Anni and Giedy's arrival in Marseille and the lesser known province of L'Estaque. Anni has gone to bed late and dreamt of her capture by the gypsies and her struggle to escape. Frantic that Aunt Anne will find out what she has done, she fights all the harder to get back to the apartment before anyone finds out.

Suddenly, she awakens from her sleep to find that she has indeed escaped and she is still in the comforting apartment with Anne, Giedy and CoCo and they are already making their own plans for the day. It is good to be awake from the nightmare. Not that she minded the lively gypsies so much, but for the fact that the fear of Aunt Anne finding out would certainly mean horrors unspeakable, such as the possibility of never being invited back to this magnificent city. That would be a crushing blow she could not sustain. Her heart, happiness and joy are here along with a dreamboat man named Lazare.

A knock comes at the door and there is no doubt who it could be by now. This time, though, Aunt Anne is coming along for the day with Uncle Lazare and Anni. One of the two greatest highlights of these visits has been scheduled for a perfectly clear, sunny day in Southern France while the rest of the world spins on its axis missing the ultimate adventure, or at least, that is how Anni feels as her imagination is speeding forward. The threesome leave Giedy to her reading as she sits on the couch and drifts in her own thoughts with her coffee. Sunlight beams across her black form and the Bible in her lap. The beads shuffle in the breeze, and the street noise begins to rise up from three floors below. It is time to leave paradise and enter Eden.

Anni takes Mony Lazare by his strong, firm hand and they set the course down the stairs, to the tram and step aboard for the ride to Vieux Port. As the tram rolls, rattles and jogs downhill though the city, it takes the three adventurers down the main street of La Canebiere (later to become affectionately known by American GIs as "the Can of Beer"). However, the crude term given by the Americans at a later date is far from fitting for the street and the sights, which are now being sorted by Anni. This is a different time. Although some things have not changed even to this day, in 1937 La Canebiere was the most infamous street in all of France if one was an artist or favored such. It is on this street that the tram passes by sidewalk cafes, wine shops, bakeries, book stores, sailors from around the world tramping the street, working "ladies," vendors of both real and fake trinkets, but most of all artisans. They come here because this is where the people are, and this is where they have invested their hopes. Anni's curiosity is drilling through her thoughts as they pass along far too fast for satisfaction. She will be coming back here on foot very soon, of that she is sure. Uncle Lazare will bring her, protect her and let her learn as Papa has told her to do so many times.

For now, the tram arrives at the stationing point for the Vieux Port, which is literally translated in English as "old man port." It is a fair and adequate way in which to describe it because this is the old city, walled in by the old hillsides and the old man of the sea, Neptune. And here is where the three now find Neptune's bounty all around. As they step from the tram, the air is filled with a plethora of sights, sounds and aromas. Especially, aromas. Here, the salt air has won the battle for ground and obtains the full attention of all living creatures, including boy, man, girl and woman. There are inordinate amounts of seafood treasures all around, and the port offers them on a silver platter in unique flavors for the temptation, satisfaction and lustful indulgence of the crowds.

Blackbirds squeal and sqauwk all around as they flitter, swoop and light in search of a morsel larger than their appetite. They are airborne thieves and have no shame. They reflect some of the human nature at this port, and it is all acceptable until caught. The blackbirds fill the skies roundabout in squadrons while the sandpipers scurry up, down and along the rocky shores attempting to ambush any fiddler crab, small fish in the tidal pools or other unwary living breakfast.

Anne, Lazare and Anni, in tow, approach the docks where the tourist transport boats are docked and lined up row upon row, crowded into every square inch of dock space in the busy harbor. As they gaze out through the alleyway of the port, to the right and at the end of where the harbor meets the sea sits Fort St. Jean, guarding the right flank. Out on the left, down at the end of the harbor again to the sea sits Fort St. Nicolas, preventing any breach of the left flank. It is a port that has seen more than most any other seaport in the world for battles by conflicting countries, religions, creeds, color and plainly obstinate souls with a grudge to avenge. But these are not the two fortresses that will set the tone for the future of the young butterfly. No, the fort she is looking for is out that bay and set in the twain of the seaside and the offset double islands in the distance.

There among the waters is a rising monarch. A guardian of a different nature and sort. It is the Chateau d'If. A daunting island fortress built to do as the other forts, protect and defend the inhabitants of Marseille, but that was changed in time and by circumstance. While St. Jean and St. Nicolas remained in their indentured servitude, D'If was altered from the fort built by Francois I and became a holder of prisoners. In direct contrast, two forts visually opposed the "Sergeant of the guard" surrounded by deep waters. It was here that Alexander Dumas set his portrayal of *The Count of Monte Cristo* and all the tales that went with it. Two forts with a mission to guard and protect what lay behind and a frontal view against a fort developed to take the very same inhabitants and hold them captive because they were considered dangerous for either their strength, politics or opinions.

Two forts kept freedom alive in its care and protective custody while the other performed the opposite evil. A fortress which took the living into its deep hollows of stone in a cold hell for preservation against threats, real and imagined, toward rulers and power magnates. The living were robbed of their freedom and disrobed of protection without any genuine care or concern. If the occupants survived, such it was. If they died, then it was done.

On this July day in 1937, Anni is heading toward one of two places where her imagination, curiosity, sense of adventure and schoolgirl heart reaches its highest level of passionate satisfaction. She is infatuated with the stories abounding of the Count and his escapades and escape. She daydreams of being a guide on these hallowed grounds. She has been here before but every time is always different, better and special. As they board the boat to make the crossing, the engine churns from its grumbling idle to a vibrative roar that deafens the passengers into relying upon their vision and touch only. Their sense of smell has been quashed by the bloated air of diesel fuel being carbonized into the air. Soon, as they make headway, the smell of salt air returns and Anni heads for the bow of the boat in anticipation, braving all meaningless threats for the best view. After all, this is about her and she is in charge of her own life. Nothing comes between her and her desire to satisfy her adventurous, curious spirit. Anne and Lazare look on the girl-child at the brink of womanhood and at the forefront of the vessel with apprehensive smiles.

They let her go of sorts to be free in her spirit and watch with caution and care. Of course, had Giedy been here, she would have trodden hard and fast down the boards to retrieve the bedeviled child and relieved her of that daring and dangerous spirit with words worse than any corporal punishment. But, she isn't here and Anni sees the island chateau drawing large in view. In a moment's time, the transport places them at the foot of the cliffs.

All parties disembark the vessel and join the other travelers arriving in other boats from ship size to small outboards and sailboats, on the wet and mucky shore. All the bodies converge in silent approach, like sheep, up the stairway that clearly, though quietly, announces, "This is the way you want to go." Single file, or by twos at best, they mount the cliff-side and reach the pinnacle of the ascent where the grounds are tumored with mud holes, stone groupings and sparse vegetation. Anni has heard the stories of the guides many times past, so she is not inclined to waste precious opportunity.

Instead, knowing the place like the back of her hand, she launches into her own foray of investigative imagination and play. She rallies around the yards and forges into the prison gates. She sweeps through the hallways escaping invisible men in arms. She takes victory with every step, jump or leap. She is free to be wild and wildly play. All, of course, under the instantly-ignored, out-of-mind eyes of Aunt Anne and Uncle Lazare. They are there, but Anni is not here. Anni has taken flight on her butterfly wings and added something new. She has let the Chateau d'If become her body. The two have become one. If the wings reflect her life and experiences, the D'If exemplifies the body resilient against all assaults throughout her life. Strong, determined, performing the task of the "Sergeant of the Guard," protecting what has been locked inside from villains, usurpers and demons.

The allotted time comes to an end, and Anne, Anni and Mony Lazare trudge back down the earth and stone walkway to the waiting boat for departure. They board the vessel with their wet and muddied shoes in hand. It is best to let them dry from the air on the ride back while bare feet cool on the deck of the ship. Anni now takes her station at the stern of the ship and endures the acrid smell of the diesel fumes from the engines so that she might memorialize the kindred spirit of the Chateau in her heart for future reference, as one would to a young love that remains forever in life, secretly tucked away for personal privacy and comfort of thought.

The vessel arrives back at the port and it is time for the trio to revitalize their strength for explorations. After disembarkation from the boat, they head to a small waterfront café and order up wine for all three. Anni is a lady now and no one argues the point. Rather instead, Aunt Anne and Uncle Lazare encourage her to grow strong and fast like a racing mare with fine muscles, sinuous heart and speed of mind. She is being formed from her own curiosity, imagination, Papa-inspired learning and encouraging supporters to be whatever she wants to be, and she wills it so.

The three travelers take in a repast of seafood and wine (well, almost, Anni chooses a sausage and her beloved *pomme frites*) and relax as the noon day edges into early afternoon. The city is bustling with hurried assignments, endeavors, dream-chasers and wanderlust. It seems fitting to pass the remaining few hours of the day taking a walk up the seedy, infamous La Canebiere and letting the girl-child experience the most dangerous circumstances for one of her age and size alone, but through the glass as it were, because she comes well guarded and held from harm.

As dangerous as its reputation is, most of the danger resides in the bars and brothels along the boulevard. In the streets where they wander now, there are artisans abounding in numbers beyond Anni's count. The painters have set up their easels, if they can afford one, or they lean their canvas against the walls along the streets and set their paint kits to the side. With collapsible chairs they sit and put natural and manmade chemicals to the test of their own imaginations and pour out their souls and visions onto the blank boards. Some will sell enough or make enough money for a humble dinner. Some will make enough to have a great meal and a bottle of wine. Others might make enough to pay the rent past due and then an elect few might make a profit. They are all here. Those that will never be known, those that were famous of this time and even the ones that are alive today in their art, though long since passed.

Marseille is truly a place to visit, a place to vacation and oddly enough, a place for a little girl to train and learn how to live her life in the future.

Back at the apartment the vagabonds arrive to find Giedy has revived herself from a late afternoon nap and stationed herself in the kitchen to make a point. She doesn't say a word, nor would she; instead, her points are in her hands. Giedy is commanding the kitchen and preparing food and feast the old-fashioned way. While she lays no claim to gourmet cooking, like Aunt Anne, she can and will show the young ones that time makes great progress and age makes refined recipes that cannot be matched in the finest of restaurants. It is home-cooking that she performs and her artistry is no less substantial than those that are packing up in the dark of the evening back on La Canebiere with their rent money in hand. Giedy can cook—what less would one expect from a matriarch.

As the three tramps make their boisterous entrance, Giedy throws her glance with perfect timing while all three are looking at her directly. Without a word she has expressed her disapproval of their wasteful ways and frivolous behavior. And for that, she will show them what they may have missed had they dallied a little too long over someone else's table. Of course, a few glasses of wine from now she will be part of the party as the troubadours amble in and that damnable bird screaming from the balcony has been brought in to sing his same old song and drink his triple sec so that the wildest animal in the jungle is appeased. The festivities continue as the bar patrons traverse the steps in both directions from the humble apartment filled with wine, laughter and song to the bar below filled with stories of wars, daring deeds upon the sea and lies as bold as gold wine in a goblet. No one seems to care whether it is true or not, it is entertaining, and this is life in their contented, happy saga.

Now that another evening of revelry has passed, the darkness of night turns to early blue morning and the approaching new day is only an hour or so away. While all are asleep in their personally assigned quarters, Giedy lifts her aging body with its metal strength from her resting place and begins to fix breakfast. It is Giedy's turn to set the day's forays and she has one daunting goal in mind. Today, we go to see "Our Lady Mother," *The Notre Dame de la Garde* (Our Lady of the Guard). The second and equal, if not superior, fortress in Anni's young life, which will remain with her for all remaining years to come.

Pork fat, eggs and hard, heavy rolls are laid out on the table, with a bowl of reddish gravy for dipping the hard-tack leftover rolls (Giedy hates waste and won't permit stale bread to be cast to birds.) The parties gather together in somber appearance, awaiting the jolt of life from fresh-brewed espresso and maybe even a tousle of cognac to ward off the evil spirits of the night before. Giedy has fixed a hardy meal for a hardy journey. There will be no expeditions into the seediness of Marseille today. No interaction with the ruffians, hooligans and desperate artisans of La Canabiere.

No, this day is set aside for the Lord and the enlightenment, encouragement and education of the lesser qualified in the group, for their spiritual development and hedging toward their holy obligations. As the threesome stuff away the undeniable "gourmet" of time impertinent, they rise and gather themselves to delve into the day that Giedy has set on the agenda. They quietly pass jokes but they love her dearly and respect her wishes. To make things better, where she is taking them is actually quite interesting place and worthy of the day's visit. It is a castle of sorts, yet, a church. Too small to truly be church, it is a fortress as big as God and belittling to the man-made objects ascribed as defenses against enemies. No, St. Jean, St. Nicolas and even Chateau d'If are weak-kneed compared to this castel of the skyline.

The Notre Dame de la Garde sits upon one of the highest hills in Marseille and is, itself, a monstrosity of a building project that could only have been completed through divine intervention. Her pinnacle is the Virgin Mary and under her skirt are the treasures of golden images, gilded walls, paintings, cultural influences from the greatest artists the world had known to that date. Her size and appearance assure the devil himself that this lady doesn't back down. During the day she looms over the skyline and the city below like an eagle on watch for rats. At night, she bastes the city forefront, around and the hills behind, facing the sea in an aura of brilliantly lit golden hue. She truly shines in the night and abates the night wolves.

The normal routine is a tram ride to the station at Vieux Port. But this time, it is a journey on foot to the "Lady." While Aunt Anne, Giedy and Mony Lazare would prefer the convenience of transport, it is a necessity to walk the half-mile pilgrimage. The reason being that Anni is plainly too much energy in one package and it is the hope and determination of the elders that the walk will take some of the energy out of the child so that when the ensemble is complete, she just might be tired to a bearable level.

They arrive at the "Lady" and she is truly magnificent. Enormous. Hovering above into the clouds with her majesty, the Virgin Mary,

Mother of Christ, firmly stands guard over the treasures beneath and inside. The colors are magnificent. There is no place left undone. Artistry inspired not by paid workers, but by laborers for God who have put their collective talents into this palatial fortress for God Himself. If the forts below failed in duty, this kingdom's throne would stand a thousand years against an army of hell. She will not be denied her majesty over the treasured seaport with all its sinful behavior and ignorance of the one true God.

Anni has explored, run through and imagined things only she holds dear to her heart today from this visit to a sanctuary that resembles Giedy. Giedy and "Our Lady Mother" are one and the same to her. More so, the Lady of the Guard is now Anni's heart and mind. Just as the Chateau d'If is her body and life's lustered living is her wings. They will return now in awe of the majesty of a God who rules the universe and in umbrage of their particular position in time and obligations to do well and be good.

As the foursome gather back at the apartment, each with their own sun-kissed, rosy-red cheeks, a smile makes wrinkles where sorrows couldn't hide. For Anni, her smiles are making trails and paths for the timelines to come—lines which will reflect who she is and how she has handled her challenges. Smiles only go where the wrinkles have been and her tender face is squinched with elation. She runs to the balcony and brings His Majesty, CoCo, to the parlor for another night of celebration with family and friends. She will soon be eleven years of age. It is 1937 and the devil has left Herod behind. He has discarded Caesar and Attila; now, there is a new being rising in the East; Hitler is replacing Bismark. Chamberlain and Churchill are in England and Franklin D. Roosevelt is in Washington. But tonight, there are songs, dancing and happiness. It is, after all, another vacation in the South of France at Aunt Anne's and Uncle Augustine's playhouse. Mony Lazare is in attendance along with the bar patrons and Giedy is sitting guard over her La Petite.

The breeze blows through the beaded gate from the sea and city life below to engulf the gypsy palace and all therein. Music rises from the heart, laughter rings clear and dance is unbearably insistent in the soul. So, she does, she laughs and begins her dance. Anni is the entertainer again. La Petite has the eyes of the world upon her. A roomful of audience and a twenty-five-year-old parakeet that sings when he is drunk, and who loves this girl-child. Anni begins her lilting sway. She dips, parries and spins. She takes CoCo and sets him upon her head as she smoothly blends her body with the breeze and song as she falters into another world. She knows she is still here but her mind, spirit and soul tell her she is not in a real place. Reality is where her heart and mind have settled in peace. As she dances, Giedy sits quietly on the sofa and says a prayer to herself and to her God. "Lord show me my baby granddaughter, show me she will be alright, safe and happy, please." As she does so, Anni slows in her dance and Giedy looks on as time stands still while Anni moves in slow motion with the silly bird perched on her shoulder.

As the room spins and an ethereal feeling permeates her spirit, Giedy sees in front of her weary eyes, a magnificent, four-foot-tall butterfly. Its wings are enormous, beyond description in color, her body is the Chateau d'If in glossy black—strong, impregnable and virtuous. Her head appears as light, gold and brilliant as Notre Dame de la Garde and it encases a mind set on wisdom and a heart fixed on faith. God has blessed her. She, Anni, is pre-determined to exemplify survivability based on strength of character, and she, Giedy, has a spiritual revelation that God gives gifts to grandmothers. The two fortresses have taken form in the little girl, child, emerging woman and butterfly to survive the future and remain intact and respectable. Full of admiration well earned, well learned and well deserved.

# A Glorious Homeland

## *"ONS HEMECHT"*
## (OUR MOTHERLAND)

*Wou d'uelzecht durech d'Wisen zelt,*
(Where the Alzette flows through the meadows)
*Duerch d'Fielsen d'Sauer brecht.*
(The Sura breaks through the crags.)

*Wou d'Rief Iaanscht d'Musel dofteg bleit,*
(Where the vine fragrant grows along the Moselle,)
*Den Himmel Wain ons mecht.*
(The sky promises us wine:)

*Dat as onst Land, fir dat mir geif'n,*
(There lies the land for which we willingly)
*Heinidden alles won.*
(Dare everything down here.)

*Onst Heemechtsland, dat mir sou deif*
(Our Homeland which we so deeply)
*An onsen Hierzer dron.*
(Carry in our hearts.)

*Onst Heemechtsland, dat mir sou deif,An onsen Hierzer dron.*
(Our Homeland which we so deeply carry in our hearts.)

*O Du do uewen, deem seng Hand*
(O Thou above, Whose powerful hand)
*Duurch d'Weit d'Natioune leet.*
(Leads the nations through the world,)
*Behitt Du d'Letzebuerger Land*
(Protect the Luxembourg land)
*Vru friemem Joch a Leed!*
(From foreign yoke and threat.)

*Du hues ons all als Kanner schon*
(As children Thou already instilled in us all)
*De fraie Geescht jo gin,*
(The spirit of freedom.)
*Looss viru blenken d'Fraiheetssonn,*
(Let freedom's sun which we have known for so long)
*Dei mir sou laang gesin.*
(Shine for evermore.)

The Luxembourg National Anthem
(Luxembourg founded 963 A.D.)

The year 1938 arrived in full force. The world seemed to be spinning ever faster on its axis as if propelled by the winds of humanity veiling its earthen body. Politics, music, song, heroics, dance and danger abounded at seemingly every inch of earth. Tragedy and triumphs ruled the news in similitude. On one end of the spectrum, the German Army entered into Vienna on March 12 and took dominance over the fate of some 183,000 Jews. Within a day, anti-Semitic laws were passed and applied instantly upon the innocents. Within a month's time, over 500 of them committed suicide. On the other end of the spectrum, the Carnival of Swing took place on New York's Randall Island where more than 25,000 Americans danced the jitterbug for nearly six hours in a marathon of revelry.

In other news, the Biro brothers have invented the ballpoint pen. Joe Louis knocks out Max Schmeling in the first round of their rematch, showing the world that Joe is still the undisputed heavyweight champ of the world. Chester F. Carlson presents the first xenographic print to modern industry.

Near the end of the year, Britian's Chamberlain and France's Daladier agree to German annexation of Czechoslovakia; the German Iron Eagle begins seizing Jewish property, branding all Jews with the letter "J" on their passports, "Kristallnacht" occurs and some 300,000 Jews are arrested, blamed, brutalized and fined for the destruction.

On the other side of the world, Orson Welles presents his radio broadcast of H.G. Wells' *War of the Worlds* regarding an alien invasion of the planet Earth. A testimony to an infamous lack of judgment and full consideration of the power of radio and media influence upon the audience. Last, but not least, *Time* magazine names Adolf Hitler as "Man of the Year."

During this same time period, in the town of Esch-Sur-Alzette, Luxembourg, young Anni has produced her report card three quarters of the school year (minus her winter schooling in Belgium) to Papa with a smile on her face and reassuring words from her father.

"Anni, you do so well, I am happy that you work so hard to make your grades," Papa graces her with the words of encouragement. "You always do so well, you have a natural gift for learning. I am proud of you. Your grades are wonderful as usual," he says smilingly as the wisp of smoke clears the corner of his mouth from the latest draw upon his pipe. Indeed, her grades are remarkable, just as remarkable as the invisible butterfly canopy of wings she is wearing. Anni makes a 58 or 59 where a 60 is the highest mark. She takes a 28 where a 30 is the mark. These are not easy-to-achieve grades. The guidelines are set under some of the toughest schooling rules of the day throughout all of Europe. Luxembourgers pride themselves on their educational system and the product of a well-educated society.

This is the year that the Neuman family moved from the humbly-warm home and hearth of Rue Ancion 17 to 68 Rue Zenon Bernard, across from the school, the church and center of daytime activities. While history lessons at school continue to focus more on the neighboring countries of France and Germany, Anni has accumulated a wealth of knowledge about her own sweet and fantastic Luxembourg. Through this year she has seen the seasons change from her early return in spring through the summer, her late trip to Marseille, and then the fall and winter months at the close.

After the journey through her first eleven years, with the prepubescence of twelve looming on the horizon, she has finished another year of school and has been advanced in grade. She was home in time for Easter with the family and traveled to Echternach for the celebration of Luxembourg's only named saint, Willibrord. The event at Echternach was of fantastic proportions. It was the celebration of the June 4, 1906 removal of the *relics* from the St. Peter Cathedral which was followed by a procession of nearly twenty thousand marchers, musicians, clerics and dancers. The parade is an annual ritual on the seventh Sunday following Pentecost and is flamboyant, joyful, and enlightening in heart. Hand to handkerchief, each member of the assembly gather and make the faithful march through the city, and the festivities follow in full force. Actually, the march is more of a dance that is unique to Echternach, a skipping of sorts through the town square. Anni has learned a lot from her travels to surrounding countries, but none are so dear to her tender heart as those experiences here in her very own homeland, Luxembourg.

The country is beautiful in its very own special way. This is just as should be expected from a country so small, yet so bountiful in culture, history, character and strength—holding guard over the heart of Europe. The tiny country is mighty in spirit, pride and presence. It is known as the second Gibraltar. In fact, the fortress in the north stood guard from A.D. 969. and its tunnels remain today as a testimony to what pride in a homeland can produce through a determined and resilient people. The populace of Luxembourg is a mixture of the surrounding countries, however, it maintains its own independence and truth of character in the fact that it has been conquered, embattled and surrendered, but recovered each and every time warfare spilled blood into its rich soil.

This small, daunting country has proven itself worldwide as the epitome of resilience, and it is no surprise that such a creature as gentle as a butterfly with a body of iron should exemplify resilience of life. Anni and her homeland are one and the same. They have struggled. They have conquered and been conquered. They have been overcome, overwhelmed and dominated. They have been taken low and risen high. They have survived the storm and drought of worldly influences uninvited. Nevertheless, they both remain today, almost as if untouched by it all. A monument and testimony to perseverance. Time is but a rain upon the rock of what God has created in both country and man, and in this case, woman. Anni is Luxembourg, personified.

Here in this small country, nearly devoid of worldly recognition, are deep gorges that fall swooning from mountaintop to mountaintop. In almost every crevice or ravine is a small hamlet, or larger city if the flow of a river is nearby. The landscape is a lush, lusty green nearly year round. Some snow will whiten it for a while but the fir trees better themselves of the skyline. The air is crisp, clean and sometimes tainted with the smell of the iron industry, but the aroma is as old as the centuries. France has all of its history, Germany the same; however, none stood, nor still stand, as nobly as the encircled heart of Europe. The bedrock-solid nation that is little in appearance is enormous in stature. A people as stout and hardy as any given on earth. Ingenious, tenacious, crafted and secluded in an identity that bespeaks what determination can accomplish.

Here is where the Moselle flows, as does the sweet wine from the hillsides. Castles, fortresses and chateaus dot the landscape like road signs. The rise and fall of the terrain protect the inhabitants inside and guard against intrusion. It is a guarded country and one worthy of all the respect imaginable and then some. Luxembourg can compete, and she does indeed; however, a shadow is falling upon her lands and the sun is dimmed by the flight of a strange creature. The year 1939 is fast approaching and stifling quiet has bathed the hearts of all its countrymen with silent apprehensions and concerns of unknown origin. There is word that an Eagle is in flight and it is headed in this direction.

Meanwhile, Anni and young Albert have gone up the stairs, through the small window at mid-staircase and onto the terrace overlooking the yard. "Anni, what is a Jew?" young Albert blurts out as the two scatter their marbles on the stone floor. "Albert, where did you get that word from?" Anni inquires. "On my way home from school. Somebody said that there was a Jew living over there [pointing toward a row of houses just meters away]." "Don't worry about it, Bubby, it doesn't mean anything, it's just a word some people use. People are always trying to make up names for everything and everybody." Soon, the attention is back on the dozen or so marbles rolling here and yon amidst the laughter of the two young Luxembourgers at play on a late winter evening's sunlit balcony.

# An Iron Eagle Flies Over Its Own Shadow

*"This is the last territorial claim I have to make in Europe."*

Adolf Hitler, Sept. 26, 1938.

This was a placating and assuring statement made by the Ruler of Germany; the Rhineland(1936); Austria (1936); Sudetenland (1938); made September 26, 1938 while in the very midst of a decisive and destructive plan to launch slaughter upon Czechoslovakian independence.

By March, 1939, Hitler honored his words to "claim," if nothing else, and on March 14, 1939, German troops marched into Prague and declared the end of Czechoslovakian self-rule. Hardly settled in his higher seat, Hitler turned his eyes toward Poland.

***"Mr. Chamberlain's reaction surprised me. He had conceived himself as having a special insight into Hitler's character. He believed, with hope, that there had been a true meeting of the minds at Munich, and that he, Hitler, and Mussolini had together saved the world from the infinite horrors of war. Suddenly as by an explosion his faith and all that had followed from his actions and his arguments were shattered. Responsible as he was for grave misjudgments of facts, having deluded himself and imposed his errors on his colleagues and unhappy British public opinion, he none the less between night and morning turned his back abruptly upon his past.***

*If Chamberlain failed to understand Hitler, Hitler completely underrated the nature of the British Prime Minister. He mistook his civilian aspect and passionate desire for peace for a complete explanation of his personality, and thought that his umbrella was his symbol.*

*He did not realise that Neville Chamberlain had a very hard core, and that he did not like being cheated. The next victim on Hitler's list was Poland. Within a fortnight (March 31) Chamberlain gave a guarantee to Poland. He was at length convinced that Nazi Germany meant war, and he contracted alliances in every direction still open. To the Polish guarantee was added a Greek and Romanian guarantee, and to these an alliance with Turkey.*

*This was no time for recriminations about the past. The guarantee to Poland was supported by the leaders of all parties and groups in the House. In this sad tale of wrong judgments formed our climax. That we should all have come to this pass makes those responsible, however honourable their motives, blameworthy before history. Look back and see what we had successfully accepted or thrown away; a Germany disarmed by solemn treaty; a Germany rearmed in violation of a solemn treaty; air superiority or even air parity cast away; the Rhineland forcibly occupied and the Siegfried Line built or building; the Berlin-Rome Axis established; Austria devoured and digested by the Riech; Czechoslovakia deserted and ruined by the Munich Pact, its fortress line in German hands, its mighty arsenal of Skoda henceforth making munitions for the German armies; President Roosevelt's effort to stabalise or bring to a head the European situation by the interventions of the United States waved aside with one hand, and Soviet Russia's undoubted willingness to join the Western Powers and go all lengths to save Czechoslovakia ignored on the other; the services of thirty-five Czech divisions against the still unripened German Army cast away, when Great Britain could herself supply only two to strengthen the front of France; all gone with the wind."*

Winston S. Churchill; *The Second World War and The Editors of Life*; Golden Press, New York; Copyright 1960.

It just didn't make sense. Something so catastrophic was happening in Europe and the whole world sat witness and left the debate and the matter itself to politicians for resolution. It seemed the general attitude of the gross population of the planet, excluding Nazi Germany and its victims, was that this could not remain and would never touch their respective doorsteps. Because it didn't make sense that a man named Hitler could do such horrible deeds without repercussions or immediate reprimand, it couldn't be real and thus it wasn't "sensed" by the minds, bodies and emotions of the world at large. Surely it was a matter of some unreal circumstances which would be allayed with immediacy and action and the band could play on, the dance floor continue to fill and drinks continue to flow with the flirting whispers of men to women and women to men. This, after all, was 1939, war was over with the Great War, World War I, and it was time to live it up. Music, movies, telegraph, telegram, radio and other media had made the world smaller and almost as if one.

Prohibition had come and gone over a decade ago in America, and while the world was getting drunk on revelry and swing, and ignoring hunger and depression by all means possible, one man was getting drunk on blood. Hitler had developed a demonic, mesmerizing personality that anaesthetized the masses. He would take his audience from beginning revulsion to delusional affirmation and admiration, all within the matter of time it took him to deliver another infamous speech.

In May 1939, the British government issued a White Paper which restricted any future Jewish immigration to Palestine to the limit of 75,000 within a five-year period. In June 1939, The S.S. St. Louis with a cargo of some 930 Jewish refugees was turned away by the Cuban government. The United States also promptly declined their request for admission and thus the innocents were forced to return to an uncertain Europe and certain terror. By August 1939, Hitler had declared that "Jews" in particular, but under the guise of "hereditary disease," should register with the government. Just months previous, the king and queen of England, on April 30, 1939, attended the $150 million New York World's Fair with all fanfare and fireworks.

By September and through October 1939, Germany had invaded Poland; Britain and France declared war on Germany; A "Fuhrer Decree" made murder by medical personnel acceptable and legal; The Russian Red Army invaded Poland from the east; Piotrkow, Poland became the first Jewish ghetto and by November, 1939, Hitler slitheringly escaped an assassination attempt on his life. On November 23, 1939, all Jews in Poland were commanded to wear the distinctive armband "Judenstern" (Jewish Star) or face certain consequence.

Meanwhile, during the same time period, the United States considered nominations for the Academy Awards, which would be awarded by February, 1940. In the run for movies: *Goodbye, Mr. Chips*, *Love Affair*, *Mr. Smith Goes to Washington*, *Of Mice and Men*, *Stagecoach* (staring an unknown actor John Wayne), *The Wizard of Oz* and lastly, in December 1939, *Gone With the Wind.* For music: "Faithful Forever," "I Poured my Heart Into a Song" and "Over the Rainbow" took honors in the Top Three category.

As of September 1939, the German *Sitzkrieg* (Sitting War) was in full swing for operation *Fall Gelb* (Plan Yellow), as the German forces came to call it because of the stalls in activity, long waiting periods and indecision. It was in parallel but direct contrast to the German *Blitzkrieg* or "Lightning." The plan was organized by Hitler himself to stretch his Iron Fist to the West. A hope to engulf the entire European continent and, undoubtedly, a biting pain in the pit of his stomach to rule the world.

Through this year, in Esch-Sur-Alzette, Luxembourg, at 68 Rue Zenon Bernard, a gray concrete and stone building stood shoulder to shoulder with neighboring houses in a secure environment. It had stood there for decades and was meant to stand for all time. In this humble home, the Neuman family lived out an exciting first half of the year only to become deathly quiet for reasons unknown to the ever inquisitive mind of Anni. It is the same year Deddy passed away and "Boma," the senior Albert's mother moves into the home.

Anni had done her "pulmonary" duty of spending January, February and March in Belgium for respiratory therapy. The spring and summer had brought wonderful times at school, Anni had made her last trip to Marseille for nearly a lifetime. Her young friend, a Jewish girl by the name of Andree' Nussbaum, had recently moved away with her family for reasons strange as a bird's flight in silence. By September, the world seemed to be growing quiet around Anni and she didn't quite understand it.

"Anni, here, now sit here and don't move and don't listen to the grownups, just watch the game, yes?" Papa would say as he picked up young Anni's light-framed twelve-year-old body and set her on the stone wall surrounding the football (soccer) field. "Yes, Papa, I will. I will cheer for your team, too. I will stay here and I promise not to listen," Anni would reply, to make her father happy, although neither believed it and neither would let it show on their faces. Anni would sit on the wall and Papa would go off to the sidelines to study the art of sports. On occasion the adults would wander nearby or stand close to Anni. Even over the wall there was a house where conversations could be heard but not quite understood. A lot of talking seemed to be going on at once. Everyone looked around as they spoke as if they were waiting for someone to arrive or expecting to be interrupted, or worse, overheard.

For all her straining to hear, the words were creatively concealed by just the right volume to communicate to the intended audience and no others. At times, Papa would stand onla a couple of meters away, and yet she still could not get her ears to hear. It was very frustrating because these conversations were obviously serious and important. "Why shouldn't I know what they are saying? I am almost grown now and I can handle it. This is silly, it is probably important for me to know and the men are keeping it to themselves. Ughh! Men," Anni would think to herself, "they make me very irritated."

While the conversations had become apparent at the soccer field that early September, they were not limited to that location. In the weeks and months to follow, they carried over to the grocery store, the church, the school, the shoe repair shop and even to the Neuman dinner table and living room. Papa read the paper as he had always done but in a way that was not at all the same. He would read and set it down. He would look up or close his eyes. Sometimes he would silently look at his wife, gaze around the room and at the children, one by one. He would lift the paper as if it were heavy in his hands. "What is wrong with Papa?" Anni would think to herself as she sat at the table doing her homework. "He always checks my work and instructs me." She contemplated but could not grasp any hints—it was boiling inside her mind.

September rolls into October and cooler air arrives. However, this is the strangest year Anni has ever experienced. It seems, and it sounds silly, that the wind isn't even blowing. Things are growing so quiet and still. People aren't as happy anymore. Sour faces are now in the place of laughing wine. Concern is taking the place of celebration. There is something very wrong and nobody will talk about it or admit it. All the adults seem so preoccupied, even though the children are the same as ever and happily so. "We aren't going hungry. Mama and Papa still talk to each other. Charly is getting bigger every day. Albert is making me laugh until I cry. What is wrong?" Anni continues to ply her brain for an answer. She hates it when she cannot get an answer. She won't rest until she understands the weird world in which she is now an unwilling participant. Yet, she continues hopefully, vehement about finding answers.

Through the end of October and the month of November Anni has become predictable. With all the "unnecessary" quiet and clandestine behavior, she has resolved that she will enjoy life and maybe everyone else will see she is right, it is silly to be so sullen. "Mama, we did good at mass today! Can Bubby and I have some francs for the movies?" Anni asks, knowing that the adults seemed only too disposed to having the children out of the house and preoccupied with better thoughts, dreams and less curiosity where it doesn't belong. "Yes, but you be careful, do not stay too late and make us worry. Watch your brother closely, you know how he likes to run off and make us all worry as if it were funny," Mama chides Anni, and Anni nods in acceptance of the authority bestowed upon her young shoulders. Little Albert is a joy and no problem to her. She knows his routine by now and no matter what he does, he always returns safe and won't get his sister in trouble. Scared, shocked, angry, laughing, concerned; yes, all the above, but he doesn't disappoint her. There relationship is one of trust and very trustworthy.

The winter months continue to roll in and the air has not changed. If anything, it has grown thicker, and there are some people moving from the neighborhood that Anni thought would be here for a hundred years. Not many, but just enough to notice it isn't normal. Meanwhile, every Sunday is church, movies or playing near the apartment. "Mrs. Rondelli, are you putting your laundry on the balcony?" she will ask of the upstairs neighbor. The Rondellis are a lonely couple in Anni's mind. They have no children and they don't say much. But they are nice people and that is fair enough. "No, Anni, you and Master Albert are free to play your marbles or whatever it is that you do." And so it goes on certain days. When the weather is not good outside and the rain comes, the laundry of the buildings' occupants will hang in the attic. However, the attic is not a place for Anni to take interest in during her flights of fantasy anyhow. Today, it is the balcony for more laughs and questions for Bubby.

December passes the baton to January and thus to February, March likewise and into April of 1940. Anni has seen Buffalo Bill a dozen times at the theatre. Her favorite movies and movie stars keep her entranced and riveted with imagination as she puts herself into the place of each actor and player. She is a cowboy riding hard and fast on a horse. She is an Indian creeping up on a firelit camp in the desert darkness of night with knife in hand. Next, she is Margaret O'Brien being courted by handsome men of suave speech and broad shoulders. Soon, she is dancing around the ballroom floor with Hollywood's finest leading men as she steps into the shoes of the adored Shirley Temple and commands all attention.

By May 1940, she finds herself carrying out each and every step of the days as the day before, determined to remain joyful but it just isn't working. She looks forward to school, playing with her friends and Bubby, good dinners at home, walking with Papa to the football field and Sunday movies. In the short nine days from the inauguration of this month, all is quiet. Evening has come as the sun has slowly lowered in tearful solitude and retreat to a darkness beyond its control for a twelve-hour forced abeyance. It is the late evening of May 9, 1940 and Anni climbs under the covers of her bed. Mama, Papa, Bubby, Charly and Boma are all in bed as well. The curtain of night is drawn over Esch, Luxembourg is going to sleep, all is peaceful and quiet with the exception of those who work in the late hours.

Meanwhile, in the grandest house of the entire little country, bags have been packed, servants scurry in great haste and perspiration is rolling on every occupant's forehead. Her Royal Highness, Charlotte, and the Ducal family are fleeing their independent, neutral country and countrymen. They are taking flight to New York by the morrow and will seek refuge because somewhere, everywhere, without a cry, scream or siren, a large black Iron Eagle has flown over this wonderful little country and a shadow has fallen, marking the territory of its landing. The Eagle will fly in lowering circles this night, return to its nest and contemplate a reenergizing leap into the morning air, bringing with it all of its evil intent.

# Part II

# Joys and Sorrows in the Dark Years

# Passover All Over Again, Two Days Before Pentecost, No Less

*"Now it came about at midnight that the Lord struck all the first-born in the land of Egypt, from the first-born of Pharaoh who sat on his throne to the first-born of the captive who was in the dungeon, and all the first-born of cattle. And Pharaoh arose in the night, he and all his servants and all the Egyptians; and there was a great cry in Egypt, for there was no home where there was not someone dead. Then he called for Moses and Aaron at night and said 'Rise up, get out from among my people, both you and the sons of Israel; and go, worship the Lord, as you have said.*

*'Take both your flocks and your herds, as you have said, and go, and bless me also.' And the Egyptians urged the people, to send them out of the land in haste, for they said 'We shall all be dead.' So the people took their dough before it was leavened, with their kneading bowls bound up in the clothes on their shoulders. Now the sons of Israel had done according to the word of Moses, for they had requested from the Egyptians articles of silver and articles of gold, and clothing; and the Lord had given the people favor in the sight of the Egyptians, so that they let them have their request. Thus they plundered the Egyptians." Exodus 12:29-36.*

*"Now it came about that when Pharaoh had let the people go, that God did not lead them by the way of the land of the Philistines, even though it was near; for God said 'Lest the people change their minds when they see war, and they return to Egypt.' Hence God led the people around by the way of the wilderness to the Red Sea; and the sons of Israel went up in martial array from the land of Egypt. And Moses took the bones of Joseph with him, for he had made the*

***sons of Israel solemnly swear, saying 'God shall surely take care of you.' Then they set out from Succoth and camped in Etham on the edge of the wilderness. And the Lord was going before them in a pillar of cloud by day to lead them on the way, and in a pillar of fire by night to give them light, that they might travel by day and night. He did not take away the pillar of cloud by day, nor the pillar of fire by night, from before the people."***

Exodus 13:17-21; *The Open Bible*, Expanded Edition;
Copyright 1985 by Thomas Nelson, Inc.

***"And when the day of Pentecost had come, they were all together in one place."***

Acts 2:1; *The Open Bible*, Expanded Edition;
Copyright 1985 by Thomas Nelson, Inc.

*The night had passed and the Grand Duchess of Luxembourg, Charlotte, with the Ducal family in tow, were in flight for New York, New York, United States of America. In the vacuum behind, her own endowed country from birth and by blood, Luxembourg was being Luxembourg without her. For common sense and reason, she had to flee for the safety of not only herself but her family and those that served her house. After all, it would only have been expected they would have been put to death or imprisoned under horrific circumstances. It was a wise and prudent decision. She was safely kept and able to plead to the world and anyone who would listen, for the help and aide of her beloved country.*

*On May 10, 1940, the entire little country of some 300,000 inhabitants had awakened to news from the night of pending terror and more was coming at an alarming pace: the leadership had left and they were left to do whatever seemed to be the most reasonable acts.*

*The most reasonable acts where such that men took charge with their very lives in hand and stood up to the daunting challenge. They took the challenge to keep throbbing numbers and scores of cities out of panic. They took the challenge to ferry the fellow countrymen to safety by finesse and favor of God's divine providence. Real men, Luxembourg men, took on roles they had never even known existed and wished it weren't so. But nevertheless, they stood up when, and even before, they were called upon. They took challenge to their will, stamina, endurance and strength of heart to act as leaders with the title thrust upon them. They took charge as need may be and became the itinerant militia of mild sorts.*

*Their only goal, purpose and genuine heartfelt desire—to see that each and every Luxembourger woman and child found safe refuge from harm. To see to it that each was kept sheltered from fear and disaster and placed into comfort while the men did their job. They were the quintessential gentlemen, thinking only as men do. The word had spread as if Moses had walked through the land that early morning and announced the time had come to pack what you may and start out immediately on a journey into the unknown. It was an Exile. It was an Exodus. It wasn't 5,000 years ago, it was 1940 and it was happening to a gentile nation of some 96 percent Catholics two days before the celebration of Pentecost. And yes, in two days to come, nearly twenty centuries later, they would be "gathered again, all in one place."*

In the second largest city of Luxembourg, Esch-Sur-Alzette was only getting trickling information as rumors filtered through the mill of the populace. The impromptu militia of Esch men were meting out the coming news at a cautious pace to avoid outright panic and alarm. The sun had already broken through the early dark hours of morning; however, one would almost certainly swear that it was getting darker. The news was not good, not good at all, and getting worse.

"Anni, get your brother up before he sleeps the whole day away. It's already past eight. I swear that boy sleeps like the dead for someone with so much energy awake," Mama calls out, and again, "Anni! you both get in here for breakfast or I am going to throw it out and you can eat tomorrow." Mama has given warning, although she is saying it from a good mood and somewhat teasingly. For Anni and the rest of the Neuman home, things had started out fairly normal this morning of May 10, 1940.

It is a Friday and also a holiday, school is out and Sunday would be Pentecost Mass and a feast of ham afterward. Mama was already preparing to cook the ham today and that made things a little brighter in the home. Anni couldn't be happier. For the past several months the secretive behavior and quiet conversations, have all forced her into a dark tunnel created in her mind. This tunnel is something Anni has developed out of her imagination and she uses it when she is unhappy, afraid, depressed or just melancholy. It is her own little hideaway inside her heart and head where she is safe, a comforting place for her to seek refuge from the storms of life and the threats of anything that steals joy.

Anni has been slowly, methodically and now, nearly completely entering back into her cocoon. All the feelings around just aren't right to her fourteen-year-old senses. She didn't go to Coq-Sur-Mer this year and she was very surprised. This week the Catholic church notified all of its congregation that the annual pilgrimage march to the city of Luxembourg for the payment of homage to Mary, Mother of God, Consoler of the Afflicted, the Patroness of the City of Luxembourg was cancelled. It was a ritual of epic proportions. Beginning in 1666, Our Lady of Luxembourg had become the patroness and guardian over the war-torn city of Luxembourg and the country surrounding it. In 1678 the Holy Virgin had been elected patroness of the whole Duchy of Luxembourg and the County of Chiney. It was from this event that the pilgrimage developed into a strong undercurrent and foundation for the religious devotees of this great, yet small, country. The solemn celebration, with all its pomp and circumstance, meant the world to Anni.

It was a wonderful time to renew her faith in God and know that the Mass would reaffirm to the entire country that they were covered under the supreme protection of their guardian Mother. To be assured that no harm would befall the small, independent nation. Mary had become a symbol of assurance to the predominantly Catholic nation that the utter destruction, such as from the Thirty Years War of 1618-1648, would never set danger at their door again. They were solemn in faith that divine protection guarded them from the evils of other nations and the dark hearts of despots.

Anni had always enjoyed the trek from the city with all the excitement through the night to arrive the next morning to a world of people. Some gatherings, such as in 1937, reached a total of between 50,000 and 60,000 people. In fact, just this past year arrangements had been made to set aside an eighty-acre piece of land to be decorated with the way of the cross. Here, special feasts were arranged, gatherings occurred and an itinerant market was fashioned to provide the faithful with rosary beads, miniature figurines of Our Lady, candles and other wonderfully crafted works.

Seven days hence, the pilgrimage should have taken place for the 280th consecutive year in Luxembourg history. Unfortunately it too was vanquished by the black Iron Eagle screaming from the sky, sweeping across the fields and advancing upon sacred soil. The irony again to this resilient and proud people was that they were set in the middle of other peoples' wars and conflict and the Consolation of the Afflicted was their heart's desire and their elected providential protector. They had done nothing to deserve this, other than being literally caught in the middle.

"Anni, you and Bubby bring me your dishes so I can get this kitchen cleaned," Boma belts out the words over the children. She is the senior Albert's mother and she is known by the family name of Boma, but her given name is Elizabeth Clesen-Neuman of pure Luxembourg blood. In her mid-sixties, she stands tall, strong and devout as the family's paternal matriarch. The children comply with her order and clear the table while Mama takes young Charly to change from his bed clothes to something more fitting. The home is increasingly being surrendered to the older women and the children are all too pleased to make way to other surroundings before they are deemed valuable help with housework and other chores. Anni and young Albert have honed their skills quite well for times and days like this, they have a routine now which leads them to their rooms quietly seeking toys. Then, they patter out like mice past the adults to go play in their fantasyland and imagination.

By noon the sun has risen high above Esch, the family has had their most important meal of the day and all have returned to their own endeavors. As the sun falls slowly to the two o'clock position, Albert and Anni have found their way upstairs to Marie's apartment, the neighbors on the next floor above the Neuman home. Poor Albert has become the victim of the most confining position for an eleven-year-old energetic boy to be in—a silent listener by compulsion to two women in conversation. "Anni, let's go, I want to play in the yard," he moans and pleads to no avail. The "women" continue their ceaseless chatter although one is in her thirties and the other in her teens. "Anni, Marie is busy, let's go downstairs and I will show you my new backflip and cartwheel," again he implores for his sister's attention. Still no success.

"Anni, look! I'm a clown at the circus, I bet you can't make this face!" He has succeeded to some degree, finally. Although Anni is not willing to surrender her grownup talk with Marie, she and Marie both break into uproarious laughter at the way in which Bubby has contorted his body and face at the same time. It is as if he were performing for five thousand people under the Big Top. "Some day you are going to get stuck like that." says Marie tauntingly, still spilling laughter from her belly. The girls almost cry from the way in which this kid acts. He is a born entertainer, he is a clown, he's funny by nature and a natural talent at bringing life, laughter and joy to everyone he meets.

As the laughter starts to fade, a sound arises from outside. It is the ever-growing rumbling of a small crowd of people. Some are walking, some stand in small groups neighbor to neighbor, others half-walk an half-run alone to and fro. It is a very strange feeling, like nothing Anni has ever felt in her entire life. It is as though suddenly the world has been turned to fast forward and it is being seen in slow motion. Her mind reels, and thinking isn't working.

Below, there comes a loud banging on the door and voices rise and fall like boulders plunging down the side of a mountain. Bouncing up and down, crashing and then quietly rolling. "What is going on!" Marie bursts forth, speaking to herself as much as to the air and the room around them. "Anni, you stay here while I go downstairs and take a look. Keep Bubby here with you, OK?" She bounds out the door and down the stairs before Anni can form an answer. Anni goes over to the window and looks down below to the front door of her home. There, three men wearing armbands, representing some sort of authority, stand speaking to Mama and Boma. There is sunshine among the clouds, looking up. Looking left and right, there are the same old buildings and familiar sights she has seen for the last thirteen years. But below, confusion, chaos and pandemonium have ruptured the peaceful streets."What in the world are they doing?" Anni asks herself. She sees it but it doesn't make a bit of sense. Someone over there is pushing a two-wheeled cart without a horse and a child is pulling on the shafts. The thing is loaded like a jigsaw puzzle of household belongings. "Where in the world are they going?" Anni is spinning in her head and her stomach. She can barely hear the commotion anymore because of the pounding of her heart. She feels sick, for no reason other than the fact that something is happening and whatever it is, it isn't good. Whatever it is, it is something even the grownups have never seen. Fear has suddenly become king for the day.

"What is it, Anni, what is going on?" young Albert cries to his sister. He doesn't have tears nor even fear, he is just bewildered at the sudden change of events and the oddity of it all. "Where are they going?" he says, pointing out the window at the neighbors from five houses over. A family of five, father, mother, and three children of proportionate ages are carrying pillowcases and shopping bags down the street and around the corner. They walk so quickly the youngest child can hardly keep up and they are out of sight before Anni can answer her brother's questions. This is all too weird. It isn't real. It can't be. It doesn't make sense. It is happening, she sees it. This is too much to stomach. "Stop, stop it!" she screams to her head. A city can't just up and leave like this, people, families walking, even running, away from their homes as if they mean nothing.

"Where is Papa, he will straighten this out and explain it" she says inside her mind. She cannot stand here and wait longer. Marie has been downstairs too long and the voices are still rising and falling in argument, cries, despair and anger. Time's up, Anni grabs Bubby and tells him to follow her down the steps. She will find the answers to more than a hundred questions that have turned her head into a spinning potter's wheel.

As Anni rushes down the steps with Albert some two steps behind, she hears the voices clearly on her approach. "You have until six o'clock! That's it. I am not discussing this any longer. You have heard what we have had to say. You must and you will get out of this house and out of Esch immediately. You have three hours, pack whatever you can into your pillowcases and you can take another bag if you believe you can carry it all night. That is up to you, we have other people we need to tell and time is running out. Tell your men to stay behind, we need them, they are not to leave." The medium-sized man of the three in the doorway discharges these final words in parting to Mama, Boma and Marie as if he were a army commandant. He isn't the biggest of the group in size but he carries his authority and voice larger than the others. This is serious, deadly serious and the women know this man is right and only doing what is best in sounding such an alarm.

"Albert! Albert!" Mama calls through the doorway (the sound of the name is *Al Behr*, the "t" is silent). It is Papa pushing through the small gathering of neighbors just outside the doorstep. "Mama, what is the matter, what is going on?" Anni begs of her mother while the younger Albert stands three steps back with a blank, pasty white face. "Never you mind, go get your things together. Take your brother. Get your pillowcases from your beds and fill them with a change of clothes and whatever else you need. Don't over pack, and help your brother, don't forget your pajamas, now do as I say. We have to leave the house." Mama is in no mood to be challenged, she appears scared in a way Anni has never seen. She is fixated on getting the distance shortened between her and her husband.

"Papa! What is going on, why do we have to leave?" Anni asks as her father enters the doorway. "Anni! Go away now! Do as your mother says!" He raises his voice in a way unfamiliar to Anni. It hurts and she wants to cry but she knows he is being the strong man that she has always loved and admired. He doesn't mean harm, it is for her good and all the good of the family. He is responsible, in charge and all the decisions fall on his shoulders. He has to be trusted without question, he is all they have now.

"It's the Germans, Albert." Mama speaks first to Papa. "Yes, I know. I heard the men at the university, so I got here as fast as I could. We don't have much time. The militia men are right, we do need to leave and leave as soon as possible. We have three hours at the most, so let's get this thing together as best we can, OK?" Papa queries.

"Yes, Albert. Boma, you take care of Charly please and gather your clothes and his while I go to the kitchen. We are going to need food and something to drink along the way. We don't know how long this will be."

"Gredy [pronounced *Greh-dee*, Papa's nickname for his wife], I'm not staying behind. They want the men here but I cannot leave you, the kids and mother alone. It is too much for the five of you and you are my responsibility. If that is a problem for the other men of Esch, then they will have to accept it. I am not letting you go alone." He is a man and a real man stands by his family. Sometimes a real man must leave his family to fight for a higher cause, if there are any, but here, this is the right thing to do for not only this man but for any man.

By six o'clock, the Neuman family has packed as best they can. Anni has her pillowcase with a change of clothes and not much else, except two books. Anni has already become an avid reader by now and, inside her cocoon, books are her life's greatest enjoyments. In fact, at times she would play marbles with Bubby with one hand and have a book in her other hand. She has been known to walk the sidewalks and even cross traffic without so much as lifting her eyes from her book.

Bubby has his pillowcase packed also, except one thing. "Papa, should I take my accordion?" he inquires with a quizzical look on his face. Bubby is as avid a musician as Anni a reader. He has never received formal education in the art, it is all "by ear" and self-taught. "No Bubby! There will be no time for music, just leave it," Papa snaps. He doesn't mean to be harsh and he doesn't want to be. But he must be pointed, sharp and disciplined right now. The amendments can be made later, hopefully.

Mama has stuffed the ham that was to be the joyous center of attention for Pentecost Sunday into a shopping bag, after having carefully wrapped it in cloth and paper. "Gredy, leave the silverware, I have a knife in my pocket, that is all we need and can afford to carry," Papa directs his wife. And she obeys. Papa is leading this family from their home at the evening hour into the streets, to the country roads and into the unknown as if it were Passover all over again. The fleeing of a people in a hurry and without time to make practical decisions, only expedient ones.

"Papa, where are we going," Anni asks as the close group of six gather on the street and begin walking. "I don't know Anni, it is war, let's get the hell out of here," Papa replies not only to Anni but the whole family. "Remember, whatever you packed, you have to carry, so if you don't need it, throw it out now!" he commands as they steady their legs for an unknown march into the night. Little six-year-old Charly starts to cry. He doesn't mean to, he doesn't want to, but he cannot help it. Held in his mother's arms, all the things his young eyes see, from top to bottom of buildings, streets and sidewalks, is utter chaos and he is frightened. His grip tightens around Mama's neck and he clings to her because she is life and he, like the rest of the family, want to live. They want to survive and find safety in the broad alleyways of hell. Find the dark places, travel light, fast and quietly. Seek hope. That is all they can do this second night prior to Pentecost. The celebration has been cancelled, but Passover has occurred while the exodus begins.

# Journey from Home, the Butterfly's Forced Flight

*"My Fuhrer! My Comrades!*
*Again we experience the hour that makes us proud and happy.*
*By your order, here stands a youth—a youth that knows no class distinction.*
*The youth of our nation is shaped in your image.*
*Because you are our ideal of Loyalty…we also want to be loyal.*
*Adolf Hitler, leader of German youth, will speak."*

Introduction by unknown speaker

*"My German youth! After a year, I again greet you.*
*You here today are only a part…of what is spread over all Germany.*
*We want you, my German boys and girls, to absorb all that we expect of Germany.*
*We want to be one people…and you my youth are to be that people.*
*In the future there must be no ranks or classes…*
*And you must not let them begin to grow in you.*
*We want to see one nation and you must educate yourselves for it.*
*We want the people to be obedient…and you must practice this obedience.*

*We want this people to be peace-loving…but also to be courageous.*
*You must be peaceable and courageous.*
*You must be peaceable and courageous at the same time.*
*We want this nation to be hard—not soft…*
*and you must steel yourselves for it in your youth.*
*You must learn to accept privations and never collapse.*

*No matter what we create today or what we do today... We will pass away. But in you Germany will live.*
*And when nothing remains of us then you must hold in your fist... the flag we tore from nothing.*
*I know this cannot be otherwise...*
*because you are flesh from our flesh and blood from our blood.*
*The same spirit that dominates us burns in your young minds.*
*As the columns of our movement sweep through Germany today...*
*Then I know that you will join with them and we know around us is Germany—in us Germany marches...and behind us Germany follows."*

Triumph of the Will 07; Hitler Youth Rally 1939; Adolf Hitler
(Attendance estimated to be between
1.5–2 million 8-16 yr. olds with others)

Here at the outskirts of beautiful Esch-Sur-Alzette, the Neuman family take their final steps in the city, placing their feet over the invisible town limits and across that same line into an undecided, hurried and bewildering journey. Many others have now joined together as they straggle from all directions forming an informal line of sorts. They are encouraged by the attending men with the armbands to keep some distance between parties for safety. It is another confusing thing to add to Anni's thoughts. "Why would we need to spread out? For what? There isn't anything around us or above us?" However, she is not completely ignorant of the dangers, not as much as the adults had hoped for. She has listened in the past couple of months while lying in bed as planes flew in both directions in the night sky above their home. Bombing runs had been incessant during the night hours leading up to this day and Anni had become somewhat accustomed to it. After all, it had nothing to do with them and they were safely nestled in between the flight patterns of the machines. Their purpose wasn't quite known in full to Anni but she had learned the difference in the sounds—which ones were coming from where, and also how the engines whined loudly on return compared to the hard droning caused by heavy payloads as they fanned out toward potential targets.

The numbers swell from staggered groups of all proportions to nearly two hundred men, women and children on foot, mostly women and children. As the exodus makes its way to the main roads leading south, a horrific screeching cry, unequaled by an Artillery shell in flight or a wounded rat, fills the twilight. It is the Iron Eagle, with its sinister laughter at coming death and destruction. This horrible cry comes from the darkest corners of evil. Its unnerving skills are being laid bare before the world and this skill being heard now is one of them, the ability to scream so loudly and terrifyingly. Yet, it doesn't pierce the air, it pierces the mind. The ears are deaf to it outwardly, but the mind is rattled and unnerved, seized with paralyzing fear.

As the exodus of Luxembourgers paces down the roadway, Anni looks up at Mama beside her with Charly in her arms, still crying but a little less now. She looks at Papa's back and, though she can't see his face, she knows there is anguish written all over it. Looking slightly behind her, she sees Bubby and Boma. Boma looks shell-shocked, staring blankly ahead as if she isn't even here. She is a stern and strong woman, but right now she seems to be more a moving stone statue of things past, no present and no sign of a future. Further back down the road sits the town of Esch, all Anni knows as home. The place where she has launched on dozens of adventures and travels. The place where her heart has always been warmed with welcome on her returns from various days, weeks and months worth of trips and education. It is the spiritual bedrock of her soul and the emotional fountain from which her life has flowed.

She cannot contain it any longer, she finds herself holding her breath, pressure building in her head, heart and eyes. Her eyes water and then tears break forth with a flood. "Will we ever see home again?" is all she can think and it is hurting beyond the fires of hell in her flesh and bones, in her young tender heart. She is being ripped from her roots for no good damnable reason. The screaming black Iron Eagle has taken his razor-sharp talons and sliced open the cocoon with a tearing snatch and the butterfly has been coldly, quickly forcefully thrust into flight from its comfortable cocoon. The multicolored creature representing all that is beautiful in youth and life, the example of love, hope, lust of life, exuberance, joy, charity and knowledge is flying for its total existence, for survival. Now, the butterfly must steel itself and draw on all its strength to become more iron-bodied than that horrid Eagle.

"Anni, Anni, not right now, sweetheart, don't cry. We will be okay. I need you, and I need you to be strong for me," Papa says with a forced, yet gently true smile of encouragement on his face. She smiles back and the tears cease. Her face is wet with the dew of despair and pain, but

Papa's words have turned her face into a wash of resolution. She won't let him down. She will be strong starting here and now. Anni is becoming a woman at age thirteen by force, but the iron and steel resolve will carry her higher than she could imagine. Starting from this darkening night, and into the forthcoming flight of days, nights, months, years and even decades ahead.

> ***"When the darkness comes, that is when we have known there was light. When the light has come, we smile and forget that there was night."***
>
> L. Story, The Author

Darkness falls, and the family continues to walk, each step growing heavy in the coolness of the night. The Neuman family plods forward toward an unknown goal and a fictitious hope. It isn't fair. It isn't right. It is a dream and a desire. But, it is the soul of continuance and refusal to give in. The quarter-inch leather soles of their shoes begin to feel like plates of steel to the bottoms of their feet. Each step starts to pound a spike of pain through the legs and up the hips and to the lower back. This treacherous journey is toilsome and brutally incessant. They, as well as the others, walk on and through the night until it is nearly dawn. Here they reach a farm along the countryside, having advanced into their new host country, France. Not by gift, not by request, not by mutual agreement, but by necessity and the reality of the fact that there is no alternative. It is indeed, if there ever were, a must.

The families, the couples and even the lost and lonesome gather together here in the grassy wet ground of a farmland that has been obliged to proffer shelter for whatever it may be worth. This morning it is priceless, even though it appears to be worthless. Values have changed in the twinkling of an eye, and the benefactors have received benevolence that is irreparably separable. The small splinter groups gather in and huddle for rest amongst the woodpiles that have been stored for the winter months ahead. Practicality has pre-circumvented itself and become useful before its due season. What will provide heat and comfort in the winter is now shelter, comforting support and blockade against the wind and the world on an early Saturday morning near Bar-le-Duc, France, some forty miles south of the wanderers' homeland. Those that travel the road in reverse will find clothing, pots, pans, paintings, books, glassware, plates, family photograph albums, toys, dolls, and items too numerous to mention scattered as they were discarded along the way in the necessity of traveling with just a slightly lighter burden.

As the morning hours wane, Mama takes out a thermos bottle in which she had secured coffee for the journey. It has been hours since it was prepared but it is still mildly warm and enough so to soothe the family in this moment of respite. This is all they can spare for now. She pours the first cup full and passes it to Papa, who then passes it to Boma, and down the line of the children and back to Mama. She continues again until there is but maybe one cup left. Cold or not, it is a reserve of liquid that is more precious than gold right now. The ham is greater than a holy lamb and not to be sacrificed so early in privation, for those in the earlier stages of hunger. They can wait, they must wait and they will wait.

As the day passes the group grows even larger. At least two hundred people or more have filled the surrounding area and knitted themselves in communication through the men scurrying back and forth with commands, comments, information and guidance, albeit slight. Things are being arranged and rearranged as information is disseminated and the overall well-being of the group is evaluated and factored into plans. Leaders are emerging and some are declining. Common sense is the rule of course, and action is based only on reason worked out through collective minds.

As this Saturday comes to a close, the activities slow within the groups of individuals. The only activity is among those that are still working out plans and trying with all their strength to save this ramshackle group of vagabonds. The Neuman family huddles close together and tries to get what little rest they can with the continuing unsettlement of the makeshift camp.

Something new is coming as they sit dazed, quietly staring at one another. Questions have become meaningless and conversation a waste of energy. There are sounds, distant and far, but not far enough. They draw in closer with each passing hour. First, it is just a faint whistle or a humming in the sky. It turns slowly into a gathering "band sound" of bumps, booms and swooshes. As the early hours of morning approach, the sounds are much more clear and distinctive. Artillery rounds are flying to and fro only ten, maybe fifteen, miles behind and west. Air activity has increased enormously, and bombing is booming in the air like five thunderstorms at once. All the while, it is coming closer with each flap of the Iron Eagle's wings.

Early Sunday morning is announced by the sweet smell of wet grass on the fields. Where they sit now, this group of outcasts, sojourners, uninvited guests and human beings begging for free air and a moment's peace, there is neither mountaintop nor valley experience. It is both. These early morning hours have brought the mountaintop hope that help is now on the way and the valley experience that hell is closing in on help. The entire group of some two hundred souls are trapped between escape and extermination. They are human beings but they feel like rats. They are unwilling participants in military strategies of nations and political leaders and their existence has become nearly meaningless in the schemes of the warmongers. They don't even factor in on the maps and plans on tables in war rooms on either side of the battle. They are but leaves brushed aside or trampled upon in the search for ground occupation in a ground war. It isn't even their ground anymore. That ground they left behind to save the spirit within and for the sake of family and friends. Their only dignity is that they are still alive, fighting to stay alive by wit and wander, and they won't quit or give in. They remain determined to survive until they succeed or until death takes its toll. They pray, believe and even somehow know that death doesn't always—win and they plan on winning. Now, here in these morning hours, on this Pentecost Sunday, something special has been arranged for these faithful believers in God and their Catholic Church. A priest has been summoned to present Holy Communion for the refugees.

Just when it seems nothing is real and the unreal has become normal, something surreal is takes place. The people gather together to hear the Father speak of continuing faith in God the Father, the Son and the Holy Spirit. They take communion and are absolved of their sins by confession one by one. Certainly, by now they each have some sin to confess. This is an intriguing question in Anni's mind. "What sin could I possibly confess for these past two days?" It is absurd. Can one live a moment without sin? Some say no. But in this cataclysmic chain of events, was sin committed by a fourteen-year-old child? Anni is resolute to comply with the request so she tells the Father in confession, "I stole some grapes." There, it is done. Sin confessed and all forgiven. It is actually worth a laugh to Anni for the first time in days as she walks from the confessional, knowing her heart was as right before as it is now, and more so because it was silliness. It deserves a laugh and makes her being feel good inside. Maybe that is why she loves God so much, He knows the truth and they can laugh together about it. Things are right between them and they didn't need a priest to make it so.

Hearts become brighter on this Pentecost Sunday. Yes, war is raging in all directions, they have marched, starved and hurt for two-plus days. They are displaced from their home and have little, if anything, to call their own. However, the Neuman family remains intact and the sun is shining. The winds and noise of war are drawing ever near and it is in this symphony of hell that the family finally sits down as one, prays in thanksgiving, and joins together in the feast of ham reserved for the holy occasion. The celebration of a time when the Holy Spirit, the Comforter, arrived on planet Earth to impart wisdom, help, affection, encouragement and solace to an afflicted people. The ham is good and it is nourishment for their bodies, but the dinner itself, to a family still united through these days, is very spiritual and infinitely, uniquely special.

As the night hours roll in, the news is disseminated to the large gathering through the gendarmes who have taken charge, continuing the lines of communications and plans for placement of the refugees. They have worked hard and feverishly without any payment other than knowing that their dedication to service of their country is embedded in their hearts and that is reward enough. They don't ask for accolades, merits or badges. They only want to see the reward in success such as someone, maybe a few, maybe more, hopefully many, will go forward and survive. That others might live. Mission accomplished. They refuse to tire or grow weary, they sacrifice it all for the sake of this simple reward and the love they feel for their fellow Luxembourgers and mankind in general. They are lovers of peace in war and warriors of hope in a time of utter despair.

The spring Sunday afternoon of May 12, 1940 drew to a close as the sun set in the west and left a red-streaked sky to weep tears of blood over a wounded and hurtful land. Pain and agony rose grotesquely from seed to seedling and the full flowers and fruit of sadistic existence were growing by the day. In this short interim from May 9, 1940 through May 12, an astounding number of incidents took place in spite of all logic and the altruistic beliefs of humankind.

On Thursday May 9, 1940, Hitler gave the order to launch operation "yellow" beginning at 5:35 A.M. The Wermacht was comprised of an enormous, overwhelming and unstoppable force.

***"Soldiers of the Western Front! The battle which is beginning today will decide the fate of the German nation for the next thousand years. Go forward and do your duty!"***

Adolf Hitler; May 10, 1940, communique to all German Armed Forces

With those words spoken, the German military machine launched 10 armored divisions, 5 motorized divisions, and 75 infantry divisions at Holland, Belgium and Luxembourg. In addition, some 2,500 tanks, hundreds of fighters and bombers from the Luftwaffe and an airborne assault force are mobilized to seize key positions in Amsterdam and Rotterdam, Holland. In a daunting, admirable challenge of courage, the French and British Air forces counterattack by sending dozens of sorties into the pitch of the air war in a futile attempt to "slow" the coming onslaught. Of 32 warplanes sent to attack the advancing forces in Luxembourg, 23 are lost in combat. By May 11, 1940, all attempts by British and French air forces are destroyed or missing in action. The fullness of Luxembourg is seized in the grasp of the Nazi Army and by May 12, 1940, the French nation proper is in great peril, as is Belgium and Holland. On May 13, 1940, the skies are blackened by the hordes of Luftwaffe Stuka dive-bombers supporting Rommel's Seventh Panzer Division as they seize the Meuse and begin to surround Sedan, France.

The amazing trait of pride in country and humankind, not pride as in boasting, but pride in something other than one's self, has mobilized a skeletal army of those with a fixed heart and purpose in doing right, whether by their belief in God or by conviction of ethics.

Monday, May 13, 1940, the Neuman family awakes from faint sleep, with the other gathered multitudes, to the sounds of vehicles rushing in and engines revving. Voices are all around and orders are being shouted as well as questions. "Mama, what is happening?" little Charly inquires. "Honey, we are going to get moving now, it is time for us to get going again, OK?" she replies. "Yes, Mama," and Charly falls back to sleep. "Papa, should I go and find out what they are planning and what we should do," asks young Albert. "No, son, I already know. I talked to the men earlier while you were sleeping. We are going to catch a train a few miles from here and hopefully we can be safe somewhere in France while things are sorted out." Papa reassures Bubby and Anni as she is obviously listening in on the conversation. A few hours pass as things get started, stalled and started again.

These past three days have seemed like three years and the family, as well as hundreds of others from the south of Luxembourg, are ready to disembark once more in exodus. They find themselves some sixty miles south of home, twenty-five miles from Sedan, where the German Wermacht is in full-blown engagement of warfare and carnage. The sounds of the war have rung in the air and rattled the ground in an ever closer encroachment and it is obvious that time for choices is running out.

Whether by force, faithfulness or fortitude, numerous vehicle owners, mostly taxis, have taken up the demand to meet the need of a deserted people to transport them to a safer haven. Things are going on at lightning pace, and hurrying is the slowest permissible speed of conduct. Anni, Mama and Boma gather the belongings of the family, while Bubby takes Charly in hand. Papa heads away to secure the path before the family moves. He returns in a short time. "We have a car waiting, hurry, hurry, now, before we lose the chance!" he shouts. They all practically stumble at the same time and fall into a frantic pace behind the long strides of Papa as they head for the car just ahead.

All the while, the bombs explode in the distance, lessening the range as the winds of war sour the air. Not only to the nostrils, but to the ears and the head, a fear of unfathomable proportions rages in this direction. It is the conglomerate of a thousand thunderstorms orchestrated by evil-hearted men with distorted values. Not that the average soldier or airman of the Wermacht is that incarnate evil. They are enlisted men, under compulsion by threat of life to carry out their deeds. Their actions are necessary compliance to the true deeds of the hierarchy that pushes them by threat of death or worse. Soldiers doing what they have to do and obeying orders. In the instant case, these soldiers and airmen are conducting a campaign of total annihilation against anything and anyone that is not of their order, the Nazi regime.

"What is this?" the driver asks. "The men are supposed to stay behind. Never mind, just get in, hurry!" The taxi operator is in no mood for deep discussion. The air is beginning to fill with Stuka dive bombers; they are not far from this point nor the area where the refugees are headed by heaven or hell. "Get down, everyone get over him and stay down!" the driver commands. One, he wishes to protect Papa so that he can go forward with his family, and two, it is safer, with the bombers nearing above and a very scary and hairy road ahead. The cab speeds forward, bouncing, bumping and banging over pothole and pit. The vehicle dodges mud holes, steers clear of open spaces and races to the point where the family will be slung out into the field where they are to confront the next challenge. Talk is of no consequence. There are no answers to questions, therefore, questions are a waste. Just sit tight and when the time comes, do what you have to do. Within a matter of twenty minutes or less, the Neuman family find themselves scrambling over one another and out of the vehicle with shouted thanks to the driver as he spins away before they can even right themselves on their feet.

"Anni! Anni! stop crying and get over here!" Boma shouts to the poor distraught soul. Anni has been in tears since the taxi started banging away and dodging along the roadway as if at any second the devil himself would appear in their path. She just can't help it anymore. She is terrified and the sight of her whole family, such strong adults, robbed of their strength and pride, crouching like chickens in the back of a taxi, is too hurtful and sad. She has lost no respect for anyone, it is just too much to witness. Her flow of tears is a natural reaction to this disaster on a rising tide.

Hardly fifty miles from Field Marshall Rommel and his infamous Panzer division, the Neuman family are sequestered in the slight shelter of fir trees lining an open field. Ahead some three hundred meters, a train is rolling back and forth on the tracks. It is hard to grasp. A train moving one way and then the other as if rocking back and forth in a pattern of despairing action. The purpose is to avoid being hit again. It has already sustained several hits from the bombers above. Anni surveys and finds that all around there are groups just such as hers, and then some that are much, much larger. In all, there are probably three to five hundred people down the line of trees and in the shallows of the ravines on the edge of this farmer's field. All with one purpose in mind. They must run. They must run with all their might. They must run without any weakness, hesitation or restraint. They must run for their lives. The Stukas have arrived overhead and are trying to destroy their only hope while they look on, to the angst of their respective hearts. "Dear God, save the train," "Dear God, let us make it across this field," "Dear God, don't let us die here," "Dear God, Don't let those planes destroy that train," "Dear God, protect us and save us all, we will serve you all our lives." The prayers go forth from hundreds of minds all at once here on the edge of a field that is more like a cliff. It is a dive into a gorge for a small river below. It is a run for life. It is a chance, however slim, to reach a hope that has become a target of death. It is insanity turned sane in the commonality of the absurd and unreal truth.

"What a beautiful day," Anni thinks to herself as she looks around at the sky, the earth and all of nature surrounding her. It doesn't make sense that such hell should be breaking loose and raging in this atmosphere of God's beautiful creation, a day perfect for springtime and joy. Up in the sky are those flying pests, like crows flying all around. They don't stay there for long. They maneuver from a height nearly a mile above in a vertical dive to as low as some two thousand feet above the earth, hurtling headlong at approximately 300 mph. It is dizzying to say the least. With it, they throw forth bombs creating holes in the earth as the soil flies away from the metal ordinance in chunks as big as cinder blocks clouded by debris as thick as locusts. In these holes rest the remains of the chunks and shards of torn metal from shell encasements and fragments. It is a pit of injury. But it is also the only possible place to dive away from the fire from the Stukas' 37 mm machine guns as they rake the field and seek to kill any moving target. The planes fly in low. So close that Anni can actually see the two-seated cockpit. Some have one pilot and others have two. They are sheer terror and she wishes for each one to crash to the ground and be consumed.

The flying airborne artillery machines ravish the field with payloads as large as four thousand pounds. Bombs strafe the earth and the innocent with machine gun fire all the while. The mission had been instructed to attack anything and everything that moved. Specific targets were trains, road junctions and fleeing civilians. There was no remorse in the killing of innocent civilians, unlike the wars to follow. A defenseless child of two was just as much a target as a man of forty or a woman of eighty years old. It was killing for sport to the pilots, the more hits, the better the boast and the higher the marks and respect among their peers, demented beings flushed with adrenaline and sadistic desires bent on spilling blood and taking life as if they were gods. Surely, enough targets hit (kills) would result in rising in the ranks with all the honor and prestige attached. Brainwashed men, pawns and puppets of an ingenious, evil demon incarnated and thriving in the body of a man named Hitler.

> ***"When Hell breaks loose, Angels build dams; when demons fly, God cancels the wind. When people die, the earth mourns. When people live, Heaven rejoices."***
>
> L. Story, The Author

"NOW!" Papa shouts. "Run Mama, Anni watch Charly. Go! Run as fast as you can, keep your head down and don't stop." The family breaks forth over the false shield of the berm they have hidden behind. They get up almost as one and just like the launch of armies pitted across a field of battle, the line of trees explodes with living souls, human beings of all ages, sizes, and sorts. Women, children, old, sick, sore, tired, angry, hurt, crying, screaming, yelling, cursing and praying. Three to four hundred people have come to make this train ride to freedom. It has all been hastily arranged and the Stukas were not a part of the plan. "Mama, Boma fell!" Albert shouts as they run. Papa is in the lead, not because he is saving himself, but because he is sacrificing his life on this field, knowing that every step he takes could lead the family into a hole filled with jagged scraps of razor-sharp metal. They could fall in and injure themselves or fall upon an unexploded bomb or become faltering targets easily hit by the airborne machine-gun fire. Young Albert grabs Boma's hand, Mama is running with Charly's hand and Anni is right behind. "Run Anni, run faster," Mama shouts. They forget they even have bags in hand, all they see is the train ahead as it continues its insane course of one hundred meters forward and one hundred meters backward. The planes have lowered their flight level and are firing all the more intensely into the running refugees. Pure innocence slaughtered like skipping calves in a field, with tree-top snipers grinning with each pull of the trigger.

"A shoe," Anni asks herself, "what is that doing lying here?" All around, as she and the family are running, she notices pillowcases on the ground, jackets, shirts, shoes, boxes, bags, luggage and, yes, bodies. "This is too much, it is too fast, I can't run anymore. I'm getting sick, Mama!" she cries. "Run Anni, damn it, run!" Papa shouts. He hasn't missed her words even though their ears are ringing and nearly deafened from the explosions and the gunfire blipping to and fro like a high speed sewing needle, punching holes and spitting dirt in their faces and around their feet.

In an instant, out of the corner of her eye it happens, a man. A man who must have been thirty or forty? A grown man. A bomb has exploded three feet in front and to his right. He flies into the air in an arc that peaks some twelve feet high, as if his body were a fifty-pound feed sack. He almost forms the position of the cross in midair and lands lifelessly with a sickening impact, and he is no longer a man. He is a discarded item with all the other utensils, clothing, shoes and such on this farmer's field in a race from inhumanity and for the human spirit and will to survive. Some live, some die. Others are injured from falls, broken bones, and bruises.

Healthy and sick, old, young and cripple, all as one. All with one goal. Make the train, if the train survives.

A girl's doll and a toy train. A sterling silver tea pitcher and a brown sock. There, lying in the grass alongside the unmistakable dark red streams of blood splashed and running down the foot-tall grass as if it were ink. All these items covered as far as the eye can see by a cloud of blue, acrid smoke. The carnage covers 360 degrees, 30 feet high and 15 feet deep as they reach the train. "Adults first!" the gendarmes shout over the incomprehensible noises. "Adults first!" they continue. There is a reason, it is just that no one else in the relay for survival can understand. It must be this way because the adults are larger in size, the children will need to be close to the doors when they are opened because children come first and they will need the most immediate attention when the time comes. It is a wise decision but one that Anni does not understand and certainly doesn't like. To her advantage, it is a decision that falls apart after the door is rammed shut and the sliding iron bar falls into its carriage sealing the seventy passengers inside a car that should hold only twenty or thirty people. From Anni's eyes, there must be ten or twelve of these cars. Actually, the cars were made for cattle, not humans. Even cattle cout not fit as close together as this.

All down the line, doors are being slid shut and the gendarmes that nobody cared for, or even hated because they took control, stand on the other side like menacing men of meanness. What the "incarcerated" occupants of the train cars do not know yet, or grasp, is the fact that these men, these unappointed soldiers with hearts of steel, are not boarding the train. They are left to die there on that scattered, shattered and bloody field, victims of Stuka dive bombers and pilots chalking up their counts. It is a thought of hope and grace that maybe somehow, some of them made the run back to the line of trees and lived to have another day.

Just as darkness falls, the train shakes, lurches, rattles and then rumbles into motion. Everyone is standing upright without an inch to spare. They are literally packed and bunched shoulder-to-shoulder and toe-to-toe. But the train is moving and they are alive, living and learning that war is hell.

From this Monday the thirteenth day of May, 1940 through Friday, May seventeenth, the Iron Eagle had flown hard and fast, decisively and destructively. By the fourteenth, the German Army had broken through the stronghold of Sedan, France. It was all but fallen. In the same day, as irony would have it, fifty-seven Luftwaffe bombers slaughtered 814 civilians in a raid on Rotterdam. The world rose in outrage and political, opinionated disgust. No one knew of the countless lives lost at the border between Luxembourg and France and it wasn't "newsworthy" to the press. After all, where was Luxembourg?

By the fifteenth, Wednesday, Paris turned into pandemonium and total chaos. French men, women and children were fleeing for their own lives to the south of France. The word that Sedan was now occupied by the Wermacht struck fear into their hearts to the point that some feeble, weak or already infirm literally failed in heart and died. They packed out of the city by the thousands—a horde of humanity afoot with no presence of mind as to where to go but "away." By Thursday, the sixteenth, the Wermacht had taken Sedan and was using it as a launch point to multiply its station and stronghold to a wider degree in an effort to seize all of France.

Friday, May 17, 1940, German troops had taken Belgium and the Netherlands. They were in full force, fighting for Northeast France and gaining ground by the hour. The French Commander-in-Chief, General Gamelin, gave the final order to all Allied forces in command, "Conquer or die." A new government was formed overnight for the weakening and dissipating country.

This Monday night, the moon is still eight days away from being full. With the half-moon light outside the voluntarily imprisoned, it is near total darkness inside the cattle car. Charly has somehow fallen asleep. Boma just stares into another world. Mamma is not far behind her. The Neumans have found their way to a corner of the boxcar and it is horrid, stench-filled and putrid inside this entrapment of homeless evacuees.

"Anni, I have to pee," Bubby whispers to his older sister as if she can give him an answer, she always did. "Papa, Bubby needs to use the bathroom," Anni queries Papa, up the chain of command for an answer. "Bubby, I know this doesn't sound good and I wish to God it weren't so, but, son, there is no way of getting a bucket over here and if we did it would be too nasty for you to look at." Papa steels the eleven-year-old child for his instructions. He first looks at Anni and warns her, "Anni, turn your head and don't listen! Bubby, pull your pants leg away from yourself and let it aim down your leg, try your best not to get your pants wet, you will be even more uncomfortable if you do. I know it isn't easy or what you want to do, son. Just be as quiet as you can and pee to the floor, OK?" He reassures his young son that, although this is abnormal and inappropriate societal behaviour, it is judiciously proper for the prevailing circumstances. Thus, Bubby relieves himself and returns to staring into the darkness trying to avoid the puddle at his feet, which he can't see but he knows it is there. He doesn't feel ashamed, only sad. It won't be very long before the whole body of people squeezed into this ungodly quarters will realize that the incident repeats itself because of necessity, with no respect of age or sex.

As the night crawled on along with the train, the passengers became quiet with fear. Slowly, almost one by one, their legs begin to weaken and give out. It started with the sick and elderly and worked its way down to the children. Everyone leans on someone else and no one really cares anymore as the entire mass of packed-in people become a huddled, half-upright mound of beings. Whether they were human or cattle it didn't seem to make a difference—the treatment was the same.

As the following day approached, the rising sun brought with it the heat and the heat found its way into the cars at a rapidly rising pace. Although they had escaped the bombing and the fear of the fields of death less than twenty-four hours ago, they all wanted off this damnable train, to cease this ride in crushing arms of misery. It was miserable, indeed, and much worse. Yet, everyone knew, this is where they had to be, they couldn't nor shouldn't get out and they had to endure the unbearable.

Through the day the train continued its slow, jogging and tossing course, weaving a zig-zag trail, making a one day's journey into four and a half days. All major cities were being avoided because the rails were needed by the military headed in the opposite direction. So here they were, traveling like a lifeless payload through the back rails and smallest of towns. As the clock slowly ticked in this rumbling machine, people began crying. Some even wailing. A man over on the other side screams from hysteria. Anni watches it all with her eyes and says nothing. The man begins screaming so loudly that no one can bear it and another man punches him unconscious with a single blow of his fist to the man's head. Of course, it does nothing for the others who are by now vomiting from the dizzying ride or illness, or both, and just when it seems impossible that it could get worse; yet again, it does.

With the day and the heat, thirst has come upon the refugees in a way that causes their head to bang with headache, their mouth to clinch until their teeth are literally cracked and broken. Their tongues swell and they sweat until the water is gone and cramps take over each and every muscle. The kidneys begin to ache and the backache becomes twice as strong and painful. It isn't long before whispering begins and then a woman breaks out with loud weeping and mournful sounds. Anni can't run from it as much as she wishes to, it isn't a choice. As young as she is, she is a witness to it and must deal with it for what it is. At times Mama or Papa try to cover her ears or shield her eyes but it is unavoidable. The woman weeping is holding her husband's lifeless body, begging it to return to life, if one could call this living. Others look on as if they were envious. The train continues without remorse through the journey. It has been two days and the stench inside the car is indescribable. It is beyond any imagination unless one has passed by a mass of human waste, purged stomachs and bloated death. Anni goes into her cocoon and this part of her life will remain here in hell where it belongs for a very, very long time.

By day three, the train makes a stop and the doors are opened from the outside. The weakened, battered, sore, tired, sick and wasted Luxembourgers are hardly recognizable as human beings. They literally fall from the train and spill out. Some too weak to walk just crawl away and sit or lie down. Others gingerly stalk the ground to stretch their legs and try to get some strength back. They won't be here very long. Hundreds of bodies cover the ground along the tracks to the left side of the train. Some bodies remain inside the stench-filled cars, too weak to move or no longer living. Some men gather buckets and try to wash out the cars while nearby farmers and small-town citizens of France bring food and water to these wide-eyed beings with souls but no spirit or self-awareness.

Having been in these "cattle cars," knowing one's self is a thing of the past. Their identity is gone, stolen by the draft of gale-force winds swept from behind the wings of the black Iron Eagle. After a couple more stops, what remains of the hundreds who fled home and hope arrive at Montpellier, France. They left the farm field on Monday, May thirteenth, and now, four and a half days later, May 17, 1940, they have been "liberated." They have also been imprisoned. They have nothing to offer and no way of knowing anything other than the fact that they have been subjected to the hatred, disdain and mercy of people involved in war. As the train rolls to the final stop, the occupants do as they have done for days, they stand on bags, baggage or even one another to get a look outside the two small windows at the top of the car. All they see is a strange land, strange surroundings and it is known by all, this is where we begin again. Without a clue, other than one step, one word or whisper at a time. "What will come of us?" Anni asks herself. No one answers.

The seventeenth day of May, 1940, one week from the late-evening exodus of the Neuman family from their beloved Luxembourg, news was spreading rapidly around the globe. Germany was out of control with aggression. Germany was forcible. Germany was fierce. Germany was formidable and Germany was fighting to occupy or destroy.

# Seclusion in a Hideaway from the Storm

*"During the night of May 9th-10th, 1940, the German forces sprang forward towards France across the frontiers of Belgium, Holland and Luxembourg. Complete tactical surprise was achieved in nearly every case. Out of the Darkness came suddenly innumerable parties of well-armed, ardent storm troops, often with light artillery, and long before daybreak a hundred and fifty miles of front were aflame. Holland and Belgium, assaulted without the slightest pretext or warning, cried aloud for help. The Dutch had trusted to their water line; all the sluices not seized or betrayed were opened, and the Dutch frontier guards fired upon the invaders.*

*The Germans broke through at every point, bridging the canals or seizing the locks and water controls. In a single day all the outer line of the Dutch defenses was mastered. At the same time the German Air Force began to use its might upon a defenseless country. Rotterdam was reduced to a blazing ruin. The Hague, Utrecht, and Amsterdam were threatened with the same fate.*

*During the 14th the bad news began to come in. At first all was vague. At 7 p.m. I read to the Cabinet a message received from M. Reynaud stating that the Germans had broken through at Sedan, that the French, commanded by Generals Gamelin and Georges, were unable to resist the combination of tanks and dive-bombing, and asking for ten more squadrons of fighters to re-establish the line. At almost all points where the armies had come into contact the weight and fury of the German attack was overpowering. All the British air squadrons fought continuously, their principal effort being against the pontoon bridges in the Sedan area. Several of these were destroyed and others damaged in desperate and devoted attacks. The losses in the low-level attacks on the bridges from the German antiaircraft artillery were cruel. In one case, of six aircraft only one returned from the successful attack. On this day alone we lost a total of sixty-seven machines, and being engaged principally with the enemy's antiaircraft forces, accounted for only fifty-three of the German aircraft. That night there remained in France of the Royal Air Force only 206 serviceable aircraft out of 474.*

*It was already clear that the continuance of fighting on this scale would soon completely consume the British Air Force. The hard question of how much we could send from Britain without leaving ourselves defenceless pressed itself upon us. Our own natural promptings and many weighty military arguments lent force to the French appeals. On the other hand, there was a limit, and that limit if transgressed would cost us our life.*

*All these issues were discussed by the whole War Cabinet, which met several times a day. Air Chief Marshall Dowding, at the head of our metropolitan Fighter Command, had declared to me that with twenty-five squadrons of fighters he would defend the Island against the whole might of the German Air Force, but that with less he would be overpowered. Defeat would have entailed not only the destruction of all our airfields and our air power but of the aircraft factories on which our whole future hung. My colleagues and I were resolved to run all risks for the sake of the battle up to that limit—and those risks were very great—but not to go beyond it, no matter what the consequence might be.*

*About half-past seven on the morning of the 15th I was woken up with the news that M. Reynaud was on the telephone at my bedside. He spoke in English, and evidently under stress. 'We have been defeated.' As I did not immediately respond he said again: 'We are beaten; we have lost the battle.' I said: 'Surely it can't have happened so soon?' But he replied: 'The front is broken near Sedan; they are pouring through in great numbers with tanks and armoured cars'—or words to that effect. I then replied: 'All experience shows that the offensive will come to an end after a while. I remember March 21st, 1918. After five or six days they have to halt for supplies, and the opportunity for counterattack is presented. I learned all this at the time from the lips of Marshal Foch himself.' Certainly this was what we had always seen in the past and what*

***we ought to have seen now. However, the French Premier came back to the sentence with which he had begun, which proved indeed only too true: 'We are defeated; we have lost the battle.'***

*The Second World War* by Winston S. Churchill and the editors of *LIFE*; Golden Press, New York, Copyright 1960; ppg. 52

The train still shivers and lurches as it comes to a final halt in the rail yard, grinding and clanging in metallic cacophony. As the sway ceases and the boxcars still, a moment of silence occurs among the occupants of the cattle car. Mama, Papa, Boma and the children stand silently still as if entranced by the loud deafness of the moment. Everyone remains in place as if the slightest move would set off an explosion of murderous proportions. Then, suddenly, someone outside grasps the lock arm of the door and loudly swings the iron bar free of its slot of security and entrapment.

The door slides freely open and the occupants are dazed and temporarily blinded by the light that illumines the car. The light awaits in relief of the four encompassing walls of stench filth, fear and tears. As the members of this particular car disembark, Papa turns to the family as a whole and gives directions. "Everyone grab their bags. Hold close to one another but stay a step behind me. When I get to the door, wait for my okay before you move behind me." He is sharp and knows that even in this humble circumstance, wisdom and caution is what keeps the family not only together, but alive. As the eldest and most educated of this tiny unit of blood relations, the burden of leadership rests upon his shoulders.

It is now the latter part of the day here in the weaving and winding tracks of the Montpellier industrial train station. The refugees have arrived at their disembarkation point and here they will be disbursed to friends, relatives or improvised refugee accomodations. As each occupant of the railcar lowers to a sitting position on the edge of the doorway and leaps down, Papa edges the family closer to the light of day brightening the open passageway from this grotesque chamber of horrors.

"Albert, where are we?" Mama inquires. "We are in Montpellier. Do you know of anyone here?" he asks. "No, Albert, Anne is in Marseille but I think we have others around this area that are family. I don't know right now but we can find out can't we?" she queries. "Yes, but for now, I guess we will take it as it comes to us. Make sure the children have everything and we don't leave anything behind," he commands in the gentlest of ways.

The Neumans approach the doorway with apprehension but very little time to consider it. In the rush of relief from the boxed-in cattle car, everyone is ready to gather fresh air into their lungs, lusting for the feeling of free space to stretch their arms and legs and look upward at an open sky free of planes, clouds or smoky threat of destruction. The clanging and clamoring continue as the family huddles itself together with Papa slightly in the lead, following the crowd. They make their way across the tracks and gravel yard to the station, where buses, cars and people are awaiting in a requiem of welcome. A welcome for these travelers that shouldn't even exist after the onslaught of the Wermacht. The Wermacht that took Sedan, only kilometers from where these wanderers originated their journey. Unbeknownst to the weary refugees, they were moments, even seconds, from a massive horde of military forces thrown against an entire nation. They missed annihilation by the faintest of imagination and grace of God.

As the massive crowd draws together around the main focal point, parties begin to evaluate and determine their whereabouts and their destinations. For Anni and the rest of the family, there is no one here to greet them. Therefore, they remain with the hundred or so refugees who are gathered and tiredly marched to the schoolhouse some short distance away, a shelter from the past four days of travel and the past week of mesmerizing emotional inferno. More buses will be arranged in the morning for the balance of the robust crowd, who will be divided and directed to new locations for temporary quarters.

As they arrive at the doorway of the schoolhouse, it is clear that little, if any, accommodations have been arranged in advance. They stagger up the stairs to the hallway where sections are cordoned off by sheets or blankets, providing a modicum of privacy. Food is brought, along with ragged, rolled mattresses useful for the barest of comfort for the displaced, wandering and downtrodden souls. Exhausted and filthy from travel, the families, strangers and survivors make the best of the ill-furnished shelter. They eat with dirtied hands and don't care. They drink from soiled cups and glasses, care or concern are vacant. Food is bread and bread is life. Wine, water or beer, you drink it and appreciate it, whether you are ten or eighty years old. Some coffee is supplied and the night encroaches deeper. The mattresses are rolled out and with them comes the plague of fleas.

As the saying goes, "Beggars can't be choosers," and they aren't even begging. They are subjects. They are human experiments to the width, length and breadth of what the average soul can endure, mindful that another minute, another hour or another day can bring a change. That the change will be something better. This is called hope. Hope is all they have and they settle in for the night's rest in the flea-infested comfort of a mattress to sleep supine after four and a half days of upright travel. Somehow, it is rest and it is better than their recent history. There isn't even an adequate place for natural relief of bodily functions but that is commonplace now and it is dealt with by the fortitude of hardened minds and spirit. Tomorrow must be a better day. Tonight the bed bugs do bite, but they are in form of fleas and they irritate Anni relentlessly. She awakens throughout the night to scratch and seek brief relief. Her body demands her return to rest and she lies back down again and again through the restless night, dreading the morning.

"Everyone wake up," Papa speaks over his family. "Get up, it is time to go. They have buses downstairs to take us to where we will stay for the next couple of weeks." He truly believes it will be only a few weeks before they can return home and forge past this horrible chain of events. The hope still continues to maintain the family. They are still together, they survived the terrors of the past week and now they are safely secluded away from the storm that has stalled north of them, raging with a fury of an inferno.

"Papa, what about the mattresses?" Bubby asks. "Leave them here, we don't need them and we certainly don't need the fleas," he says with half a smile, trying to keep some cheer in the cheeks of his older son. "Where are we going?" Boma asks.

"To Castries, it is just a short ride north of here and the French are making arrangements to find apartments for all of the refugees until we can get a safe plan to return home." Again and again, these words will spill forth like water upon a plant. The farmer ever hoping that the next day the fruit will appear. Here, the "fruit" is a journey back home to where life may not be as it was, but at least they will be home again and they can survive from there.

Once again, the Neuman family is on the move. This time the day seems just a slight bit brighter and the ride is a little more comforting. They board the bus, with pillowcases in hand, and roll away from Montpellier to the smaller city of Castries. Here they disembark and set out on a new journey of day-to-day living and whatever that means.

"What's your name?" the man asks the senior Albert. "Albert Neuman, why?" he replies. "We are trying to place everyone as best we can with what we have. Do you have any family here in the south of France?" the man inquires. "Yes, but not here, down in Marseille, why?" Papa replies again. "Because, if you have family we will try to put you with them. We cannot afford to put up every refugee from Luxembourg and Belgium at the expense of our war-torn and exhausted French government, that's why!" the man retorts with some indignation toward Papa's inquiries. It isn't that Albert Neuman is ungrateful or lacking in acceptance of help under forced circumstances. The fact is, he is still a man, a strong man, and this is his family. They have already beaten the odds and survived together intact. Most families were broken apart or never even afforded the opportunity to unite. The have been greatly favored and blessed by God and he, Albert Neuman, is not going to squander that precious gift.

"Alright, we have a place for you and your family. There are six of you, no?" the Frenchman inquires. "That's correct," Papa answers while glancing at the committee member and gendarme from Luxembourg. "Follow us," the two state as if one. And thus they go, Boma, tired, elderly, strong but worn, her bag in hand and her eyes far fixed from her soul. Mama, her bag and pillowcase in one hand and Charly perched on her hip and held tightly with the other arm. Her face is dirty, tired, and distant. She moves, her body moves, but her life has left her for the moment. Bubby strongly grabs his pillowcase and prepares for the longest of marches. Anni looks at each one of them and takes it all in. It is heart wrenching and sad, yet she finds some solace in her pride for her parents and even Boma.

These adults are people of true and genuine character. Their generation exists here and now but the future may not be so secure without the likes of them. People with resolve to save and be saved so that they may again pass the baton of learning by experience to the under and uneducated in years to come. The simple lesson that life can be hard. Life sometimes will be hard. Life is living, and living sometimes requires plain surviving. They are a testament of resiliency and flexibility to all that hell has to offer, confirming their faith that someone higher is watching.

"Some march, I didn't even get to fight a Nazi three times my size," Bubby whispers to Anni as she breaks into subdued laughter. She cannot laugh out loud but that boy has done it again. He is so funny. He knows just how to make her smile, and to him it is worth any price he pays. To see her smile is worth more than any price of ticket for admission. "Bubby, shoosh!! This isn't funny, we are a long way from home and look at Mama and Papa. We are lost in plain sight. People see us but we don't exist. We are just animals from some distant land." He knows she isn't angry, just being "Anni," the big sister that loves him dearly and is keeping him from saying something that others might hear and get him into trouble he doesn't need, trouble he can obtain easily enough without additional effort.

It is nearing noon time and the gendarme and French refugee-committee person have led the family, intact, fifty to seventy yards from the bus stop on the main road. Ambling up the alleyway, they face the discouraging sight of a vintner's home, warehouse and blending barn. Here before them stands a barn of sorts with a short-house at the base. Less than a house, it is more akin to a cave carved into the mound of stone, mortar, cement and dirt. It is a place built by unskilled hands, ramshackle and yet sturdy enough for the charge. As they approach, they can hear the bellowing laughter of grown men in the small room below the new "home" for the Neuman family. It is immediately disturbing to the women, Mama and Boma, their collective looks are almost aghast, but Papa steels his back and glares to the family with a look of don't touch, don't think and follow me. It is an unsavory and unsafe place for women young or old, but it is all they have.

As they mount the steps of dirt to the tomb of the so-called "apartment," the desperation and disappointment increase. The party enters through the doorway of their newly acquired accommodations to find a filthy hole-in-the-wall, single-unit room with two beds and a place called a "kitchen." There is one window and no facilities for human comfort. Papa looks at his pale family and assures them, "We're together, now. This is what we have and this is where we will be for a while, maybe a few weeks. We will be okay." He checks each face but no one says a word. The place is filthy, disgusting. Animals shouldn't be in this dungeon, but they are not animals, they are refugees. *Refugee*, a word attached to the lost, forsaken and forlorn.

"Thank God that we're together. We won't be here a long time," Papa reiterates, even though there is water building in his eyes. It is there because he looks to the love of his life, his wife, and sees tears flowing from her broadened stare and down her stern cheeks. For all the hell they have survived—evacuation within hours of notice; bombings, bloodshed, death and near death; a train ride through hell; displacement into the unknown, subject to time without end in sight—the family has remained intact. They, the six of them, are still one.

The Neumans are family and they are here to show the world that one family, with sacrifice, grit and grist can beat the odds and be a people, be human, once again. They are determined to show that they can couple their strength and resolve with their faith to face adversity, death and deprivation head-on and come out on the other side with words of wisdom for those who inquire in later years: Keep your hope. Hope is sometimes all you have, but, if you have your family, your faith and your hope, you can conquer death, hell and demons. Hope is eternal and it is a matter of the heart. Be true to your heart.

The officials leave and the family is left to its own methods of activity and action. Boma starts immediately doing what comes natural for a woman her age and of such strong European heritage. She begins to tackle the dirtiest jobs first, getting the dirt out and the clean to come out from hiding after God only knows how long. Mama moves over to the left, near the corner of the open, single-room shelter. There, she lifts open a large chest with rounded crown top and peers inside to find it is empty and cedar-lined. This is where the family will pack their clothes. Six people's belongings and all their clothes will fit into this valueless treasure chest, some two feet wide, four feet long and two and a half feet high. To Anni it looks life a coffin. Though no body will lie in it, the contents for the near future are surely grave clothes for the living. They are officially refugees and they have a committee somewhere outside that represents them with the French government and local officials. Arrangements are always being made, but of course the refugee is always the last to know.

"Albert, come here, please!" Mama summons Papa. He strides across the room as if it is a stretching exercise for his legs. For too long they have been cramped, weakened and unused. After all, he is a former Olympic gymnast and now, well, until now, a professor of the sport. "Look Albert, behind the partition through this door." She points as the door is pulled gently open, looking as if it might fall into her hand from the mere movement it hasn't had in ages. "Let me see if there is a light in there," Papa tells Mama. He steps inside the dark and immediately bumps the wall. It is a shallow passageway not even a meter wide. He feels his way through the dark tunnel slowly, sliding his feet to avoid stepping upon trouble. One hand grasps the dank air, open-palmed to feel any obstacle that might come to his face without warning. Halfway through, although he doesn't know it is that far, he feels a light bulb dangling from a wire in the ceiling. He feels for the chain and pulls just hard enough to not pull the fixture from its place, nor to break the chain, but to make the contact work, and work it does. Light illumines the hidden back walls to reveal a hearth for cooking and a sink for washing. That is the limit of the kitchen.

"It's okay, Gredy, you can see for yourself. It isn't much but this is what you have to work with. At least we can have hot meals and stay somewhat clean." He is trying his best to reassure her fumbling through without causing tears as only a man can. His efforts are all of encouragement. The hallway is the length of the entire room on the other side of the paneled partition and it has its advantages and disadvantages. It is the only area that provides privacy. Otherwise, it is nearly worse than cooking over an open campfire. It is hell's kitchen to the womenfolk. The men and boys will steer clear of it the whole time they live here.

"Animals live better than this," Anni tells herself. She is disgusted by the sights, sounds and smells of the place. It is squalor and even, glancing around, "Rats won't live here." And she is right, for rats only go where there is food and shelter and here there is only shelter, but for a rat there must at least be a way of escape. For the new occupants, this is the place they have escaped to. As Boma continues to make tidy the two beds offset from one another across the room and to the immediate right of the entrance, Mama and Papa reemerge from the alleyway called the kitchen. The two of them talk quietly for a moment as Papa holds his wife close to him and talks to her face-to-face and eye-to-eye, his right arm around her tightly and his left hand gently upon her face.

"Bubby, do you have to go to the bathroom?" Anni asks her energetic cohort and sibling. "Yes, Anni, I did already, right over there by the ivory tub." He laughs mischievously while pointing to the center of the room. He is not being mean, rather it is his feeble attempt to once again be the clown/comedian and make his sister laugh at the absurd. "Bubby! I have to go!" she insists. "What should I do?" "I don't know, ask Mama or Boma," he replies.

"Mama," Anni interrupts her parents with great caution, "I have to go." Papa looks with great consternation on his face and then looks to his wife. This is obviously something for the women to sort out and now they are forced to deal with it quickly. "Come with me," Mama replies and walks across the room taking her daughter by the hand as she strides through the door and down the dirt steps. They pass by the lower room/apartment where there are several men, maybe eight of them, sitting at a table drinking from bottles of booze on the table, playing cards and cursing in the worst fashion while pipe and cigarette smoke billows through the veiled room. It is a rough and vulgar sight and a danger to no end, that is a certainty.

Mama and Anni walk quickly past in hopes of not being noticed and maneuver across the street. Just down the slope and into the brush there is a fig tree. "Here Anni, I know it is difficult but this will have to do for tonight. I will try to find us something better, but for now, this is where you must go, and stay clear of those men. Only pass by when they are laughing because then you will know they are not looking out the door. Don't pass if they are talking. Do you understand?" she inquires. "Yes, Mama." She understands. "Only pass when they are laughing and move as quietly and quickly as a mouse back upstairs. Do not ever talk to them no matter what and don't let them even try. You keep to yourself and stay close to your brothers, Papa and me," she makes the instructions clear. Mama waits patiently back by the roadside just in the shadows of the brush-line until Anni returns. The two practice what Mama has taught her young, beautiful and innocent daughter—how to deal with men and remain clean from the evil that can arise in the most sincere man's heart and mind. Women live by cunning and it is a necessary tool. The two wait just before the doorway until the room bursts into laughter, and without a moment's hesitation, Anni's arm is nearly yanked to pain as Mama follows the shadow of the wall in three steps pulling Anni past the open door. Now Anni knows how to do it. How to move when the men are not looking and how to not get their attention.

Through these years Anni has not been given the slightest teaching or training from her parents about how to attract a suitor's attention, how to speak to a boy or even how to be a girl. The one thing she has been taught is how not to be seen by boys, how not to talk to boys and that it is not a subject to be discussed. At this time and place, it is a workable solution.

In the meantime, Boma has done some amazing magic for a sixty-plus-year old woman. The room is clean, the beds are made, as well as can be expected, and some bread with leftover ham and wine mixed with water are laid out on the table for the family to come together in humble reserve and peace. They all take their seats and bow their heads. They make the sign of the cross and begin to eat in silence. For the first time in nine days, the Neumans are at a table eating dinner. It is dim, dreary and dank but it is a meal while sitting, and sitting together. There is still something to be said for thankfulness.

As the table is cleared, weariness appears on every face. Words are too much work and not worth the effort unless absolutely necessary.

Boma, Bubby and Anni will take one bed, while Mama, Papa and little Charly take the other. As they gather into their sleeping quarters, Papa slips out a whispered "goodnight," turns off the light and the day is closed. *(May 18, 1940 in Castries, France; while Paris is falling into the hands of the Third Reich and tens of thousands set out on another exodus of their own.)*

No sooner does Anni's head hit the pillow than she falls fast asleep—dirty, tired and worn but willing to succumb. The night is cool, but inside this cave-like room, the heat begins to build. The single window offers some night air, but it isn't enough. Nevertheless, it is not important enough to be bothered by anymore. Within an instant, or so it seems, the light comes on in the middle of the room. It is Boma standing there already dressed for church. "Anni, Bubby, Margaretha, get up, wake up. It's time to get dressed for church," she commands them, woman and child alike. There is every excuse in the world for the family not to arise and go to some strange church after all they have been through. Certainly, God would understand, but not Boma. There is every reason in the world to go to church, for the facts are clearly evident just by looking around. They are still together and have survived, they have much to be thankful for and it is a duty, by Boma's standard, to thank the One above for their answered prayers. Papa will stay behind, there is much work for him to do improving their new accommodations and much information to gather from the refugee committee, the other refugees and the French hosts in this small town.

As the five of them, Mama, Boma, Anni, Bubby and Charly arrive back home more tired than when they left, they find men standing outside the doorway with Papa. Or course, the door to the lower apartment remains open for fresh air; the men drank all night and are still sleeping away the day.

"Here's my family, now. Let's go up and talk about this," Papa says to the two gentlemen standing with him. The whole family meanders up the dirt steps and into the stone and mortar cavern. Inside, although it is still day outside, the light remains lit. The window doesn't provide sufficient light, even for such a small area.

"Here," one of the men says, while handing a basket and a paper bag to Mama, "it isn't much but it will have to do for now. You have chocolate, baguettes, some wine and a couple of francs to use for your most pressing needs." "Thank you," she replies and places the packages on the table. She can already see the hunger on the faces of her children and it can't be soon enough that the business, or whatever it is, should be dealt with, leaving them to eat in humbleness and peace. "We will bring more in the morning, enough to last you the week. The refugee committee has assigned each family or group eight francs for adults and four francs for children. With that, there will also be voucher books supplied with sufficient credit to purchase food to sustain you. You will get the same amount every month so long as nothing changes with the number in your party," he finishes. "Months!" Mama exclaims, now fighting back tears and trembling, visibly shaken. Just when it didn't seem possible anymore tears could come, she has them flowing as she rushes to Papa's side.

"Yes, ma'am. I am afraid so. We have not only your friends, family and the others from Luxembourg to help as best we can, but now tens of thousands of our own people have fled Paris and the surrounding areas headed here to the south. There is only so much we can do. You will have to make the best of it as you can. Sir, [looking at Papa], there is a small pond nearby, you may have already seen it. I would suggest you try fishing for extra food. We will continue to discuss matters among the committee and the local government as well as the French authorities to stay informed for further actions. In the meantime, it has been arranged for the children to start school tomorrow, if you can spare them. The convent is just up the hillside. The nuns will do their very best to continue their training." Having said these words, the men leave the room silently, tipping their hats to the ladies and looking past the children. They have gone.

The Neuman family gathers at the table, gingerly testing the seats to determine if they will hold the weight of their respective bodies. Boma and Mama begin to serve the food to the children first and Papa next. They save the remainder for themselves. It isn't much for nutrition, but it is abundant enough in quantity to meet their immediate needs. "Children, after we are finished eating, I want you each to get ready to go with me to the pond so that you can bathe and get cleaned up. Plus I want to see this thing and look for a way to fish. Gredy, the kids can bathe in the clothes they have, to clean them as well, and can change to their pajamas when we get back. OK?" Papa instructs and inquires. "Yes, Albert," Mama replies. With that having been said, Boma leads the table in saying grace and they begin to eat in silence in accordance with Papa's rules.

The meal has been eaten and the table has been cleared. Just as Papa has directed, the children go to the box, withdraw their pajamas and lay them out for their return. They discard any unnecessary outer garments and prepare for the walk to the pond with Papa. Mama and Boma busy themselves clearing the remains of the meal and frustrate themselves with how to preserve what they have in such poor accommodations.

"Children, let's go," Papa says with the start of his first footstep. He isn't one to wait and when he says go, he expects it. He, himself, is disciplined and he expects it from his children as well. "I'm ready Papa," Bubby chimes in as he falls behind his father on the way to and through the door. Anni rushes behind and little Charly is a foot behind her, reaching for helping hand. Anni grabs the young boy up in her arms and heads out the door. It is easier to carry him than to hold his hand and drag him along. The group meanders down the street to a slope of tall, lush green grass that heads down some twenty or thirty feet to a still pond where the wind whispers through the tall weeds and grass. The pond is rippled from the breeze and it is a serene place to contemplate what, when and where life is for this day and moment.

"Anni and Bubby, take Charly and the three of you get into the water. Here is a bar of soap [he tosses it to Anni to catch]. Go into the shallows and rub the soap on your clothes and your bodies. When you are done, get out, take off all of your clothes except what is respectable and rinse the rest until they are clean. We will hang them to dry when we get home." Papa gives all his directions for the moment although his mind is occupied elsewhere. He wanders around the large pond and searches through the short and sparse trees, the rocky ground and the shoots of willow, reed and grass. He finds what he is looking for, takes out his pocketknife and cuts off about six feet from the top to the root. He has found his "fishing pole." A tall, sturdy, pliable reed to which he can attach a string and start his fishing. This is not fishing for pleasure or for sport, but for the hungry bellies of the women who depend upon him in his role as man, husband, father, provider, leader, strength, steel and encourager. His task is daunting, he is willing, he is able and he truly is all that a man should be.

As the daylight starts to give way to twilight, the foursome head home, damp and cold in the evening warmth. They shiver somewhat but hold their spare clothing close as they walk the street in utter humility, as only refugees know, aiming quickly with hurried steps to the place they now call home. Papa leads the way and any bystander or curious prying eyes are sufficiently dealt with by this man that knows who he is and gives back a look that makes its statement without a word. "This is my family, this is me, you mess with us and I will break you. Don't look down on us.

We are here because we have to be, if you don't like it then speak up or come to me. I will show you what we (I) can do, so don't even try if you are smart." This of course is kept inside his mind and spirit, but it is clear in his eyes. Anyone daring to stare will turn their head because he is like a wounded lion and far too dangerous to deal with. Leaving the refugees alone is a good idea. They are hurt, wounded, desperate and hungry. That is all that is required to create a potentially bad situation. It is better to help them than to hurt them. Thus, brotherly love among human beings can begin to foster between the homeland and the homeless.

The family unit arrives home damp, cold and clammy. They dispose of their garments without hesitation or shame. Mama and Boma assist and direct Anni in how a female does these things. Obviously, she cannot change her clothes as easily and circumspectly as the boys. When all is said and done, the children are in their pajamas and ready for bed. They are, unlike most children, truly ready for the escape into rest, relief and sleep.

Mama takes the wet clothing and hangs them around the room to dry while the children fall fast asleep. Boma quietly leads herself to the bed in tiresome agony and lays her body beside the children. Papa takes his seat at the now empty table, reaches into his vest pocket and withdraws his pipe. He reaches into his chest pocket and retrieves his tobacco. He methodically packs the pipe and lights the comfort of thought, imagination and the war plans for the coming day and days.

"Gredy, tomorrow get the children off to school. They need the comfort of conformity and continuance of their education. You will need the respite from their company and I will need to think things through and gather information from the other families and the committee," he instructs with a kind spirit. "Yes, Albert, I have already gotten the directions to the school, what the children need and there will be a few other children to guide them out the door, down the street and off to the school. They will be okay and we can do whatever we have to while they settle into this strange place. Also, I spoke with a woman today who said we can use the telephone at the post office to call family, if they are near here, and have them come assist and visit." She is glad to encourage her husband with that news.

"That is good news indeed. Maybe Anne can come up from Marseille. The children would be elated and it would be good to have her here or nearby. Let me know what you find out," he finishes. "Of course I will, Albert. You need to ready yourself for bed and I will be there shortly.

I love you darling. You have been wonderful through this all and you have done right. You have kept us together and the children are safe. My love to you." She whispers across the small room as she turns back to the door for the hearth fireplace and sink with dishes in hand. Papa quietly receives her words and ponders the past week's events.

> *"When we were evacuated, I grew up fast. I was fourteen, but thinking back sometimes I was ten; sometimes I was thirty or forty. Each day was different. We did not know what was happening back home—it was very hard on my parents and grandmother. I helped in some vineyards. There were dark purple grapes, not exactly sweet, and some white ones. Muscadel taste. I was always in a vineyard. Nobody could bother or disturb me there. My father went fishing for eels. He caught them with a fork, it was absolutely awful. I never ate any, they would squiggle and squirm even in the pan as they were dead and cooking. It was disgusting to me and made me sick to my stomach. Boma would leave the room.*
>
> *The French nuns were kind and very holy. They felt bad for us youngsters. My aunt came from Marseille to visit us 30 miles away to my other aunt's house. My father and I used bicycles to get there and see them. We had two flat tires along the way. I wanted to go home so badly. I missed it and I was miserable. Life was miserable even though so many people tried to make it better for us (refugees). I became angry and hateful, I tried not to and prayed to God for belief and that it would all soon be better. Those four months were terrible. I wanted to just run away so many times to the Mediterranean down in Marseille. At least there I could get a decent bath and real food.*
>
> *I didn't want to be away from my family and especially Papa. He was so much a man and so good to me. He kept telling me, 'Anni keep a stiff upper lip!' He was so strong and leading. People admired him and looked up to him because of his silent wisdom and strong physical body. He was all muscles and very, very strong in both arms and legs. We all just wanted to go home and leave this place. It wasn't so bad, the people and such, it was just not having anything to live with, I mean nothing, it was bare and hard living. No comfort just hurt inside, pain and suffering and longing to go back home. I cried a lot and turned into myself. I created a tunnel to hide in, inside my mind. I would go there and hide for minutes,*

*hours and days. It stayed dark there and that was where I felt safe. No one could see me crying and no one could see my hurt. I could face it alone and hide until it went away, but it never did.*

*Usually it was Papa that brought me back out. Sometimes Bubby or Boma. They both loved me so much and I loved them. Mama was always busy with Charly. It was hell. We were always dirty and looked at like intruders. Most accepted us but we still knew this wasn't our home and we didn't belong here. We just existed, waited and prayed it would end and we could go back to our home and Luxembourg. God, we missed the place so much our memories began to create visions and dreams of it being greater than it was. We had truly loved our land and lost it. We wanted it back, desperately. We would have done anything to go back."*

ANNI NEUMAN ADAMS; July, 2003;
direct quotation through interview by author

"Anni, Bubby! Get up, it's time to get ready for school," Mama commands from the doorway to the hidden hearth and sink behind the partition wall. The smell of coffee has already filled the room. Over on the table by the window are two plates with baguettes and cheese already placed in portions for the children. Their clothes are lying at the foot of the bed. "Bubby, Bubby, get up so I can get out of bed." Anni literally grabs his pajamas with both her hands and rocks his body back and forth. "I'm up, I'm up!" he whines, still tired and sleepy-eyed. Since time immemorial, boys have loved sleep more than girls at that age. The two straggle from the warm bed and embrace the coolness of the room in their bed clothes. At the foot of the bed their clothes have been carefully laid out by Mama. Anni and Bubby both reach for them at the same time, then laugh. They didn't feel like laughing, but it happened anyway because it was absolutely hysterical. Their clothes could stand on their own. The garments had hardened from the pond-washing the day before and the overnight drying to a stiff shell. The laughter ceased quickly and sadly though as the two began to change into the roughened garments. It was horrible. They were rigid and uncomfortable. They still smelled of soap and pond water. Immediately, dismay and sadness displaced the laughter.

The two make their way to the table to eat and ready themselves for their first day of school. "Mama, how do we get there? What are we going to eat? When do we come home? Are you taking us?" The questions come out from the twosome like a chorus without so much as a breath for

Mama to answer the first one. "Sssshhh!" Mama replies, placing a finger to her lips. "Let the others sleep, you are going to wake them with all your silly question. I made arrangements yesterday and I went to the bakery before I woke you up. There will be some other children along shortly that are headed for the school. The nuns have made arrangements for you in class. You follow the others down the street and through the vineyard up the hillside to the convent. I have already packed your lunches. You have baguettes, chocolate and wine mixed with water in thermoses." She lays out her carefully made plans to the two returning students. Life is supposed to return to as normal as can be expected under the circumstances and everyone is brought to task to make it so.

A knock comes at the door and it is Ms. Chavais. She is the owner of the winery which surrounds the small barn-like accommodation in which the Neumans reside. She is the landlord of sorts and has a fourteen-year-old daughter of her own. "Mrs. Neuman, the children are leaving for school. You should send yours out now so that they may learn the way. I hope that you slept well and I will see you again maybe this afternoon. I have much to attend to, but if you need anything, come see me up the hill at my house." She is very accommodating and kind. As the time progresses, young Anni will develop new colors to her wings representing her friendship with both Ms. Chavais and her lovely daughter.

The children depart and make their way up the hillside through row upon row of grapevines and over the top to the convent where school has now resumed. Anni and young Albert will make this trip a hundred times over the next four and one-half months. They will stop along the way and pick the grapes to appease their appetites in the mornings. Although they have had breakfast, there is never enough food to satisfy the hunger. Everything is rationed, and it is irrational to the stomach of the refugees. Just steps from view of the school, Anni and Bubby look over each other's hands and face to make sure there is no evidence of the stolen fruits. No stains, no dribbling and no evidence. They aren't thieves, they don't mean harm, they just do what kids do, or anyone for that matter when plenteousness abounds next to dire living standards.

When the school day draws to a close, young Anni and Bubby make their own way home now that they know the path. Since it is the two of them, they are in no hurry to return to the dreary dwelling place they must call home. Instead, they zig-zag through the vineyard and play hide-and-seek, laughing all the while so that the game is far too easy. Realistically, they do it in such a fashion because making it easy is one of the few things they have control over in their tender lives. All else is harsh, and too harsh even for adults. They didn't ask for this and they hate it. They don't want it, but it is theirs to deal with; therefore, they play and forget, or at least try to. It is good they have one another. Anni and the junior Albert will be friends like this throughout life, and the years ahead are filled with just as many highs and lows. Anni will survive and Albert will pass to his own playground. In the meantime, they are here and they laugh, chase, hide and say words they aren't supposed to. They are truly filled with love and admiration for one another. It is indeed a very special brother-and-sister relationship.

Upon reaching home, the two children notice that Boma is sitting outside on a stone garden wall. As usual, she is facing into the distance with a stare far from her body and close to her thoughts and soul. They dare not disturb her. She is sweet and kind to them and they love her, respect her and accept her unusual ways. That is Boma and she is quite some lady.

Inside, the children soon discover why Boma is sitting outside. Papa is laughing for the first time and the antics seem to be at Mama's expense. There in the room is a pail with two squirming eels, each approximately two and a half feet long. They are grotesque creatures of monstrous proportions. "Albert, kill these things and get them clean, at least," Mama implores Papa as he stands still grinning. "OK, Gredy, I'll take them outside and skin the little critters, but you are going to thank me when you have a taste of good, hot eel," he banters and laughs as he takes the pail outside.

He takes the eels and puts them up to a tree just outside with a nail to their heads and while their bodies continue their frantic flipping and flopping, he makes a cut with his pocket knife and starts to pull the skin from the sinewy bodies. He cuts below the head and returns the fresh catch to the pail and returns inside. Anni, all the while following and watching, is sick from the sight but so inquisitive she cannot resist following and learning. Her curiosity is stronger than her stomach. Returing into the domed dwelling, Papa presents Mama with his first fresh catch of the day. She makes haste to rinse the wriggling, lifeless beings and places them in a skillet heated in the hearth. Anni watches intently from beginning to end. As Mama places the skillet over the indoor grill, the eels writhe with contractions and contortions although now long dead. It is a physical phenomenon that intrigues Anni but is too much for her young appetite. She is disgusted, sickened and resolved not to eat these wormy things and will do without if need be. Let the others have her share.

Each day passes with new ideas on how to survive in this surreal world. Bubby begins to pass his time, when not with Anni, by playing soccer with some of the other refugee children. The refugees develop a routine of Saturday night get-togethers on a hillside overlooking the valley with the beauty of the stars and moon above. Some sing, some dance, others talk; but all dream, wish and pray for it to be home where they gather like this, and maybe it will be again.

As the weeks turn into the first couple of months, Aunt Anne arrives from Marseille with an excellent assortment of cheeses, wine and some meat. She stays some thirty miles away at another aunt's refugee site. Papa and Anni pedal bicycles borrowed from Ms. Chavais to make the trip. Two flat tires, half a day's traveling and half a day's visiting later, they return to the rest of the family with wonderful baskets and bags of treasure. The next two months are spent merely surviving. Anni becomes weak, tired, angry and rebellious. She hates it here and keeps it inside. Inside the cocoon it is darkening and it is not a good thing. It will haunt her for many, many years. Still, she maintains her steel of character and resolve. She cherishes wonderful moments in time such as picking blackberries with her father. Bicycle rides with Papa and having great philosophical discussions. Of course, nothing about boys, those were "Anni, ask your mother" questions. Anni would borrow books from the church to keep reading and play in the vineyards with Bubby. If the weather permitted on school days, they would have picnic lunches with their meager bread, wine and water on tables outside on the playground.

The existence went on unbearably. After seeing the eels, Anni was resolved to never bathe in the pond again. She was diminished in pride by the humiliating circumstances for her young and tender soul. Always creatively trying to find a way to use a real bathroom facility rather than dare the disgust and despair of the fig tree. Having to sometimes steal food to satisfy the pain in her stomach. Watching Boma knit socks of wool (God only knows where she got the wool) for days upon days and pairs upon pairs. All insanely useless in this sweltering heat of summer. It was Boma's escape just as other family member's had their escapes from reality. Papa with his long walks and fishing, Mama with her trips to the market with Charly in tow, and Bubby clowning or playing soccer. Somehow, it worked. They lived this life in the grasp of death, disgust, despair, anger and humiliation for four and a half months.

News came in early September. The Germans had taken control and all Luxembourgers were being repatriated to their homeland whether they liked it or not. They were being shipped back to the country that was no longer theirs. Back to the newly annexed property of the Third Reich and Nazi rule. It was like falling asleep into a nightmare, awakening to find it a dream and then returning to sleep and the nightmare continues. Except here the awakening was a dream and the nightmare is real.

**Author's Postlude:** *The wind is torn in two and the sky is a divisive battleground. The Iron Eagle flies to heights beyond comprehension to the butterfly. Yet, the butterfly flies flitting circles and dance of flight, fancy and windsong that the eagle cannot conceive. The two are at war and yet they have no knowledge of one another. The eagle will fly in its self-absorbed confidence and damnable strength. The butterfly will lilt upon the breezes as she flows without clear direction. She will fly as the air carries her and she will prove her resiliency, determination and resolve as the superior force to be reckoned with. The Iron Eagle will fall flat to the ground with a resounding crash when she breaks forth from her cocoon and shows the fluorescent, iridescent, menagerie of colorful wings built on steel and borne like flakes of snow. Her power is overpowering to the eagle. She has something he does not have and it is his weakest point. He has determination and will for self-purpose. She has hope, faith, trust, care, concern and a willingness to give to the final point of breath for someone, anyone, other than herself. Therein lies the difference. One is absorbed by self and the other for others.*

# Returning Home

*"Mir Welle Bleiwe Wat Mer Sinn!"*
**(We Want to Remain What We Are!)**

Luxembourg Credo

By June 22, 1940, hardly a month into battle, the French Army and its country behind it, or what remained of it, surrendered to occupation and armistice. For the preservation of approximately a third of the natural property of the country called France, all remaining territory and confines within were surrendered in a humiliating fashion as orchestrated by Hitler himself. He wanted full retribution for his own inadequacies during his soldiering in World War I. His vengeance was wrought with his maniacal enjoyment of replaying a surrender of arms at the same site and location as the previous war between the two countries. His jubilance was clearly evident, without any flinching of concern for the pain, murder, anguish and blood poured out under his ego and fragile fingers. His masculinity was enmeshed in the sacrifice, hardship, suffering and whole-hearted martyrdom of his own countrymen. They were the true warriors, while he rode upon the winds of his own words as his only controlling strength and yet, strong they were. He had no muscle in his arms or legs. He only had a black heart, black mind and evil soul. It served him well, at least, for the time being.

On July 25, 1940, Hitler appointed Gustav Simon, Gualeiter and administrator of Luxembourg. The Volksdeutsche Bewegung movement was formed under the lead of Damian Kratzenberg to direct the Luxembourgers "Home to the Reich." The VDB, as it was called, became the Grand Duchy's only authorized political party and enrolled nearly 84,000 members, the majority of which joined for the sole purpose of remaining employed. Without membership, employment was not permitted within the "New Germany." By August 6, 1940, the German police took over all police activities and the remaining gendarmes. The Luxembourgish language was banned along with French, and German was the sole language to be spoken. Any variance was subject to harsh punishment. French language schools were closed, the Luxembourg Constitution was declared void and by August 26, the Reichsmark currency was introduced to the annihilative diminishment of the Luxembourg currency. By September 7, 1940, the Germans imposed the Nuremburg laws and applied them to all Jews living in Luxembourg as a matter of escalating anti-Semitism and determination to eventually see the Jewish members of all occupied land methodically weltered away and exterminated. Luxembourg became a part of the "new order" and was pooled into the putrid growth of the so-called "Greater German Reich."

By the last week of August and through the first week of September 1940, the words were becoming clear and a matter of fact. The refugees were to be gathered from all corners of French land and returned to the new "Gau Mosselland." Luxembourg no longer existed. In hindsight, this was quite an extraordinary reality in light of words of the German government on or about May 10, 1940:

> ***"The German Government expects the government of the Grand Duchy of Luxembourg will appreciate the situation created by the sole fault of Germany's opponents and will take the necessary measures for insuring that the population of Luxembourg will put no obstacles in the way of German action.***
>
> ***The German Government for their part desire to assure the government of the Grand Duchy of Luxembourg that Germany does not intend, either now or in the future, by these measures to impair the integrity and political independence of the Grand Duchy."***
>
> The World at War; The Grand Duchy of Luxembourg;
> by Richard Doody

On or about September 6, 1940 word had made its way to the small town of Castries, France and the doorstep of the Neuman's refugee quarters. As the sun melted away into the sunset, hearts were melting as well. "Albert, please don't go, please. There has to be another way. There must be. We got here through worse. Can't you stay with us? I don't want to do this without you." Mama expresses her broken heart, spirit and feelings of desperation. Her husband is about to depart from the family out of the ongoing necessity to continue surviving the backwash of war. "Gredy, if there were any other way I would do it but, I have looked at it from every way possible and talked to the other men. There just isn't any other way to get it done. I have to leave ahead of you and it is going to take me at least a week. I believe the best time for me to go would be about four o'clock in the morning." He lays out the plans further to the family. "Anni, come over here with me," he directs his cherished daughter. Meanwhile, Mama staggers over to the table to seat her trembling body as her tears pour forth.

"Anni, I am counting on you. You are a big girl now. You are becoming a special young lady and I know how strong you are. I know I can count on you. Take care of your mother, Boma and the boys, OK?" he half asks and half directs the girl; she's growing up fast before his very eyes. She has a look on her face as blank and empty as a stare into black night sky. Inside, she is torn in two or, more to the point, completely shattered. She is aching and yet trying not to show it. One part of her wants to stay strong and prove to Papa that she can make him proud and the other part wants to run screaming and crying away. Not away to any place she can think of, she can't think that clearly. She just wants to run, cry and run some more. From here, away from here, as far as her feet can take her, if she had wings she would fly. What more could extinguish the spirit of a butterfly but to be entrapped and unable to lift its wings. Anni is grounded and she must stay this way for the sake of her father, her family and because there simply isn't any other choice.

"Albert, what are you going to do? How do you plan to get back," Boma asks, breaking her silent vigil over the whole family and her quiet internal prayers. "I spoke with a guy over in Gignac at their refugee area and he has a bicycle. He said he could meet me here. I bought a used bicycle and I have it over in the ditch. We've already agreed to go together. He's from Esch also, so we can stick together and follow close to the east border. We traced it out on the map and I think we can avoid most of the steep hills and mountain areas enough to make it in seven or eight days," he replies, but more to the whole family than directly to Boma. He wants the whole family to know where he is, what he is doing and to have some sense of safety and comfort knowing he will be working hard on their behalf. He's going ahead once again as the leader and take-charge man that he is. He will get to Esch before his family and prepare the house, or at least, find a place for his family to return to some kind of life worth living. He knows the Nazi soldiers and police are there and it is better that he sees things first and prepares for the worst.

Shortly thereafter, Boma and the children settle in to bed for sleep while Mama and Papa sit quietly at the table occasionally pressing out soft words in solemn discussion. It is another sad night for the family but there is hope that once the family gets back home, things will be better. To Anni, it has to be. This place has been a nightmare, even with the sparse lighter times gathering with semi-friends and the few treasured times with Papa on walks and bike rides. Even a few times they went blackberry picking like the old times.

At four o'clock in the morning Anni looks out of the corner of her eye and sees her father in the dim light of the room. She immediately feels like crying again. She has a feeling in the pit of her stomach as if she is never going to see him again. Her heart aches with loneliness already. He blouses his pants legs and dons his round-topped, brimmed hat of wool meant to cast a circular shadow over the head and neck all around. Right now though, the only shadows being cast are from the dark thoughts and heavy hearts. It is enough that the family has been ripped from their home in the night, traveled through the byways of hell and spent four-plus months in exile, but now this. Somehow, they all know, except Charly, that this is a new beginning to the same song and the song is an incessant dirge. Papa leaves the room to go outside and Anni rises out of the bed and follows him to the door, watching him pedal off on the rickety old bicycle with the back end overloaded with all that the man could carry with him. He rolls down the road and is soon out of sight. She realizes she is holding her breath and lets it out, turns and goes back to bed with a suffering soul.

As the morning grows outside and slivers of light break through the window, Mama and Boma make breakfast for the children. Charly is already up and busying himself without any playmate, just whatever he can find to occupy his six-year-old mind. "Mama, when will Papa get home?" Charly asks, looking up at his mother. "Charly, Papa left. He is going to find us a better place to live and we'll all get back together in about a week, so don't worry yourself?" she says with a faint smile on her face, made especially for placating the child and nothing else.

"Bubby," Anni whispers to the junior Albert, "do you think Papa will be okay? I'm afraid for him. I hate this, I hate this place and I hate the Germans. What does any of this have to do with us?" She asks the questions but no answers are coming and none are truly expected. "How long do think we will be here before we leave, Anni?" Bubby queries back in response. "Papa said it would be about a week so I guess we will be leaving in just a few days. I'm ready to go home but I don't feel like moving or doing anything. All I think is, we are nothing but animals to other people and nobody cares or wants us. That's all I know and that's all I think, Bubby," she says coldly with a deadpan stare on her face.

"Children, get out of bed and come eat your breakfast," Boma tells the two, and they comply. There isn't any talking at the table. It isn't so much that it is Papa's rule, rather, it is just the melancholy feeling they all share. Then something unusual happens. Because of the uncertain times, Boma tells the children to bow their heads and she begins to pray for Papa's safety and his successful return. The children raise their heads again, make the sign of the cross, say amen and return to silence.

After three days, the refugee committee comes to the little hole-in-the-wall of an apartment and tells the women it's time to leave. They are told to pack all their belongings and be ready for the buses coming early tomorrow morning. This is it, the hour has arrived for Anni and the rest of her family to take flight once again as unwilling participants. The cycle is becoming nauseatingly repetitive. They are leaving their meager hideaway and feel as though it is none too soon to their imposed-upon hosts. It isn't so much that they are disliked or looked down upon, it is just the fact that, to the French neighbors who are war-weary also, seeing the refugees day after day has been a constant reminder of how bad things have gotten. With the refugees leaving, they can at least pretend that things are getting better and maybe even hope to go back to the way their lives were some five months ago, before all hell broke loose in the belly of Europe.

With bags packed and in hand, Mama, Boma, Charly, Anni and Bubby say no final farewell or even look back at the single-room dungeon where they have existed for four months. There are some symbolic goodbyes to temporary acquaintances and friends, but that is all. They trek down the small alleyway and board the buses to Montpellier with the other refugees of Castries. There are only a couple of men remaining in the group. The few that were there before have all left just as the senior Albert. It wouldn't be wise for a healthy Luxembourg man to arrive on the train at the border checkpoint which lay ahead. The checkpoint is now controlled by the German police and Nazi soldiers. The new occupying forces are not pleasant when it comes to any man, or older boy for that matter, coming any closer to their homeland of Germany. Such actions are taken as highly suspicious.

The family's arrival in Montpellier is a repeat performance of the worst kind. Just as before, the refugees are herded into a school, although not the same one, for bedding down and "out-processing" through physical check-ups and documentation. The process takes four days. Ration tickets are taken back; the refugees won't need them anymore. The hours are agony, hunger and silent anger. Once the group has finally been cleared, from head checks for lice to proper identification, they are permitted to board a train. This is the one thing different that is actually a pleasant surprise and a welcome relief. There will be no cattle cars and sweltering heat and stench. The cars are actual passenger vehicles, clean and shiny, and there is even a wash closet at the rear of the car. Each person actually has a seat, some food, wine, water and rest. Some of the elderly and infirm are placed into compartment cars for a bit more comfort.

Anni still cannot overcome her feelings. Even in the improved environs, she has passing urges to just jump from the train to escape being tossed around, moved, shuffled and treated like an animal instead of a person. She is fostering some very bitter feelings and she has no place to let them go. Instead, they get stuffed down inside and compacted into boxes that she will store in her mind for many, many years to come.

Outside the train window the French countryside speeds by and Anni wonders where Papa is right now and how he is doing. She pictures him pedaling hard and fast along country roads and aiming for home. Actually, Albert Neuman and his travel partner, Robert, have traveled some 240 miles. They have come from Castries, through Montelimar, beyond Valence, Lyon and passed Bourg-en-Bresse. They are aiming for the border-line to remain out of sight of soldiers, police and anyone else that may hinder their mission. They have sweated, sweltered, crossed back roads, bumpy fields, briar patches, farmlands and woods. They have slept very little, have eaten when and what they can and pedaled until their legs ache so bad they nearly fall to the ground when they come to a stop and try to dismount. Already halfway into the cross-country marathon of misery, they are beaten, bruised, bitten by bugs, sunburned and filthy. Their drudgery turns to anguish and then the anguish turns to agony through exhaustion. They begin to appear near catatonic and move almost robotically in fashion to keep moving. They have taken a mental step outside their bodies to avoid the sensations of blistes, bloodied wounds and pain.

As the night cloaks the small country with darkness and quiet, the train rolls on through the night while, somewhere along the border of France and its Eastern neighbors, Papa and Robert find an old abandoned barn to seek shelter from a late summer rain in the waning hours near midnight. They will rest for three, maybe four hours if possible, and start out again. They know that as bad as things are, it is better to get the best miles in before the merciless sun flexes its radiating muscle on their blood-stained flesh, bruised bones, burning lungs and spasmodic, cramping muscles. They have work to do and will sacrifice it all to get there on time and get done what is best for their families. These men are in a class of a very rare breed: true family men.

By September 12, 1940, the sun has come up upon the third day of travel along the rails of the French countryside. The inside of the traveling train car has become a permanent mental picture for Anni and her family. People all about have settled in and it is hard for them to believe that they will be arriving tomorrow to finally return to their precious home of Esch for whatever might be in store. Home is only a day away.

In the aisle, Charly crawls along the floor pushing his toy truck, running from window to window and peering out then bouncing back to Mama to make sure she is still sitting where he left her five minutes before. He is full of energy, content, and oblivious to the seriousness of the travels. Not because he doesn't see it, but, for his young mind, it is better to ignore it and believe it isn't there and so he does.

As Boma and Mama sit quietly chatting, their attention is divided between each others' faces and the children as they maneuver about the car. Anni has grown silent and morose inside her cocoon, looking out the window as a visionary escape into an empty unknown. She reflects upon the years of her life and feels as though she has bounced like a rubber ball from one age to the other only to arrive back at her present circumstances.

This is perfect timing for bringing in the clown and thus he appears with fake mustache upon his soft upper lip and a harmonica in hand. He falls over into Anni's lap with his head flipped back and bent awkwardly with feet deftly planted on the floor, his back arched over her legs and his head thrown back with that absurdly silly moustache protruding from under his pencil sharp nose and soft mouth. He grasps the harmonica quickly with both hands and breaks forth with a tune to change the astonished look upon Anni's face into unbridled laughter. What a joy he is to her heart and spirit. He brings her life and light when all seems dead and dark. He selects his song in an split second of whimsy and it fits perfectly, she will never forget him, his antics nor his song. He blasts the notes and the song pierces the air, almost all around recognize it and even appreciate it. It is pure Luxembourg, it is who they are and it is what they are all about.

The song is called "De Feierwon"(Fire Chariot) and goes as follows:

***"Ready stands the fire chariot,***
***It whistles through the air and off it goes.***
***Rattling over the iron roads,***
***Proudly the neighbors it shows,***
***That we now, too, found our way to the great League of Nations.***

***Come (you) here from France, Belgium and Germany,***
***We want to show you our homeland.***
***Go ask all around how contented we are,***
***"Mir Welle Bleiwe Wat Mer Sinn!"***
**(We Want to Remain What We Are!)**

De Feierwon; 5 October 1859

Anni's somber mood is suddenly broken and shattered into splinters of rainbow-colored lights and laughter. Bubby has done it once again. He is a magician of humor. He can fabricate laughter not only from thin air, but from total darkness and despair. Her laughter begins to match his, between his facial expressions and gasps for air, she begins to bellow laughter uncontrollably. It is a saving grace and one only God could have foreknown.

On this same day, September 12, Papa and Robert roll their bikes to a halt at the checkpoint manned by German soldiers and police at the France/Luxembourg border. The sun has brutalized their skin and their bodies are battered and torn from the elements and nature. They are immediately approached and questioned about their purpose and identification. Both men present the documents they have, proving their reason for leaving Esch in the first place—frail family members, women and children without help. They did the right thing and now they face the brunt of indifference at the border crossing. Mercy is not a commodity here at all. However, their reasons and report are valid, and mercy does find a place to put one foot forward. The men are allowed to pass. They struggle back on the hard seats of the cumbersome bicycles and wobble toward home to secure their family's safety from the storms of war around them.

By the following day, at the same checkpoint area, near the rail tracks, the train carrying the balance of the Neuman family comes to a shuddering halt. The train belches, steams and whines at the end of its journey. The aches of travel tremble through the metal carriage and the occupants absorb the exhaustion of the vehicle as a chill through their bones. As the noise slowly declines to a bearable hush, the doors open and in walk German soldiers and police. Their uniforms, their language, their attitude and their coarse behavior and indifference to liberty of others make them unmistakable; they have no respect except for themselves and their seniors. The soldiers stand by, armed with machine guns, watching over the crowd as the police give their orders and directions to the occupants. "Each person, woman or child, or man, [as they look to one poor soul seated cowering in his seat, all too well familiar with his ill-fate of having only one leg] each will sit and remain as you are until you are called upon. Once you are called you will proceed to the back of the car and into the partitioned car adjoining for processing and clearance. Once you are cleared, and if you are cleared, you will disembark the train. Once outside the train you will proceed to the station. Do not wait for anyone. Do not wait for friends or family. You will move directly to the station and wait there." And so the order goes.

Eventually, the Neuman family is called off, one by one. Anni greets her turn with a steely glare and distant soul. She does as she is told, but it is clear she is not here with them. She is somewhere else. She will do what she has to, but they will never know nor see her, personally. They will never know Anny Neuman, because that girl was never there. They call for her to disrobe to a respectable degree. It has all the potential of humiliation, but she has removed her pride with her spirit and both soar above in the clouds away from this moment of time. The body below is subjected to inspection for lice in the hair, rashes, bruises, markings, sickness, illness, disease; peer into the ears, look into the eyes and stare into the opened mouth. They search for all things contrary to purity or good health. She passes, rather, it passes. The body below has been cleared. She resumes her shell, takes charge of it and her clothing and departs the train in a direct line to the station. She vaguely takes notice of the sweetness of the air and weather around her. However, her heart does leap seeing her family at the station and the familiar surroundings of her beloved Esch-Sur-Alzette.

After clearing their final checkpoint within the station and having their papers inspected, Boma, Mama, Charly, Anni and Bubby are pointed to the door leading to the streets of their hometown. They are home and they all want to cry, walk, run and collapse at the same time. It is too much to bear, but, bear it they do. They gather quickly and head out into the open street lit by the last light of the evening and aim toward home, only a short walk away. As they arrive at the door, they have already noticed the difference in "home"—it isn't anymore. There are Germans here and yon. German police walking the streets. Very few of the population before are here now and they don't smile, wave or even notice one another. It is eerily quiet. They open the door and find Papa seated at the kitchen table. He attempts to rise slowly and gains his footing only to slide back into his seat with a fixed smile upon his face.

His family gather to him quickly and they embrace him and the questions begin to flow. For only a brief moment there is the joy of reunion, then the disparity of heartfelt abandonment returns to each as if a wind had blown it through the window. The house is a wreck. Torn, strewn and used in ways by wandering soldiers and God knows who else as a place to ransack, pillage, plunder and desecrate. It will take a lot of work to return the building, this house, into a home once again. Nevertheless, this is where it will begin because they have to, it is survival. Papa is dirty, worn and bloodied and looks as if he has wrestled to uproot trees and run upon a thousand hills. Never has Anni seen her father, the professor of gymnastics, so close to ruin's door, physically. "Papa, are you okay? What happened to you?" she asks from her broken heart. "Don't ask. Do not ask me that question again. I don't want to talk about it, do you understand?" he replies. "Yes, Papa," Anni answers. And the questions never will come again, nor will they ever be allowed by Papa for all his years. It is between him and his God and no one need know.

# What Have They Done to Our Homeland?

"**Attorney General:** *I wish to call Mr. Alfred Oppenheimer. The witness will testify in German.*
**Presiding Judge:** *I gather that you speak German?*
**Witness Oppenheimer:** *Yes.*
*[The Witness is sworn]*
**Presiding Judge:** *What is your full name?*
**Witness:** *Alfred Oppenheimer.*
**Attorney General:** *Do you live in Luxembourg?*
**Witness Oppenheimer:** *Yes.*
**Q.** *And you have lived there since 1926?*
**A.** *Yes.*
**Attorney General:** *Just by way of explanation, Your Honour. Most of the witness's testimony will focus on the concentration camps. But since we have had no testimony about Luxembourg, I will allow myself to go through this matter briefly with him, in order to complete the picture.*
**Presiding Judge:** *We did have something about Luxembourg.*
**Attorney General:** *Only documents. But we have a witness, and I would wish briefly to take advantage of this opportunity in order to present several matters.*
*[To the witness] When did the Germans enter Luxembourg?*
**Witness Oppenheimer:** *On 10 May 1940.*
**Q.** *Tell the Court briefly about the operations of the Germans, after their arrival, against the Jewish population.*
**A.** *On 10 May, when the Germans entered Luxembourg, they confiscated above all the contents of the drawing rooms, studies,*

*other furniture and so on. After the radio sets, and then there were various operations, handing things over—everything one had, one was only allowed to keep a pair of shoes—one had to hand over all one's bed linen, personal linen—one was only allowed to keep one shirt and one pair of drawers and one vest, one had to hand everything over, so that is was practically impossible to change one's underclothes. Then we were—we were rounded up, together with refugees, in a monastery—that had space for some 30-35 people, all Luxembourg's Jews, little by little, and from there the transports left for Auschwitz, for Theresienstadt, for Poland....*

**Q.** *What happened to the Jewish community?*

**A.** *Most of the Jewish community left 10 May, and at first, till civil government and the civil administration took over—that was July or August, 1940—things were still relatively peaceful for the Jews and a good proportion of the community was able to leave the country somehow.*

**Q.** *How many Jews were there in Luxembourg up to the outbreak of the War?*

**A.** *There were around 2,000-2,500 local Jews, and there were in addition somewhere between 800 and 2,000 refugees.*

**Q.** *If I might, Your Honour, digress slightly, I should like to say here that Luxembourg was one the few countries—the Grand Duchess of Luxembourg and her Government, unlike other countries, opened their doors wide and gave all Jews—all refugees a temporary entry visa, in order to allow them to look in their own time for another home. Luxembourg thus saved the lives of many tens of thousands of Jews, and I should like to make this point here.*

**Presiding Judge:** *Very well.*"

The Third Trial of Adolf Eichmann- session 68; Testimony of Alfred Oppenheimer, Session 68, Vol. III, p. 1254

**Author's Note:** *Out of some 3,000 plus Jews living in the country of Luxembourg in 1940, only 58 survived; the remaining were killed within days, weeks or months from occupation and the balance were interred in concentration camps to meet their final demise under Nazi rule. No known Luxembourger Jew is known to have survived the concentration camps through liberation in early 1945 by Allied Forces.*

"Gredy, I am sorry. I have only been here since early this morning. I was going to try and clean things up a bit before you arrived." Papa shares his dismay with his wife. "Albert, the house be damned, I am just glad and thankful to God that you are alive and here with us again, my husband. I love you!" she responds out of the hearing of the children. "I guess so, we are back together once again and maybe, by God's mercy it will be for good and we can go back to a normal life of some sorts," he answers with hope.

Meanwhile, Anni has begun to wander around the first level of the house and take inventory of the sights before her eyes. It is unimaginable, or at least it would be if it weren't right here in front of her face and within the reach of her fingertips. She peers into Mama and Papa's room. All the bedding has been piled into the small room along with the damaged armoire. She approaches the doorway slowly and steps over the threshold only to be repelled by a violent attack of nausea. She clasps her hands over her mouth and nose as much to keep from screaming as to keep from smelling further odors or vomiting. People, human beings, have used the mattresses to urinate upon, to defecate upon and the bedding is sliced and ripped out of some freakish reasoning through violent, animalistic absurdity. It is impossible to absorb it all into her mind. They have been treated like animals for no reason and here in their own home, supposedly free human beings have conducted themselves as if they were animals by choice. It is totally and inadequately insane.

"Anni! Come give me a hand with these things. You too, Bubby!" Boma calls out to the children. She is wise and knows that work is the best way to redirect the thoughts of the children, get their minds off what they see and occupy them with activity. She stands by the bags and stuffed pillowcases encompassing the belongings of the Neuman family. "Let's get all this stuff out on the veranda and then we can get started cleaning up this mess. Let's get busy, children." The young Albert and Anni both immediately comply and gather the makeshift baggage and begin lugging it to the place Boma has designated. Once done, the children begin to look around again. It is a lot to absorb, considering the condition of their home when they left five months ago.

"Anni, you and Bubby go upstairs and check on your beds and see if the room is okay for you to sleep in tonight. Make sure you check the beds closely for filthiness. If you need to, strip them down and try to wipe down and clean the mattresses for now," Mama commands as she heads to the war-torn kitchen to start somewhere, somehow, anywhere, just start. It is a total disaster. The house has been so damaged and disgustingly abused that it will take literally days, even weeks, to bring back some semblance of order and home again.

Anni and Bubby leave the room with Mama and Boma attacking the kitchen with grist and grind to make cleanliness of utter filth and putrid disregard. Charly sits quietly near Mama's feet and Papa remains seated silently at the table with his head bowed, almost nodding from sleep deprivation. His body is worn to its end of strength, but his thoughts and mind are still speeding along inside and he is floating away from it all in his spirit and soul. He just needs a few minutes and he will be alright. He will gather his strength again and rise to start cleaning along with the rest of the family. Rest will not come soon enough and there will not be much rest to come for days and even weeks. It is a known fact and that makes it all the more depressing, yet accepted so that each one may continue to function with that end in sight.

Bubby and Anni check out the condition of their room upstairs and find it to be in a much better state of repair than the facilities below. However, there is still plenty of work to be done to make it as it was before they left. Anni searches under her bed and finds that by some miraculous intervention, her treasured reading books are still there to feed her hungering lust for knowledge. It is a small thing in appearance but a blessing larger than planet Earth to her heart's desires. The two children return downstairs to give report on the condition of their quarters and to further investigate the status of matters below with the rest of the family.

As they amble down the steps, Marie, from the apartment above, falls in behind them with quiet surprise and jubilation. They rejoice in the presence of one another with questions flying about like a swarm of bees and not one answer to be found. She accompanies the two youngsters downstairs to find the same free-spirited response from the remaining family below. Even Papa arises from his distant ventures and greats Marie with a hug and a grateful welcome to these humble surroundings called home. Marie has brought some bread and a little wine to share with the Neumans just in case they have had privation for days.

Fortunately, the Neuman family isn't starving, but the gift is immeasurable and there will never come a day when the favor, love and genuine thought can be returned. It is the kind of thing that makes the most deadly, poisonous circumstances nullified before the human spirit and will. It promotes camaraderie among the suffering. Souls with common experience share their collective wills to make preparation to fight for another day and another breath of life. Although death would be easier, and life is hard, life is the choice because only life can reproduce. Death is an end. Life is a new beginning each and every moment of each new day.

Mama comes from the kitchen long enough to make short conversation with Marie. Although her heart and spirit have soared, she still has much to do before getting the children ready for bed. She hugs Marie and leaves her to the queries of Papa, Boma and the children. She walks over into her former bedroom and begins to re-pack what stuffing she can obtain into the nearly destroyed mattresses.She strips them of the filth and cleans them the best she can in preparation for a comfortable place where she can take her husband in her arms and hold him close and fall asleep together for the first time in over a week. It is a moment she knows will only last a few minutes in their exhaustive state, but, it is a moment she will treasure forever in her heart. Having her strong husband next to her and reassuring her that he is here to make his family safe from the hell just on the other side of the front door.

The evening filters into the midpoint between night and early morn and the children are shuffled off to bed as Marie departs in return to her upstairs accommodations. The dew is already beginning to dampen the street outside and each member of the family falls to sleep in their respective corners of the home with memories branded from the days past, this day and wonderment for tomorrow. Sleep takes charge as they fall victim to their own tiresome labors. Night has come and a new day awaits, though it is as clear as the smell of the breeze through the windows that tomorrow is written already with pain in addition to the present. It isn't going to end soon and sadness is commonplace. They are living but they don't have a life. Not yet. This is going to be a battle of wills, a battle for survival, a battle for family and a battle for self. A war is not only raging in the countryside of all Europe, but in the hearts and minds of the occupied subjects victimized by the whole of it all and situated in the midst of mindless mayhem.

While Mama and Papa lie side by side in bed, they whisper again to one another Marie's news: "The Luxembourg currency has been devaluated and whatever you have on you or in the bank is worth about one-tenth of its previous value. I heard that in another week or so it won't have any value at all." Papa makes plans to rise early and get busy with business. The bank first for money, if it is still there, and then to the town hall for instructions and news. Meanwhile, Anni lies in her bed thinking of how the basement looked with the washbasin broken into large chunks of concrete and mortar. How the house has been desecrated and how the stench of other people still wanders the halls of their home. They have electricity, but the lamps, bulbs and stands have all been bent, broken or otherwise rendered useless. What a horrendous squalor of waste. Although she has never seen a ghetto, this must be what it is like to live in one. Her beautiful home of Esch is a ghetto for refugees come home. She falls to deep sleep knowing that tomorrow it won't be a dream, it will be another day of pure challenge, and her strength is waning fast.

The morning arrives with a knock at the door. A German police officer asks for Papa and he comes to the door to find out what is expected of them. Papa must go to the town hall and get his instructions for the family and start completing paperwork. In the meantime, Marie comes down from her upstairs apartment with bread and coffee for the family. She has been a wonderful neighbor and the Neumans have developed great appreciation and admiration for her. Especially Anni. It is good to have an older woman outside the family to talk with and tp share her thoughts.

The morning is filled with activity as the women talk with Marie about their experiences. All this is done as they go about, with Anni and Bubby, cleaning what appears to be an endless mess. Somehow they persevere and make their way through the process until the place starts to look like home. It is a special gift that God has given to women to take such utter ruin and transform it into a comfortable cocoon of sorts. By late evening the home is almost completely restored to the temporary satisfaction of Mama and Boma. While the women are taking a short break at the table before trying to conjure up something for dinner, Papa returns from his full day at the town hall. It has been grueling for him and the look on his face shows that life is not in any wise returning to normal, nor the way it had been five months before.

"It is very sad outside, Gredy," Papa says with a downcast look upon his face. "The street signs have been removed and they are replacing the names of the roadways with new German names. Anything sounding French is being wiped out as if it never existed. It is unbelievable," he states in a manner that makes Anni think that he is going to shed tears. "I sat there for hours while they questioned me about everything under the sun. It was ridiculous and embarrassing. Absolutely humiliating the way they talk to us. I don't know how I am going to keep my tongue. Somehow, we all are and we will, or face unbearable punishment," Papa continues with insight into his day's experience. "They did give me some ration tickets to get us started," he says as he passes them across the table to Mama. "Take those and get what you can in the morning. Right now the bakery is about the only thing open. I think the Italian store at the corner will be opening in the next few days or so. We will have to make do with that for now. They said that we can take trips up north of here and get horsemeat without ration tickets, but we are very restricted as far as traveling. We cannot cross back over the border into France for now. We have to get IDs for everyone in the family and there is a curfew in place so that no one is allowed in the streets after 6:00 P.M.

"Gredy, it is not good at all," he whispers to his wife. Now in a voice too low for the rest of the family to hear, "Gredy they have killed people. They have taken people away to Luxembourg City and put people in jail. It is not good at all. They hate the Jews and have all kinds of extra rules, beyond the hundreds they have for us, regarding how we are to act around them. We basically have to act as if they, the Jews, do not even exist. What they have done to them is horrible. They have seized all their property and personal belongings. They are not giving rations to the Jews in the same amount as us and they are not permitted to work. They must wear armbands identifying themselves in public. They cannot walk in the street or on the sidewalk. They must use the gutters. We cannot even look at them, much less talk to them. How are we supposed to exist like this? No one even talks to one another as neighbors anymore. Everyone walks around with their heads down or looks the other way to avoid even making eye contact. Everyone is so afraid that they might be accused of some kind of manufactured suspicious behavior. The whole town is living in the grip of fear."

Now, back in a voice that the whole family can hear, Papa passes along the instructions he has in his hands and in his head to the rest of the family. He repeats how the children are to address, or not address, the Jews. Anni is shattered. Her sweet and kind friend, the girl at the shoe shop, and her wonderful family are Jews. How can she ignore them or pretend they don't exist. They mean the world to her. She has made up her mind already, before Papa is finished, that she will not obey such absurdities.

The night passes in solidarity of silent reflections. The members of the family are completely engrossed with their own thoughts and how this situation has come to be and what it may come to be. Only young Charly is immune to the circumstances as a whole; however, even he can feel the gravitational pull of concern and dismay. Plainly, he isn't much of a playful child right now and for every good reason. He quietly sits and occupies himself in a manner very uncommon for him, his nature and his personality. It is amazing what oppression can do to both young and old alike.

"Gredy, in the morning you and I will go to the Nazi party table and make further inquiry regarding these instructions they gave me today. Boma, please watch over the children and see if you can find out anything more particular as to when they might register, enroll and begin school. I don't want them away from their studies this long. They should begin as absolutely soon as possible." Having given charge and challenge, he slumps back into his seat to withdraw his pipe and disappear in his own thoughts and consternation.

The morning sun arises and the children wander from their beds as in a sleepy stupor. Boma has just returned from the bakery with some fresh bread, cheese and coffee. She begins to prepare the table for the children. While they were still deep in slumber during the early dawn, Mama and Papa had already risen, dressed and departed for further inquiry into their present standing. They are on a mission to secure all instructions as to how they may comply with the new ruling authority and make their family safe, at the same time evaluating the costs it may entail.

Toward the end of the day, as the sun begins its descent in the western sky, Boma starts frying some small potatoes with butter and noodles she obtained at the Italian grocery store with Maria. There is a large loaf of bread on the table and a fresh pot of coffee on the stove. While Anni and Bubby are deep in conversation, the front door opens and Mama and Papa head directly to the table to sit down. They flop into their seats as if they just fell from their feet, with no signs of life in their bodies or on their faces. In all her life, Anni has never seen her parents with such a look on their faces. They are distant, non-human, blank, catatonic and unknown. They have never been this way before and it is clear that they will never be the same again. They are changed and completely different people. They are still Papa and Mama, but, something has drastically changed them and how they will conduct their lives from this day forward. It is a day for her to never forget—she has no choice—something has turned their world upside down again and it is spinning in cyclonic proportions to the point of making one nauseated in trying to visualize.

"Albert! What is the matter? Tell me now and keep nothing from us. The children are not children anymore and I am sick of keeping two stories. Let's just get it all out and deal with it as family and harden our hearts for the pain and suffering together, do you hear me?" Boma demands of her son, mostly from frustration but also from near collapse and breakdown. It is time to come clean with everything and let all members of the family read from the same page of news. This is the only way they will make it and her wisdom has shown through like the cutting silver edge of a thunder cloud. She is right and Albert knows it.

"Boma, Gredy and I went to the bank first to see what we had for money. It is useless. What we had is worth about one-twentieth of the face value. We are broke and what little we did get is here in my pocket. Maybe it will see us through another week if we stretch it. I need to find work immediately. In order for me to do that, I have to 'prove' to the Nazis that I, and my whole family, are not Jewish; because of our name being Neuman, we are under suspicion. I have thirty days to trace our family history by birth, marriage and death back to the year 1750!" he exclaims in anguish. "I have to chart my parents, your parents, our great-grandparents for both me and Gredy all the way back over two hundred years! All to show that no Jew existed in our bloodline! We pray to Jesus and He was Jewish, we believe in His salvation through His blood and yet we must deny that same blood! It is insane!"

He can hardly take it after all he has been through today. With his wife at his side he has had to submit to the humiliation of having to salute the Nazi soldiers and German police by lifting his right arm high and reciting the necessary "Heil Hitler." A bastard of a man that he never liked, hardly has known and now hates. He pounds his fists on the table and the whole family winces in shock as the thunder of it sounds through the room as if he were breaking a ton of wood beneath his massive, muscular arms. Silence fills the room in the aftermath of the explosion and tears form in every eye. "My family will not perish," Albert covenants with himself in his thoughts, as the family silently looks upon him in way they have never seen him before and they are in awe. What a man he is, they see it for the first time. He is a rock, their fortress and their refuge.

For the third night, darkness falls upon the town of Esch-Sur-Alzette, Luxembourg; however, it is no longer that city by German standard. It is part of the Gau and the Deutschland. Luxembourg no longer exists and neither do any of its honored traditions or character. Its people are either Germanic people by race or human waste for servitude, indentured slavery or disposition upon the pile of inhumanity and discharge into heaps of nothingness.

The dawn brings a glittering of color and shadows upon the walls as Anni rubs her eyes and gains her perspective of the new day. In the bed next to hers, Bubby is still steadfast asleep as is typical for young boys his age. He could sleep for two days if left alone. "Bubby! Bubby!" Anni shouts to him, much to his consternation and dismay. "What?" he replies in a high-pitched, whining voice. "What is it?" "It's time to get up. We have to go get our identification cards. Get dressed and meet me downstairs for breakfast. I'm leaving in twenty minutes and you better be ready because you have to go with me. If you don't then you can explain it to Papa and he will be very, very sore with you!" Anni chastises him in advance for any uncooperative behaviour. "I'm coming," he laments and starts to stretch, curl to sleep and then pulls himself from his place of deep departure from the worldly demands of life.

"Good morning my little lady," Papa greets his daughter as he sits at the table sipping coffee and puffing his pipe. In front of him is a stack of papers and some scratch paper with notes he has been writing. His pen is still poised in his hand and ink has darkened his fingers. He has been diligently at work trying to make notes of what the family can and cannot do, setting a plan for survival and tracing his family history for the report due on their Germanic lineage.

"Good morning, Papa," Anni announces in reply with a genuine smile on her face. Mama is standing over the stove and watching matters over her shoulder, including young Charly seated at the table and playing with his bread and butter. He dips it into his watered-down coffee and sops it into his mouth. It is very unappealing to Anni but Charly seems all too happy with it, so let him be. "Papa, Bubby is on his way down now. As soon as we can get ready we will go get our identification cards like you said. Is there anything we should do special or not do? Will we be okay or should we take someone or go with someone else?" she inquires of her father. "No, Anni, just do like I told you. Go to the town hall, go directly in to the section table where the German police are and tell them you are there to get your IDs. They will take your picture, get your birth information and give you your cards. Don't go beyond that, just do as they say and keep your mouth shut. Don't ask questions, just be polite, quick and leave, OK?" he quizzes. "Yes, Papa, I understand. I will and I will make sure Bubby does too." She shows her strength of character and her willingness to be as strong as the man in front of her.

After the younger Albert has completed his tardy breakfast, the two embark on their journey through the streets of what was once very familiar and now, completely disorienting. The street signs don't exist or have been changed into German. Windows are shattered here and there, and pockmarks two inches deep and four inches wide are riddled on building sides, windowsills and doorways—markings of machine-gun fire from combat on their home streets just a short memory ago. It is an eerie reminder that this is not home anymore. They make their way to the identification post and, much to their surprise, young Albert does not need one because of his young age. This is a grateful reward to Anni. She submits to her photograph being taken, waits through the unbearable time and questions, receives her card and they depart for home. Before they leave, the brown-uniformed German soldier reminds her to keep her opinions and conversation to herself. "Avoid suspicious behaviour, report anything that seems as such, ignore the Jews, keep your card with you at all times and don't forget to bring in all your sewing needles, knitting needles, hairpins, safety pins and all other metal items for the greater good of the Wermacht and the Winter War Campaign. Be a true patriot of Germany." She is warned and sickened at the same time. But she bites her tongue and dares not speak, not just for herself, but for Bubby so innocently standing by.

As they wander back out onto the street, Anni and Bubby notice in silence how things have changed. They look at one another without speaking a word. People walk right past them as if they don't exist. People they know and recognize have faces worn as if tens of years have passed, and they don't even lift a hand in recognition of the two children. Neighbors long known are distant beings haunting the streets in person but their spirit has departed to another place. No one smiles. No one laughs. No one talks. No one shares life. No one is happy. They are all here and they all survey the streets and see the gray-uniformed German police watching their every step, movement and word, if any. They are prisoners with the freedom to walk about but they are also rats in a cage, observed at every moment and examined for treachery.

"Bubby, I have to go do something very quickly. I won't be long but I need to check on something. You go ahead of me and take your time. Stop along the way and make your return home slow, OK?" Anni asks in trust to her brother. "Don't hurry but don't be late, either. I will be home shortly. If Papa or Mama asks, just tell them that it took longer for me since I had to get processed on my card and I sent you home because it was taking too long and you didn't need a card." "Yes, Anni, I will take care of it. I have some thoughts to think out on my own and I will get home in about half an hour. You should be there soon after, right?" He is much more mature than she has realized and his answer is wise in the giving. Do what you must, but don't be foolish, is the message.

Anni hurries her steps to a near run as she redirects her path to her objective. Bubby departs along the same course they had been traveling but he slows and ambles along to stall his arrival at the Neuman home. Anni passes by some fellow citizens of Esch, but the most disturbing sight is the soldiers in brown uniforms with rifles strung across their shoulders. Also walking the sidewalks are the German police in their green/gray uniforms with leather belts and leather suspenders supporting their ammunition pouches and side arms. There is a lot to be afraid of. She is only thirteen and these are men. Grown men with guns and authority. She is taking her life into her own hands and risking much more than words permit. In less than a second she could be taken for many reasons: for questioning, imprisonment, rape or abuse beyond description. She ignores the obvious dangers and carries herself as if she is innocent and free of their powers. She has a goal in mind and she will make it only because she has belief in her goal and nothing interferes with her beliefs.

Anni is the only butterfly that can fly among the bees and the serpents to find the flower she seeks and not be harmed. The flower she seeks is that which is filled to overflowing with joyous reunion; the companionship of one who has freedom of flight and the one that is in need of dreams for truth, justice and fantasy to fly. She is a deliverer of hope. No one person can carry any higher priced gift than the one her heart has proven invaluable, evidenced through her loyalty to justice. She is a living example of purity toward righteousness, justice and a hatred of wrong.

Anni soon narrows her path from the main streets, down the alleys and eventually finds herself at the front door of the shoe repair shop. It is here that her girlfriend, Rosa, whom she has missed so much, lives. This visit is far removed from all the visits she used to make here before the evacuation. The cobbler and his family are Jews.

Anni looks around quickly and then knocks on the door. As it is swung open, Rosa's father stands looking worn and astonished at the girl before his eyes. "Anni Neuman!" he nearly shouts with a smile on his face. It is clear that his heart has been touched, warmed and revived in spirit. It is an amazing thing to him that this young girl would risk so much of herself and even her own family to come and check on the welfare of his "branded" family. "Come in, come in!" he encourages and calls out to his daughter. "Rosa, hurry down, Anni is here!" The entire family comes to greet her, with one exception. Andre, the oldest son is not here and will not return. Anni will never know why.

Outside the windows, through the drawn curtains, Anni and the rest of the family can see the German military vehicles passing by in the streets. They speed by on a set course for various reasons. It is also a good reason for so much fear and apprehension inside this shop and home. The father tells Anni all about the things that have happened to them while Rosa sits quietly beside Anni holding her hand and smiling amid the sadness of it all. He reaches into his pants pocket and withdraws the yellow armband with the Star of David emblazoned upon it, indicating to all the world they are Jews. Anni knows she can't stay long and that Bubby will be nearing their home soon. She hugs her young friend, kisses Rosa's tear-stained cheek and hugs the rest of the family. "I will come back again. Take care of yourself and if I can bring anything, let me know. I trust God that you will be alright." The father sees her to the door and repeats the statement in his own fashion, "Anni, we too are trusting God and it will be okay for us. You be careful and don't come near this place if you see any German police, soldiers or vehicles close by. You will jeopardize your safety and your family's safety. We will be alright," He half-heartedly reassures her.

Soon Anni is speedily stepping along the street that leads back to her own door and home. The military vehicles continue to speed by in both directions and Anni notices that all the shops once owned and operated by the wealthy Jews are closed and shut up tight. They are nowhere to be seen and she senses in her gut that they will never be back. It has hardly been a week now and the walls are closing in on her, she feels like she is trapped and imprisoned for no other reason than being alive and living here in this place that was once such a lovely home and town, now turned into a open-air prison. Danger is at every step and fear rules the streets like the black Iron Eagle that squawks and hovers above with its shrill and evil laughter.

"Anni! Where have you been?" papa belts out the question before she can even get the door half closed. She knows there is no use in lying and doesn't care to anyhow. There will be enough of that with the Germans, no need for it to poison the family. "I went to the shoe shop, Papa. It is terrible what these Germans are doing to the Jews. It isn't right." "Anni, don't rock the boat. These people are very bad and very dangerous. You can't be doing that kind of stuff anymore, do you understand me?" he chides. "Yes, Papa, I understand you but I don't understand anything else," she replies with tears welling up in her eyes. "Come to the table so we can eat," Papa directs her as well as the remaining family members. They all take their seats and Mama and Boma place the potatoes, noodles and bread in front of their plates.

Each member of the family begin to take their portions and put the small samples of food on their plates quietly reflecting in silent thoughts. The pressure seems to be building inside Anni and she cannot explain it or understand it, but she is starting to feel dizzy, angry, and about to burst. "Anni, close the curtains to the window, the Germans have ordered that no light should leak out from the house or we will be bombed," Boma directs her as she points to the black blinds fashioned earlier in the day by the women. Then it happens.

Anni lets out a piercing scream and falls to the floor kicking with all her strength and pounding her fist into the floor with all her might. "Dirty Germans! I hate them, I hate them, the dirty Germans! They are monsters." She screams and cries until she hardly has a voice left. All the while, Mama, Papa, Boma and the boys just look on without moving. They look to one another in silence and wait. Marie comes running down stairs to see if everything is okay. She has heard the screaming and is scared herself. "It's okay, Marie, everyone leave her alone. Just let her get it out. It will be good for her, she needs it. Let her alone for now," Papa commands the room. There is no reason for him to be angry with his precious daughter, he feels the same way himself and maybe somehow, Anni is doing it for each member of the family. They all want to scream, cry and hate, they just don't have it in them to let it out, yet. And so it goes as the night comes again and the weather turns cold outside. They have no heat to warm themselves, only blankets, and soon it will be time to sleep.

The train tracks to France are still torn apart and dismantled from the bombing and war. The walls of the city are forever etched with machine gun fire. German police and soldiers haunt their every move and they are literally interred in their own city, imprisoned by the war, politics and an evil dictator named Adolf Hitler. It is no longer their "Homeland." Thus the war wages between the will of the Iron Eagle and that of the steeled butterfly. By daybreak, Anni will have a renewed challenge in her blood and she will again be strong. She will outlive the horrid creature flying above and she will have the last laugh. It is written in her faith and that is something no one can erase.

# Learning the Way of the Iron Eagle

September, 1940. The world was watching Europe and most particularly, Germany. It appeared that one-third of the world was at war or near war. In fact, nearly the entire world was on the brink of war on a scale such as never seen before and, God forbid, should ever be seen again. It was the same month that Maurice and Richard McDonald started their first McDonald's hamburger restaurant in Pasadena, California. In Luxembourg, all Jewish owned businesses had become "Aryan" property. Monstrous attacks were launched over London by the German Luftwaffe. By the end of the month, Germany, Japan and Italy signed the Axis or Tripartite Pact. In Luxembourg, two Boy Scouts, Josy Wengler and Josy Wirol, had been arrested by the Gestapo at the ages of thirteen and fourteen for suspicious behavior, clearly leaders of a budding resistance force to fight the unwelcomed occupying forces. The Grand Duchess Charlotte had arrived in New York and by early November 1940, she arrived in Montreal, Canada in her flight for freedom for her tiny country.

In America, more than thirty million citizens own radios. Franklin D. Roosevelt is elected to an unheard of third term as president and Ernest Hemingway's For Whom the Bell Tolls is published. Meanwhile, fifteen thousand Jews have been or will be deported from the Rhineland on their way to camps in France via Luxembourg railways. The camps consist of transit camps, work camps, concentration camps and, eventually, extermination camps. While it is most common to hear the term "concentration camp" associated with the Holocaust later discovered by Allied forces, at this time, the dictator Adolf Hitler has several names for the camps that will swell in excess of five thousand sites, all for the "Final Solution" and greater purity of Germany and its newly occupied lands. On November 15, 1940, the Warsaw Ghetto is sealed and thus with it, the fate of approximately half a million Polish Jews. A German "Blue-Blood" by the name of Gustav Simon is Chief of Civil Administration and Gauleiter of the Moselle and all of Luxembourg.

September 23, 1940 is a Monday morning, and Anni is awakened by the smell of coffee brewing on the stove in the Neuman family home. They are home again, although appreciation of the thought is short-lived. It just isn't the same, and there isn't anything they can do to change it or make it different. They can only do what each day requires and hope, pray and believe that they will outlive, outlast and outendure the God-awful demons, ghosts and monsters outside their door. The air is already beginning to cool in the late night and early mornings and it won't be long before winter makes a full announcement of the change in seasons. Anni wrestles the covers over her head and tries to squeeze ten more minutes of the blissful deep, dark sleep that occurred somewhere in the night. It is useless. Thoughts begin to run through her head of all the things she has seen, hasn't seen and speculation as to what she will see. It is dizzying and her adrenaline is already flowing from the swing and sway from fear to dread and from dread to unhappiness, all in a never-ending cycle.

Today is not only Monday. It is not only the week after what should have been the Catholic celebration of the Holy Cross at church, but, it is September 23, 1940 and it is her first day of school in the "new" land once called Luxembourg and her city, Esch. She throws the covers down about her waist in one quick thrust and tumbles out of the bed. Her first focused thought is that Bubby is already out of bed. The ratty-haired child, the one who could sleep through a thousand thunders, is awake and out of bed before her. She is immediately astonished. It is clear that the young Albert is ready to get back to the business of school. Not because he loves learning, cares for formal education or anything of the sort. It is because he has an audience awaiting him and a new one at that. It is time for the performer to take the stage and delight his fans. For a while, a short while, he can go to school and escape what he sees at home and all around town. There, at school, he believes he will be able to return to his well-honed skills of clowning.

After a quick breakfast and a briefing by Papa about conducting themselves with quietness and keeping their heads down, Bubby and Anni head out the door to their respective schools. Bubby needs to go only a short distance across the street, around the back way and into the front of the school that sits near opposite the Neuman home. Anni, however, must trek nearly a mile to her upper-grade school for girls, at the same old building but "new" as a state building. She hardly rounds the corner of her home street and heads up the road that meets at the three-way intersection where the church sits, before she sees him. Big, bulky and smelly is all she can think. She doesn't even truly know the latter, but that is how she perceives him in her mind. Wearing a green/gray uniform of pants, high-top boots, and buttoned down jacket. The collar is sharp-cut and crisp around its three to four-inch band forming an upside-down V at the throat.

Both sides of the lapels are emblazoned with the sharp square patches of gold and black with a thin center line, indicating a German police officer. His shoulders bear the same gold/black patches covering the length of the shoulder. He wears his unit patch low on his left sleeve and has a harness of sorts made up of a belt at the waist with shoulder straps as suspenders on left and right, from the hips over and to the low back. Under his left arm is a pouch, almost like a woman's handbag, attached to the belt. Therein lie all the tools of gathering and marking information. Pad, pencils, booklets, orders, rules, regulations, and on. Across the brass belt buckle to the underside of the right arm is the distinctive heavy-laden case wherein resides the officer's sidearm, a pistol which is used just as easily as the pouch on the other side. It is fully loaded just as the carrier is "loaded" of mind to use it at his matter-of-fact choosing between left and right.

Anni has heard that you are not supposed to look at them. But then again, you are supposed to recognize them and salute them, or is that only for the soldiers or SS troops? She can't think fast enough. What should she do, which should she do? She does a little of both. She looks up and straight ahead into his steel gray eyes and with great sickness in her stomach, looks down to the ground and steps far away and around him as he walks on by, not even noticing she exists. She is truly angry now. "That is ridiculous. This is stupid. How can we live like this? How long do we have to put up this stuff?" she asks herself. That was just the first one and the first time. "How am I supposed to do this every day and all the time?" She continues her inward conversation as she straggles onward for the schoolhouse. "I hate this, I can't stand it. I am not going to be able to do this for long. It had better end soon or I am going to get into a lot of trouble for sure," she tells herself. This is a very, very bad situation for a girl nearly fourteen and just as strong in body as spirit, the way her father raised her. He never knew it would be for this purpose as much as life in general.

Anni finally arrives at the doors of her school to begin anew her studies as she has dreamed of, especially getting new books to read and study. She passes through the doorways, as do the other children and meanders to her assigned class. It is clear, here too, that things are much different than before. It is in the air. It is in the solemnity of the children, each having come here almost as if it were a wake being held for the past months of evacuation and occupation that no one wishes to recognize or verbalize. "Let's just get on with school and life now" seems to be the consensus among the children. It is immediately noticed that the nuns and the priest are not a part of the program as they had once been. The teachers are all true Germans from Germany herself and they are ready to reeducate the Luxembourg girls in their "heritage" of Germanic origins.

"*Willkommen, Stellen Sie Ihre Zukunft mit Begrenzung fest.*" The class is greeted by the middle-aged woman with staunch posture and clothing to match while the children sit rigidly in their seats. "Welcome, you determine your future with restraint." Anni knows just from this introduction that this is not going to be a good year in school. She wants to dive out the window and run, but she can't, she must sit like stone in the seat and pay attention. She looks down at her class schedule and compares it in her mind, line by line, to the way it was when she left:

| **(Luxembourg)** | **(Gau Mossellland)** |
|---|---|
| **Religion** | **Religion** |
| **German** | **German** |
| **French** | **History** |
| **Math** | **Geography** |
| **Writing** | **Art Education** |
| **Natural Science** | **Counting and Math** |
| **Geography** | **Manual Work** |
| **Gymnastics** | **Typing** |
| **Travel** | **Body Exercises** |

As the day proceeds, Anni's heart is crushed all the more, along with her spirit. Everything is so cold and calculated. There are no moments of laughter or lightheartedness. Everything is very strict, disciplined and examined in such a way that you don't only feel as though you are being watched, but that your whole family is under the spyglass for espionage. She only came here to learn and to love education; instead, she must learn to survive under the rules of the Iron Eagle and all its menacing and diabolical ways of perverting a mind. She is constantly scrutinized for any hint of deviation from conformity and even worse, subversion by her own will or knowledge of friends, family or acquaintances that might be involved in undermining the German Way. This isn't school, this is a form of compliance to daily duty and surviving under the rules of engagement during a time of war.

As the school day draws to a close, the children are lectured by the schoolmaster about some new matters of conduct expected of the students. They are required to take notes of certain things they should and should not do outside the school grounds. It is an imprisoning thought to Anni that the school authorities are so united with the authorities outside the walls of learning. It is an interwoven system she is unfamiliar with and it is eating her by the bit and bite. "Jews," the word resounds time after time. Rules, Jews, rules, Jews, Gypsies, mixed races, Christian names, dress codes, recognition of officers, both civil and military, requirements to report suspicious behavior and obligation to do "what is right" even if it is against family. This lecture is cancerous to the butterfly's gentle being. She is adamantly opposed to it all and determined to do what she knows is the right thing to do. Press all they want, she will be Anni Neuman and they can all be damned as much and more as they already are for hell. It is sorrowful, but they are who they are and they chose their present and their ending. She will not be a part of this wrong. She will do what is right in the eyes of her God.

The students are finally released after their first indoctrination day, which was supposed to be for genuine education. A total farce—a spit in the face of faith and truth. School turned into a campground of political and ideological poisoning and brainwashing. Anni wanders down the street, ignoring the soldiers with their whistles and taunts at her feminine features by the German beasts. She is only thirteen, nearly fourteen, and she is drawing attention that makes her feel dirty, hateful, angry and tearful.

With head bowed and eyes as far away as her mind, Anni makes a sudden decision to soothe her soul. She quickly alters her path and makes way for the shoe repair store to see her girlfriend and inquire of her family's well-being. Upon approach, she notices something very strange. She knows in her gut that it is horrible beyond words and it means something that is dangerous, foreboding and unbelievably scary. Prominently displayed in the front window of the store is a large yellow six-point star of David. The building has been branded as a Jewish place of business and only Jews may conduct business there, as if there were any business left to be done. They are being literally starved from existence. Anni nearly collapses to the ground as her knees go weak and tears dam behind her eyes. She knows she cannot approach, especially with a German police car parked half a block away with the engine running. She remembers the warnings she was previously given and turns toward home, completely in emotional turmoil. She will be back, but not today. Today, she must obey and go home to be safe for another day. It has been a very dark day in a very dark age.

Once at home and inside her cocoon, she feels safe and clean again. She is once again Anni and the world has been shut outside the door. Here, safety is found in the comfort of having her brothers, her mother, grandmother and, most importantly, her staunch father for protection. This is her hiding place from all that is ill beyond their walls. Here she can read, write, study, relax, talk and sometimes even laugh. Life is okay, not great, but okay in here, and this is where she prefers to be. Her once adventurous spirit is folded inside her soul just as if her ornate butterfly wings had collapsed into the hard-shell encasement that prevents them from damage. All her thoughts and memories of this life, or survival to put it best, is being folded and tucked away neatly into the boxes she keeps for storage in her mind. There, the boxes are concealed from prying eyes of all others and she, she alone, has the ability to open them. However, it will be a long time before she does open them and for that, she has every good reason. The day will come when she will do it for herself and nobody else so that she, like the world in later years, can heal from the bloodied war wounds inflicted by talons of the Iron Eagle.

A few weeks pass and it has already seemed like years to Anni. It is nearing mid to late October, 1940, and the air has become cleaner without the steel mills yet, operating but the silence is deafening. "Anni, I want you to take this letter for your Aunt Anne over to the store and have them post it. Don't stop along the way, just go straight over there and come back," Mama instructs the child. "Yes, Mama," she replies and takes the envelope in her hands, grabs her coat and heads out the door and onto the sidewalk. As she walks toward the store a few blocks away, she looks down at the envelope in her hands. Her stomach is filled with a rolling feeling and her eyes squint in anger. Her head spins a little and she stumbles then regains her steps. There on the front of the envelope, on the right upper quadrant shadowing her beloved aunt's name and address is a despicable reminder of the times. A large Luxembourg stamp, overstamped with the Iron Cross and German writing with "Deutschmark" set for currency. She ignores the passersby just as they ignore her. It isn't that they don't care for one another or happen to be rude, it is only that the soul of the city of Esch has lifted and left. It hovers somewhere in the unknown, far away from the dreary little place where they once rejoiced with great and magnificent feasts and festivals. Celebrations of life. Now, it is just living.

As she enters into the store, the bell above the door jingles and Maria, the stout, grey/black haired Italian woman of middle age, pops her head up from behind a stack of boxes. "Hi Anni, what brings you here today?" she says with a disarming smile on her face. She has clearly been working hard in her store and making room on the shelves for items that have long since been ordered and have finally arrived. "Mama asked me to give you this letter to see if you could get it to Aunt Anne down in France," Anni states. "Can you do that?" "Why certainly, sweetheart. This isn't just a store, you know, I have the telephone here and I am the official post office for the time being," she says again with a great smile that comforts Anni. They meet halfway by the counter where the cash register sits among many other items of display, fronted by a single row of six or seven barrels. Some barrels contain Italian noodles of wide variety and a couple hold flour or other basic staples for rationing. "I will see to it that this gets out in the morning, you assure your mother it has been done. How is she anyway?" Maria inquires while she looks over Anni with a quizzical look on her face. "She's doing okay, I guess," Anni answers still looking at Maria and wondering why she seems to be sizing her up. "Well, I better get back home. Mama said to make it quick and not to wander around, so I better go. I will see you again soon." She tries to close the conversation so that she can complete her task as assigned.

"Anni, I know you must return home quickly but I wonder if you would do me a favor?" Maria asks in a suddenly lowered voice that draws great curiosity, though quiet, from Anni. "Yes ma'am, I am sure I could. What do you want me to do?" she asks. "I know the church is just up the way from your house, would you mind carrying this letter over there to someone for me. I can't remember the gentleman's name but he will be the only one there and he will call to you when he sees you. He is expecting the letter and I know he has been there a while praying. Just tuck it under your blouse and keep it safe and tight. Don't tell anyone you have it or drop it. Mail is very important and should always be handled carefully." Maria completes her instructions with an expression that has turned from charm to concern. "Yes ma'am. I will. I'd better hurry," Anni states as she goes about fulfilling her new instructions while making way out the door. Maria watches silently from behind, following to the window and guarding Anni with her eyes as the child heads down the sidewalk and off to church and then home. "She is a good girl," Maria says to herself.

As the church comes into sight, Anni feels suddenly strange. She can't quite figure it out. Is it because she doesn't usually go to the church this time of day? Is it the cold silence of the streets? Is it the solemn, ghostly appearance of the Gothic-styled building or its tomblike emptiness? It is none of the above. It is the fact that she is delivering mail. She has never done this before, especially not to a person whose name she doesn't know, nor how they look or even how she should do it. It is all very surreal.

The hinges of the heavy church door announce her arrival, giving an aching groan of squeaking metal that seems unusually loud in the sanctuary. Just as Maria had said, a man is seated in the back row all alone, bowed as if in prayer. He immediately notices Anni. "It is lovely in here this time of the day isn't it?" he starts without giving her a chance to answer. "I like the solitude and time alone with no one around. It helps me to think and reflect. Don't mind you coming in though," he follows up and continues. "I don't mind seeing such a pretty young face lighting up this dark place at all, in fact, I was hoping someone would come along. Did someone send you?" he asks almost too innocently. Anni catches the clue and responds in kind, "Yes sir, Maria at the store said that it would be a good thing to stop by the church on my way home and say a prayer just for the safety of us all. She is not showing her cards fully and neither is the gentleman. This is a test through cryptic words orchestrated by life or death circumstances.

"I told Maria that I would be here praying in case some word came for me from my family. Did she send anything with you?" he asks innocently again. "Yes sir, actually she did, My name is…" "Stop!" he reacts quickly. I don't want your name. It is better for us to just be strangers for now. You are a sharp young lady and you have a great future ahead of you.

So, if you have something for me, I would appreciate it and in fact I have a little change here for you for being such a kind and sweet child," he finishes. Anni scans the sanctuary round about and then passes the envelope into his hand. It deftly disappears as if it never existed. She refuses the change, however, and departs the church in silence. It is getting close to late for her return home. The only words spoken are goodbyes as they part their ways. She leaves first but she knows it will be only minutes before he leaves also. She will never know because she enters the door to her home and closes out the crazy world outside, glad to settle safe and secure in family and home, her hideaway once again from a storm brewing out of doors.

After school the following week, on Wednesday, October 23, 1940 to be exact, Anni arrives at the street corner of Rue Du Brill and De L'Industrie near their home. Bubby has been waiting for Anni to arrive from school and he has a very strange look on his face as he stares south down the way toward the 168 Road and the train tracks. The weather has turned quite chilly and Anni asks, "Bubby, why are you still sitting out here. You don't have to wait for me, you know that, you should have gone on in."

"Anni, listen. Do you hear that?" he asks. "Hear what, Bubby, it is all quiet around here except for the trains down there," she says, pointing in the direction he was looking. Then it dawns on her. There is something odd, something out of place and strange. "The trains, Bubby, what are they doing down there? It isn't even time for the afternoon train and it sounds like a dozen of them," she says but knows that he is wondering for the same reasons. "Anni, I want to go down there, will you go with me?" he queries. "Bubby, you know we need to get home or Mama is going to be angry." But on second thought, her curiosity is too much for her practical side and she tells him to come along.

The two head down Rue Du Brill to where the railway tracks from the northeast fork into a track turning north and a track turning south. As they approach, they hear the loud clanging and rattling of the trains moving through at a slightly higher speed than usual. One train, the first one they heard, is gone out of sight and the second is near its end without a caboose. As they peer down the tracks looking behind the cars, they can see a third train approaching. As it passes, they feel the rush of air and the mixed smell of diesel, dirt and grime. The cars clack by, about fifty in number, she suspects. Bubby turns to Anni and asks, "Why are they moving so many animals? Where are they coming from? Are they emptying the farmlands from the North to France?" He continues in quest of an answer from his older and wiser sister. "I don't know, Bubby, it is very strange," she replies. "We better get back home right now though, we shouldn't be here and there are some German soldiers coming this way, let's just go." Then it hits her. Out of the breeze blown up from the passing cars, an odor permeates the air. Immediately she lurches over and starts to vomit. Before she is even aware, Bubby's eyes water and he is shaking. The smell is the same horrid, putrid smell they endured on the cattle cars to France months ago.

As Anni tries to regain her composure, grab Bubby's hand and run away, she sees something out of the corner of her eye. The last few cars on the third train. There is barbed wire on the windows at the top of the cattle cars. "That is weird. Why would they do that for animals. I have never seen that before," she tells herself. The third train is already bearing down hard and fast, but she isn't waiting to get any more answers. In her last glimpse, she could swear that she saw a frail and fragile human hand opened as if trying to catch the wind from the barb-wired window. "No, that couldn't be. It was just something else. My mind is playing tricks on me," she tells herself as she and her young brother begin to break into a run toward home.

Unbeknownst to Anni and the younger Albert, they had just been eye witnesses to some 214 cattle cars on four engines pulling over 15,000 Jews from the Rhineland to their relocation to an internment camp on the east border of France. From there, the Jews would eventually be removed again and forwarded in transport to camps such as Dachau for annihilation of the race in the evil design for a "pure" Germany. It was just the beginning of sights that would flit and fly through their individual minds and dreams for years to come. The Nazis were monsters from hell. Real, living demons on earth in human form, and Good and Evil were at war.

A couple more weeks and winter is making itself known all around to the occupants of the tiny country of Europe. Anni has taken to knitting sweaters to earn extra money. The sweaters are given to her by Maria at the store and are quite large when she first receives them. Her job is to take them completely apart row-by-row and thread-by-thread. Once this is done, she must wash and clean the material thoroughly and let it dry for two days or more, weather permitting. After it drys, she begins the process of using patterns to knit new sweaters in her sparse spare time from school, church, studies and other activities outside. She can make a fine profit of two dollars for each completed item returned ready for resale at the store. It is long, arduous and painstaking work, but rewarding to a small degree in profit although large in her determination to push ahead. Anni is resolved to make a living for herself and her family. This is not an attitude that will expire or dissipate, rather, it will grow in years beyond the willingness of the average person.

This is how the evenings are mostly spent approaching the infamous holiday of Armistice Day, the very day Anny Neuman was born at 11:00 P.M., for November 12, 1926. As Anni and the rest of the family sit about the living room of the house on the tenth of November, Papa has an announcement to make. Bubby puts down his accordian (the only music they listen to since radios are strictly forbidden unless it is German music and Papa has made the rule of no radio, period, to be safe) and the family listens to the patriarch. "Ma, Gredy, children," he starts. "tomorrow is Armistice day and the Germans have decided that we should not celebrate the way we have before. They do want us to participate and join in for a time of festivities marking their presence here and their great achievements for the betterment of the Aryan Nations. I had to purchase a German flag today at the store just as all our other neighbors have done. We will have to fly it from our window in support of the parade that will follow tomorrow. That is about all the "festivities" there will be, thank God," he says genuinely. "We are no longer permitted to have the Luxembourg flag and we are required to tear it into pieces, which we may keep to use as miscellaneous rags to clean and such." Now his eyes water but he clears his throat and continues, "Gredy, make sure that our flag is done away with tonight. I will put out this stinking flag tomorrow and bring it in as required to the minute, but I don't want to see the repulsive thing unless we have to do it again. OK?"

"Yes, Albert, I will tend to it immediately. You are not to worry so much," she tells her husband. "Gredy, if we are caught with the flag of our homeland we will be sent to a work camp as punishment for a term of no less than one full year. No trial, no defense, nothing. We may all go or just me. They decide as they please and many people do not come back after the year, understand?" he makes his point. "Yes, Albert, I understand," she concedes and bows her head. "Anni, I know tomorrow is your birthday but since it is a Monday, well actually Tuesday (he smiles), I have set aside a treat for you to go to the movies with your brother and a friend if you wish to take someone," Papa informs his daughter much to her amazement and delight amidst such a terrible time. It will be something to look forward to for the whole week and a wonderful opportunity to disappear into a movie, a real movie. It has been a long time.

Saturday, November 16, 1940. Morning has come and dawn is fading fast to the bright sunshine of a white, snow-crusted Esch. Anni is ready to make the two-hour "vacation/escape" to the movies. She has no friend to take since her only true girlfriend is Jewish and that is not possible. So, once again, it is her and Bubby. The matinee starts at noon and it is now 11:00 A.M. The two of them excitedly gather their coats and wool gloves and dart out the door. Anni has the jingling change in her pocket to purchase their entrance to the dark, intriguing world of other countries, other people and fantasy galore. It is dream time and flights of fantasy. She is so excited that her wings almost spread forth from her body in the ethereal realm unseen by the people on the street and the Nazis, but well-viewed by God and all His angels. The two take hands and run, slip and slide on the icy sidewalk—one-part dance, one-part skip and one-part circus on foot. In a matter of minutes they arrive at the theatre and purchase their tickets. Their spirits soar along with their hopes that things are actually getting bearable and maybe even going to get better.

Just as Anni and the younger Albert settle into their seats after challenging the darkened aisles with unadjusted sight, the silver screen starts to flash and flicker as the film starts to roll. Over their shoulders they hear the click of the projector in the booth above. Music starts to pour forth with the sounds of horns blowing, trumpeting the tin sounds of military influence. The screen suddenly jumps to life with an opener of German news from the front and homeland. Everything is in the German language and the reports incredulously spew in loud volume the great marches, leaps and bounds forward of the greatest nation to ever grace planet Earth. Pride, vanity, purism, calls to war and calls to incite and encourage gurgle from the garbage of celluloid. Anni is vehemently disturbed and disgusted. Once again, the Nazis have invaded and been the spoiler of joy. She deliberately makes a joke with Bubby about the silly stomping toy soldiers and the stupidity of the cartoon-like film that is supposed to be serious. It is not going to spoil the occasion—they will wait it out and enjoy the movie.

They do wait and once the movie starts, it is clear all over again. The movie starts with a German title, words, music and credits to all the Germans who made it possible. It is a German movie. What a sarcastically wonderful waste of time, she thinks to herself. She has had enough of this and would rather be at home knitting. "Bubby, let's go," she tells her brother. "I am not staying for this stupid stuff, it makes me sick." "Yeah, Anni, I am sorry it wasn't better for you. I wanted us to have fun and I was hoping you would have a good day. I am sorry," he states humbly. "Bubby, there is nothing for you to be sorry about, you didn't do this and it isn't your fault. I know we will have fun somehow, it just won't be here. Let's go back home," she finalizes, and he nods in compliance.

It has hardly been an hour away from the outside world, and as the two step out onto the street and into the blinding light, they can hear the rumbling of the iron ore cascading through the overhead tunnels. The iron and steel factory, once owned by Arbed, will soon be running again. Also, there is something else to take notice of while they were inside: Someone, and it isn't hard to figure out who, has placed posters all over the lampposts, the storefronts and other conspicuous places along the walkways. Anni and Bubby aproach the first one outside the theatre on the power pole directly in front of them.

***"AUFMERKSAMKEIT: AUF BEFEHL VON DEM FURHER SOLLEN FOLGENDEN RICHTLINIEN DAS BETRACHTEN IRGENDWELCHE UND ALLE JUDEN BEFOLGT WERDEN:"***

**(Attention: On instruction of the Furher the following guidelines regarding any and all Jews are to be obeyed:)**

1. **Jews are not allowed to go outside after 8 o'clock at night or before 6 o'clock in the morning.**
2. **Jews are not allowed to shop in any stores other than those stores that are considered Jewish shops and only during the hours of 3-5:00 P.M.**
3. **Jews are forbidden to attend theaters or the movies.**
4. **Jews are not allowed to have or possess radios.**
5. **Jews are not allowed to have boats.**
6. **Jews are forbidden to take part in any athletic activity in public.**

7. **Jews are forbidden to visit Christians in their homes.**
8. **Jews must attend schools designated for Jews Only.**
9. **Jews are not allowed on public transportation, cannot ride buses, trains, and all bicycles possessed by Jews must be turned into the Police.**
10. **All Jews are required to wear a 6-point yellow star. It must be sewn on the left-hand side of outer garments in exact accordance to location.**
11. **No Jew shall hold any government, or government-related jobs.**
12. **Non-Jewish citizens are forbidden to visit or attend Jewish doctors or Jewish lawyers.**
13. **Jews are not permitted to teach in any place, in or out of designated schools, other than those designated by authority as Jewish schools.**
14. **All stores owned by Jews must display in a conspicuous manner the word "Jew" on the front of business doors and windows.**
15. **No Jew shall marry a non-Jew.**

**So Ordered this 16th day of November, 1940.**

As Bubby and Anni read in silence together, their faces mirror utter shock and dismay. Bubby now knows what a Jew is and he also knows what injustice some humans can inflict on others. They both look to each other with astonishment upon completely reading the list of rules and remain speechless as it sinks into their minds. "Anni, this can't be real, can it?" he asks his older sister. "Yes, Bubby, I am afraid it is. Look down the street, there are more them. They really mean it," she says while the anger is burning inside her. "Let's go home, this is stupid!" As the two wander down the street back toward home, they see the signs time after time. With each new one appearing, they both burn with anger and rage but they keep their feelings to themselves and show no outward emotion, for safety's sake. God forbid that a German soldier or police officer see them visibly upset, distraught or reacting to the despicable iron fist they have fallen under.

"A Jew cannot even own a bicycle. Can't even borrow one or ride it! That is so stupid!" Anni shouts once inside the home. "What next. What else are they going to do to them and to us. When will they turn on us like the Jews?" Anni asks to no one in particular, only to Bubby, and now

Mama's listening ears. "Anni, I saw it too on my way back from the store. You know they are serious, so we have to comply. Do as your father has said and don't rock the boat. Somehow it will pass and things will get better. We just have to wait and be patient. It can't last forever," she reassures her children. All the while, the look on Boma's face disagrees in silence. She turns, shaking her head, and walks upstairs to get away for a while. She is a devout Catholic and Catholics are taught to not hate anyone and especially not Jews. It is not only "stupid," it is insane. Nothing good ever comes from hate, unless it is evil itself that is hated.

By the time Christmas comes, things are not much different outside, in the world gone mad under the Nazi presence, until the actual holidays themselves arrive. The Nazis have given new orders: No parades, no festivities, no celebrations, no gatherings of family and friends, "black-out" periods of total darkness at sunset and the list goes on. They are permitted to go to mass but even that is stood over by the German police and the now-foreboding presence of the black-suited SS troopers. They stand watch over the crowd of worshipers gathering and entering the church. Each and every man, woman and child is under suspicion and can be taken aside or even taken away for however long, whenever the "authorities" desire. There are no courts to answer to, no one to plead a case to or ask for relief, no one to give a defense to. The Nazis rule and everything is subject to their rules. They have a rule for everything. If they don't, they can make one up. Madness has taken charge of the city and the citizens cower in fear for their lives and families by force of evil minds.

For Christmas the Neuman children get special plates hand-decorated and adorned with candies. All other festivities are in short supply. It almost a formality rather than a joyous occasion. They make the best of it and let it pass in the silence of the night. By January 1941 it is getting bitter cold outside and the spirit of the city has grown cold with the weather. Now things are not only dreary in the hearts and minds of the average Esch citizen, but the surroundings themselves are gray and dreary. The Gestapo have escalated their appearance and are preparing new agendas. New rules are made almost daily by the Nazi SS, and soldiers, along with German police, patrol the street in numbers that are probably one German for every four Esch citizens. Not just because of the weather, the days grow dark almost as early as the morning light tries in vain to bring a better day. The battle of joy and sorrow is now fully engaged.

By January and on through the year events continued to unfold on a pace with the Apocalyptic rider of the Pale Horse. Just when one shock was settling in, another occured. All common laborers in Luxembourg were required to join the Deutsches Arbeits Front or face being unemployed. Both men and women were conscripted for service to the Reichsarbeitsdiet (or the Realm Work Force), in other words, the commoner was now a forced laborer for the German occupying forces and all those behind it and above it.

From January through December, 1941, the world continued to be full of headlines apart from the war as it gathered steam in Europe. In the United States, John Ford's How Green Was My Valley won the Academy Award and Best Actor was Gary Cooper for Sergeant York. In March, Adolf Eichmann became the supreme leader, next to Hitler himself, over the Gestapo and Department of Jewish Affairs. In April, Germany invaded both Yugoslavia and Greece. In May, Rumania instituted forced labor upon its own Jewish population. In June, the United States cut its quota of immigrants allowed into U.S. territory by 25 percent. Germany invaded the Soviet Union, and in Vichy, all civil liberties and rights of French Jews in North Africa were revoked. The German Wermacht began using Einsatzgruppen (mobile killing squads) to institute mass killings of Jews in occupied territories of the Soviet Union. The "Final Solution" was in full form, working toward complete extinction and annihilation of all Jews that were within bullet or club range of a Nazi hand.

By July, the U.S.S.R and Britain had signed a military pact, Jews were systematically and brutally killed in Lithuania and American Actor Cary Grant donated his complete earnings from his starring role in The Man Who Came To Dinner to the British War relief effort. In August, the Polish-Russian Agreement permited Polish refugees to be freed from Siberia. September rolled in and with it, the American Hero, Joe Dimaggio, The Yankee Clipper, batted safely for fifty-six consecutive games. October became the second most eventful month of the year. The Germans had advanced and were marching on Moscow, "The City that Would Never Fall." Auschwitz II (Birkenau) was opened for "business" as an historical site of real-life horror scenes and General Hideki Tojo attained the position of Japanese Premier. On December 7, 1941, the Japanese bombed Pearl Harbor, exacting heavy damage and casualties on the United States' military and civilians. December 9, the United States declared war on Japan. In retributive alliance, Germany and Italy declared war on the United States. Now everyone seemed to be involved, everyone in the world seemed to be at war with someone else.

The beginning of the year finds the family adjusting slowly and hesitantly to their new surroundings and the rule of foreigners. In their hearts, they are still Luxembourgish and no name change on a map is going to take Luxembourg from their hearts, nor will it deter or silence them from gaining their country back and its identity.

Papa has found work as a teacher again by complying with the indoctrination process disseminated by the Nazis. He doesn't care about politics and despises war. He has only one driving concern: work and provide for his family. That he does, he begins teaching once again at the school and starts working within a new program offered by the Germans to gain his gold-level title in gymnastics. With it, comes a professorship, a much coveted position, and a higher salary to feed his family. He bends and bows in humility through strength of character to meet the requirements of the monsters in charge and salve the wounds of his beloved family. He has to raise his right arm in salute symbolizing loyalty and dedication to the Reich, a creature he doesn't even know and hates all that it represents. It isn't about his loyalty to the Reich or his determination to survive for himself. His family is his only waking thought and that drives him to utter humiliation inside and staunch compliance on the outside. He will do what a man has to do to keep his family safe and pray for the storm to end.

The only news of war comes in the night. As Anni lies in bed she hears it clearly, distant but too close for comfort. She tosses and turns but sleep doesn't come easy. "Keep your windows closed and don't let out any light or they will bomb you!" The words echo in her head as she glances about the dark room with her eyes now so accustomed to the dark that she sees as if it were dimly lit. She can see all about the room, Bubby sleeping beside her, the dresser and table, the fan above, the ceiling, the walls and the door. The window she avoids. There is something scary out that way and she won't look.

The sound is distinct with each overflight. All through the night and the nights of months to come, the heavy, deep-throated drone of bombers carrying massive payloads of destruction from east to west and in similitude, from west to east. Bombers from England pass bombers from Germany in the night skies as each head toward the other to break loose their hellish fires, explosions and death, as a woman whose water breaks when giving birth. Except this is a birthing to death itself. It is concise and retributive. Tit for tat, one for the other. The Brits bomb Germany and in turn, Germany bombs Britain. An aerial exchange of warfare. As the night wanes away into the early morning hours she can hear them again. This time the droning has turned to high-pitched whining as the airborne engines reach their highest rpm, without the cargo they once carried, in a hurried race to home and safety for the pilots.

Months seem like years as things continue along the same course day and night, all the same. School is tedious and boring, although scary at times for the Neuman children. They come and go through the streets on their travels among the other citizens of Esch all under the watchful eyes of the German police and now, the presence of Gestapo and SS troops seems to be increasing. The citizens clearly are not trusted, and almost feared, as if they could actually thwart the Nazi's iron grip. It is absurd, the way in which they are scrutinzed, and every suspicious act, however ludicrously derived, is hunted down and thoroughly investigated. On Easter Sunday, nearly the entire town turns out for a special day of Easter Mass at church and picnics permitted by the Nazi Civil Administration for the one time only. It is a seemingly wonderful break from the spirit of heaviness under which they have been cloaked, as if wearing water-soaked wool jacket that weighs a hundred pounds. For a moment, the cloak is lifted, flowers are budding, the grass is green across the fields and the sun has warmed the earth in this tiny part of the world. It is indeed a good day, weather-wise, for a picnic. Maybe for a while, each family member hopes and prays, they can have a day of fun together as family and enjoy one another's affection and companionship.

Although rations have been sparse and Papa's pay as a grade-level teacher meager, Mama and Boma manage to put together a wonderful basket of food for the family outing. "Anni, Bubby, Charly, get your clothes changed into something you can play in. We are leaving in twenty minutes!" Mama shouts to the children as they race through the house to their rooms, already making the change before the order was even given. "Papa can we take the soccer ball?" Bubby asks his father. "Of course, why wouldn't you?" he responds to the silly question. For him, it is something that is nearly mandatory. The family gathers at the door, files through, and regroups to walk off to the cemetery and city park. On Sundays, for as long as Anni can remember, the people, families and friends of Esch gather in the park and cemetery for social gatherings—gossip among the women, politics and sports among the men. Children play, fight, make up and play some more until the evening comes. It has always been that way, fostering a strong, close-knit community.

The family arrives at the cemetery where generations of Esch family members have been laid to rest. It is a solemn, peaceful and yet very pleasant place for a picnic. Some reminisce while others gather or wander off into small groups. The children race off into the open grassy areas and begin their various games. Some children forge into the small woods surrounding the cemetery to play hide and seek. No sooner have they all scattered and barely begun their cherished routines, it becomes clear once again that things are not the same and aren't as enjoyable as they should be. The German police arrive one and two at a time and walk around the cemetery, in and along the line of woods, standing, strolling, brooding over the gathering like a snake watching a gaggle of small chicks.

"Anni, Anni come here!" Bubby shouts to his sister. "What is it Bubby?" she asks as she approaches the lean and slightly muscular boy fast becoming a man. He is standing at a stone marker. "What is it, Bubby?" Anni inquires again, almost sounding irritated to have her desire to play soccer interrupted before she can even get to the grass.

She walks over and stands next to her brother. Immediately she becomes aware that this is not the same stone. Here, where Grandfather Neuman is buried, rests a new stone, and his name has been changed. "Those dirty German monsters!" she hisses under her breath where only Bubby can hear. "It isn't enough that I have to change my name from Anny to Anni and we all have to change our last name from Neumann to Neuman, but, they desecrate Grandpa's grave! And look, they have done it to a lot of the other graves too!" she points out to Bubby. "Why the graves, Anni?" Bubby asks. "For the same reason they did this to us, Bubby. Anything even sounding Jewish is changed and you can't even be dead without it affecting you! The dirty Germans change the street names, change our names, change gravestones, store names, it just keeps going on and on! Where will they stop? I don't think they will stop until it is just them and we don't exist anymore, that's what I think," she finishes and then looks at her brother and realizes she may have said to much. The two walk back to the blanket where Mama and Papa sit and tell them the bad news. The picnic will continue, but now it is tainted with filth and stench from the mere presence of these uncaring people. In their spirits the picnic is over, but they wait out the rest of the day.

Spring gives way to summer and everything remains somewhat constant with the exception that food, clothing and basic needs, such as metal items, are falling into even shorter supply. Obviously these things are being gleaned by the Germans for themselves, with the remaining gatherings forwarded to the various war fronts in several countries, in support of the German military. By July, the Neuman family is down to two meals per day. The children still have some bread and coffee in the morning but not much else. Dinner usually consists of small round potatoes cut in half and seared in a frying pan or noodles boiled with butter, and bread. Sometimes a few chunks of pork make it into the noodles. Occasionally, the family has a pear each from the farm where Anni wanders off to chat with the upper-class neighbors, filling her pockets from the orchard on the way home.

"Albert, tomorrow I am taking Anni with me to Clervaux. I am sick and tired of feeding my family potatoes and noodles seven days a week," Mama announces to her husband this on a July afternoon as she clears the table from the day's last meal. "Gredy, you do what you have to do. I understand. I know it is frustrating for you. I also know that you try hard and you have done wonderful. No one is complaining," he reassures her. "Thank you, Albert. I just think we could all use the extra food and to actually get some meat. Even if it is horse meat, it is better than what we have been living on for months now. The children are looking thin and unhealthy. I can't wait any longer than this," she states her case. "Gredy, it's okay! I understand. I know all too well how my income only meets the basic requirements, and I know how much you do to stretch the rations. I truly understand. You do what you need to and travel carefully. You know there are more Germans in the north and they watch the trains closely. I will give you what you need for money to get there," he says. "Yes, Albert, thank you. I am sorry, I don't mean to make you feel bad, I just want to try and improve things for us and the children." She closes the discussion as her words fade away from her tearing eyes and she turns to the sink to avoid being seen face-to-face. She feels shameful and all for no good reason.

"Mama, I'm ready when you are," Anni states as she arrives back downstairs to the kitchen where Mama and Boma are packing a light lunch for the trip. "Ok, Anni. We will leave in just a minute. Boma, thank you for seeing the boys off. I will try to be back tonight as soon as possible and before the curfew," she concludes. She picks up the bag of humble food portions for her and her daughter to make the 120-mile round trip to Clervaux in the northern countryside of Luxembourg. Or at least what was once called Luxembourg. They head for the train with their identification cards in hand.

At the station, they go through the arduous tasks of clearing travel arrangements through both the Nazi Civil Organization (police) and the now ever-present Gestapo. It is frustrating and humiliating but neither woman nor child can show the anger and bitterness boiling in their insides. They finally board the train and in nearly an hours time, they are traveling to the north with short funds in hand and little to eat. Only the travel makes Anni feel better. She misses traveling. She had done so much over the early years of her life and it is good to her soul to see the cities and countryside as the train barrels along the path to its destination.

There are several stops along the way and each one snatches her back from her flexed wings into the cocoon again, back inside to the dark realm where she can hate the German soldiers pacing up and down the tracks and trains outside. One thing she does admire and that is the beautiful German shepherds. She knows they are trained for evil and are used in terrible ways, but, they are only animals doing what their masters have required of them. Otherwise, they are beautiful creatures. They have such strength, character, intelligence and appearance of pride in their work and performance. Both the male and female dogs have a certain masculine grace. Oh how she would love to have such a puppy and raise it to play fetch and do things good dogs can do. She would even like to send one to chase down a nasty Nazi for a good biting, but she hides that thought as her own personal joke. It would be funny and it would be fair. She doesn't dare to share that thought, at least not until she gets back home to tell Bubby. She smiles and retreats again while waiting and watching the dogs.

As the train slides to a graceful, slow-rolling halt at the Clervaux station, Anni's heart leaps inside. She is instantly in love. Her heart and spirit soar inside and she can feel her butterfly wings begging, aching, longing to stretch and take flight into the wonderful landscape. Clervaux is a wonderland of enticement to her wanderlust. Anni is mesmerized by the lush green grass on the rolling hills and tree-lined hillsides. The wide open fields as far as the eye can see. It is truly gorgeous country and it is overwhelmingly inviting to those who have a free spirit and long for the freedom of such expanse of nature to explore and dance upon. But for her, today, there will be no dancing. She has a mission to complete with

Mama but she is also determined in her heart that she will return here some day. When she does, her wings will be stronger and all the more painted with both bright and dark colors. She will stretch them as one stretches idle arms upon awakening, reaching for the corners of each side of the room, tugging the muscles taut and full to the very fingertips. She will leap upon the wind and fly up along the fields, high above the trees on an uncharted roller-coaster ride on the winds of this magnificent place. But not today.

"Anni, stop staring. You will get their attention and you know better than that. We don't need trouble here this far away from home, as if we don't have enough there as it is!" Mama breaks Anni from her trance. She wasn't even aware she was staring. "Mama I'm sorry I didn't mean to, I didn't know I was staring. It isn't the Heinies, it's the dogs. They're so beautiful and marvelous, Mama!" she exclaims without thinking. "Anni! shush your mouth! You want to get us killed!" Mama bears down on Anni leaning over her shoulder and gritting her teeth as she seethes the words into her daughter's ear where only the two of them can hear. "Where did you get that word? Don't ever, ever use that word again. That will get you killed. I mean it. You could get our whole family thrown in jail or put on a work farm for a year or even life for that word!" Mama makes her point all too clear. Anni begins to get sick to her stomach with dismay and anger all at the same time. She certainly did not want to upset Mama, she just has grown so far in hating these grotesque excuses for human beings that God has somehow permitted to walk His earth. "I am so sorry, Mama. I won't, I promise you. It is just so hard," she replies to her mother's now softening face. "I know, my baby girl, I know. Please forgive me, I just want to get this over with and get us safely back home to your father and the family." She concludes the conversation at the station and the two depart for the town streets looking for food and bargains.

As they walk down the brick streets past the hundred-year-old buildings, they dart their eyes back and forth, to and fro. There is so much to take in of this quaint, but ornate, city. Flowers literally seem to bubble up, out and over from the balconies on every level of the buildings. It is almost as if they are walking through an upright botanical garden. The colors abound gloriously and call to the loving and living side of what makes a woman appreciate beauty differently than a man. The two women are enlivened and there is a faint sparkle in their eyes.

As the hours pass, the two make great strides in getting fresh produce from what has been brought in from the surrounding famlands.

Even the potatoes here are much larger and hardier than the ones back home; however, they will pass on potatoes. There are plenty of other vegetables here to cherish and carry home. The final stop is reserved for the heaviest cargo, meat. The two step into the coolness of the butcher shop and away from the July heat outside. Immediately Anni's stomach grumbles so loud that it draws a laugh and twinkling eye from Mama. They both smile at one another as only a mother and daughter do and keep the moment like a pressed flower in a photo album, tucked away in their mind's memory book.

"Anni look around the window cases and see what you think is a bargain. I want to speak to the butcher by myself, OK?" Mama states. "Yes, ma'am," Anni complies and moves to another part of the room and begins looking over all the heavenly stacks of plenty. She wishes she could take it all home. Sausages, at least a dozen different kinds; hams, large and perfectly marbled with just the right amount of fat; chicken, beef, she can hardly stand being blocked by the glass from selecting the entire inventory. Her stomach is echoing its own voice as well as the one inside her head, telling her how hungry she is. Meanwhile, Mama stands slightly bent over the arched glass casing and inquires for a third time. "How much is it if I get two pounds of the "hoof" meat and one pound of the slaughter meat?" The butcher answers patiently with the amount.

He has seen this a million times if he has seen it once. It breaks his heart but there is nothing he can do. He has a family to feed also and the Germans take his best before he can hardly even see it. What they are talking about is the fact that here in this farm country there are two types of horse meat. The other meats aren't even a question for Mrs. Neuman because of the high prices. Horse meat is the cheapest because of the size of the animal and greater numbers of them. The subject of "hoof" and "slaughter" is a matter of plain fact and nothing Mama wants Anni to hear. "Hoof" meat means that the horse either died from work, old age or injury within the past day or so and was butchered by the farmer or soldiers that worked the horse. It died "on the hoof" and the price is cheaper because the meat will be tougher from the horse having not been properly bled and "dressed." Slaughter meat is meat from a horse that, most likely by some poor and starving farmer, has been sold alive to be properly slaughtered and cut by the butcher. Mama makes her choice and packs away the meat.

"Come on Anni, let's go." Mama draws Anni's attention back to the task at hand with a faint, encouraging smile on her face. They leave the store and as they do, Mama passes along some fresh farm eggs, maybe five in all, to Anni. "Keep your blouse tucked in around your skirt but pull it loose around your waist and hide these carefully until we are safely on the train. Don't dare let them get broken or we will have trouble for sure with the guards," she directs the young girl. Anni does as she is told and upon arrival at the station, just as expected, they are thoroughly examined both by identification and physically for anything suspicious or unauthorized. It isn't that the eggs aren't permitted; however, they were purchased without rations and are more than they are permitted to have. Also, these men are well known for taking whatever they want for themselves. Things are progressively getting worse and it doesn't appear that the Nazis are so inclined to winning the hearts and minds of the Luxembourg people anymore. The two women finally return safe and are at home by late evening. Another day under the shadow of the Iron Eagle has passed with all its challenges and experiences, never to be forgotten by this innocent butterfly hiding and waiting her turn to fly. Anni will fly again, she keeps her mind made up on that fact. She just doesn't know when.

For a few days, and even stretched a little into more than a week, the Neuman family has "real" food on the table for dinner. It is a time for them to be thankful to God, grateful to Mama, appreciate Papa and his work and have hope again. For a short while the dangerous and arduous journey pays up its reward as it is so deserved. The family can have a respite from culinary deprivation and a mental break from the constant reminders of oppression by looking down at their plates in contemplative silence. For a short while, they can lift their heads up, look around the table and feel good about themselves and each member of the family. They are still together, they are living by their "smarts" and becoming wittier and wiser by forced inclination but nevertheless, they are showing the whole God-forsaken Nazi Party and the world that they are true survivors.

The coolness of October arrives and with it a fresh sense of coldness from the Nazis, Gestapo, SS men and soldiers ply the streets of Esch-sur-Alzette and all of Luxembourg, Belgium, the Netherlands and France. No one even seems to remember that a short few years ago, there was a place called the Rhineland. All thanks, ingratitude, honor and dishonor go to Adolf Hitler, the son of Satan himself. The sadness is that he is not an only son; there are many more offspring just like him lingering from times past, haunting time present and lurking in the dark clouds of time future. For Anni, it is all the more reason to keep doing what she is doing.

She continues to make her little mail runs with envelopes that carry no stamps, just addresses or sometimes, now, no address at all. She doesn't ask, she doesn't fully know and she really does not care. It is her own little way of fighting back and kicking the shins of the stupid, arrogant monsters clogging her alleyways, streets and cities.

Today, Anni has gone to the store on a return trip from church and brought Marie a letter, again no stamp. She smiles and passes it to Marie, who in turn takes it and hands the child candy for a reward, although none is needed, she has reward enough in her heart. Thinking of such things is useless so Anni does what is in her heart; she goes to visit her dear, sweet friend Rosa and the Jewish family languishing in deprivation and starvation, shut out of business and succumbing to the cold of a new winter on the horizon. Anni has not failed nor refused them even against the stern warnings of her own father and Rosa's father. Anni walks the street as if she is happy. All to fool the idiot police that are scared of a little girl and yet so dumb as to think she is unable to harm them. They always let her pass.

As Anni turns the corner, she waits in her usual fashion, pausing and glancing all around within a blink of an eye. She moves forward in an almost straight line for the door to the shoe shop, ignoring the warning posters and signs indicating who lives there or who is supposed to live there as well as those who shouldn't. With her left foot she steps on the shoestring of her right shoe and pulls forward to draw it loose. Two more steps and she looks down to see her shoe is untied. Neatly timed and in place, she stoops down and methodically reties the string, using the opportunity to survey each and every avenue or hiding place where danger may await. No one is in sight. She bounds up the two steps and bangs on the door; silence. Again she knocks. Silence. Finally she tries the door and steps in. Everything seems in place but it is empty. "Rosa!" she calls out. No answer. She looks around the room. It is darkened by the evening but clearly no one is home anymore. She notices some papers on the desktop where Rosa's father kept his store records, books and such. There is a letter only half written: "Dear Sister, Things have gotten much worse. It has only been two weeks since they took many of us from our homeland to Funkbrunnen. I do not know what the future holds for us but we are certain for leaving if at all able." Thus the letter ends incomplete. No finishing statement, no signature and no addressed envelope. (*By October 16, 1941, some 1,074 Jews were led from their homes and places of business [or hiding] to be transported to their final destination of the Lodz Ghetto in*

*Poland. To this date, Anni Neuman Adams has never been able to account for her beloved friend, Rosa, nor her much loved and loving family.)*

**Headlines January through June, 1942:**

**January 1:** ***Frank Sinkwich leads Georgia to Orange Bowl title over Texas at 40-26.***

**January 20:** ***Wannsee Conference: Details of plan to murder 11,000,000 European Jews are drafted.***

**January 30:** ***Hitler speaks at the Sports Palace in Berlin, "The war will end with the complete annihilation of the Jews."***

**February 15:** ***Singapore falls to Japan.***

**February 27:** ***The Allies are routed in the Battle of the Java Sea.***

**March:** ***Jewish aid organization reports over 240,000 Jews massacred in Ukraine.***

***88 Allied and neutral ships are torpedoed by U-boats in the Atlantic.***

***Mrs. Miniver wins three Academy Awards.***

***The Japanese land in New Guinea.***

***All Dutch Jews are concentrated in Amsterdam.***

***Japanese still residing in California are told they must evacuate within 24 hours.***

**April 10:** ***Japanese capture Bataan and 36,000 troops.***

**May:** ***Wendell Wilkie brings 80 paintings and drawings from China to the Metropolitan Museum for display.***

***More Allied forces and neutral vessels are sunk by German U-boats in Atlantic.***

***Surrender occurs at Corregidor.***

***The Japanese are defeated at the Battle of the Coral Sea.***

**June:** *RCA Victor sprays gold over Glenn Miller's recording "Chattanooga Choo-Choo" for having sold more than 1 million copies—the first "Gold" record.*

*The Japanese are turned back at the Battle of Midway.*
*Over 100,000 Jews have died in Warsaw Ghetto.*

*Eisenhower is appointed Commanding General of the European Theater of Operations.*

*Germany and Italian Armies reach El Alamein and prepare for attack in Suez.*

*The world is at war. Planet Earth is witnessing the most devastating assault on its own soil and nearly all of humankind is killing, dying or attempting to survive, shocked by the brutality of a world gone mad. It is World War II.*

# Prelude to a Four Year War Song

*If it made sense, then it would be normal, and if it were normal, then it wouldn't be life. Since when does life make sense? From the beginning of mankind all that makes sense is a facade and therein lies the most comical of all black comedies. Why should it be so disturbing for us as human beings to find laughter or laugh at the most horrific, morally reprehensible and distorted acts of our fellow beings? Until you have filled your nostrils with the tainted air of acrid smoke fed into your lungs or tasted the remnants of war winds from incendiary bombs on your tongue, don't laugh. Until you have felt the jolt in the middle of the night from an artillery shell; heard the heavy, head-aching drones of planes plying the skies in the early morning through the midday until evening, dumping a payload of destruction, then you don't know black comedy. So what is so funny about it?*

*Well, it becomes quite simple when you are the one living in this menagerie of hell and daily life. You can either laugh or cry, and laughing feels better. Not only is it the better emotion, but it is the key to survival. So, you make dark jokes, why not? You live in a dark world and everyone surviving with you makes the same jokes and encourages the same laughter, to keep each other knowing that tomorrow it could be either entirely worse or unimaginably better. Thus, the humor of it all. For tomorrow, who knows, we may drink cognac, eat buttered baguettes with strawberry jam, sing songs of liberty and dance until the morning light rises through the window shades. Even a bird can teach us as the sun*

***rises that there is, by the grace of God, a reason to sing, a reason to dance, a reason to hope. Chances pour les petite enfants! (Sing for the Children)***

L. Story, The Author

May 17, 1942 started out just like any other day now under the oppression and daily disappointment. Anni expected nothing new or good of the day. Some days there isn't any hope even in her, the butterfly that can soar to places in her imagination that others cannot even dream.

Anni dresses and comes down to the kitchen, with books in hand, ready to eat her bread and drink her coffee before rushing off to school. In doing so, she notices Boma sitting quietly in her chair, head bowed, arms wrapped around her waist, as if she is half holding, half hugging herself. It strikes Anni as unusual but not to the point that she is worried. It just seems a little strange.

"Anni, come here a minute. I want to talk to you," Boma says as Anni clears her plate at the sink. She is almost startled, thinking that Boma was sleeping. Anni had eaten quietly so as not to disturb her and now she feels as though she has been watched all the time. "Yes, ma'am," Anni answers and walks over to kneel beside her grandmother. It isn't hard to see the weary look on the matriarch's face and to notice that she is indeed very tired but not sleeping nor even sleepy.

"Anni, I am praying for you. You need to keep praying, too. Things will change, they always change. That is God's way of assuring us He is here with us always. I get concerned about you acting a little too big for your britches, but I know you will be okay. I love you. Keep praying, promise me?" she queries. "Yes, Boma, I will. You know I do. I will be fine," she reassures Boma. "I know you will," Boma says with a half-smile as the corners of her coffee-stained lips turn upward. "I know you will," she repeats again as if she knows something Anni doesn't. Has she just talked to God and seen the end of things? Has she visited the future in her prayers. Anni knows the answer already. "I must get to school, Boma, I will see you when I get home, OK?" she gives her parting words. "Yes, Anni, I will see you soon. You have a good day at school and pray," she reaffirms her point to make it resonate in Anni's head all the way to school as she walks her usual course. The words are fixed into her mind to pray and so she does. She doesn't quite know what for or how right now, but she just carries on a private conversation with the God she sees in her mind and leaves it at that. It is personal and no one else need know where she is.

On the walk home, the sun is shining and Anni looks up at the sky. For once it is clear of planes and quiet. It is a beautiful spring day and summer is coming soon. Birds fly over and Anni takes notice. Not that they haven't been flying here every day, it is just that she hasn't paid attention in a long time. She has been so used to making this trip with her head down, afraid to look ahead, much less up. She doesn't want to draw that God-awful word that haunts them daily, "suspicion." A guilty word borne on their backs like pack mules loaded with anxiety and fear, distrust and anger.

The warmth of the sun on her face makes her feel as if she has been recharged with energy and it feels oh so good. It fills her spirit. She wants to fly up to the birds and soar around them. She smiles to herself and continues toward home, now a matter of yards away. As soon as the door turns on its hinges, something ethereal permeates the opening and the interior of the home. Anni senses immediately that something has changed. Something very big has occurred once again, and she is right.

"Anni," Papa says to her as she closes the door and notices other people in her home. "What is Papa doing home this early?" she says to herself. "Come here, Anni, I have something to tell you," Papa draws her to him by his low-spoken words. "What's going on, Papa?" Anni is already nervous. "Anni, Boma passed away this morning, just before noon. She was very tired and sick. She loved you and you shouldn't be sad, OK? She is in heaven now watching over us. I need you to be strong for me and I know you will. She was a strong lady and had great faith, she is happy now and you know she is with us always." He tries to reassure his precious daughter as he sees the tears forming in her eyes. They come out eventually and Anni turns away without a word or any notice of any other person in the room. Shell-shocked, she goes upstairs to her room, falls on her bed and begins her grieving process. She cries, stops to pray, think and cry some more. She will pass all the hours until night turns to the darkest hours and she will sleep briefly only to awaken in three hours or so and wonder if it was a dream. She knows already, it wasn't. She can feel it in the house, death has been here up-close and personal. She only wants it out and to go away.

For this day, Anni is sent to relatives while Mama and Papa make arrangements. Even in death, the Nazis are still in charge, lording it over not only those who remain, but the bodily remains of the departed. Mama and Papa actually have to prove the passing to the German Security Police (the SP) and purchase a permit to transport Boma from home to church for the funeral and further permission to bury her in the cemetery. The rules of government are grotesquely cold and hard. There is no bending nor mourning in their souls. Apparently, they have given up their souls to hell somewhere along the way.

Anni returns home the following day. Family and friends have gathered at the house to view the body and look into the glass-encased casket, taking in a memorial look at that face of a strong woman. A woman of godly character who ran across a field under dive-bombing planes with her family. A woman who fed and nurtured her son, his wife and her grandchildren in exile. The woman that looked German police, soldiers and the Gestapo right in the face with spit on her lips, piercing blue eyes and a spirit inside that kept it all under control. She stayed and she prayed. Her prayers were never unanswered. She left when she knew somehow that her family was safe now and safer without her. She had somewhere else to go and no one could go with her. But she didn't go alone. Elizabeth Clesen went into the hands of her Lord and Savior, Jesus, the Christ. Anyone who knew her, knew that is what she believed and they believed her. You couldn't and wouldn't dare argue it with her. You would certainly be the loser. After all, she was born on Christmas day, of all days, in 1874.

As the sun nears its highest point on this hot May day, the knock comes to the door. It is time. The family gathers together, dressed in their church clothes, and follows the horse-drawn wagon carrying the casket to the church down by the cemetery. Inside the sanctuary, the formalities are conducted and somewhere in here is at least one stranger. A German police, no doubt, in plain clothes. Trying to blend in and still ever watching for the suspicious behavior. Outside by the grave, the family, friends and neighbors gather as the priest finalizes the ceremony and prays aloud that God now receive Elis Neuman into his guard. "Her name was Elizabeth, not Elis. It was Elizabeth Neumann, you monster Nazi heinies," Anni mutters the words for only her and heaven to hear. She is hurt and angry. She will save her request for forgiveness, just as Boma would expect of her, for another day. But, not this day.

# Strawberry Fields Aren't Forever

*"Anny, Anny, du muss opstohen, das zeit, mer mussen goen."*
**("Anny, Anny, wake up. It is time to get going—we have to go.")**

In the early morning hours, Mama calls to waken her naturally beautiful fifteen-year-old daughter. It is time to go to the bus. A neighbor has an uncle who owns a strawberry farm due north of Metz, France, an hour or so from Esch. The hardy, robust skins of the berries veil the soft, delicious fruit inside, which is grown row upon row throughout this northern French countryside. It has been nearly a year since Anni last went anywhere outside her own hometown of Esch. Her last trip to Clervaux seems like a million years ago. The year is going by slowly but thankfully is half over. Things are still getting worse by the day, week and month under Nazi occupation. However, maybe today she can enjoy the beauty of the deep green grassy fields and trees, the countryside of Metz, France. She will hope and wish, but not hold her breath. She does as she is told and after a quick breakfast she is on her way with Mama.

Still groggy from sleep, Anni boards the bus with Mother, neighbors, friends and strangers. The warmth of the sun already penetrates the cool June morning, even before the sun itself appears on the horizon. Looking for a place to lay her head, however awkwardly, Anni tries to snatch a bit more rest as the bus rumbles along. The good news is that they are permitted to cross the border and leave behind the horrid oppression of the Nazis and their endless rules, resulting in death if disobeyed. The added hope is for something besides the usual fare of potatoes, noodles and horse meat.

As the bus rambles and bounces through the early morning, it heads its way to the fields just south of the Luxembourg/France border to the town and countryside of Metz. All too soon it is time to rise from the sleepy comfort of her curled-up position on the bus bench, from a mother's lap to the sweat and dirt of field labor, simple yet exhausting. Gathering the strawberries is a family endeavor, yet, her own stomach, her own hunger, drives Anni to do this "man's work." She and mother enter the field surrounded by many others of both sexes, young and old alike, to harvest sustenance for themselves.

You pay to enter the field and harvest the berries. If you wish, you can collect extra baskets of berries to return to the farm manager and receive a discount on your purchase. It is a fine example of democratic European living. Both the community and the individual benefit.

This strawberry season has become different, though. The close-knit friends, family and strangers straggle out through the long, wide fields, absorbing themselves in the task at hand. Some whistle, some sing, some chat while others go about their picking in quiet reflection. The wind gently breezes through the fields and the late morning dissipates along with the dampness from the earlier dew that ushered in the dawn. As the sun rises above and nears the overhead mark, a disturbing feeling fills the air. It sings into the gut and makes your head swim suddenly from the job at hand into a bursting flurry of thoughts, not one comprehensible or solid enough to hold on to.

"*Anni, dig a hole*!" "NOW!" "*Anni, dig a hole and get down*!" It is the voice of a mother, almost like a songbird without a song, screeching to her chicks to take cover. Now, Anni hears it. She can hear the drone in the distance. "Oh, my God, they're coming again." "Why? Why, why do the Americans hate us so much?" "What have we done to deserve this?" "Damn them." "Damn the Americans and their bombs, their planes, their war on us." We know it isn't France or Luxembourg that the Boeing B-17Es (the Flying Fortresses) are coming to bomb. They have "intelligence" information. They are coming to bomb strategic sites where Germans have been seen encamped or traveling on patrols and in support lines. But in this simple strawberry field, in the beauty and brightness of a sweet summer day, the drone is turning into rumbling drums and thunder.

"Anni, dig!" Mama cries again, and dig Anni does. With both hands she casts the box of strawberries on the ground beside her, close to her bent legs. She kneels there in the dirt between the rows that were being carefully searched for berries only a moment ago. Now, time is slowing, the heart is pounding, the mind is racing. Suddenly, everyone that was in the field has disappeared; although they are still there, they cannot be seen. The only sight to the eyes of the fifteen-year-old child is three feet of dirt in front of her. Fast and furiously she digs with her bare hands to make a shallow to lie in. "This is crazy, how can I dig a hole to hide in while they are already nearing the open air above us?" But, dig all the more, she does. The drone, drums and thunder have now turned into a deafening roar engulfing the entire world and the pounding rolls through the woods and across the fields. Whoompf!! Whoompf!! The bombs, aimed at a farm truck that was supposed to be a German tank unit or anti-aircraft gun, "walk" their way in all directions. Anti-aircraft fire sounds in the distance but it is far from here. It is far from this field and has nothing to do with us. It has nothing to do with Luxembourg, or does it?

"Anni, get down!" And she does. Just in time. But not quite so fast as to forget why she came here. Why she is here now in this ungodly horror. She reaches for her box of strawberries and thrusts it into the shallow trench, flattening her body and covering them with her chest. Just in case she doesn't die today. Just in case she gets the chance to rise up from this barrage of war birds and the devil blasting enormous holes into the ground all around. If she lives another hour, she will be hungry. The family will be hungry and will need the strawberries to live. In it all, there is the strangest feeling. On Anni's face is a smile. It can't be so but nevertheless there it is, a smile. She is laughing somehow through this insane situation because she can see herself from outside her body huddled in the dirt hole. She looks silly clutching the strawberries beneath her like a mother hen and now she has strawberry stains on her dress. It is a comical sight.

Is it a black moment? Yes. Is it frightening? Yes, beyond words. Is she crazy? No. She has just fallen into that zone where you don't see anything, yet you see it all. You hear the world thundering, roiling and breaking in two around you, but, you are in another world. Here is where black comedy exists. Here is where nothing matters anymore. Here is a place where time has stood still and there is nothing you can do. You are immobilized by the instinct to survive. You have to wait. That is all you can do. You wait like standing in a storm. The lightning strikes all around with pure death electrifying the air, but you stand firm. You don't flinch. You don't realize how tense and tight your muscles have become until hours later.

"Anni, you can get up now."

The planes have gone. They have come in by threes, by tens, by twos, even dozens at once. They roll in and roll out like the flat tide on the beaches of Southern France. In the wake, Anni sees a man out of the corner of her eye. He is walking with a look that reminds her of the face on a little girl's doll. It is blank, empty, without any show of awareness. His arm is missing. As the deafness fades and the sounds return, it is no longer a beautiful day in the strawberry field. There are screams of adults and children. There is crying, wailing, pain, anguish and anger. Some sit in the field just looking around. Others run for help. It is hard to comprehend.

"Why do they hate us? I hate them." Anni knows she doesn't truly, but her young heart has suffered enough already, now this. Yes, there were probably some German soldiers in the woods a quarter mile away, and yes, there most certainly had to be German soldiers moving equipment or deploying their operations on the roads, hillsides and woods a mile or ten away. But they weren't in this field picking strawberries, laughing, and even though the work was sometimes hard, they weren't here imagining of the taste of a cool strawberry, filling the mouth with a flood of sweet flavors this evening on the bus ride home. No, there weren't any German soldiers at all to be seen. But, there was hell to be seen. Yes, war is hell. Here is hell and somehow, she laughed in its parlor, she laughed in the dancing devil's face. She had seen something funny about herself. Thank God. Strawberry fields aren't forever.

# SURVIVING IN THE DARK

*What is it like? Take this exercise of imagination:*

*Close your eyes and rest a few seconds. Breathe a few deep breaths and relax. Let your mind go black. Take a good, close look at the darkness in front of your eyes. Now, place your hands over your eyes and press firmly enough that all light is completely shut out. You are sitting upright in a chair, hands clasped over the eyes and total, black darkness and silence. Now, imagine that the chair where you are sitting is wooden, painted black and in the center of a twenty by twenty-foot concrete room. Walls, ceiling and floor all cold grey concrete. You can see the room from the picture in your mind but you cannot open your eyes. Keep staring into that blackest of darkness.*

*Now imagine someone else in the room. Don't open your eyes, just know that someone is there and you can hear them, feel their presence and sense it from the wafting movement of the air around you as you sit straight up in your chair. You cannot and are not allowed to move. Just keep your eyes covered, focus on the dark black place you have entered and picture a large man in a well-cut, leather strapped and belted uniform pacing the floor in a circle around your chair. He is about 220 pounds, over six feet tall and has a holstered pistol and fists that are huge and meaty hanging from his arms and broad shoulders. He is a monster of a man and these are his weapons. You, however, must sit with hands upon face, perfectly still in your chair listening to the pacing boots walking around and around, inches away from you. You are in total darkness in your mind and in your sight. Blind to not only the room, the chair or the man, but even forgetting what you look like after having your eyes closed to the darkness for so long.*

*Continue this picture and put into the scene the added fact that this man is going to take his huge bear-like fist and punch you in the back of the head. He is going to do it. You know it; and it is certain. There is no changing that fact. He is going to give you a blow to the back of your head with an unbelievable amount of force and you wait. You sit, wait and listen. The steps clap in your ears with each footfall of the boots on the concrete. Shhht, clomp, shhhhut, clamp, sshhht, clop. Incessant, merciless waiting in this blackest of places with your mind fully alert and whirling at light speed. He has all day but you know it is coming, you just don't know when. Dread comes in and your heart pounds, your body leaks with sweat all over until you find yourself wishing it would just go ahead and happen so you can come out of the dark. Out of the fear of the unexpected. Out of the unknown. Then it happens, suddenly and without warning.*

*A blasting thunder rings your ears and dizzies you as your head feels heavy and parted from your body and other senses. Immediately stabbing, shrilling rings echoing inside your darkness, but there are also dancing bright-lights and the feeling of something cool running down the nape of your neck. You feel yourself falling as if forever until you hit the hard cold floor and immediately become sick to your stomach. Nausea so bad you wish you were dead. You are still in the dark.*

*Now, do you want to come out of it and live? Or do you just want to lie there and die. You won't because you can't. That is what it is like surviving in the dark. And that is how Anni Neuman lived, her family lived. All of Esch, Luxembourg and every other country occupied by the Nazi armies, security police, SS troops and Gestapo. Not for the moment of this exercise. No, they lived with that same apprehension, fear and anxiety day after day, month after month, for four years. The worst years are coming. Remember as you read, take time to close your eyes and remember.*

The summer of 1942 is increasingly filled with world-wide activities, all circumnavigated by the winds of war and destruction. So much has happened since May 10, 1940. It seems to Anni that the years past were an entirely different life and this one she is living is completely disconnected. It is as if she lived some foreign, beautiful, happy, fairytale-existence and then became sequestered in a twilight zone of sorts, only to burst back out in another plane of existence to discover the world was a horrible place to try and live or even survive. Merely surviving is a daunting puzzle of the mind and circumstance, with an abundance of facts and lies all thrown together.

July 20 arrives—Bubby's birthday. There isn't any fanfare, only good wishes for his passage into his teenage years. The younger Albert is now thirteen years of age and will begin the ascent into manhood with all its wonderments, and yet the day is unremarkable. Times are getting tougher, life is getting harder and people are more open with their distraught and heavy-laden spirit.

By August 5, Bubby has heard the trains rolling south of home. This time, he wants to know what it really is all about and why so much cattle would be moved through their town from the Belgium tracks across to Germany or whereever. Anni, with great hesitancy but loyal to her beloved brother, follows down Rue Du Brill once again to the fork in the railways where the trains pass by. This time is far different from October of 1941. This time the trains are rolling day and night. Over the horizon in both directions. Again, the air is filled with that putrid, rotting smell made all the worse by the August heat. The two teenage children stand so they can see, but out of sight of the Nazi soldiers, watching the cattle cars rumbling by at a fast click.

The odor brings flashbacks of their own nightmares. This time, there is no denying what they both see. There are indeed hands extended through barbed-wire fencing around the top windows of the cattle cars. Not only human hands but human faces peer out. Some are crying, some have a distant look upon their face, others are clearly in pain and gasping for air. It is a horrible sight, too shocking to register in either Bubby or Anni. They stare blankly at something that isn't a movie—that is where it should be, but it is real. It is here plainly before them. For some reason unknown to the thirteen-year-old boy and fifteen-year-old sister, the Nazis are transporting live human beings like cattle, like rats packed in a box for a train ride obviously stopping in hell. They don't know why and they don't understand. They won't even discuss it on the walk back home. Things are getting far too strange for words and inside they know, for their own sake and family's sake, it never happened. Not for now, not today. Maybe they will revisit it in their memories when they are older. God willing they should live that long.

> ***"In June, 1942 the Nazis decided on the first deportations from Belgium. August 4, 1942 the first transport of Jews from Belgium left for Auschwitz. In the course of 1942 exactly 16,882 Jews were deported from Belgium—of which none were Belgian citizens. Starting in the summer of 1942 the Germans to deport Jews that were Belgian citizens. In the course of 1943 and 1944 more than 8,000 were deported to Auschwitz. A total of 28,500 Jews were***

*deported from Belgium during World War II—only around 1,000 of them were Belgians."*

Copyright: http//www.holocaust-education.dk

Earlier in March of the year, Gauleiter Simon had issued a decree authorizing the seizure of all property belonging to Luxembourgers who were considered to not be "friends of Germany." August continues to bring changes almost too fast for young Anni to keep up with. However, she remains resolute in participating in her "mail deliveries," which have grown now into grocery deliveries also.

On August 17, round-the-clock bombing begins under a campaign by American Army Air Corps with B-17 bombers making daytime strikes with fighter escorts into targeted locations of Germany proper. On the same day, a full-scale rehearsal of an invasion by Allied forces takes place, with little historical reference in years to come, at Dieppe, France. The operation is a disaster. The losses are overwhelming, the German occupying forces in France were underestimated and the plan fails. However, it sets a benchmark in lessons learned and what not to do, and the plan continues for "Operation Overlord," which would be a total onslaught of Allied forces upon the coast of France for a time yet uncertain and future.

*"In a referendum organized by the Nazis, 98% of the population vigorously expressed themselves against becoming German citizens, which drew a series of reprisals. People were beaten, harassed and imprisoned by the Gestapo, and as early as 1942, young Luxembourgers, who had organized public strikes against the Nazi occupants were court-martialed and shot the next day in the concentration camp of Hinzert, Germany.*

*Already and earlier, several young men had escaped and, after risky trails, ended up in Great Britain to join allied forces being built up. (As such, there were Luxembourgers in the British commandos, Free French, SAS, Belgian Artillery, unit "Brigade Piron," later on even some in the U.S. Forces, and numerous armed resistance organizations.) Nazi oppression became stiffer and penalties became more and more brutal. In late 1942 the Gauleiter started conscripting Luxembourg youths into the RAD (German Labor Service) and the Wermacht (Army). Young men were forced to join under threat of their families being deported or prosecuted if they did not comply. During the same time, the Nazis also started prosecuting the local*

*Jewish community. All these measures only resulted in the Luxembourgers holding even more together; gradually resistance, which in the initial stage was rather insignificant, because of fear of reprisals, organized itself into the networks that had contact with similar organizations in other occupied countries. As such, Luxembourgers assisted shot-down allied airmen to regain unoccupied zones in France, hid about-to-be conscripted youths, or organized clandestine actions against the Germans. People who got caught by the Gestapo (German political secret police) or the SP (Security Service) were sent to concentration or death camps; many of whom were never to return."*



By mid-August more news came directly to the doorstep of the Neuman home. The month was hardly half over and school was out but young Albert, "Bubby," had drawn the attention of the local German government. It wasn't that his grades were spectacular—they may have been satisfactory, but Bubby was a play-king not a serious student. Nevertheless, he had special qualities that made him attractive to the German administration. Bubby was a teenage boy of fine years, strong and good lines in physique, blond-haired and blue-eyed. He was a perfect specimen to breed in a new pure-blood Aryan Nation. He was what the Fuhrer himself called the epitome of Germanic purity and origin.

At the end of school, on the last day of bringing home papers and reports, Bubby presents his father with a peculiarly large package. It is sealed with the "Iron Eagle" stamp reflecting the Greater Deutschland official flavor. "Papa, they told me at school to give these papers to you to fill out and said that you should bring them back yourself tomorrow or the day after." The young Albert presents the package to his Papa. "What is it?" Mama inquires as she walks over from the kitchen table to Papa's chair, where he is sitting with his pipe clasped precariously between his teeth, but secure from years of practice. He peers over the cover sheets and riffles through all the paperwork filled with row upon row of questions. The most outstanding language grasps his attention, flying up off the page to his wrinkled and squinting eyes. "Your child should be prepared and ready to depart according to the enclosed information no later than 20 August 1942." He drops the pages into his lap in silence, looking at Gredy. "What is it, Albert!" she states again, raising her voice in a way which Papa has never heard her use with him. He fully understands. "Gredy, they want Albert to go to Germany to study," he replies blankly.

"Study!" she shouts. "Study what! He is studying here and getting by fine in school. What do they want with our son!" she continues frantically, looking about as if they are going to burst in and snatch him away. All sorts of thoughts fly through her head of how to hide him, send him to Vichy France, send him away to anywhere but here. She knows she can't. It is too late and they would surely punish the whole family for any such act of treason. "NO Albert! No, please Albert, no they can't take him. Isn't there anything you can do? You are about to become a professor at the school. You go to Germany, isn't there something that can be done?" She is crying out loud now. Not hysterically, but with great anguish and fear. "Gredy, you know that if he stays here they will conscript him in two years. Then we will lose him to the Wermacht and he could be killed. It is better this way. At least we will know he is safe. We have no other choice. I'll do the paperwork and we should prepare to let him go. God knows, he will be back soon. I can see him when I go to competitions and keep you informed of his health. It is all we can do," Papa says sadly, and for one of the few times ever seen (by Gredy only) Papa allows tears to trickle down his solemn and quiet face.

Two days later it is official, Albert Heinrich Neuman is set to leave from the train station and depart to the upper lands of the country Germany, proper. To be exact, he is sent to Pommern Ostpreussen. Since the day of the news until now, Anni has not ceased to grieve and become all the more angry at the unknown hierarchy that has propelled such black-hearted misery upon such an innocent family. "Why us, why can't they just leave us alone? Don't we continue to say 'We just want to be who we are,' but we can't because of what? Why. We did nothing but live in the wrong place at the wrong time and for that we are punished beyond pain and sorrow?" She demands an answer from God as she speaks these words in her mind. She begs and pleads for His divine intervention and at the same time for the safety of her family and her very special friend and brother. Will she ever see him again? The way things have gone now as they approach 1943, it would appear not likely.

August 30, some ten days after Albert H. Neuman's departure, a call of conscript went across Luxembourg by the order of the Gauleiter, and a national strike ensued. Upon declaration of martial law once again, twenty-five leaders were rounded up and shot point blank without benefit of inquiry nor trial. High school students that participated in the strike were rounded up, desegregated and taken away to work camps in Germany away from their families for a minimum one-year summary sentence without defense, aide nor excuse.

> ***"September, 1942: The State Department of the United States grants permission for 5,000 Jewish children to enter U.S. Initiative fails because of Vichy Government stalling; September 2nd, Sternbach cable arrives at the Polish Embassy in Washington, recounting the deportation of 100,000 Jews from Warsaw to death camps. October, 1942: Morton Cooper of St. Louis wins Most Valuable Player as St. Louis wins 4-1 over the Yankees in the World Series. November, 1942: Shostakovitch's Symphony #7 is sent to the U.S. on microfilm through enemy lines before its performance by Toscanini and the NBC Symphony; U.S. Forces land in French Africa with British naval and air units assisting; The State Department confirms the existence of Nazi extermination camps and the murder of two million Jews to date; North Africa west of Algiers is subdued by Allied forces; Major counter-attack by Red Army in the Stalingrad region. December, 1942: Don Hutson of the Green Bay Packers sets an NFL season scoring record, with 138 points on 17 touchdowns."***
>
> Copyright: http//www.holocaust-education.dk

The cool breezes of October find the Neuman family scrambling for coal to keep the firegoing in the belly of the iron stove. Winter is fast approaching and the world outside is getting darker than ever before outside. It a constant gray from morning to evening, fading to black. By six o'clock the windows are covered religiously with the black curtains that Mama and Boma had made for this very purpose; to not get bombed by mistake in the night. Off in the distance some two miles from home, Anni can hear the sound of the German anti-aircraft guns firing through the night as they guard the steel mill against bombing. She lies in her bed only a few feet away from the empty bed where Bubby slept. She turns away from the sight of it and faces the wall. Tears come again as if there is no end to them. She thinks to herself that her tear ducts should be all dried up by now but just as the emotions redevelop, so does the water supply to her weary, reddened eyes. Boma is gone, Bubby is gone, Mama and Papa hardly talk and Charly is starting to ask too many questions. Even he has come of such an age to notice this odd world around him.

This mid-October Saturday morning Mama asks Anni to go to the store and get some noodles for the dinner meal. Only the week before, they had once again gone up north to their cousin's home in Clervaux and obtained more horsemeat. "Yes, Mama, I will be back as soon as possible. Is it okay if I stop by the church on the way home, though?" she asks, knowing that Marie will have some brief duty ready for her. "Yes, Anni, but not too long," Mama replies. On her way out she passes by Papa as he squats by his tobacco plants, looking them over. He gently gleans the brown edges of dead leaves and places them into a small brown paper bag. It is enough to smoke in tonight's pipe. He leaves the green leaves to flourish briefly, then turn brown as the weather takes its toll. "Papa, I am going to the store for Mama. I will be back in an hour or so, do you need anything?" she asks. "No, Anni, you do as your mother has told you. I am going down to the football field for some practice. Don't forget, I have to leave tomorrow for Hamburg. I have two more tests to get my medal, and I will inquire about Albert for us, okay, my little one?" He smiles and encourages her with his strength. "Yes, Papa, I will miss you but I can hardly wait to hear how well you do, and maybe Bubby can talk to you by telephone or get a letter home," she replies with the greatest of hope in a faint atmosphere.

Just as certain as it is another day, so is the fact that as Anni arrives at the store to retrieve the noodles Mama has asked for, she is prevailed upon by Maria to carry a bag of a different kind of noodles. These noodles are mixed with some other things in a paper bag and carried inside a crocheted carry-basket. It is clear to see that this is more than mere groceries to Anni's now well-trained eye and she knows that after looking at it, she must forget its existence. She takes the package to the textile store just a few blocks away from home. They make mattresses, provide bed-linen, bed-clothes and cloth material for the making of clothing. Here she meets her new friend, Georgette, the daughter of the store owner. She promptly delivers the bag to the mother and starts a conversation with Georgette. The two have struck up an immediate friendship, even though Georgette is some three years her senior. They agree to go to the park tomorrow after church. Anni returns home in good time with her task complete.

Sunday morning arrives with a chilly drizzle of rain. Mama, Anni and Charly go to church across the street and return less than two hours later. Papa has rested and read some of his book of proverbs to get his day started. By this afternoon he will be on a train to Germany for another contest beginning Monday for the final qualifications that, should he be successful, will result in his tenure as a teacher and his promotion to a full-fledged professor of gymnastics, with all its entitlements and, most importantly, an increase in pay.

Anni quickly changes clothes, informs her mother she is headed to meet with Georgette and spend some time in the park. This information is fine with Mama—she needs the time to spend with her husband before he leaves for the week of training, competition and travel. Charly busies himself with his toys and makes no complaints. He is a contented child, happy wherever he finds himself. His childish imagination is still strong in his eight-year-old mind. He is already showing signs of his great and unique independence. He is somewhat introverted, but happy to be so, and that is good enough for the times. Anni bounds out the door and heads off to meet her new friend. Her spirit lifts with hopes of a day of girlish conversation out-of-doors in the park, escaping adult life for a while and being only a teenage girl, if only for a couple of hours.

No sooner has Anni exited the house and started down the street than she begins to take notice of the flyers posted on the street posts and doors of various shops along the way. The Nazi party is making it clear that there is a meeting being held in the park. The meeting is for those that wish to come and hear various speakers about the greatness of the parties' existence, its accomplishments and how wonderful being a member is for those that dedicate themselves and join. Anni is disgusted. She doesn't even bother to get angry anymore. It is of no use and no value. This is the way they are going to live the rest of their lives. Here in a hell created by a madman she has never met and a group of people determined to control not only the bodies of people, but their very souls. "Good luck!" she says to herself. She personally is resolved to go along as she has to, but only God has her soul and she would rather die than surrender it. The opportunity exists every moment of the day, to her great sadness.

At Georgette's the two girls decide that it would be better to study, and make a pact to become study partners for the coming months. Although Georgette is three years older, she and Anni are on the same intellectual level because of Anni's love for learning and her father's guiding hands. They grow close as they meet often on school afternoons. Some days they just sit and talk, other days Anni sits quietly while Georgette practices piano or takes lessons. Anni needs a friend now that Bubby is gone. No one can take his place, but at least, by God's grace, someone has stepped into Anni's life where someone else has stepped out. This seems to be an unending cycle for this unique butterfly that hides away in her cocoon when people leave her life. Just when she turns into the darkness of her tunnel, God somehow rescues her with a new and fresh face to draw upon her inner strength, wisdom and simple yet pure character. Neither she nor the new person in her life can fathom which one is blessed the most. God seems to keep it equal, and for that, she is daily thankful.

By late November, some good news does come after Papa arrives back home from the gymnastics competition in Germany. By now he is getting some unusual, even insulting looks from neighbors for his trips. It disturbs him because he knows his heart and loyalty are to his family first and his country second. However, the two are almost one in his mind. He loves Luxembourg and despises the politics and the war. In his mind though, these are events beyond his control. What is in his control is his hard work, caring for his family, his love of his sport and teaching. These things he continues to perform with excellence.

"Anni, Papa's home!" comes Mama's shout from downstairs. Before Mama and Papa can part from their "welcome home" hug, Anni is at the foot of the stairs, racing for her father with a smile big enough to trip over. "Papa! It is so good to see you. I missed you. How was your trip? Did you hear from Bubby? Are you done now? Did you win?" She rapid-fires the questions at his smiling face. He breaks in with a laugh that stops her chatter. "Anni, slow down. You are going to blow out a lung talking that fast!" he jokes with her. "Yes, Anni, and my dear Gredy, I did not only win, I got this!" he says with a broad and beaming smile on his face. He opens his hand out, palm up, and a blue ribbon is strapped over it. As he does so, a large, glowing gold medallion falls heavily to the full extension of the ribbon and Papa raises it like an oversized pocket watch for his ladies to see. "Albert, it is beautiful," Gredy says. "Yes, I think so and not only do I have this to show for the training, but with it I have been given my professorship." He can hardly hold the words back, making an even more blunt impact to his wife and daughter.

"I will cease my teaching position at the school after the Christmas holiday and start immediately at the college," he informs his small audience. "This is cause for celebration," Mama says as she turns for the kitchen to see what magic she can start for the afternoon. Just in time,

Charly arrives home from school, and he immediately sees Papa in the house heading for his seat to rest a moment. “Papa, you’re home!” he exclaims, glad to see his strong and manly father. “Yes, I am, Charly, how are your studies? Are you doing well in school?” Papa asks. “Yes, Papa, I am doing very well. I expect high marks by the end of this grade period. How was your trip? What is that?” he inquires upon noticing the huge gold piece in Papa’s hand. “It is my Achievement Award for reaching the level of Expert Gymnast and with it I am now a professor. It also means that I won’t be seeing you at school anymore, Charly. I will have to start over at the college after Christmas, do you understand?” he carefully and almost sadly asks his youngest son. “Oh that is great, Papa, I mean that you won that. I don’t want you to leave the school though. I know you have to, I will be okay,” he reassures his father as he straightens himself to show he is a young man. Papa looks at his son and stares with glistening eyes and a smile. It is good news and a great day for the family.

As Christmas day approaches, things have settled somewhat after a month of life having Papa home again and a glimmer of hope. However, outside with the cold and snow, life under Nazi rule is getting colder and more dangerous. The Sunday before Christmas Anni, as usual, goes to confession. However, as she enters into the confessional something strange occurs. She has an overwhelming feeling that she is being watched or listened to by more than just the priest. In fact, she knows in her stomach and mind that someone else is in there. Then it dawns on her. The dirty Gestapo have started listening in on confessions, threatening the priests with certain death and mayhem should they not cooperate with their secret little activities. Even the church has now been poisoned by these insidious creatures. They lurk behind the shadow of the church confessional in all its sanctity to listen and just maybe entrap a repentant sinner in crimes against the German government.

Anni’s head spins as she mutters the words: “Father, forgive me for I have sinned.” Thus begins the new way in which she will make confessions from this day forward. Her sin this time, a stolen apple on the way home from school. Each and every confession from this day forward will be the same. A small harmless, make-believe sin because her truest heart is now behind closed doors where she will confess straight to God for anything she feels she should. Her spiritual connection on earth has become a victim and a prisoner of evil.

Christmas day arrives and Mama sets out the best she can come up with for the celebration feast. Christmas will be the barest ever this year—only a dinner with two distance relatives as guests. It is overshadowed by Boma and Bubby's absence. Anni has now taken more interest in Charly. But he continues to be independent, spending most of his time alone or with close neighbor children. Except for occasional visits with her aunt after school, or short trips to Georgette's home, Anni is finding herself more and more alone. This day, the day to celebrate the birth of One that has introduced Life eternal to mankind, falls sadly upon a meal that Anni will never forget. As they sit at the table, Anni is introduced to a distant cousin and her husband.

In an unusual change of circumstances, Papa is talking, and so are the other adults at the table. "Albert, I am telling you, you should come by and visit with me more at my office," the man continues his speech to Papa. "There are many things I can do for you. All you need to do is become pro-active with us and get on the wagon," he entices Anni's father. "Look at what I have at home and what I am accomplishing. It is the only way to go now and it is better for us all. We should join in and not be so terribly obstinate and resistant." Anni feels sick to her stomach and hardly touches her food. She knows this man. He is one with an evil heart and a mind poisoned by the Nazi demons. He sells out his neighbors and his family for favors or money, sometimes both, to the Germans. He treats the Germans favorably and deprives his own people and nation. He is a traitor, an adulterer, a liar, a thief and all that goes with being self-appointed to pride and rejection of Godly character and morality. He lives a lustful life and sees no shame in his acts. He is a black mark upon the family and Anni disavows any recognition that he is related. In fact, but for the fact he married this cousin, he would be sitting at someone else's table. How she wishes now that it were so. Most certainly, if he knew of Anni's "mail runs" for Maria, the whole Neuman family would be in a prison in Luxembourg City or worse, serving a year or more in the work camps.

January 1, 1943 heralded in a new year and the world at war for the second time had nearly very existence (or at least that of mankind) pressed into a corner for survival. The search for atomic weapons was full-blown and the use of such instruments in the wrong hands could have turned the entire planet into a vast wasteland. The odds were being weighed out in high-level meetings. "Should such abilities be obtained by our nation or the nation of another what will come of us?" was on the lips of the leaders of Britain, Germany and the United States.

On the years' news front, the following headlines pour forth over the months:

**January:** *U.S. State Department is informed via Switzerland that in one Polish location six thousand Jews a day are being killed; 18: The first armed resistance occurs in the Warsaw ghetto.*

**February: 2:** *The Germans surrender at Stalingrad. Russia begins reconquest of Ukraine.*

**March:** *The Japanese are routed in the Battle of Bismark Sea off New Guinea; The Cracow ghetto is liquidated; Casablanca wins the Academy Awards with Michael Curtiz winning Best Director. Paul Lukas wins Best Actor award for his performance in Watch on the Rhine.*

**May:** *Final Assault on Tunis by Allied troops begins; U.S. decides to use the atomic bomb on Japan instead of Germany; At a War-Bond rally at Gimbels' basement in New York City, Jack Benny's $75.00 violin is bought for $1 million by Julius Klorten, president of Garcia Grande cigars.*

**June:** *Duke Ellington gives his first Carnegie Hall concerts; An Axis garrison at Pantelleria, in the central Mediterranean area, surrenders after six days and nights of heavy bombing.*

**July:** *DDT is introduced in the United States and hailed as a boon to farmers; MacArthur starts the Allied offensive in the Pacific/New Guinea Isles War; Polish resistance courier Jan Karski gives an eyewitness account of the Holocaust in a meeting with Roosevelt; Allied attack on Sicily begins; Revolt in Italy: Mussolini is deposed by Badoglio.*

**August:** *Revolt in Treblinka; Selman Waksman discovers Streptomycin and coins the term "antibiotic."*

**September:** ***A bill is introduced to allow refugees who won't endanger public safety to be allowed to enter the U.S. temporarily. The bill dies in office; Invasion of Italy by Allied forces/Italy secretly signs armistice with the Allies/The Allies land in Naples; Rome is occupied by the Germans. The German Army now controls most of Italy.***

**October:** ***Clark's forces enter Naples, Italy; Stan Musial wins the batting title for the St. Louis National League team with an average of .357; 400 Orthodox rabbis march on Washington from the Capitol to the White House. The President refuses to see them. However as a result, public hearings on rescue in the House and in the Senate are held; 600 prisoners of Sobibor's Camp #1 revolt and try to escape. One crematorium is destroyed. Most of the prisoners are eventually caught and killed.***

**November:** ***In a few days, 50,000 Jews in the Lublin region are deported and shot in ditches behind the Majdanek gas chambers; The U.S. State Department demolishes FDR's plan to set up refugee camps in North Africa and Southern Europe; Tehran Conference: Roosevelt, Stalin and Churchill meet.***

**December:** ***Sixteen Allied vessels are lost by Axis bombing at Bari, Italy.***



By January, February and March, things have grown progressively oppressive; as hard as that might be to imagine. Because of early darkness and increased bombing activities between the Axis and Allied bombers, blackouts are required thirty minutes prior to nightfall and curfew is pushed back to 4:00 P.M. Anyone caught on the streets without expressed written permission, except in an absolute emergency, is subject to interrogation, removal for imprisonment or execution on the spot without question. Anxiety, fear and depression are taking a heavy toll on the citizens of Esch and many have become physically ill as a consequence. Some have literally become insane and had to be hospitalized, others, such as Anni, disappear into their own little worlds and hide inside themselves in the darkness of their own minds. Anni no longer makes stops at her aunt's house on the way home from school for cookies or other treats and conversation. No more friends to play with, it is too dangerous—parents aren't allowing their children out of sight. It is as though there were some horrifying dragon flying about the skies that snatches children without warning. In truth, it does exist, but it is the black Iron Eagle with its blood-soaked talons.

April comes and each walk to and from school has become a mental minefield for Anni. She still makes her "mail-runs" for Maria on Saturdays and Sundays but her outings from the house have become nearly nonexistent. She is solemn and plainly unhappy. Day and night, vehicles patrol the streets. If one doesn't see a civilian-attired Gestapo goon, then there is an SS troop marching in numbers of two or more along the streets and alleys, sometimes even knocking on doors. Household inspections begin to take place by the SP (Security Police) without warning or permission. It can happen anytime around the clock, day or night, to anyone of their choosing. Sometimes Anni is awakened from her sleep to hear that horrid wailing siren as it pierces the night air with the distinct sound "Erraw, Erraw" pitched in and out, up and down at high volume. With it comes the immeasurably evil men who snatch people from their beds, children from their parents, wives from their husbands and husbands from their families. Very few, if any, are ever seen again. When that truck comes, people go and people are gone. Sometimes there is even a flash in the night and the sound of pistol fire. Some don't go with the men, some go to their graves at the cemetery, if the family is granted a permit to bury them.

Time continues to pass slowly under the skies filled with war machines as if it were Sunday traffic rolling along invisible highways lain out amongst the clouds. They go by in groups of dozens or more, this way and that. Germans, British, Americans and Canadians. Fighter escorts take each group of bombers safely by while Luxembourg lies below their highways as if it were the bottom of the ocean for sailing ships. Each group of air machines has a destination on either side of the small country. Somehow, even through all hell is breaking loose on the ground and in daily life, they are safe from the skies. They are territory that is like the side of the road on a highway—insignificant as a military target, merely a mapping point for direction to where hell's fury is ablaze on both ends of the spectrum.

"Papa, do I have to wear this? Can't I be sick like the times before?" Anni asks her father, already knowing that she must. "Anni, we have used that excuse beyond its value. If we say it again, we will draw suspicion and then what?" Papa makes his point. "I hate this, I don't want to, can't I find something else to do along the street, maybe?" she pleads imploringly. "Anni, put on the outfit and get down there for the parade. Argument time is over and you have to go!" Mama sharply intervenes. "It is enough that we have managed to get Charly out of it with church. Some things you have to do, like it or not!" She has had it with the bickering, and her nerves have grown sensitive from her emotional pain and anguish. She doesn't want it anymore than Anni does but they have to comply with the orders. It is humiliating, but part of survival. If they want to live and stay together, they must "play along." "OK, Mama, I am sorry. I know you hate this and them too. I'll be back as soon as I can, I just hope I don't throw up!" she states and goes upstairs to change. There Anni puts on the white shirt and the blue skirt. A uniform. A stinking, stiff and stifling Nazi uniform for children. "I am not a Nazi and these stupid clothes won't make me one," she says to herself. "I will go and be as mean and nasty as I can be. They will regret that I was in their stupid parade. The whole rotten lot of them."

Out in the middle of town, Anni arrives in her hated attire to join all the other children of Esch as they gather for the grand march in a grim parade of hollow German pride. It is a celebration called up by the German rulers, the Nazi Party members and the Gestapo to try once again to sway the Luxembourgers into believing that they too are German in blood and should be proud of their new homeland. It is absolutely sickening and even sadly comical to Anni's eyes. Every child here is angry and bitter toward these people who must eat their own children and enjoy abusing others'. They gather in the hot June sun and make the march amidst the fanfare of tinny musical instruments and drums. They wait at the park at the end of the march to listen to the incessant, monotonous drones of Nazi Youth Rally speakers. Anni wants to vomit. "You got me into this stupid dress, but you will never have me. I would rather die first," she tells them as loud as she can scream in her head but not her mouth. Here she stands, silent outside, screaming inside and wanting for the first time in her life to truly do unspeakable harm to another human. To her, they aren't human, they are animals, beasts, demons, monsters. The event ends and Anni races home as fast as she can without running, all the while making sure that she gets the clothes as dirty as possible by rubbing up against walls, kicking up dirt from the gutter and any other way she can find to soil the garments meant to soil her spirit. She wins.

Near the end of the school year, Anni and other students from her school, ages sixteen and older, are taken on a special field trip orchestrated by the Nazi government. It isn't the kind of field trip that the children are used to. Unlike the winter trips before the occupation when the children went ice-skating or out-of-doors in the spring to observe nature, this trip is organized by terrorists calling themselves government. Anni and her classmates are loaded onto buses for a special occasion that reflects the political climate in which they live. There have been several uprisings across Luxembourg and in other countries. Rebellion and resistance has taken shape all across Europe under the grip of the Iron Eagle. The Nazis want to make a point and this they do.

As the bus pulls into Luxembourg City, Anni fondly remembers the days of years past when she, Mama, Boma, Giedy and Albert would participate in the annual march to celebrate the church, and the carnival atmosphere afterwards. Those days seem as if they were in another life. As the doors open on the bus, a man in a crisp black uniform steps in and stands tall, blond and blue-eyed, like steel in front of them. At first, he doesn't speak. He just glares around the bus as if taking inventory and sniffing for fear. He finds it quite easily. He is intimidating and menacing. His steely eyes penetrate the hearts and conscience of each child. This is definitely not a trip for an education toward higher learning. "My German youths," he begins. Immediately Anni feels sick again and anger builds while she is shaking on the outside. "Today we wish to welcome you to visit our headquarters here in the capital city. There have been some very poor acts and misbehavior through uprising and resistance on the part of some criminals against our country. We wish for you to see that we are taking care of such troublemakers for you and want to assure you that we are making every possible effort to keep you safe from such miscreants. We want you to feel safe knowing that we will protect you from those who wish to bring undue hardship and suffering upon you who are loyal to our cause and our country. Please follow me." He turns sharply and marches down the steps as the children slowly rise one by one from their seats and with sweaty face and palms, begin to exit the bus. No one wants to be directly behind this walking, talking machine ahead of the group.

The chaperones herd the children like sheep being led to the slaughter and they all enter the cold concrete building that harbors the ant-like accommodations of Gestapo and SS headquarters. Inside, it is a fearsome sight. All around are men in and out of uniform. Some wear the black of the SS, some are in brown from the Wermacht, some in the Grey/green of Security Police and others in the dapper attire of Gestapo. At some tables and desks sit civilian Luxembourgers. There is no strict guideline as to who is being questioned. At one table sits what appears to be a husband and wife. At another, a boy, apparently of their own age. At yet another desk sits an elderly woman with crutches and missing a leg. The entire place smells of fear, dread, discipline and dark soullessness. Evil incarnate is at work here behind typewriters, telephones and a network of spy operations and police work.

They are briefed as they take the tour. "You see, my German youth," the SS man continues, "this is where we find out who would be so dishonorable as to plot against you and your government. As I am sure you are aware, the vehicles that often visit your streets in the day and night, sounding sirens, are searching out the very ones who are not good for you. Well, this is where they come. Here we interview them and get the answers we need to keep you safe. They are well-treated if they cooperate. However, should they be designing evil plans against your safety, it is our job to make sure they understand that we will not tolerate malfeasance. Follow me." He again takes up the lead and the children fall in line behind him and file downstairs to where the prison cells are and to an open room. "This is what happens to those who would be so cowardly as to wish to overthrow good and proper leadership, organization and your future." He gestures with his hand, sweeping their eyes to follow and take in every element of their surroundings. It is horrible beyond words and the children are terrorized by what they see.

The cells have people sitting in them. They have obviously been beaten, abused and bloodied. Some clearly have broken bones and burn marks on them from electrical shocks and wounds from whips and clubs, all untreated. The smell is nauseating and putrid. In the open concrete room the bloodstains on the walls and on the floor are clearly visible. Various instruments of interrogation and torture are strewn about and chains and shackles hang from the walls. "You see, my German youth," the machine in human form begins again, "we will leave no stone unturned nor turn our backs to criminal behavior against the Fatherland. We are working hard for your safety and well-being. Your obedience brings you this sense of security. And through your obedience to your country, we trust that you will work with us in building a better Germany. We wish you to be a part of a greater good and help us dispose of the evildoers you see here. These animals seek to keep you from peace and safety and would see your families harmed. We know, now that you have been here and seen with your own eyes, that you will help us seek out, find and confront those that are traitors to the Nazi Party, to your beloved country, your families and yourselves." He turns and leads the children back upstairs and to the buses outside.

Out in the open air, more buses can be seen arriving for the same tour. It was a short field trip but clearly educational as to how the Nazis operate. They have no love, no humanity and no souls. "I am sure that you will take this matter to heart and remember this place as you go about your days and nights. We are protecting you and we know that you will, each and everyone, do the right thing in protecting your country. There is great reward for you as you grow and learn. If you ever have suspicion of anyone, family or not, you can approach us and we will reward you for your loyalty to building the greatest country to exist in history. You can be a part of the making of the world's strongest and best-educated country. We can all be a part of a new world where only good exists and criminals no longer exist. Farewell. Heil Hitler!" He stomps his high-top boots together thrusting out his right arm, hand stretched toward the sky, and the children respond in kind without even thinking. It is a reaction out of terror rather than intention. They solemnly mount the bus and return home. Anni returns home without ever speaking a single word for the day and not even the evening to come. It is worthy of forgetting but the doing of such is not impossible but impractical.

Each day is filled with a sense of impending doom and disaster. Anni cannot help but feel it. It chills her spine even in these hot summer days of July and August. What little escape she has now is an infrequent trip to the theatre with Marie or a weekend "mail-run." She will not stop running the errands for Maria at the store. She realized more and more that it is dangerous and something is definitely going on, but the less she knows the better, and it stays that way. At the movies, the newsreels continue to spew forth great news about the advances that the German war machine is making in Europe, Africa and Russia. Clips of troops marching into cities around the globe are exhibited. They are greeted with much fanfare and welcome. The news depicts the Allies as weak, mutable and soon-to-be defeated. Newsreels roll off visions of literally million-plus audiences of farmers in one scene and youth rallies in another, all gathered to worship the greatest leader in history, the Fuhrer, Adolf Hitler. Anni passes such news time by closing her eyes and ears mentally. She takes herself to Marseille or some other place until the movie starts. Again, the movies are German, but at least they are about something other than war. They are B-rated movies, poorly made and poorly attempting to reflect romance or heroism. They are pitiful but it is better than the real life just outside the doors.

By October and November, not a day or night goes by that the skies are not overrun with a beehive of activity. The war is ever encroaching and Anni has no idea what is actually happening. One thing she does know is that it is still getting worse and stranger things are happening. For one, she doesn't see people that she once saw. Those that were handicapped or mentally ill. They apparently go to the hospital but never seem to get released. Anni no longer seeks this kind of education. For all her curiosity and crushing desire to learn, she isn't willing to investigate and find out where they go. She only knows that they aren't here anymore, they go to the hospital and then they are gone, never to be seen again. One other thing she notices: Mama is always sick, especially to her stomach. Mama continues to reassure Anni that it is just a cold and nothing is wrong. Anni knows better but leaves it alone. Worry has become commonplace and room for more doesn't exist. She finds time to occassionally play with Charly or read her books. Someday this hell will pass and she will be on the other side of it.

*What Anni doesn't know, she will soon find out in the months to come. Mama has been pregnant since late June or early July and will give birth to a new family member. Such things are kept very secretive by her parents. She is a girl and girls are not supposed to know such things. Winter wind is bringing cold and snow. With it a new year is approaching and on the winds of the year comes the Iron Eagle with his one last bastion of hope and insatiable desire to do even more harm through death, cruelty and destruction.*

# The "Oatmeal" Farm

**January:** *13th day this new year of 1944—Eisenhower leaves to Europe to organize "Overlord" Normandy operation; Southern California University defeats Washington University in the Rose Bowl; Jewish underground in Budapest is set up. Forged documents workshop is formed. By the end of 1944, 10,000 people have been supplied; Roosevelt establishes a War Refugee Board.*

**February:** *First Japanese territory invaded at Kwajalein.*

**March:** *German Army invades Hungary; War Refugee Board evacuates 1,200 Romanian Jews and moves 48,000 to shelter; Horse racing is banned because of the war; Bing Crosby wins Best Actor in Going My Way by L. McCrary, who wins Best Director.*



This winter in Esch has been especially hard and cruel. Rations have been reduced drastically due to the overwhelming needs of the Wermacht to maintain some semblance of survival on its own accord. Not only food is meager but so are all other basic necessities of life such as soap, cloth, metals and so on. Very little of anything remains on the shelves at the store almost immediately after its arrival. In most cases Maria just sells things right out of the crate, burlap bag, barrel or box. It still isn't much and the same goes for the hopes and dreams of nearly every citizen.

As the coldest months have now passed, March rolls in on cool winds and dry hearts and souls. Everyone seems worn-out, cried-out and pushed out. The city is turning into a ghost town of sorts as young and old alike are either "called up" for conscript in the military or taken away to work fields and work service. Papa's class is about half its normal size and he has little to work with, just as all others fortunate enough to be employed in any position. Even the gentle and kind souls that were once called neighbors and friends are turning on one another out of anger, bitterness and gross instinct for survival. It has become a torturous existence. A hell without flames. The only fires that exist are the ones in the eyes of the oppressed people.

On March 2, 1944, Anni is called to Mama's side in the kitchen where she and Papa have been having another one of their low-voiced conversations. "Anni," Mama begins. "your Papa and I have something to tell you." "Yes, ma'am?" Anni waits, hating the suspense. "Well, um…there is going to be another child in the house soon. You are going to have a new baby brother or sister," Mama finishes quickly, intending to stop the whole thing there. "Anni," Papa jumps in to prevent the onslaught of questions he knows Anni is about to machine-gun fire off, "Mama will be going to the hospital in a few days or so and she will come home with a baby. Don't start asking questions or getting worried, she will be alright. She just has to go away and then she will be back and you will have a brother or sister to help look after, OK? I don't want any questions, just understand that you are going to need to take care of Mama's chores and cooking, OK?" He finally lets her speak. "OK, Papa," she answers. She can tell by their faces, the way they are already dismissing her from their presence, that she isn't going to get one good question in edgewise. "I just hope it isn't another boy!" Anni says to herself and walks away to take in the news. She goes upstairs and starts her homework and mulls over the facts. She knew all along something wasn't right but those two, Mama and Papa, keep secrets about girls' and boys' stuff as if it were the life of a nation depending on it.

It doesn't take long for Anni to learn a little about where babies come from and how it starts. The following day, actually night, of March 3, 1944, Anni has hardly closed her eyes to sleep when she hears Mama scream with pain, calling out to Papa. Anni runs downstairs to find Mama standing in the doorway of her and Papa's room, doubled over in obvious pain, gripping the doorjam, with Papa standing beside her. "Anni, run upstairs and get Marie! Hurry!" Papa yells out to her no sooner than she has hit the last step. "Anni, go!" he says again while she stares with a slack-jawed look on her face. She turns to do as she is told but there is something that catches her eye and every thought in her head as she leaves the room—there was drops of blood on the floor and water around the hem of Mama's nightgown.

Anni doesn't even need to reach the door upstairs to knock. She is met halfway by Marie who has a clear and distinct look upon her face reflecting the fact that she already knows and has known all along. Anni briefly feels a little betrayed that Marie didn't share this with her nor anyone else. They all knew except her and she is disappointed in them, but only for a moment. For now, she is more concerned about Mama. Both Marie and Anni return to the bottom level to find Mama and Papa now standing by the door as Papa helps Gredy put on her longcoat. Although it is early March, is is a cold night and there is still some snow on the ground outside. Marie runs past Anni, and Papa tells Anni to go back to her room. The women are headed for the hospital and he will stay here with both Anni and Charly, who is now coming out of his room to investigate. Both children are directed to their beds by Papa, and Anni heads back upstairs completely confused and dissatisfied with the whole matter.

At approximately nine o'clock at night and long past curfew, Margaretha Neuman and her good friend and neighbor, Marie, walk to the hospital nearly three-quarters of a mile away. A couple of blocks from home, they are confronted by a German security policeman. They could easily be shot and killed right there on the spot for violating the curfew. What espionage or suspicious behavior were they up to? Obviously, the officer feels it is something criminal and begins his questioning at gunpoint. "What you are doing out past curfew and where are you going? Tell me now. If you lie, I will shoot you, women or not!" he demands. Marie, holding Margaretha around the waist, points to the ground and the snow behind them. "She's pregnant and having the baby now. She needs to get to the hospital, she's losing a lot of blood, you see?" she exclaims in rapid fashion. Immediately, the SP takes notice of the blood trail behind them, the stains at Mama's feet and then stares up the road in the direction they are headed. It makes sense, they are headed for the hospital. He makes no apologies but does actually try to clear some snow for them to walk without falling. There are no ambulances available nor cars for assistance.

The two women reach the hospital in time, but only by minutes. Gredy has lost a lot of blood. She gives birth to a baby girl, Mariane Neuman, that night of March 3. She remains in poor condition after the delivery and will have to stay in the hospital for ten days to recover. In the meantime, she receives the birth certificate of her fourth child. Little

Mariane has become Elfriede Neuman. Mariane sounded too French for the Germans and thus they changed her name, just as they had done to every other member of the family. The child will be called "Elfie" for short. Mama had the name all picked out but at the last minute they were forced to change it. Even here, they have no true charge of their lives.

The following day, Anni asks Papa if she can go see her mother in the hospital, but Papa immediately forbids it. He is still determined to keep Anni in the dark when it comes to human sexuality and facts about God's own blessing, procreation. "May I at least go see Grandma Giedy?" she asks. Papa bends and permits it, "Go straight to see your cousin Renee and don't be late home. Remember, you have to cook dinner." Anni goes out of the house and soon finds herself knocking on the door, only to find out that Giedy is in the hospital, too. Although she is not at the same hospital. Anni discovers from Renee that the maternal matriarch has tuberculosis and has been quarantined at a hospital for people with contagious ailments.

Just as the real world seems to be collapsing not only all around Europe, but the entire globe, Anni's world appears to be collapsing around her. She has been kept in the dark about a major family event. She has lost her best friend and brother to another part of the world it seems, while he is in Germany. Boma's absence from the family is still felt. Charly has his own world to live in. Her best friend Rosa has disappeared with her entire family in the middle of the night, and now Giedy is sick. Not only is she sick, but she is in the hospital, and so is Mama.

She takes in a deep breath and heads for the hospital to see Giedy. Even if she can't see Mama, nobody said she couldn't see Giedy and she isn't going to waste time asking. Anni starts up the hillside where the hospital is perched, off from the main part of town. All the while as she walks, she can only think of the train rides to Marseille. She reminisces about the summers in the south of France with this beautiful, loving and tough grandmother. She thinks of the dancing beads at Aunt Anne's apartment, the singing, drunk bird and the parties they had with even Giedy getting a little playful as Anni danced away the night. It seems like it was a hundred years ago.

Upon arrival at the hospital door, Anni is met by a man coming out. He is the security guard in this place where people are imprisoned for being sick. No unauthorized personnel are permitted in or out. The sick come in and stay. Friends, neighbors and family are kept out. There are no bars, no locks nor armed men, but it is a prison of sorts. Immediately the man tells her she cannot come in and she had better find another place to go. He has rounds to make and doesn't have time for argument or discussion with her. He turns and walks away to survey the surrounding property, and as he does, Anni walks right inside and starts looking for her grandmother. The man had his back to her and made the mistake of thinking his size, gender and stern words of warning were enough to chase away a "rabbit" like that little girl. He was dead wrong. It wasn't the first and most certainly not the last time, that Anni Neuman was underestimated.

She meanders down the hall, trying to make herself invisible to the staff, without cloak or hiding place. By some miracle and against all odds, she does find her grandmother in the rows upon rows of beds for the infirmed. Arriving at her bedside she can see the pallor on the face of her grandmother and hear the rattling breath emanating from her cracked and broken lungs. She is obviously in distress but holding onto life with the same strength she once held onto Anni's hand as they walked the dangerous roads of Marseille amongst the drunks, thieves and hardened sailors.

Now she is here in the fight of her life, and by German order she is going this road alone and without family. Well, this time Anni takes another shot at the established order and the Iron Eagle. Her determination and grit have pierced another hole in the old bird's armor without him knowing it. Giedy is delighted to see Anni, and her face radiates with joy. They don't have long but they share the minutes like hours and Giedy will rest easy knowing that she has a loving granddaughter and family outside the walls, praying and missing her. Anni has the reassurance that her beloved Giedy received that very small reward. She holds her grandmother's hand and kisses her forehead. "I love you, Grandma," she whispers. "I love you too, honey." Those are their last words exchanged, and Anni walks back down the hall and out, just as invisible as when she came in. One would think that maybe a butterfly had been in the room and escaped through an open window. Certainly, no trespasser had entered.

March 5, 1944, Albert Neuman walks into the hospital to see his wife, Gredy, and their new baby daughter. The child is beautiful and healthy. The father takes a moment to enjoy the pride of this new life added to his, but he keeps it bottled inside like a treasure map. He comes to his wife's bedside to encourage her and inquire about her health. She has suffered greatly and lost too much blood. She is weak and pale, yet strong enough to rise up and greet her husband. In an instant she sees it.

"It" is one of those things that, through the history of all mankind, a woman can see on a man's face or smell in the air no matter how hard he tries to hide it. "What's wrong, Albert? Is Mariane okay?" she asks. "Yes, Gredy. She is fine and beautiful. Are you eating yet?" he asks, trying to change the subject. It doesn't work. "What is wrong, Albert?" she queries again. "Gredy, Giedy passed away this morning. I just heard a short while ago on my way here. I will be making arrangements."

He assures his wife, all the while knowing that there will be no way his wife can leave the hospital to attend her mother's funeral or view her one last time. It is a very sad moment for everyone, but for Gredy, it is one of the hardest days of her entire life and yet she keeps it to herself. In two days' time she has delivered a precious new life to the world and has every right to take great pride in her God-given gift of being a woman, but now her life is bittersweet. She has a son lost from her protective arms, a child at home growing fast, an older daughter that she worries over to no end, a new baby to think about, a husband that could be taken or killed any day and her mother is gone. Her pain is silent and indescribable. It will take years for her to make peace between this day and her soul.

By March 15, the family is once again gathered at home. Several are missing and one is new. It is an awkward situation for anyone to handle, particularly when cheated by circumstances and ruled by the greed and ego of people in power. Their personal difficulties have no meaning to those above them in the chain that links their lives to the unscrupulous warmongers.

Mama begins her convalescence at home with Elfie and tries to make the best of her newfound legs after lying in a hospital bed for ten days, plus. Papa made funeral arrangements for Giedy as best he could according to his promise to his wife. However, because Giedy had a contagious disease she was ruled by the German authorities to be a risk, even in death; therefore, her bodily remains were to be removed and discharged without proper Catholic service and burial. A memorial service was all that was to be had and it was a sad one at that. Although ruled by circumstances, Mama, Papa, Anni and all who knew her kept vigilant memories and never let her die in their hearts.

The successes of war depend on speed and the element of surprise. Those two combined can make massive inroads toward a successful campaign or victory altogether. However, the speed of war and its remnants of surprise can exact a toll of epic proportions upon the innocent bystanders and underlings. Unfortunately, like most Luxembourgers, the

Neumans are just that, mere underlings in a greater scheme. No one would be able to convince them that they mattered, and it is obvious that in cigar-smoke-filled rooms where cognac flows and harlots abound, men are making decisions as if no one is impacted by their own personal appetites.

Two weeks after Mama has come home from the hospital with baby Elfie, a funeral mass is finally held at the church for Ann Linninger "Giedy" Bost; February 22, 1876–March 5, 1944. Although she had lived nearly all of her sixty-eight years in Esch, the turnout is low. Too many people have become terrorized by the Nazis and fear attending any gathering other than routine Sunday Mass or the mandatory gatherings and parades held by the Nazis. For the others not in attendance, it is because they are too tired, weak, hungry, sad or no longer living here in Esch. It is a formality and dispensed with as such. Giedy's bodily remains were long since removed and handled in the Nazi regulatory style for anyone that had the misfortune of being anything but "perfect" in life or death.

A week later finds the Neuman family semi-intact but suffering sorely under the harsh conditions that are befalling occupied countries and particularly Germany itself. Unknown to Anni, the war is fast being lost by the German Wermacht. They are now in a bitter struggle to regroup and retake. Although she doesn't know, news has spread far and wide into the reaches of the SS, Gestapo and German police. Their efforts to stop uprisings and espionage are made an offensive tactic. They don't wait anymore for suspicious behavior, instead they are now routing people out of house and home, church, workplace, factory or streets. People are literally being shot where they stand. Others are taken away never to be seen again.

On this final day of March, Anni and her classmates gather at the windows on the third floor of their school. Outside and across the grassy field stands the college where Papa teaches. The children have been instructed to watch and learn a new lesson for the day. Much to Anni's surprise, she can see the teachers, staff and professors from the college being led out single file along the side wall of the building facing her school. The Nazis SS, Gestapo and German police are all in attendance. The men are lined up against the wall and told to salute with the obligatory "Heil Hitler." Although the words cannot be heard in Anni's classroom it is clear what is happening. All the men raise their arms as quickly as possible to comply with the order. However, some are a little slower than the others and for that they are suspect and are shot immediately.

Anni is in utter shock, for right there in that line is her own father; she accidently lets out a scream. Then, as a final reminder to remain loyal to the Reich, a Gestapo leader walks along the line, counts off one through four and stops at each fourth man. He raises his pistol and fires point-blank into the forehead of the unfortunate number four. By amazing grace and mercy Anni quickly counts down the line and at about the time the killer pauses in front of Papa, she realizes he is number three. Her heart pounds so loud she can't hear and she stops breathing in apprehension. Just as certain, the man standing next to her father is dispatched as a "number four." The remaining men are turned and marched back inside to continue teaching their students. No one dares to ask why or question it. It is evil—done on a whim. These men are no longer soldiers or police, they are blatant cold-blooded murderers.

The following week, with Papa's permission, Anni and her friend Lillie, from school, leave on a Saturday and travel to Luxembourg City. They have an opportunity to leave school early and volunteer to enter into their conscript to mandatory RAD. RAD is the short term for Reichs Arbeits Dienst (Realm Work Force). It is usually a two-year service that all "Germans" must serve as civilians for their country and government. There are some thirty-nine farms and other such labor camps throughout greater Germany proper. After one year of labor on farms and in factories, the second year must be fulfilled by more dangerous work such as working in the munitions factories or other sites supporting the military. Anni and Lillie have collectively decided that volunteering would speed them to a better chance at higher education. Should they volunteer and complete one year now, the reward would be having their time cut short and also being permitted to go to school in Nancy, France for college-level learning. For the two of them, they know it is the right thing and best thing to do, not only for themselves but for their families.

Upon return home, Anni provides Papa with all the paperwork he must complete and sign so that he can release his precious older daughter into the hands of the monsters that already have taken, with his pride, his oldest son. It is not much of a choice for him; he hates it but he does it. If he doesn't do it, he may lose her here in this hell anyhow. Also, he hates the thought of thinking so practically, but it is one less mouth to feed and his family is slowly starving. He believes that she will at least have food and shelter and in Germany proper, no one will be trying to kill her without cause or reason. For Gredy, it is one more loss among all the recent losses. Her grief has taken her away from herself. She goes through the motions, pouring all her tears inward and into her soul. Her heart beats but doesn't bare itself anymore. She will love, nurture and care for the remaining three, Papa, Charly and Elfie, and resign herself to doing or saying anything else. After all, what would be the point?

By early April, Anni and Lillie leave Esch at dawn Friday morning for the long journey to the RAD farm they have been assigned to. They embark from the train station at Esch and go on to Luxembourg City. There they switch trains and head to Frankfurt, Germany, where again they switch trains and travel to Wurzburg. One last change of trains and they arrive between Wurzburg and Stuttgart in a small village near a bombed-out ammunition factory and the farm where they will serve out their requirement. As the two travel along the dirt road to the farm, it is clear why they were sent to this place to work. The munitions factory is an annihilated pile of rubble, the obvious target of incessant bombing by Allied forces. In fact, for nearly a mile around the factory, the fields, hillsides, woods and some small farmhouses are just as ruined. The trees have been stripped to bare, blackened needles pointed skyward and the ground is pockmarked by overlapping, gaping holes where the ground has been displaced again and again. The two girls stare at each other in amazement and disbelief. This is where they will be staying for the year to come; it is a bad thought and they are already wishing they had made a different decision.

By the time they approach the farmhouse where they are to stay, they realize that they are not just assigned to this place, but by the looks of all the property surrounding them, they are replacements for the workers that were here before. It is amazing that the farmhouse is fairly unscathed, although it shows some minor wounds on the outside walls. There is no doubt that the workers here before them have been killed or wounded in the bombing raids. It is insanity that the Germans permitted the work farm to continue operating and put young girls in a field certain to be hit by errant rounds of ammunition hailing from the sky to strike the munitions factory.

The girls knock on the door and are greeted by an older, stout German woman. She brings them inside only long enough for them to drop their meager belongings and take the mattress bags they are handed. "Take these to the barn and fill them with straw. This is what you will be sleeping on. When you get that done, get back here, take your belongings and go into that room [pointing across the hall] and take a bunk. Once you pick it, that is where you stay. There will be no arguing or moving, understand?" she says harshly. "Yes, ma'am," the girls reply in unison and head off as told. The get their mattress bags stuffed as best they can with the smelly, damp straw and carry their heavy load back to the house. This is going to be a long and grueling year of work. This is only a taste of the labor they will be forced to endure. It is a dreary spring evening and the smell of whatever is cooking doesn't excite the stomach. The girls go to the room, which has approximately twenty wooden beds lined in rows around the room. They pick the only two that are side by side and start to settle in as best they can.

By dinner time, they have hardly seen a soul except for the woman at the door. Then a dinner chime is rung and everyone seems to shuffle in on tired feet from out of thin air. There are five women here to run the show and run roughshod over twenty girls doing forced labor in field work and farm life. As they all gather to the table, the food is ladled out bowl by bowl. Whatever it is, it stinks to Anni's nostrils and she knows she isn't going to like it. As the pot is passed to her, she takes the ladle and fills it deep and pours the strange concoction into her bowl, passes the pot and looks silently at it and then at Lillie beside her. The mixture in front of her makes her gag and nearly vomit. Anni looks only long enough to try and decipher what exactly this terrible stuff is. What she finds is a boiled watery mush made with last harvest's near rotten carrots, beets, the greens from the beets, oatmeal and tapioca for thickening. It is disgusting beyond any pig slop Anni has ever seen. If she wasn't here looking at it, she would swear that no one in the world ever ate such stuff nor did it exist. But there it is and this is all she will get. She refuses to eat. She would rather go hungry and thus she does.

After being excused from the table, the new girls are given their army-style red wool blankets for bedding, long muu-muu type dresses made of burlap, and scarves to cover their heads and keep the hair and sweat out of their eyes for tomorrow's labor. They go to the room and make very little conversation as they adjust to the girls around them from all different cities and places. The other girls don't seem to care much for conversation. They are all dirty, tired and worn. It is apparently a daily regimen that doesn't change nor end. Just as the lights go out and they close their eyes, hoping for sleep to bring relief from the itchy blankets and the prickling mattresses, the drones are heard. The same ones Anni is already familiar with from home but this time they sound different. They are not flying high overhead on a distant course, they are flying low and coming in louder and louder by the minute. They are coming to bomb here or near here and Anni knows there will be no sleep tonight. The bombing goes on all night and rattles the house at times as if forty thunders were released simultaneously in a summer storm.

The girls stir from their half-sleep to the still-dark morning hours in this land that seems ethereal. Still dressed in their gowns they all drag themselves to the table for a 5:00 A.M. breakfast of bread, jam and what they unaffectionately call "make-believe" coffee. It is obviously some form of chickory bark that has been boiled down and dubbed "coffee." The bread is stale and tough, the jam is thick but old and tasteless just like the "coffee." This is the breakfast they will eat repeatedly, morning after morning. Anni is the only one at the table that pauses to say grace. Even she isn't quite sure why she is doing it other than it would be a sin not to and there is no place for her to confess it. Plus, plainly put, she needs all the help she can get. After the so-called breakfast the girls are sent off to dress in their work clothes and clean their area. They report back for duty outside at 6:00 A.M. as the morning sun is rising in the sky. Each day brings warmer temperatures indicating the summer heat to come.

Anni and Lillie are assigned their duties. They will raise carrots—row upon row. It is their job to till the soil, plant, cultivate, nourish and harvest the maximum amount and there is no room for failure. The girls are drilled by the older women and they expect perfection in performance and unceasing efforts of labor that grown men could not accomplish. It is as though they were in the military itself and being subjected to the grueling challenges of basic training.

At the end of the day, Anni and Lillie follow the other girls from their respective and distant positions into a gathering of sorts by the side of the house. Here they all take turns using a water hose to wash their hands, face, neck, feet and whatever else they can manage to splash water on without soaking their already sweat-soaked garments. Water on burlap is a cardinal sin punishable by a following day of wearing hard, rough clothing that will literally sand your skin away from your flesh. Especially when it is encrusted with deep-rooted dirt. No, they only wash the extremities and this is all the bath or cleanliness they will have for the entire stay here. There are no other facilities save a toilet.

This cycle repeats itself throughout April and May. Then as June comes to the calendar, a strange thing happens. Not one night has been silent and even recently the bombings have occurred during the day. In fact, the girls cultivate the land like minesweepers waiting at any moment to be blown to pieces from an undetonated bomb. It has happened before and is an everyday concern. But for some reason on June 6 the skies are quiet. Quiet enough for a bird to sing and be heard. It is very, very eerie and Anni senses that something very big, bad and ugly is happening. That night they try to sleep, but it is impossible. The air is filled with horrendous noise of airplanes of all sizes and sounds. In the morning the girls go outside to look. Above, the sky is nearly black with literally thousands of planes flying from east to west, north to west and south to west. It appears that every plane ever made by man is in the sky over them and they are all headed west. The sun is nearly blocked by it all throughout this day and the next. Whatever is happening, it is the biggest world event since young Anni left Esch on a dark May night four years ago. Her only prayer is that her family is safe and that good and not evil will win this battle for a change. Just maybe, this time, good will win.

Throughout June things continue to get more difficult. The girls work the fields as best they can but planes continue to ply the airways and bombings have increased all the more. Now, a mile or two away, massive lengths of armored vehicles can be seen moving rapidly along the roadways to the west. Something of epic proportion is occurring; Anni has known it since the day the planes filled the sky like a plague of locusts straight from the Bible.

Each day the girls awaken to oatmeal and water for breakfast. The rations are meager. They are isolated—no deliveries come nor go from the farm. Anni supplements her diet with the carrots she grows or beets, potatoes, anything she can barter or steal rather than eating that horrid mush they serve day-in and day-out for lunch and supper. They haven't been to church since they have been here. On Sundays before that black day of metal birds, they would be given a few coins to go to the coffee house in the village and get sweets but that is over now. Even the portions of the pig slop they are fed are getting smaller. This is getting to be a very, very desperate time and it is written all over the faces of the old matrons haunting the house.

The month of July brings with it the full force of summer. Nothing has changed, except to a greater degree the military is omnipresent. Yet, they continue to insanely perform their tasks and duties in filth with unwashed bodies and clothes not laundered from the day they were first issued. By the first of August, they are down to bread and water for all meals. The girls are too weak to work the fields and there is nothing worth working for; the land is dry and unfruitful. War is the only thing living—all else is in a state of decay, and with it the human spirit of each person here.

During the first week of August the girls are greeted by some men from town. They are Germans for certain. Why they are here, no one knows. In a matter of an hour they leave. The matrons gather the girls and dole out to each one the equivalent of eight dollars. They are told to gather their belongings, not to steal anything or they will be killed and leave. Go back to where you came from. You are on your own.

Anni and Lillie once again look at each other silently, slack jawed and open mouthed. They feel their souls part from their bodies for a brief moment. Then, reality kicks in and they hustle to gather their belongings and leave this God forsaken "oatmeal farm" from hell.

# Freed for Leaving and Finding Home

*That early morning in August, 1944, the girls at the "Oatmeal Farm" had just finished their breakfast when their attention was drawn to the local men at the door. From the time the girls had downed their breakfast, prepared to work another day, the hour to follow was mind-boggling and confusing. They had been hailed as "good workers" and "the best group of girls," then told that the war was not over but they were not needed here. They were consistently "comforted" with words of encouragement by the matrons that Germany was intact and that this was only a part of war. They would soon have it all won and they should be proud. The parting words of the senior matron, as the girls returned from their room, changed into the clothes they arrived in, were "Sieg Heil!" It made a lasting impression but one worth cherishing as an epitaph to the Iron Eagle falling like lightning from the sky to a certain fiery crash and burn. The girls from Germany and Luxembourg were permitted to leave but reminded that they were the future of Germany. What no one knew was that the lines had failed, the Wermacht was in ruins and in retreat; and a man named Charlie D. Adams, from Brooklyn, New York, with thousands of other men from the United States of America and its allies with them, were pounding their way across France, Belgium, the Netherlands, Luxembourg and into Germany on their way to Czechoslovakia and Poland. The Third Reich was becoming the "last Reich." Men from Britain, Canada, Belgium, France, Netherlands, Luxembourg and the United States of America were drawing the blood of their enemies and spilling their own blood in toil, sweat and tears of combat, but successfully so in every inch of ground they recovered for those to whom it belonged, as God meant it to be.*

The girls quickly enter the room and begin to shed the sack-clothes that they have been wearing for months now. They toss the filthy garments in a pile at the foot of each bed and pull from underneath the clothes they first arrived in, still semi-fresh and clean. Hurriedly they pull over their blouses and don their long skirts, wool socks and high-top leather shoes. They make no time for conversation or pause to reflect upon anything. They stuff the money into the pockets sewn into their skirts and look for the last time at the straw mattresses that have pricked and tormented them for so many long nights.

Lillie and Anni walk out of the door of the house without so much as a look back. They fall in line with several other girls walking the dirt road to the small town over the hill some three miles away. As they walk along, the planes continue to fly in all directions above their heads and it is an eerie feeling for Anni. Somehow with all the noise above the total silence as they walk makes a surreal contrast. Deafening silence amongst the raging noise of air war. The planes are of all sizes and types—bombers, fighters and escorts. Even as they walk, Anni can hear some of the planes engaging in combat, with their machine guns and bombs falling in the distance. The war has come all too close once again for Anni and she is determined to get home as fast as she can, however she can, even if it means she has to walk the whole way. What she doesn't know yet is that is exactly what she will end up having to do.

At the train station, it is evident that not many people are willing to risk being out of doors. Some must stay because it is home and others must because they cannot afford to leave but, overall, it has become an exercise of wisdom to move about as little as possible. The train station is practically empty, with the exception of the girls from the farm. It is an eerie scene as the train finally takes on passengers and Anni and Lillie move quickly to secure their place, praying silently. What little money they had has nearly all been spent on this ride. The past hours have been far too long for both of them and their anxiety has reached a fevered pitch.

"When are they going to get moving!" Anni exclaims in frustration. "Anni, be quiet, you're going to get us into trouble or get us killed," Lillie responds. Lillie, shorter in stature but stout, is more concerned with the slightest imagination of drawing attention even in this near empty place. She had been that way nearly the entire time the two young girls worked their carrot rows back at the farm. Anything Anni said seemed to cause her alarm and dread that they would be killed for no apparent reason. It was amazing the two had maintained their friendship but necessity saw to it.

Finally, the train engine revs and the movement becomes evident to the passengers. The anxiety is not Anni and Lillie's alone. A collective sigh of relief is heard throughout the passenger car from the few others that sat there waiting to be bombed to pieces at any second. Slowly and methodically, the train presses forward against its own weight and gravity. As the machine takes up speed, Anni and Lillie look out the window and down the hill to see the farm that was to have been their unhappy home for at least a year. Thank God that has changed. They both are nearly in tears as the feeling sinks in that the torment has been shortened.

No sooner have the girls settled into their seats than the train begins slowing, much faster than it started. The wheels screech against the steel rails. "No, now what? What are we stopping for?" Anni cries out. They have hardly made some ten or fifteen miles of headway toward Wurzburg before they find out that the bombing has damaged the railway systems as much as all the other targets. The tracks are blown out ahead of them and there will be no more train ride and most definitely no refund. It will be dark in a matter of hours and the only decision has already been made for them. They, like the few others caught in this trap of war, must disembark and start walking toward home. Lillie begins to cry and Anni just looks blankly at her and permits it without a word. After all, what is there for her to say?

Anni puts her hand on Lillie's shoulder and looks at her silently as if to say, "I know, I feel the same way. Follow me." And then turns and begins to walk in the direction of Wurzburg. Their plan was to catch a train from there to Frankfurt and from Frankfurt to Luxembourg City and finally home. The travel plan remains the same but the method of travel has been changed drastically.

Walking along the distorted and disfigured tracks reminds them miserable of their present circumstances. The coolness of the summer night comes on the rising winds of the evening as the sun sets in the west. They follow the waning orb as if it is their own personal beacon from their families calling to them. It gives them the strength and will press on and survive the journey, no matter how difficult it may be. In fact, everything is difficult anyhow. Life has been difficult, each day is difficult; difficult is the norm. "So who cares anymore? Just keep moving forward," Anni thinks to herself.

By nightfall they have walked nearly twelve miles and can see the outskirts of the large city of Wurzburg, but only in shadows and the brilliant flashes of white phosphorus bombs leveling the city to ruins and ash. It is an otherwise "black out" city, and it appears that by morning it will only be a name on a map with nothing else to represent itself.

"Lillie, we are not going to be able to get a train there. That is certain. We need to get close to the main tracks and find the sign that says 'Frankfurt.' Then we can follow those tracks a few meters away without getting too close and getting bombed or shot." She advises Lillie of her plan. "It's a good plan. We can do it, just be patient with me, Ok? You walk faster than I do," Lillie states, showing Anni her own strength and resolve. "Let's go. I think we should walk as much at night as possible and take short rests in the day. That way we are less likely to be seen by anyone or get into trouble," Anni concludes. "I don't like walking in the dark and I know you don't either, but what else can we do? It is our best hope." Young girls in a foreign place and far from home, the two of them become a team of spirit and fortitude.

All through the night the two teenage girls walked along the brush near the tracks, sometimes seeking smoother and less rocky ground but keeping within eyesight of the tracks. Along the way, as day approached, they would find little sheds where farmers kept tools, seed and supplies for tending their fields. There Anni and Lillie would sleep, sometimes for several hours and other times much less. They would steal food from the fields, orchards or vineyards. They didn't gather quantities of anything—just a quick snatch and run with something to live on. The guilt, shame and fear were enough punishment. They didn't like it but they wanted to live. Getting caught could have easily been deadly in times like these.

After several days, the girls found themselves on the outskirts of Frankfurt. Here, they felt as if they were halfway home but this also was a very dangerous place for them to be. The road ahead was hung with black billowing clouds of terror awaiting their approach to rain down on them. In the darkness one night, Anni and Lillie literally walked into two German soldiers. They walked right into their arms and the soldiers wrestled with the girls, trying to contain them, all the while asking questions. Anni's terror inflamed the adrenaline in her body as well as Lillie's. "Run, Lillie, run and don't stop!" Anni screamed out to Lillie as the older girl broke free. These were grown men, soldiers and monsters to the girls. It was a fate worse than death for them both if something didn't remove them from this disaster. Something did. From reflex Anni kicked up her knee with all she had, as if she were aiming for the head. The blow was successful, straight to the groin and the soldier dropped in his tracks, letting go of Anni just long enough for her to run past the other soldier.

She caught up with Lillie on the dark path and didn't slow down, only told her to keep running. Anni did slow enough to keep Lillie in sight. They kept running for what seemed like hours. No distance could be far enough to satisfy their fear of the soldiers. Eventually, they could not take another step or draw another breath and they hid in some bushes to catch their breath and wait. The soldiers never showed up.

Eventually, the two girls began their trek again toward home. Home—that was all they could think of. But they still had a long way and days to go. After nearly five days of walking, the girls faced another two days' journey to get to Esch. They made it to the first bridge at the Rhine only to find that it had been bombed out and more soldiers were there. They are offered a lift to the nearest existing bridge and finally get across at Rudensheim, Germany. From there, it was more walking, with some helpful rides, until they reached the Luxembourg border. At the border they walked some more, then received a short lift to Luxembourg City. At last, the girls were able to ride the train home and meet their families at the station.

*At this point I would like to make note of some things the reader should consider. This story is real and it is true. It happened. Throughout this writing process, Anni and I, the author, have struggled diligently to be accurate and truthful. During the writing of this chapter, some four weeks after the death of my brother, during the two weeks preceding our leaving for three weeks in Germany, Luxembourg, Belgium and France, Anni and I fought hard to resolve what we thought would be a short chapter. As you can probably tell by the last working paragraph above, things became somewhat vague and less descriptive.*

*For two weeks, Anni and I met and discussed this chapter to get the facts straight. Each time she would tell me the stories, I would listen and take notes. I would go home and attempt to write. Every time, I failed. I would research the area I was to write about and the events in the larger picture of the war. Things did not add up. The problems were simple at first—Anni could not remember the name of the city where the farm was located. This was astounding to me because Anni has an uncanny memory. Even after my prodding and pushing to remember, to the point of nearly causing her to become angry, no answer to that question would come. I tried gently to let it go.*

*I spent hours searching maps and cities, presenting them to Anni to look at and still no answer. I was researching and writing seven days a week and sometimes a total of twelve to fourteen hours over the days and nights. Anni would have one problem, only to have it resolve a week later, and then something new. This went on to the point of total frustration on our part. The worst of it came two days prior to our departure to Europe for our final work and research and book promotion. Anni was admitted to the hospital emergency room where she was a volunteer. The past month had taken a heavy toll on us both. After being cleared from the hospital (because she refused to stay and miss the trip), Anni returned home where she and I, along with Jean (Anni's best friend), met for a late dinner and one more look at the map.*

*I returned home this time certain I had it and could write it. It didn't work. It was all wrong. Not what Anni had told me. What was wrong was who or what happened over that time frame. It had nothing to do with Anni's memory and yet everything to do with it. Her mind was sharp and clear, but her "memory bank" had a black hole in it. A vortex of sorts that had sucked in the mental pictures and images of a part and time of her life when hell was too simple to describe the war, the weariness, the sorrow and most of all the fear. It was the fear that had caused the blank.*

*During my writing attempts over the past two days, I was afforded the privilege of receiving a copy of Chuck Dean's book, Nam Vet: Making Peace with Your Past. As I read with great interest (I had four uncles in Vietnam and my Army instructors in 1980 were predominantly all Nam Vets), I came across his description of post-traumatic stress disorder (PTSD) and how it affected and still affects people in and out of war. One particular passage stood out to me and I will quote it here directly by Chuck's permission:*

> ***He hardly ever slept. He drank coffee continuously, and took other things to keep himself from closing his eyes. How he lasted so long without sleep is beyond me. He was afraid to sleep because he would have horrible dreams about the war, but he would never tell me about them. He would just walk around like a zombie for days after having one of these nightmares. Staying awake was his only way to protect himself.***
>
> ***Last year, while on a trip away from home, he died in a motel. He died in his sleep. The autopsy showed nothing unusual, but the doctor's report stated he died of fright. He died from a bad dream.'***
>
> *Nam Vet: Making Peace with Your Past*, by Chuck Dean, copyright 2000; p. 66

*After reading this passage from a woman who lost her husband after he was already "safely" home from Vietnam, some important issues started to dawn on me. For the integrity of this book, I will try to keep it brief and finish this chapter, however, it is extremely important. The key word to me in post-traumatic stress disorder was the word* stress. *When you add trauma to stress you have a cocktail for physiological, psychological and organic poison. I had shunned two years of a living hell and refused to talk about it, using this book to escape from what I had been through. This was compounded by my loss of a family member and memories of my own past. Anni and I openly and honestly share our past with each other. I brought back memories I had hidden away and even "forgot."*

*At the same time, I was impressing upon her to "relive" and replay this time of her life in her mind. She had painted it black with impermeable ink and nothing, no way, was going to bring those pictures back. This is how we sometimes deal with trauma and stress. Thinking about the trauma raises the level of stress. In Anni, her body began to react to her mind, her fears, anxiety and emotions, all mixed with the daunting challenges of returning home to make peace with some things in her life and revisit where she grew up for the first time in ten years.*

*In my own case, I became physically ill—tired, fatigued, irritable, anxious, sweaty around others. I would rather have died than talk about anything that might make me crack open the door into my "world." This was all a byproduct of stress, anxiety and fear. These small- sounding words are killers of the most evil kind. I wish to encourage everyone who reads this book to reflect upon your own life and find your stress, anxiety and fear points. Identify, seek help and talk to others that are genuinely helpful.*

*The Bible states, "As a man thinketh, so is he." Your thoughts control your body and your body is not ignorant. It reacts in physical ailments seemingly unconnected, strange and uniquely from "nowhere." Personally, it is this author's belief that the only way out is through a sound mind based upon spiritual reconciliation to the past and looking to the present and future. This, to me, is done by a confession of faith and firm belief in Jesus Christ as my personal Lord and Savior. It doesn't mean being perfect or trying to be. It means to be yourself, accepting who you are and knowing Whose you are. This transforming power can bring health and healing to your body, soul and mind. It removes the anxiety, the stress and destroys the fear. It is our opportunity to fight back against whatever attacked us first; and we can win.*

*In the end, Anni and I returned from a successful trip to nearly all the places mentioned in this book and took in all the sights, sounds and memories.*

*A most remarkable trip down memory lane for Anni. She came back refreshed, renewed and young all over again. Finally, after another month of vicious research, I found the name of the town and RAD camp number:* **Wechterswinkel, Germany; RAD 6/194.** ***Mission accomplished.***

Lonnie D. Story; the Author.

At the train station in Esch-sur-Alzette, Anni is greeted by her overjoyed mother and father, with tears in their eyes. Lillie is greeted as well by her brother. The two girls hug and agree to meet again in a few days, but for now they are anxious to get home and be with their families. To reunite and celebrate being at this humble place like no other—home.

The first thing Anni does that evening in August, 1944 is stand at the sink, skirted with a makeshift curtain by her mother, and bathe her body, washing away the dirt from months of being at the work farm and walking for nearly seven straight days through the darkest pit of hell. In less than a month's time, the Germans and Nazis will flee the streets like rabbits. In their place, soldiers from the United States Army will stand guard with kindness, affection and genuine concern for these people. They are liberated September 11, 1944. The butterfly has outlasted the Iron Eagle.

# Part III

# She's One in a Million: The War Bride Era

# Margot's Birthday and Three American GIs

Slightly more than five months after Luxembourg had been liberated, it was now being placed back into the hands of its rightful government and the people were being repatriated to their beloved land. One other pleasant surprise had awaited Anni in the month of August, 1944. Her much beloved clown and brother, Albert, had arrived home ahead of her. His circumstances of getting home were not totally unlike her own with its inherent fears, dangers and stress. But for the younger Albert there was one much greater added danger; he had not been released like his younger sister. Instead, the young Albert was facing immediate forced induction into the Wermacht at the front lines, fighting against the massive onslaught that was hammering down the defenses on the Eastern Front. The Russians were coming and defeat was likely, as was death. Both were coming in large quantities. Under those circumstances, Bubby would be a conscript to be used as fodder for the German Army to hide behind as it retreated and tried to regroup and fight back.

Seeing his friends leave at all hours of the day and night, he knew his number was coming soon. However, he had a better answer. It wasn't his war, his fight, and it wasn't his country. He wasn't going to waste his life and he most certainly wasn't going to let someone else sacrifice it for him. That is not the way he was raised. His father taught him to be a man and he wasn't about to let his father down. At approximately three o'clock in the morning, of the first week of August, 1944, he left everything behind. He knew the clothes on his back were his only protection and the lightest assets he could carry. All his belongings meant nothing if he weren't here to use them. He knew he had to travel fast and that meant traveling light. To travel light called for fast feet, quick mind and empty hands. At any given moment he could and would be faced with the necessity to fight for his life.

He slipped out in the blue, dark night and escaped, literally running for his life. He made his way from Northern Germany to home at Esch in a record time. It was a physical feat befitting his family name. His father and all Neumans had much to be proud of. Now, the months had passed with further events of epic proportions. Both Anni and Bubby had reunited and almost immediately fell comfortably back into their close friendship—the lady of the palace being entertained as ever by the court jester.

The two teenage Neuman children were back to their near inseparable status in spite of some new and disturbing circumstances in Anni's eyes. Bubby was now smoking at age fifteen, using language she was not used to and she knew for a fact he was sneaking drinks with the older boys. He was acting like a man while having to be one but his act wasn't as good as his being. He was still a hard worker and with Anni, took up semi-employment at a farm to the west of Esch.

In fact, it was here that the two of them were working one early morning when the sounds of rumbling machines, gurgling rocks under their massive steel bodies, literally shook the ground and the leaves of the trees as they approached. The young Albert's immediate reaction was for Anni to come along and quickly hide their bikes in a ditch. Bubby grabbed grass, and anything he could find to cover the shiny reflections of the bikes. They were in a precarious position but curiosity was stronger than wisdom.

As they lay there in the cold, wet grass, they witnessed a fearsome sight. The Infamous Third Armored Division with its full might and power was displayed for the world to see and be struck with awe. The first vehicle to pass was an open jeep with a mounted machine gun and gunners in the back. The third jeep back was unusually clean and different in style and appearance from all the others. That one had flags flying with stars on it and a stern-faced man riding high in the back seat, raising and lowering himself as he looked back at his army and then ahead, gazing toward the horizon. It was General George S. Patton. The kids had no idea what part of history they were seeing. It wouldn't be the last time Anni saw the man, but on this day, it was a sight that could scare the life from the strongest lion's heart.

These men weren't mean and menacing like the Germans, they carried a different look. They looked sincere. Not sincerely kind. They looked deadly serious and they looked like they were ready to take it all on and take care of business in a judicious, decisive and clear manner. They were a force to be reckoned with and anyone seeing them knew it. What the two teenagers didn't know was that this army was being called from its original intentions to inflict a direct blow to Germany soil proper. They were hailed because of a surprise attack and overwhelming of the 101st Airborne to the north in Bastogne. The German Army, with its panzer divisions, had encircled the elite unit and had a stranglehold on them. These men were on a mission of speed and endurance, needed for all the damage they could inflict. They wouldn't fail that promise; they made it, they meant it and they did it, along with the Fourth Armored Division and other units close to the call.

From the sixteenth day of December, 1944 through the next six weeks, Esch-sur-Alzette went almost entirely underground. It was another onset of dark days in the uncertain times of warfare on their doorstep. The Neuman family took up residence in a bomb shelter or "bunker" built between the standing walls of the house and the street. It was here that for hardest part of the battle of the Bulge, these innocent bystanders took up residence. They would occasionally, at great risk, leave the bunker for fresh water, mild rations and the opportunity to relieve themselves outside the hole in the ground, entombed by concrete. It was a rare opportunity to use toilet facilities outside the bomb shelter. Around the clock, the sounds of planes, huge and heavy metal vehicles pounding the roadways and thunderings from the distant artillery and other implements of mass destruction resounded in the ears of each person in this "hell hole." However, it could be worse; they had certainly been through worse and this was just another stepping stone in survival. Another day of breathing air that was tainted by war and another night left sleepless from the noise, anxiety and fear. They ate when they had to, not when they wanted to.

By January 10, 1945, the Fourth Armoured Division had run to beat the doors down at Bastogne with the Third Army and open the gateway to relieve the entrapped 101st. Of course, in true esprit de corps, the 101st took the lead in the assault on the retreating Wermacht as an anvil of American fortitude and retribution for those who strike the first blow. In contemporary fashion the 101st would lead the way against those who had come so close to executing them from the mortal plane. They may have been hurt and endangered, but they were also aroused to anger and vengeance—a driving force in the American soldier that even the officers find hard to contain when it is aroused from its status as a sleeping giant. Meanwhile, the Fourth was steered unwillingly from the run with the bulls of the 101st due to another "fire-call" back down in the south of Luxembourg. The call was for an upcoming battle thrust into the very heartland of the Third Reich itself, directly on the soil of Germany.

By early February 1945, the "all clear" signal had been given once again to the fragment of remaining citizens. The town was no longer anywhere near its size prior to the war. The Neuman family returned to the humble walls of home, still standing some seven feet distant from the furthest point of the bomb shelter. Again, they had survived intact and remained an indomitable example of family strength weighed against the military might of the world and all countries and forces within. Family stays, family works and family wins.

Nearly two weeks passed since the family was afforded the chance to try again at a sense of normalcy in their lives. Anni had taken up the charge upon herself to take her baby sister, Elfie, outside for a stroll. The two bundled up large and tight against the harsh winter that had set records for its time. Fully packed into her stroller, Elfie sat silently and took in the sights and sounds as her teenage sister pushed the heavy stroller through the snow-brushed sidewalks. It had formed into a weekly routine for which Anni would attempt three to four day-trips. Leaving home for hours, the two would meander down the streets and sidewalks to the house of Anni's cousin, Margot, and her Aunt Sisy (pronounced *zizzy*). Here, Anni was only a short distance from the college where her father had taught sports. The facility had now been turned into a place for quartering of American soldiers on Rest and Recreation (R&R).

On this particular day, February 24, 1945, the most important "accident" of Anni's entire life would take place. On this dreary gray day of winter in the lower parts of Luxembourg, one young teenage girl, nearly eighteen, would meet a man that would change her life eternally. Charlie D. Adams from Brooklyn, New York, aged some eleven years older, would meet the young woman that would become "the" woman of his life. Out of the two, only one knew it and the other couldn't imagine it. Yet, in all the turmoil, heartache, pain, loss of good friends and family members all to war, the two would cover a multitude of sins to see each other through their own eyes and without the judgment or prejudices of an outside world. A war-torn American soldier had met a war-torn Luxembourgish girl. Age made no difference. Their hardships, pain and suffering were a common ground and a building block for the future.

As Anni arrives at her cousin Margot's house pushing the baby stroller, she rings the door bell and is greeted by her smiling Aunt Sisy and her cousin. At that moment, the trail of soldiers passing by on the sidewalk produce three American GIs that immediately take interest in the beautiful Luxembourg ladies. The three of them and their ages aren't of the greatest import. They are beautiful women to men that have been hard at war for months on end. The GIs stop and take notice and even pay compliments. Mostly, courtesy of the babe in the stroller but also to the young ladies and the youthful mother figure standing close by. They were gentlemen in a place where it was least expected. They certainly had an "American Way" about them and it showed in their strong bodies, mild manners and respect for the opposite sex even through all the bawdy days of conversation amongst fellow soldiers. That language was left in the field.

After some mild conversation, it was time for the soldiers to keep moving along their way from the R&R house to the town where they could get in some congac and maybe some music and a dance, if they were lucky. But just as Anni clears the final steps to the door and Margot stands ready to bring in her cousin and mother for a birthday celebration, Sisy turns back to the sidewalk by the street-way. "Hello! GIs, American!" She calls out, getting them to stop in their tracks and look back at the siren sound of a female voice. "You Americans, you want cake and coffee, please?" She calls out in a second. "Come here and have some coffee and cake with us. It is my daughter's birthday and it would be our pleasure to share with you!"

The soldiers look at one another in a brief glance and without a word, start back to the gate to meet the ladies at this most unusual invitation. After all they have been through and seen, this is an invitation of delight in contrast to invitations of the past to hell. The sudden change is heady to say the least, but they regain their composure and start back to the place where Charlie had questioned the motherhood of the minor child in the stroller. As much as Anni had insisted that the baby girl was her sister, the soldiers seemed to feign acceptance, all the while reserving their true belief that Anni was a teenage mother.

By two o'clock in the afternoon, the GIs have found themselves cordially welcomed into the home of a native Luxembourg family. While Margot's father works steadily in the basement with his printing press, his daughter, newly turned fifteen years of age, is upstairs with Mama, cousins and three grown men, all eating birthday cake and drinking the worst of "coffee," chicory coffee. Not the real thing. To Charlie D. Adams, Dick Gordley and Herschel Mays, it is heaven, and they are in no hurry to end the invitation. As the conversation grows lively, Herschel entertains the women with his gift of gab and "Gordley" entertains the baby, Elfie. Meanwhile, the thin-framed and rough-edged Charlie cannot take his eyes off of the young lady with the sparkling eyes, athletic build and innocent demeanor. Anni has stolen Charlie's heart from the first look and she doesn't even know it.

After the birthday party and festivities come to a close, the men say their good-byes and well-wishes. Likewise, the three ladies and a baby see them to the door. On the sidewalk, as the men begin to turn the corner of the building and head back up to the barracks, Charlie looks longingly at Anni once more. "Are you sure that isn't your baby? You two look a lot alike," he states his challenge. "No, she is not my baby, she is my sister, wouldn't that explain why we look alike?" Anni retorts after growing weary of the inquisition and erroneous guesses. "Then would you consider meeting me again sometime soon for a cup of coffee or a walk?" Charlie dares the question. He has a little sweat on his hands even in the cold of the day, and this from a war-worn soldier. "I would have to ask my mother and father. If they say yes then I can come meet you at the school," she states, pointing up the street to the college where her father taught until the American soldiers took over and made it into a barracks. "Ok, just ask for me at the guard's gate, they will know me. My name is Charlie Adams, OK?" "Yes, Charlie Adams, I will ask my parents and if they say yes then I will come to the gate on Saturday, but no promises," she concludes. Charlie smiles with a twinkle in his eye and turns to catch up with Gordley and Hersch.

The following morning at Margot's house, Aunt Sisy opens the door on her way out to the market for the day's shopping. As she pulls the door open, a large bag of oranges drops to the ground from the door handle.

She is completely baffled and befuddled as to where in the world and how, oranges would be here on her doorstep. Margot is seated inside at the table having her breakfast when she sees it. She looks quizzically at her mother and at the oranges. "What a strange thing," she thinks to herself. She cannot figure it out but strange has become normal in these unusual days and times. However, the gifts keep coming. Someone is providing them with oranges and even other surprises over the coming weeks and it will take some investigation to discover who this present is for, and why. At first, they dare not even open nor eat but as no one comes to claim the gift, soon they are enjoying their treat with great relish among the difficult days of rationing. Someone is smiling upon this humble home. It is a blessing to behold and cherish.

On this same Saturday, February 24, 1945, Adolf Hitler addressed his disintegrating empire by radio address in an attempt to bolster resistance and final sacrifice into the fires of raging defeat. Even in sight of overwhelming loss, he continued his absurd and insane rantings of how this "empire" would sustain itself and he would lead it through his own personal sacrifices. Throughout his discourse, he raved about the past victories of Germany and hurled insults at the Allies and Jews. All the while, he continued to express, with numerous references, a providential destiny and the Creator's favorable design for his empire. It was a sickening broadcast—an attempt by the most vile of human blackhearts to declare his evil works as divine in nature and attempt to deceive his own countrymen that God was on his side. In his final words practically begging each man, woman and child to die for his cause, he feigned his own sad song of pain in an attempt to manipulate innocent Germans to die an unnecessary death. Calling for sacrifice of sons and daughters, blood of all for his last-ditch hope of self-attainment and deliverance. His final words: "Twenty-five years ago I predicted the victory of our movement. Today, filled as always with belief in our nation, I predict the final victory of the German race." In the end, he didn't die with a gun in his hand facing his enemies such as he demanded little children to do; instead, he shamefully and selfishly took the gun to his own poisoned mind and head. He couldn't find the backbone to face a single enemy even though he had urged and encouraged hundreds of thousands of innocent and deceived people to do so on his on behalf. They believed in him, he believed in himself, but deception had run its course and the course led to the truth. There is a right and a wrong. No gray. No maybes. He was evil and he died for it. Good and right had prevailed in a wholly unnecessary bloodbath. All because of one man's greed, avarice and lustful desire for power.

# Who Is Charlie?

With snow still faintly on the ground, spring is still weeks away. The American soldiers, having defied death and presently not being shot at, are suffering their own version of an early "spring fever." The citizens of Esch-sur-Alzette suffer their own version of euphoria from having so many men in town to barter, sell and trade with; to communicate with kind people and to be out from under the iron fist of the Nazis. It is a concoction of joy, rampant emotions and celebration throughout the cities and in the homes where some, by God's grace, have survived and have already fixed their hearts and minds on the future. Of course, in the Neuman home some questions are being asked.

"Mama?" Anni begins gently in her conversation with her mother at the kitchen sink. The family having just completed dinner and the two women cleaning the dishes, Anni feels this is as good a time as any to make her case for a social life. "Yes, what is it, Anni?" Mama replies. Papa has gone to his chair and is out of earshot of the conversation. There he readies his pipe and fades off in thoughts of his own. The boys have gone their own directions and Elfie is already busying herself on the floor looking for things to pull down and put in her mouth.

"Mama, I met a man today and he asked me if I would go with him for a cup of coffee or for a walk. I would like to go, if it is okay with you and Papa." She steels herself for the worst. There is a long silence and then Mama begins what will become a secretive and lengthy conversation over the sink. "Where did you meet this man? Is he Luxembourger? How old is he?" She starts in with the first battery of questions. Anni is almost reeling with thoughts of where to begin. "His name is Charlie," is all she can reply. "Who is Charlie?" Mama raises her voice, still in a whisper from Papa's ears. "I met him today at Aunt Sisy's house. She invited them in for Margot's birthday cake. He seems like a very nice man and he is very respectful. He is an American. I don't know how old he is, though." She finalizes the answer, hoping to daunt the age problem that is certain to come. Although she doesn't know how old Charlie is, she does know he is an older man and this is going to be a tough challenge to overcome from the start.

"I think this is something we should take our time on, Anni," Mama replies as they continue to dry the now cleaned dishes and close out the chore. "How about we just keep this between you and me for now and we will go over to your Aunt Sisy's house tomorrow for a visit," Mama says with a smile and a nod toward an unaware Papa. Anni smiles back at Mama with gratitude written all over her face, just knowing that she has made it this far. It is the end of the evening and time for bed. Once again, as she has done so many times, Anni goes upstairs to the room where she and brother Albert share their last moments of the day.

"Anni, tomorrow night I want to go out with some of the boys. Will you cover for me with Mama and Papa?" Bubby asks with a mischievous grin on his face. "Bubby, you know you shouldn't be sneaking out after dark. Just because things have gotten better doesn't mean it is safe outside. You know the curfew is still in force with the Americans, too!" She chastens him, but all the while she is already nodding in agreement to keep his secret. After all, what good would it do to say no, he would do it anyway. There is no way to hold back this young buck. He is ready, willing and able to run through the night. She is afraid for him and worries, but she has a sense in her gut that he is unbreakable and uniquely supreme. Anni loves him for his friendship, admires his adventurous spirit and even envies his manhood and that men can do so much more without a guilty conscience. She also knows that he will be safe because that is just the way it is with this family.

"Bubby, I met a American soldier today at Margot's. I had seen him before, about a month ago, but we met today. He and his friends came inside for birthday cake. I think he likes me." She divulges her secret to her brother now that she has his confidence as well. "What's his name?" Albert asks. "His name is Charles, but they call him Cday or Charlie," She answers. "Charlie? Who is Charlie?" Bubby retorts with a squinted and quizzical look. "I just told you, he is an American GI. He is much older than me but he is very nice and polite." She closes as if she were finishing an argument. "Well, sis, good luck! Just don't let him kiss you or I will have to come over and knock his teeth out!" young Albert says with a laugh. Anni, knows he is only jesting but she wouldn't put anything past her brother. He does brood over her at times.

The next morning after church services, Mama and Anni stroll out onto the portico of the church and pause at the top of the stairs. "Anni, I want you to go down to Marie's and get some coffee for Papa. Tell her I will be by in the morning to pay for it, OK?" She descends the steps to cross the street to home and dinner preparation. "Yes, Mama," Anni replies and steps away off to her left and down the sidewalk to the end of the block where the store takes up the larger share of the corner. The door of the store faces the street they live on and she can see either one, less than seventy meters apart. At the T-neck of the street, the train tracks loom overhead where she and Bubby have seen so much sickness. She casts aside the thoughts and spins inside the door of the small market. "Hi Marie!" she says, smiling. "Well hello, Anni, aren't you light on your feet this morning. Did you have a good service?" Marie queries. "Yeah, it was alright. I need to get a bag of coffee for Papa. Mama says she will bring you the money in the morning, OK?" Anni starts right in as if ready to turn and go. "Hey, what's your hurry?" Marie asks. "Oh, nothing," Anni replies. "I just feel hungry and want to get home." She tries to be polite. "I don't know…there is something different about you." Marie looks over Anni and into her eyes. "You have a funny look." "What funny look? No I don't!" Anni retorts. "Yes, it is there, what is it, what is new with you?" Marie asks teasingly. "Not much, I did meet an American GI at Margot's in case you didn't already know. It was just yesterday!" Anni states, exasperated. "Oh, now I see!" Marie smiles as if she knew the secret all along. It was just that hunch women get and it was accurate again.

"So, what are you up to?" Marie pries again. "His name is Charlie but they call him Cday and that is all I know, OK?" Anni says, blushing and a bit frustrated. "Oh my, aren't we a little tender to touch, little girl?" Marie teases even more. "And just who is Charlie?" she finishes her taunt. "I told you. He is an American GI and that is all I know. He is a nice man and Aunt Sisy and Margot had a good day." She is near tears now from being put on the spot about such things. "Well, you tell this Mr. Charlie to be nice and I will see him soon, I am sure. Here's the coffee and give my best to your mother and father." Marie smiles as she releases Anni from her chains of conversation.

On her way home, Anni makes up her mind. She is not going to talk about this anymore. "So, the guy might like me. So, he is nice and kind of good looking. So, we might talk again. So, what?" she says to herself. "I am not going to answer anymore. It is as though people think I fell off a truck and keep telling me I 'have an accent.' They can keep their questions to themselves." She closes her self-educating conversation and goes into the house with her task complete. "Gee!" she says to herself. "Who IS Charlie! I don't even know, so everyone, stop asking! Really, 'who is Charlie?' I wish I didn't know his name," and with that she closes the argument in her head but her mind is still working.

The following morning, as Anni is getting up from sleeping in after Bubby's late arrival, Mama comes back from the store having paid for yesterday's coffee. "Anni, let's go for a walk up the street to Sisy's, I want to know who this 'Charlie' is," she states. Anni changes into her dress and puts on her shoes. As the two of them walk up the street, Mama starts to ask more questions about how her daughter met this man and what Anni is thinking. The questions go on for the entire walk until they arrive at the doorstep of Aunt Sisy's apartment. They hardly knock before they are welcomed inside. On the table can clearly be seen a large bag of oranges. "Where did you get those, Sisy?" Anni's mother asks. "Well, I can't actually say I got them, it is more like they were given to me," she replies. "It is a very strange thing. I opened the door not too long ago and there they were, on my doorstep. That's why when you knocked on the door, I answered so quickly, I thought maybe someone had made a mistake and came back to get them," she continues. "I think it has something to do with the Americans.

"The Americans?" Mama starts. "Hum, that is what I came here to talk about. Anni tells me she met a very nice gentleman here yesterday." She finishes with a slight smile on her face. "Yes, it was Margot's birthday so I thought it would nice to share with the men. They all seem so lonely at times and it is better than them hanging around town. Plus, I thought it would be good company and educational for the girls." She finishes with her own reassuring smile. "Well, if you approve, then I guess it is okay. What harm can come of it? Just so long as they are here in the house. Do you think they are coming back?" Mama asks. "Well, by the looks of things," Sisy says, pointing to the oranges on the table, "I would say someone made a good impression and I do believe that some interest has been struck in the heart of one particular gentleman about your lovely daughter." They both smile and look at Anni. "Well, she is getting to be a real head-turner and a good young lady, isn't she?" Mama asks Sisy. "Indeed, I think so Marg, I think so." Again they both smile.

The conversation continues and the visit is well spent. Eventually, both Mama and Anni return home by the same path. However, while the path is the same, things and the times aren't. Mama has a lot on her mind, as does Anni, and the walk homeward is much more quiet than the walk up. "Who is Charlie?" Mama ponders to herself in her thoughts. "Who is Charlie?"

# Charles Adams and the "Breakthrough Fourth"

Charlie, what a name. It seems so unfair. There are so many "Charlies" and we know them from books, films, etc.; we read about them, hear about them and even know some. But this was Charles Donnell Adams, a blue-eyed baby born March 5, 1915 in the depths of the city of New York. This was a different Charlie. This was "CDA" (pronounced see day) as they called him, and of course the amenable moniker "Charlie." This was a man who grew through some twenty-nine years of life to reach the close-knit town of Esch-sur-Alzette in a small European country, Luxembourg, with all its richness of history and culture. Here, on February 24,1945, Charlie met Anni Neuman. He had not arrived there instantly nor easily. His journey had been one literally wrought with experiences that Dante couldn't paint and Hemingway couldn't describe. Spielberg has finally made some inroads to the visionary picture of it all. Charlie had traveled from the beaches of Normandy and managed to live long enough, while literally hundreds of thousands of fellow soldiers fought, died or were wounded in the push through France, through Luxembourg, through the Ardennes to the Battle of the Bulge at Bastogne, the Rhine, Germany, Czechoslovakia to fall back to rest in the arms of a quaint city of wonderful, grateful Luxembourgers amid the beauty of the landscape and, of course, one particular lovely young lady in Esch.

"Dear God, what in all of hell am I doing here!" were Charlie's first words as he stepped into nearly three feet of briny water from the ramp of the landing craft. His pants soaked and his rifle held shoulder high, he strode through the water as quickly as he could and ran out of breath long before the halfway mark. The Fourth Armored Division arrived at the beachhead in Normandy on D-day plus 36. The beach was secured but constantly under haunting attack by air assaults and sometimes sniper fire. The water blipped occasionally around him in reassurance that the German Army was still at war with the United States and he was here as a personal representative of the combat forces of his country. He was one man, unique in his own way, but he was among thousands of brothers-in-arms.

Tech. Sgt. Charlie Donnell Adams (the Donnell being his mother's maiden name) was to lead his Headquarters squad out of harm's way and into the sandy trenches and bulwarks that had been established by the blood of men over the days before him. Even as they waded through the water with all the strength their legs could muster, they felt like soccer players in four feet of mud. With one major difference. When a watercraft moved from the sea to the beach, it got special attention from the air. The German Luftwaffe, under the command of Hermann Göring, was still strafing and raining machine-gun fire on everything that wasn't water. They were assaulted and deafened by the roar of the aircraft in combat above and the ground artillery firing antiaircraft rounds skyward, delicately attempting to avoid hitting their own Allied air cover who were heavily mixed in combat on the wind above the sea and sand.

This was some sight to a Brooklyn boy, now a man, previously a court reporter from New York. From the very beginning of this July 11, 1944 morning, it was clear that this was not going to anything like the training they had done back at Pine Hill, New York two years prior. For Charlie and his Headquarters Company and the entire Fourth Armored Division, the waiting was finally over. They had waited impatiently back in Britain to get across the water and join the foray into what they firmly believed would be the "end-all" to the war. They had waited countless boring hours and days for an invitation to the "dance." The invitation finally came and they accepted wholeheartedly. The welcome they received upon arrival made them wonder if they should have been so hasty in their acceptance. But they were well-equipped, well-trained and very much ready to get it going. The sooner the better, and maybe they could help bring this whole force of American war power to destroy Hitler once and for all.

It was a noble idea, but it was not without enormous price in pain, suffering, hatred, anger, bitterness, death and fear. Sweating in summer and freezing in the winter to come. It was not going to be a "dance" unless you enjoy dancing in the devil's parlor. It was war, combat, blood, horror and terror unspeakable and sights indescribable. No matter how gifted the writer, no one can put it in perspective—perhaps if they have seen it with their own eyes, but even that is doubtful. It isn't something anyone should truly desire to see. Many men in this war of wars, and those before and after, returned home with silent lips, never to discuss what their eyes had seen, what their hearts had felt, what their mind had done and the dreams that reminded them of their witness to such unbelievable horror and disaster.

Charlie and "company" didn't get to enjoy the "beach life" for very long and that was fine with them. The "beach life" consisted of seeing what was coming back from what lay ahead. It was gruesome. Bodies beaten, broken, shot apart, torn, bleeding, screaming, burnt and missing body parts. Charlie was amazed they could still actually be living. Orders to move came quickly and it was time for the Fourth Armored Division to relieve some of the battered warriors up the road and continue on a path that would run on for the next ten months. Of course each minute seemed to take a day off their lives as they made the treacherous journey. They had landed at Omaha and Utah Beach on July 13, 1944, and within four days were already getting their first look at dead German soldiers and coming under sniper fire. Casualties were light and sporadic but the future didn't look bright.

By July 30, Operation Cobra was fully underway. The Fourth had met their first major encounter with the enemy at Avranches, France. It was their first initiation into full-blown fighting and harrowing combat. The city would eventually be taken with costs, and within four more days the Fourth would repeat the same combat situation in Rennes. By August 6, they battled hard at Lorient; August 16-21, they made Orleans and there again hell was welcoming with open arms. By this time they had seen so much death, blood and bloated animals, it was almost difficult to get sick anymore. It had become a common feeling to be inside a top-rated horror movie, but it wasn't fake, it was real life and life was precious until you made up your mind you were already dead. That was when one could function as a soldier and probably at least half the Fourth made their mind up that would be the case. Because of that, they were able to function beyond better, they functioned as the best fighting unit they could be.

They fought through Troyes by August 29, and then clashed into the worst of it all since Normandy on September 13 as they rolled into the boiling pot of their worst fighting to date. From that day until December 8, they battled with guts and grit at places all around the east and south of Metz. Fresnes, Bayen, Arracourt Luneville, Fenetrange, Rohrbach—and the list goes on. With a lull in the battle, they moved forward north to an already liberated southern part of Luxembourg. On the way, the call came. On December 19, the 101st Airborne had become surrounded at Bastogne. The Fourth moved quickly to aid and deliver. They punched through with iron fists into the panzers and the rest of the German Army. For the Fourth, the battle for the Bulge lasted from December 20 through January 11, 1945. For twenty-two days they fought, froze, pushed, battled, and were wounded. Some died, and others survived the bloodiest conflict of their journey. The disposition of units was finally made in the south of Luxembourg, mostly Esch-sur-Alzette, where Charlie met Anni from January 12-30, 1945 (for the first time). They moved on to Koblenz, Germany, then south to cross the famous Rhine River at Oppenheim on March 24. The "Breakthrough Fourth" had fast become the "Breakout Fourth" because of their speed and conquests. They were relentless in pounding down the roadblocks, war machines from the air and ground and all that the Wermacht could thrust at them in trying to keep them at bay. It was futile. The Fourth would not stop and it did not stop. It rolled on.

By March 27, 1945, the Fourth had made Frankfurt, Germany, the very heart of Deutschland. By May 6 they had battled their way into Czechoslovakia and it was there that Charlie saw firsthand the lengths of brutality and evil to which the Third Reich was willing to go. The day before, the Germany Army had officially surrendered but it was still killing men, women and children by the thousands. Not necessarily by gunshots anymore, but their own previous acts were still taking a toll in all forms of starvation and disease from brutality and cruelty. With their own eyes, Charlie included, the Fourth became witnesses at Ohrdruf, Czechoslovakia at the North Stalag III, a Jewish concentration camp. No words will ever complete the picture.

In the end, the Fourth Armored Division had lost 1,519 soldiers and brothers-in-arms. They had taken over 90,000 prisoners, killed more than 13,000 enemies and wounded at least 30,000. They had captured hundreds of tanks, more than thirty-six hundred vehicles, more than a thousand horse-drawn wagons, over a hundred locomotives and had shot down one hundred twenty-eight enemy planes. In the end, Charles D. Adams was one of thousands to receive honor and medals for their sacrifice. Charlie received a total of five Bronze Stars. He fought for his country and by God's grace, he lived to go home. He talked of it very little, if ever, and then only with those men that had been with him or in units like his. Those that knew war up front and personal the way he did would carry on that conversation with him. It wasn't out of spite, bitterness or hatred, but out of respect for those that came back with less of a body or mind than when they left. Those that came back to face losses at home and broken hearts. Those that never came back or came back only to be buried. It was conversation saved out of respect and honor for the fighting men, the warriors and even the women of World War II.

# Translation Dictionary Dating Game

*By March 1945 the winds and tides of war were moving in one direction. A piercing sword of deliverance was being thrust into the heart of Nazism, Fascism and the maniacal empire of the rising sun. The sun was no longer rising, but in every direction, on every sea and on every field, justice was turning good against evil and the battles still being fought were bringing a victory to the entire world at war. Germany was losing its grip and reeling in near total ruin. Italy, France and Belgium had fallen free into the hands of liberators and the rightful heirs of inheritance, the people and general populace of the lands. Finland joined the fight and declared war on Germany, while Germany embattled itself against Hungary for retreat grounds. The Allies finished the month having taken Cologne and Burma while the Soviets seized Danzig. The final assault for the remaining north of Italy was in place, ready to finish the job in a month. Spring was not just the season but it was the action word and work of Allied forces pouncing upon their prey, annihilating their power, strength and strongholds.*

"Launifch!" Charlie says as he looks up from the thick reddish-brown dictionary lying in his hands. He looks at Aunt Sisy and then back at Anni. "Moody! You sure are a moody little girl!" he spouts out again, grinning from ear to ear, suppressing his frustration. Aunt Sisy laughs and Anni pouts. "Not!" she says in the only answer she can give in English on such short notice. "Yes, you are!" Charlie retorts, now more than ever enjoying his teasing and watching the brown-eyed beauty in front of him get fiery mad. He is only joking with her, enjoying immensely the fact that he has been provocative as a test to see her in such a mood and successfully so. She is beautiful even when she is angry. Charlie takes great delight in capturing the butterfly that floats through his thoughts, brushing her wings and tickling his heart. She has captured him and he is completely "love-blind" to the reality of the whole situation. It is a great comedy being played out such as is common to all mankind from the very beginning and Charlie, wise as he is, is the "caught" not the "catcher." Charlie shakes his head and the memory is there but his body is somewhere inside the battle lines of Germany.

The weather is getting warmer and so are the conversations between Anni and Charlie. After their meeting on Margot's birthday, the two don't get to see each other much again because Charlie has to move forward with the Fourth Armored into German territory. He finds himself overwhelmingly raptured by this young, brown-haired, brown-eyed girl in Esch, all the while, leaving for weeks at a time to face almost certain death in a war that continues outside his paradoxical thoughts. He daydreams and night-dreams of the lovely creature and yet he hears explosions day and night from the sky above and all the earth around. Sometimes he doesn't even remember which place he is in. He faces times of staggering exhaustion, but at the moment of awakening, he is walking beside the love of his life, again.

From times of actually sitting at the table in Margot's house to walking the streets of Esch, Charlie gets short respite. He is more often riding in a truck or jeep to a new location where headquarters will be set up and the tents will be raised for the night and sometimes a couple of days. They stay on the move as the battles push and pull his unit in all directions. He is now up to his fourth Bronze Star, a seasoned combat veteran, with a living memory of death, disease, wounds, blood and horror indescribable. He has seen bodies from both sides of the battle, some living and some dead. He has seen the burned, bullet-ridden, broken and blasted. It is a menagerie of hell and yet he always finds his mind wandering now in a fog to a bright day in Esch beside his beautiful Brown-Eyes. More than ever, he is determined to survive, because she is his victory prize, not the war. Even if he has to win it by himself, consider it done. Charles D. Adams of Brooklyn, New York has a war prize on his mind and a war bride is what he wants to win.

The whole thing is about as bizarre as it gets for war time and soldiers in the midst of it. But it isn't a first for a soldier, only a first for Charlie. And it is a last, so long as God gives him breath and will to live and make another day. He has reached the respectable rank of Tech

Sergeant, E-6, and it comes with some privileges from working directly under Lt. Colonel George L. Eatman, Division Finance Officer, who controls the payroll of an entire division. Charlie is given some leeway when a lull falls upon the fierce fighting and in a blink of an eye, he will hop a jeep, truck or ambulance to race back to Esch for even so little as one day to see Anni. It restores his soul, fills his "tank" of memories and keeps him alive.

As he walks the streets, through leveled buildings and rubble on each side, he hears the snipers firing metal slugs of destruction. Rounds are often heard whirring by and then the rattles of machine gun fire, accompanied by grenades, keeping clear the path they take on these days. He walks among the conquering mighty Fourth Armored as it takes back Germany from the hands of the Nazis. His mind wanders again and back he goes to just a short three days past when he and his Brown-Eyes were walking along the street near curfew time in Esch.

The two of them had taken a change of pace and the beginning was an uncomfortable one. Charlie had arrived late in the night and left word at Aunt Sisy's that he would be up at the barracks and to please have Margot stop by the Neuman's home on her way to school. He had asked that Margot catch Anni before she headed off to school in Luxembourg City and ask her to please come to the barracks and wake him so they could spend the one day together. Charlie retired to the barracks for what few hours of dark morning was left and fell asleep sitting up in a corner with a blanket near the barracks doors.

By 7:30 A.M. Margot has accomplished her mission and given Anni her message as she stands sleepy-eyed at the door. They both smile and go their own way. Anni quickly dresses and heads for the barracks up the street, past Aunt Sisy's apartment. She comes to the gate where two American GIs stand guard.

"Well, aren't you the one," one of the men says to Anni as she approaches. "Are you here to see me? I'll be off guard in another hour, I'm tired but I've got time to chat with a pretty thing like you!" he boldly crows as if he might have a chance and risk is all he is used to anyhow.

"I see Charlie?" Anni says with the little English she is learning from her dictionary. The book is thick and the size of a hymn book. "Charlie? Who is Charlie?" the other guard says with a big grin on his face. The poor girl has her hands full but she has been through her own war just as they have and she is every bit as tough. "Charlie Adams!" she states firmly, looking at them as if they were already in trouble.

"Charlie? Oh, CDA. Not him," says one guard. "You don't want him. He is a gambler." "What is a gambler?" Anni asks with a quizzical look. "A gambler!" The other guard reaches into his pocket to pull out a deck of cards. He takes the cards and shuffles them once in his hands and pretends to deal. Then he reaches into his pocket as if to pull out cash. He then puts the cards back in his pocket and pretends to deal out the money, scoops away the invisible pile and claps his hands clean as if to say, "All gone." Anni gets the message. "I see Charlie," she demands. She doesn't care what these men say. She knows a person the minute she sees them inside and out. Charlie isn't a bad guy.

After a little more hassle, Charlie is produced at the gate and the two of them begin their walk to Aunt Sisy's with the English/German translation dictionary in hand. Actually, it goes back and forth as the two say their greetings and begin their language course for the day. They arrive at Aunt Sisy's (the official meeting place for dating now), and have a light breakfast. Aunt Sisy enjoys the company as her husband is already working the press below and Margot is off to school. She keeps her distance and helps with the language barrier as the need arises, and it often does.

For hours, Anni and Charlie sit at the table and use the dictionary back and forth to catch up on each others' lives since the last meeting. It is slow, rigorous work but they both love it and the educational experience it brings. Before long, the time has crept away and they both find themselves startled as Margot comes home from school for lunch, the biggest meal of the day in Luxembourg. Together, the whole family and guest have a hearty meal and the girls clear the table as Charlie looks, wounded that his help was refused. He likes it that these women are so traditional, but it is humbling to sit idle when he is the strongest of the group.

"Charlie, Anni!" Aunt Sisy says to the two now seated in the parlor, "go, go for a walk. Go to the park. I need to do things around here and we will have dinner at five o'clock, now go!" She shoos them out the door and away. They must take their dating game elsewhere and so they do. For several hours the two walk along the streets of Esch. They pause in the park for rest and continue their ongoing effort to search one another's heart and draw close in a bond of affection. Charlie is becoming very special to Anni and she knows, as well as Charlie, that he has set his mark on her and she has hung the moon for him.

As the dinner hour soon approaches, the two have walked and talked themselves back into an appetite and head for Aunt Sisy's. They arrive just in time. Unfortunately, both of them know that this will be a short dinner because of the curfew and because Charlie will be leaving again in the morning. The food is hardly set upon the table before all are busying themselves and conversation lags as they eat quickly so the two "lovebirds" can walk Charlie back to the barracks.

Twilight has descended upon the streets and city outside the doors of the apartment. Anni and Charlie say their good-byes to the family at the door and cross the street headed north to the barracks. In times past, and even this morning, the two have always used the sidewalk closest to the door of Aunt Sisy's apartment. But this time, they mindlessly cross the street and head up the slow incline that will take them to the front gate of the barracks.

"Secret!" Charlie states again. "I have a secret, but I don't want to tell you, yet, OK?" he finishes. "Secret?" Anni states. "What is 'secret'?" she inquires as to the strange sounding word. "Here, let me show you," Charlie says as he reaches for the dictionary in Anni's hands. "Let me see…" Charlie holds the left side of the book and Anni holds the right. They both walk along oblivious to their surroundings with their eyes glued to the book and their shoulders sweetly and innocently close. They both feel the elation of being so close and not guilty for having such a good reason.

Suddenly, without warning, all goes horribly black. Sick to their stomachs, they free-fall from the safety and security of their sidewalk path. Completely in another world, they have walked directly into a construction site and fallen into a manhole over seven feet deep. Charlie's uniform is sullied, as is his pride, and Anni is a little skinned at the elbows but neither is much worse for wear. They don't know whether to laugh or cry. They look about strangely at one another, the wet, damp walls of the tight quarters and both reach down for the dictionary.

"Are you alright down there?" comes a voice from a few feet above their heads. "Yes, I think so," Anni replies in her native tongue of *Lëtzebuergesch* to the man at the rim of the opening. "Hold on, I will get a ladder and get you out," he instructs. The two look at each other and laugh, but it is only funny down here. When they climb the ladder and reach the top, they are exposed in all their foolishness and embarrassment to a small gathering of laughing Luxembourgers. It was a funny sight and they know it, but they both are red-faced with the humiliation of being caught in-love and careless. They brush themselves off as best they can, and with short thank-you's, shuffle at a quick pace away, with Charlie gently steadying Anni by her arm.

Charlie, once again, leaves his Brown-Eyes and under the most bruising of circumstances to his ego. The poor child of eighteen years old must walk home alone along the same route. By tomorrow he will be gone and it will seem as if all of Esch has heard the story. Anni will be looking forward to taking the train first thing in the morning to Luxembourg City for school and won't be in a hurry to get home. Let it fall to time.

# The Aftermath of War, Courage and a Proposal

*"Mom, when will they let Papa come back home?" Anni asks Mama. "I don't know Anni, we just have to keep praying. We know that he didn't do anything wrong. He will be all right. God knows he saved us and he didn't do anything wrong. He will be home soon. They just have to do this because it is a part of the way some things go after a war. We will all be together again," Mama reassures Anni. Young Anni is no longer a child. She never really was, but now she has grown even further than that. She has done everything Papa taught her and gone in every direction his finger has pointed. He is the grand architect of the Butterfly of Luxembourg but no one will know it for nearly eighty years.*

*He has no tobacco, no pipe nor rest in his soul. He coughs and looks at the concrete floor beneath his feet. He holds his head low and then lifts it high to stretch his neck. He sits on the edge of his bunk and thinks of his family. He has no watch, he doesn't know what time it is and he is all too aware of what day it is. The day is too long. Whatever day they put it on the calendar, it is too long. Minutes, hours, days— they go by like watching a worm work its way through sand. It is too frustrating to consider. For fifteen minutes you can stare at your boots and study your shoelaces. For ten minutes you can try to recall the names of your great-grandmother and grandfather. For an hour you can remember the day at the soccer field and the training session when the forward wouldn't do his job and the halfbacks were too weak to compete against the French team. Hunger comes growling into his belly. As taut and trim as it is, it gurgles with an undeniable request. He can't answer. He wishes he could. He wants to, but, it isn't his decision. He will get something when someone in control says so; they make the rules and then change them for their own convenience.*

*It was only four days ago that the senior Albert had sat in his chair, pipe propped up to the corner of his mouth as he discussed with his oldest son what the future might hold for them as individuals and as a family. The conversation had come upon the disclosure of the younger Albert that there was an offer to join the circus. A real, honest- to-god circus, where he could perform as a gymnast and make his father proud. He could also make money and send it home to help in these difficult days of recovery. The conversation between a father and son, man and man-to-be, ended in a growing bond and newness of understanding. Papa was watching his first boy make his first manly decisions and he agreed. "It will do you good and keep you from trouble. Go, don't be a fool. Watch your pocket, your time and your friends, son. Come home as often as you can and Mama will have something for you to eat." Something to eat. The words ring in his head as his stomach reminds him about the need to eat. The desire isn't pleasing.*

On a late evening in March, Anni arrives home at the Neuman residence after her usual day at school in Luxembourg City and the train ride home. Immediately, she feels a chill run over shoulders and down her spine as she turns the handle to enter the house. Inside, there is weeping and a deafening silence rolling around like a fog beside it. Anni sees Papa's chair and the table next to it and knows in an instant something very, very wrong is happening. She sees the watch Papa always carries and then the pipe beside it. Two things that would never leave the man's body except in his sleep. She is petrified. She turns to the table where Mama is seated with her head in her hands and bowed low to the table in a shaking heap. Marie, from upstairs, sits holding her in her arms trying to rock her and whisper away the pain and anguish.

"Mama!" Anni cries aloud. "Where is Papa? Is he okay? What happened? Is he alive? Mama, where is he?" She fires off the questions as fast as her mind and thoughts are churning. Marie looks up with tears of her own, directly into Anni's eyes with a piercing look of pain and sympathy. "Anni, they have come and taken your father away. They are taking him to a camp with others from here, from the big city and from other places. It is the resistance force, mostly. They have even taken young teenagers. They are acting rashly and it will have to come under control. You know how things are right now. People just get paranoid. Too much suspicion or rumors have taken a toll." She looks back down at the weeping, distraught woman in her arms. "I sent for Elise and Josephine. Maybe they can come and help with little Charlie and Elfie while your mother and I get more information. Right now, there are just a lot of accusations going on and people are being taken for questioning. They mean the best for us, I am sure, but they still feel they have to know who was with the Nazis and who was against them. It is terrible, I know, but your mother needs you to be strong right now." She continues her calming words of glue, trying to hold the situation together.

Anni's head is reeling from the information that is coming at her in light-speed slices. It is too much, far too much, to comprehend. After all they have been through. After all the upheaval, the evacuation, the miserable existence displaced from home, the past four years of fear and tortuous living conditions. The bombings, the battles as recently as Christmas up in Bastogne. The work camp, not knowing where the younger Albert was, his return, hiding in a bomb shelter for a month. Just now, when something called "life"seemed to be knocking at the door, terror has taken its place. "When will it ever end!" she shouts out loud, not even noticing that the words were screamed from her mind to her mouth. "Why Papa! Why take Papa? He hasn't done anything wrong! They can't do this, not now, it isn't right. We have to get him back!" She is crying and shaking uncontrollably and Chuck, with Elfie standing beside him, comes out from hiding to witness it all. They too are shaken, scared and near tears. It seems to Anni that her joyful life as the colorful butterfly girl is being cursed for daring to laugh and dance where devils sneak, creep and crawl. She only wanted to know the joy of life and look at it with the attitude and training that her father gave her through proverbs. Now, it all seems too black for outside and the cocoon is the only safe place. Its walls are evermore strengthening and thickening due to this latest disaster.

Over the next few weeks, Mama tries her best to make the family as close to "one" as she possibly can. Daily she shows strength of character and refuses to shed a tear in the presence of her children. For Anni and Mama alike, the hour of darkness when prayers are said before sleep, that is when the tears come and with them, anger, hurt and longing. By mid-April, the younger Albert, Bubby, is making trips home from the circus at least once or twice, sometimes three times a week. Each time he brings money for Mama, chocolate or other treats for Anni, the little Charlie (now called Chuck) and for Elfie. He also brings home unannounced guests of the opposite sex, much to Mama's concern. Nevertheless, at least he does bring the young ladies to meet his family; however, the concern is that he almost never brings the same one. He is becoming far more than just a clown, accomplished musician and gymnast. He is clearly displaying his fondness for tomfoolery.

"Mama," Bubby starts in as he introduces yet another young lady to the matriarch of the family, "The circus is making camp and performing just a mile or so from here. We will be there for the whole week. It is also not far from Papa's camp. I checked and they will let you bring food and see him." He smiles. The delight on Mama's face is more radiant than the sun's reflection on a silver cloud. "When can we see him?" she asks. "Today is Tuesday, so I would think that you could go Friday, Saturday and Sunday," he continues. "They are being more understanding now and feel safe with families visiting. I believe it will get better soon." The news is good and brings great joy to the entire house. They may not have Papa sitting in his chair yet, but they will see him soon and that is all that matters.

"Gredy, Charlie, Anni, Albert and my little Elfie!" Papa exclaims from his side of the fence, hands clasped against the loops of metal. It is clear that even though he has been lacking in good nutrition, he has maintained his muscular form and physique. He is not one to let anything interfere with the performance of the body he treats like a machine. Always fine-tuning, honing, changing and improving performance. It is a lifecycle that has always been and he will carry it with him all of his days. Physical fitness is the blood in his veins and the storm of thoughts in his mind. "How is everyone?" he calls out as they approach. "Anni, how is school? Little Charlie, you're getting bigger by the day. Elfie, my pet." He continues to show his family that his will is just as strong as his body and that he is not going to permit them to hang their heads or act with shame. Inside, his gut is making him sick and his eyes want to water, but that will wait for later. Now, his family must see that he is okay and that they needn't worry. He is still every bit a man as he has always been, and will provide for his family even from here. Even if the only provisions he can give for now are encouragement and hope. That, in itself, is strong food.

The family is permitted to visit but it must be through the fence. No one is allowed inside or out. However, the food and small items that are permitted can be, and are, exchanged through the fence or through the guards. Papa has a bag full of things that will cheer him and sustain his will. More than anything, seeing his family still together is the best of all sustenance to his soul.

"Bubby, how is the circus life? You are working more than chasing women I hope?" He sort of chuckles. He knows his son well. In fact, he knows each and every one of his family almost better than they know themselves. His wisdom is unique and his plain manner disguises it well. The family will have their visit and there will be more to come, but in a few more weeks the circus will be gone and so will Papa. He is moved away from the camp to the city and placed in a facility to await trial. His charge is conspiring with the Nazis. It won't be long before the news gets back to Mama, Anni and the rest of the family.

Now the second week of May, Charlie has been gone for more than three weeks and Anni receives only a fistful of letters. The man is a soldier, and he is still in the thick of some fighting somewhere in Germany or Czechoslovakia. No one knows but Charlie and the men serving with him. To the rest of the civilian world, the war is considered all but won, yet soldiers from all of the Allied forces are still taking casualties and men are still dying every day. However, on this one particular bright day in May, a surprise comes to the school where Anni is studying in Luxembourg City. "Charlie! What are you doing here!" she exclaims as she sees him just outside the doors of the building. "You look dirty!" she says laughingly. "Well, that is because I had to crawl all the way here to see you, Brown-Eyes!" he taunts back with a big grin. Now she feels a little low because she knows that this man's love for her is strong enough that he probably would do such a thing, and his being dirty is from doing some very dirty and dangerous work. She is glad to see him and yet she still is afraid to untie her feelings for fear of the worst. She cannot let herself truly love him with all of her being the way it should be because of the constant apprehension that any day he could be gone, she could be gone or more war changes could happen. She won't even let herself believe that the Germans are never coming back to rule. No matter what Charlie, Mama or the newspapers say.

Charlie and Anni catch the train to Esch and as they ride along it is clear that other Luxembourg ladies her age on the train want to gossip. Some are jealous of her because she is with an American GI and they sit alone. Others look at her with contempt as if she is less than a lady for being with a soldier so blatantly in public. It isn't worth concern to Anni. Let them think what they want. "People are always going to do that," she tells herself.

"Charlie, they have taken Papa to a jail back in the city. His trial starts in two days. I will miss school and go to the trial so if you want to stay in Esch, I will see you afterwards." "Anni, you silly girl. You think I would let you go all by yourself! I won't be leaving for five or six days, so I am coming with you."

Anni is now all the more perplexed as to just what kind of a man this is that would run such risks for her and get so involved with total strangers. This Charles Adams from New York is a strange man, but a very good one. He is such a contrast. On the outside he is as clear as day and on the inside as deep as night. He is a lot like Papa. Simple, smart, strong and caring.

The two arrive in Esch and spend only a few minutes together. Charlie has to get to the barracks up the street to report in and Anni has to get home and tell Mama her plans. The following day they meet at the halfway point, Aunt Sisy's house, their usual place of meeting. The two of them travel back to Luxembourg City that morning to see Anni's father at the place where he is being kept for trial. By now, Anni and the rest of the family have told Papa about Charlie, but the two have never met. It is a hard thing for Anni but she is at peace with the meeting because somehow, something inside tells her, it will be alright.

Indeed, it is alright. Charles D. Adams presents himself plainly and clearly to the senior Albert Neuman and both immediately recognize the commonality of their kindred spirits, character and fondness for, concern for, an eighteen-year-old innocent girl named Anni. Both men want the best for her, believe in her and would do anything to make it happen. They both share the belief that she deserves it in God's grace, plan and design.

The senior Albert Neuman can size up a man as fast as radar can pick up a blip on the screen. This "Charlie" is a man, no doubt. The two are like old friends from the beginning. Papa knows his daughter is in good hands and this man, whoever he is, only means good for her and would no doubt die for her. That alone puts his mind and heart at ease during this sad time. They talk for hours about many things, but mostly about the history of the past four years, how and why Albert Neuman is sitting in this deprivation of liberty, and for what cause. Albert Neuman never joined the Nazi Party. In fact, all his actions, words spoken and things unspoken, showed his detest for the Party. He never actively engaged in any activities whatsoever that would further their cause nor harm or tarnish the pride of being a Luxembourger. He was clearly a victim of circumstances. He did work as a professor in the predominantly German-staffed college. He did teach and train German youths in gymnastics. He did attend and compete in sporting events in Germany. He did do his job as best he could.

He was a professor of sports and he was working to provide for his family. Politics was something he hated all his life and now it was "politics" that desired to destroy that life. Charlie saw it clearly from the beginning. A man forced to salute "heil Hitler" and yet stand before a firing squad outside the college. A man forced to wave a flag from his home window that represented an evil cause in direct conflict with his own home, nation and national pride. All of which was his to swallow and endure as a man. He would stand trial for doing what he had to do. Necessity had constructed one more victim among the countless millions. Conspiring with the enemy. Work with, or die by, the hands of the killers in their town. Save your family or let them suffer. He made a choice to survive and now he was being tried for his decisions.

The train ride home is mostly silent as Charlie looks out the window, thinking about what a strange world he is living in, and Anni listens to the whispers around her. By the time they get back to Esch, things seem to be back more to the "dating game," but much more solemn. Charlie is still expressing his love and adoration but in a different fashion this time. It is out of genuine concern for Anni and her family. He has grown to love these people, these strangers, as if they had been family all along and no one ever told him. He feels very much at home with them and even loved by them. "What a unique people these Europeans are?" he muses to himself. He has already made a command decision and is resolute to speak on behalf of Mr. Neuman before whatever tribunal there is and he will do it because he believes it is the right thing to do. His attorney father in New York would be proud of his son. His father has told him that things like this happen. Charlie had never seen such a clear case. Some people fall between guilty and not guilty. They themselves are victims of circumstance, but man, in his befuddled attempt to outline justice, makes rules that don't always fit. However, they are still applied and used.

Back at the Neuman home, the discussion is quiet and melancholy. Mama has already been told that the family is not allowed to attend, and that only Mr. Neuman's lawyer and the appropriately called character witnesses will be permitted to speak on his behalf. The decision is made that Mama will stay home with the children and trust God that her husband will be home soon. Charlie and Anni will go back for the trial.

The sun rises hot on this May day outside the courtroom in the old building now appointed to house the decision-makers weighing lives lived and whether or not they behold them to have been conducted properly by their rules and standards. At the door to the courtroom, Anni is immediately told that she is not permitted to enter the room nor witness the proceedings against her own father. She is devastated but Charlie is in a position of awkward power and authority. He is a liberator, a man who has risked his life for this very court to even exist. He cannot be denied entry. He is in full uniform and Tech. Sgt. Charles D. Adams of Brooklyn, New York has "told" this court he has something to say. Charlie speaks with his best eloquence and heartfelt persuasive words. Other witnesses speak on Mr. Neuman's behalf, including a fellow professor that served at the same college and acted no differently than Papa but yet he stands free of accusation. It appears to be all in the numbers or being in the right or wrong place determined by the eyes and minds of willful people with their own sense of justice.

With all said and done, Charlie returns from inside the room and tells Anni the news. Her father has been found guilty of conspiring with the "enemy" and is sentenced to four years imprisonment. Justice has fallen to passions. Well-intentioned people have made a devastating decision, but it is binding and there is no turning back. Albert Neuman will be incarcerated for the next four years. Fair or not, that is left to God and no one will ever know how easily it could have gone the other way. It is done, past and gone. Right or wrong. It happened. He was never a Nazi, never a traitor and never a German. Even long after and to the day of his death, he loved "his" Luxembourg and remained a Luxembourger at heart. He never spoke ill or evil of it. He remained a man of honor and good reputation.

"Anni, learn." The words echo in her head. Her father's words to her over and over, they are a part of her life. He has said it a million times over the past eighteen years and she is still trying to make him proud. Whatever happens, good or evil, for better or worse, she will learn. She learns to accept that her father is safe and that at least no harm will come to him. She will be able to visit him and still have him to talk to. He will be back all in a matter of time. They have made it this far, and life continues to go on, and she will go on learning. She becomes thankful and grateful rather than bitter. Bitterness would only make it worse and there is nothing to learn in that. Papa has always said to count to ten before you ever speak or give an answer. His patience is her patience. If he can wait so can she. This is something she will learn from all of this, she will learn to be patient.

From that third week of May, Charlie left once again to his unit, back to the business at hand and to an occupied and surrendered Germany. He was not the only one fighting. Nor were all the Allied forces the only ones to fight. Aside from the men and women in uniforms for the Axis forces, there were other people, multitudes of people, not enlisted in any army or commissioned to service, but they too fought. The people whose lives were affected. The ones that lost family members, had tanks roll through their farms or bombs fall in their fields. They endured machine-gun fire from aircraft and rifles strafing their homes and a front doors. Dirty boots marched mud into their streets, onto their sidewalks, into their schools, hospitals and bedrooms. War is an evil, pervasive thing and it penetrates much more than just a battlefield. It penetrates the soul and spirit of all mankind, whether anyone likes it or not. It is a hard, cold fact and reality.

Even in the blackest epochs of human conflict, the human spirit has a desire to drive forward and even dare to dance when the firewalls keep out the flames. Three weeks after their last meeting, Charlie and Anni are back together again. In the ebbing tide of the misery, it is a time to smile and laugh. A time to pretend all is well with the world. A time for this couple in love to dance and she will even sing for him. She will think about what she does have instead of that which she doesn't. He will savor every minute of peace and discard the raging sounds of war only days behind him. It is a Saturday in Esch and it is early June. Tonight, there will be a dance at the hall with modern music and drinks. Mama encourages Anni to go and make the best of life as she has it.

Charlie is an unwilling victim of this episode. He doesn't dance. He does not even like to dance. But, if he wants to keep his Brown-Eyes happy, he will go to the dance. It is against the rules and regulations. He is not supposed to be out of uniform at any given time. He is not supposed to breach the Army's curfew. He is not supposed to attend this function. So he borrows a suit from Margot's brother and takes his darling to the dance. He finds very little peace in it, constantly watching the door for MPs or some other form of trouble. He fears getting caught. They have even asked Bubby, who is home this weekend, to guard the door in secret. Anni gets her dance with Charlie and Charlie gets to hold his Babychen in his arms. He may scuff her shoes and stumble on his own two feet, but they hold each other and for this night, there is no war. In fact, there is nothing at all but them and the music. They even share a kiss. At the end, Anni goes home and Charlie spends the night at Aunt Sisy's apartment instead of the barracks. By Monday, Charlie is gone again and neither know when he will return.

On June 19, 1945, Charlie Adams has leaves the war-torn countryside of Germany once more and finds himself seated across a table from Anni's father at Luxembourg City. "Mr. Neuman, I want to ask your permission to marry your daughter, sir." Charlie states it plainly but with much nervousness in his stomach. "Charlie, you are a good man and Anni needs a good man. Have you asked her yet?" is Albert's reply. "No, sir. Not yet, I wanted to speak with you first," Charlie answers. "Then, in that case, good luck!" laughs Anni's Papa. He knows his daughter and knows she is a much tougher sell than he is. Charlie has more of a challenge awaiting him in Esch than he does here in this room. They both chat longer and enjoy the company. They have already established a friendship and a bond is building between the two that has a firm, lasting and true foundation.

On June 20, 1945, Charlie is standing in the middle of the dining room at Margot's house. He politely asks Sisy to leave the room so that he can speak with Anni. Aunt Sisy smiles, she already knows what is coming and she leaves the room beaming. Charlie has prepared well by speaking with both Aunt Sisy and Anni's mother the evening before, without Anni knowing. Anni sits at the table, staring back and forth between the two of them, not liking the uncomfortable feeling she is getting from all this secretive behavior. She is far from naive to unspoken words. But she is struck with awe at the words that come next.

"Anni," Charlie starts as he takes a seat across the table from her, "would you consider moving away from here?" He states it fast and firm, then steels himself for the answer. "Go where? I want to go to Nancy [France] and become a gym teacher, why?" She is annoyed by the strange nature of this conversation. "Anni, come to the U.S. and marry me!" he blurts out, and the man actually appears to be sweating. "No, I don't know the language or the people," she replies. "Don't you love me?" Charlie pleads. "Yes, but what does that have to do with it?" she responds in a way that is so practical that it would make her father roar with laughter. Charlie is taken aback and briefly wounded, but he is determined that this "no" is not a "NO!" He is just beginning the fight.

"Anni, I have to leave this afternoon. You should think about it until I come back. Will you do that?" he requests matter-of-factly. He seems certain that some time will change her mind. "Yes, I will. I will think about it. I promise." She doesn't want to hurt him and she also means it. She does want to think about it and she has learned to count to ten before giving her answers. She wants to talk to some people—family and a few friends. She wants counsel on such a major decision. Her prudence is astonishing for her age. Her wisdom has been adopted from her father and it works well for her.

# Two Weddings, an Unusual Honeymoon and Love Letters

Anni discusses the matter of marriage with her mother, her brother Albert, her aunts and friends. Her father, lastly. The bottom line is undeniable. Everyone feels it is in her best interest to marry the man. That tall, skinny guy from the United States, Charlie Adams. Mama especially encourages her daughter. "Anni, look around. It is going to be a long time before things get better here. With your father gone, I have my hands full with an eleven-year-old son and a two-year-old daughter. Bubby helps, but I have to depend on my own two hands and the love of neighbors. The man obviously loves you and will treat you good. He is a good man. That is a hard thing in life for a girl your age to find. Here, you will only have a simple life for certain; in America, you can do or become anything you want. You have much better opportunities there. Go with the man, marry Charlie and be happy." Mama finishes her small, impactful speech. They both know it is the truth. Anni's hopes and dreams are best nurtured in another country, in a foreign land. The times and circumstances have seen to it. Though she loves Luxembourg and wants to teach in France, both countries have years ahead of rebuilding and the need for strong arms of construction are more necessary than teaching sports. Her goals have still yet a chance from the time she danced with wings flared in Marseille to a new garden in a land of plenty. In America she can spread the newly-colored wings and wait for a breeze. The right breeze. The one that will lift her to the place where she belongs: in flight and happily fulfilled.

On the last day of June, Charlie returns to Esch-sur-Alzette with one thing on his mind. His entire trip from the other side of Germany, near the Czechoslovakian border, is one of silent thought and reflection. He only speaks as required. Transferring from jeep to car to truck and even on foot, he makes his way to the city where his heart is. He already told his commanding officer about his proposal and was met with much opposition, all to his surprise. The officer had been kind and generous toward Charlie and it came as a shock and a disappointment that he would be discouraged from marrying someone he has only seen approximately twenty days in six months. The war is over, Germany has surrendered and Hitler is where he belongs, in the halls of true justice, an eternal flame. Yet, Charlie finds himself still involved in battles. This time they are the battles of other people's wills. He isn't one to quit.

Late on the same evening, Charlie arrives at Margot's house (Aunt Sisy's actually), and again approaches Anni without wait or warning. "Will you marry me?" he asks. "You have had time to consider it, and I know you well enough to know you kept your promise. What is it going to be?" He has hardly entered the door before the challenging words are presented and Aunt Sisy leaves the room before his sentence is complete.

"Have you made up your mind?" he asks bluntly. "I think it will be okay. But you are going to need a lot of patience," is Anni's answer. "Just learn to speak English and we will be fine," are his words of reassurance to the "yes" that was never spoken. "I knew all along you would!" Charlie laughs and reaches to hug his soon-to-be bride. She hesitates and is still awkwardly shy. She doesn't know how to react but the joy of the man so close to her is radiant and she cannot help but be bathed in it and feel joy mix with her apprehensions. "I will go back tomorrow and confront Lt. Colonel Eatman, my commanding officer, and this time, I won't take no for an answer. I will get his permission and be back as soon as possible."

Charlie, a man known for patience, has become the most hurried individual in sight. He is exuberant. Flying in his own fantasy world, nothing else matters. He is completely taken by the emotions and feelings that genuine love can bring. He is not about to waste a minute today, tomorrow, next month, year or years to pour out this love in his being. It is his life's desire. He has been granted his dream and wish. Indeed, it only takes Charlie another fifteen days to go back across Luxembourg and Germany to secure the Lt. Colonel's reluctant semi-permission, and return to the place where he heard Anni accept his offer. He offered himself and all that he could ever hope to be, and he is determined to be more than this young girl could have possibly imagined. Her happiness is his happiness and he feeds on it like a desert lily does a sprinkling of water. However, no sooner does one battle end than another one begins.

On July 16, Charlie stays at Aunt Sisy's house as friends and family start to receive word from one mouth to the other. The news travels fast. There is going to be a wedding in the family and it will be tomorrow. There isn't much time to make formal arrangements. They will have to do the best they can because there is no postponing this event. Late that same evening, Charlie receives word from his CO, Colonel Eastman, that approval has been granted, against the ranking officer's " better judgment." Best wishes are sent with the message, and as a gift from his fellow soldiers and leading officer, arrangements will be made in advance for his honeymoon. A thoughtful gesture by his commanding officer and the rest of the "boys" in expression of their happiness for Charlie. After all the hell they have been through, it is a small measure in the scheme of things. They should all be so happy. That night, Anni goes home to be with her mother, Chuck and Elfie. Charlie stays at Aunt Sisy's with her husband, Margot and some other relatives. He is comfortable and "at home" with his newly extended family.

By early morning, Anni, Mama, with Chuck and Elfie in tow, arrive at the door to the town hall where the license is to be secured and the brief ceremony conducted by a clerk of the marriage division. Coming down the street from the north is a small band of family with Charlie at the lead, heading to the same location. Once inside, the entire party goes to the counter and Charlie, with some translation help from Anni, expresses their desires and presents the proper identification and papers to qualify them for this momentous occasion. The paperwork is handled in the usual formal fashion, all placed neatly in order and made perfectly legal as paperwork goes. The only thing left is the ceremony. The clerk reads from a well-used outline on a worn sheet and thus, in the presence of the family, announce Charles D. Adams and Anni Jeanne Neuman as husband and wife. They are given the traditional parting gift to newlyweds, a gift from the city of Esch, a cookbook for the bride. Charlie finds humor in it but keeps it to himself. In his mind, he is married. But not to Anni.

Outside, on the town-hall steps, pictures are taken of the newly joined couple with family. However, Anni has a surprise for Charlie. "Now we have the papers, are we getting married today?" she asks. Charlies' face is as white as a sheet. This must be a joke. But it isn't. To Anni, what just happened was getting the paperwork done. She isn't married until she stands before God, a priest and witnesses to holy matrimony of which she is the bride, and at a fit and proper Catholic church. Charlie is as weak as wilted leaf. "We are married! Babychen, we are husband and wife now, see?" and he holds out the papers with them listed together. Anni sees the name Adams added to her first name but it means little. What means everything is in the eyes of God, a priest, a church and family. That is a wedding, that is a marriage and that is the only way it can or will be done. The little, stubborn Anni gives battle once more to the downhearted CDA.

"It's okay, hon. I understand," Charlie states quickly, thinking on his feet. "We have the license and papers, so we will go to the church across the street from your house and see the priest, OK?" Anni agrees and the entire wedding party travels down the sidewalks back to the daunting building across the street from the Neuman residence. They file through the doors and call out for the priest. He presents himself and listens to the request of the party. His answer is a quick, succinct and emphatic no. He does not believe the couple have had time to properly think out a lifelong commitment to the sanctity of marriage. He even expresses his distaste for Anni's marrying a foreigner, and last but not least, Charlie is not a Catholic. They aren't married. Anni reaffirms it to Charlie and then the questions fly again as to how he can win this battle. The answer: Try another church.

By now, the day is progressing. At ten o'clock this morning, Charlie had a wife. Now he doesn't. He is befuddled, has a wedding party on hand and a reception scheduled for 5:00 P.M. It is nearly noon and they must leave for Luxembourg City to visit Papa and return. They also must meet with Ambassador George Wallace to obtain the "good graces" of the American government in acknowledgment of this new union that doesn't exist. It is getting far too strange for Charlie, who hasn't eaten and is getting dizzy from the spin of the earth on its axis and a bride that isn't a wife. They go to the church where Anni received her first communion and plead their case to the priest. His answer is nearly the same. He cannot do it against church policy.

"Well sir," Charlie states, she is my wife. I have the papers and license here to show it. We were married hours ago at the town hall and tonight I am going to sleep with her, with or without your permission!" Charlie in a moment of genius knew how to get his baby's wish granted. The priest becomes totally alarmed and beseeches them, begs them, not to do anything yet. He will ride his bicycle all the way to Luxembourg

City and obtain the permission from the Luxembourg bishop and get a special dispensation. The answer is fair enough. The wedding party returns to Aunt Sisy's, a priest pedals hard and fast on a July day for an eighteen-mile bike ride and the married-not-married couple ride to see Papa and the ambassador.

They promised to meet the priest at eleven o'clock the next morning, July 18, and that is what Charlie and Anni will do. They meet with Papa and garner his joyful wishes and know that he is fighting his emotions. Nevertheless, the senior Neuman is very pleased with Charlie and his daughter. He will be with them soon and happier days are coming. Ambassador Wallace "rubber-stamps" the marriage and it is official in the eyes of the United States Army and the United States government. Now, the only thing to do is to return to Aunt Sisy's and have a half-celebration and wait the night for a priest bicycling his way to achieve the permission of God to conduct an act recognizing the union of two people as one. It would be amazingly comical to Charlie except for one last insult added to injury. As he turns in for bed, he takes his wife into his arms and hugs her. He kisses her cheek and she lies down on one side of the bed, Charlie walks around the bed and lies down on the other side. In between, Gredy (Anni's mother), will keep vigil and slumber between the two young adults through the night. She will await tomorrow's wedding day when her daughter will be transformed from bride to wife.

At 11:00 A.M., July 18, 1945, Anni Neuman becomes Anni Adams. She and Charlie kneel at the side altar, in the presence of Anni's great-aunt, her mother, Aunt Sisy and Margot. It has all come together at the last minute. The priest still has perspiration drying on his skin as he gives the Holy Matrimonial Communion. He had bicycled all the way to Luxembourg City, accomplished getting a special dispensation and the approval of the bishop. He then made the return trip that very morning to match the battle lines that Charlie had set. This time they are married. Anni's Aunt Lucy sings "Ava Maria" as they join hands and turn to the witnesses announcing their indefinite union. Anni commits herself for life to Charlie and all that goes with it. She is scared, nervous and confused, but she knows in her heart that she has made the right choice.

The newlyweds are provided with a car-ride to a hotel in Mondorf where arrangements have been made for the two of them for a spectacular honeymoon with complete in-room services. They arrive late in the evening, exhausted. What they don't know or foresee is that this hotel is being used by the Army as a rest and recreation site. Soldiers are everywhere and they are mostly filled with cognac, wine and song. It is not exactly the right place to bring a lady.

Charlie sees the fear in Anni's eyes as he tries to make the best of it. Champagne has been provided in their room. They drink about half of it and go to bed tired and weary. All the two of them want to do is sleep but the revelry outside the door, up and down the hall, is too much. They both finally drift off, only to be awakened time after time by drunken soldiers singing, yelling and making noise. It is a disaster.

Charlie and Anni try to keep the best spirit they can and make their way downstairs for breakfast. At the table the waiter brings them their food. Cooked eggs and fish. This is not what Anni has in mind. They try to ignore the soldiers but the word is out that they have just gotten married and the soldiers, with best intentions, make matters worse. By late evening, the two find themselves back in their hiding in their room. Room service will bring their dinner to them and maybe things will go a little better. When the dinner arrives the final stroke is made. As Charlie lifts the silver dome from the plate, Anni peers over his side to look upon a ghastly sight. There on the platter is a large black-skinned fish with its grotesque head still on and eyes glaring at Anni as if it were all her fault. That does it, she wants to go home and Charlie certainly understands.

The next morning the two hitch a ride with two soldiers in an army jeep to get back to Esch. The family is surprised to see them but Mama makes the best of it. Charlie and Anni stay at the Neuman home for a few days while Charlie makes arrangements with the Lt. Colonel to find a better place to stay in Mondorf and actually have a real, honest-to-god honeymoon. After several days it is finally arranged. The two, with much trepidation and uneasiness, make the return trip, determined to enjoy the remaining days of Charlie's leave before he has to return to his unit. They won't see much of each other again after this time and they both know it. It is a hard way to start a marriage and even harder to keep it from the beginning. The loved each other and want to be happy but the surroundings are nearly impossible to bear, much less enjoy.

This time, they make their way to a place that is indeed quieter and without all the celebrating soldiers, the Parc Hotel of Mondorf. They have a peaceful stay up on the third floor. It is a nice hotel and the two enjoy sleeping in late. They take walks during the day and evenings. They talk to one another, and Charlie is truly a gentleman. Anni is slowly becoming more secure with her husband, but the days go by too fast and all too soon it will end.

However, even these few days make the honeymoon disquieting and uneasy for Anni. One horrid thing looms over the otherwise sweet occasion. Each and every evening, Anni and Charlie peer out their bedroom window across the hotel yard to the other side of the meadow. There in the window, like clockwork, for hours, stands a fat man in his gold/brown uniform. He leans out, filling the entire window with his presence, head held down as if in silent reflection. He does this each and every day for hours. It makes Anni horribly afraid and sick. She recognizes the man, she has seen him and seen his work. She know him. Charlie knows who he is, too.

His name is Hermann Göring, the former second-in-command to Hitler and the Third Reich. He no longer possesses his gold dagger, opulent belts adorned with jewelry and rings upon his fingers. His brooch is gone from his neck. He is no longer the "fat Herod" of the Nazi leadership. He is an evil, stark creature filling window space. He occupies the space in the same manner as a captured animal or demon, chained against all odds of escape. Still brooding and wanting his power back. He is there awaiting his trial. He will be judged at Nuremberg for not only war crimes but crimes against humankind and all that is good. He is on his way to hell, and Anni and Charlie stare at him in his descent. In a sense of justice, they are starting a new life as the man across the way is seeing his ending. They are free and he isn't. The butterfly in Anni can fly on the gentle breezes flowing through the streets of Mondorf with her beloved husband and the monster, the graven image of the Iron Eagle is broken, humiliated and loathed. He even loathes himself, yet, deems himself a righteous king of evil and the fair owner of it.

Except for the curiosity of the caged animal across the way, Charlie and Anni have a much better time for their final days of the honeymoon. It is a long and sad ride back to Esch, but they have some wonderful memories to cherish, and now is not the time to dwell on ups and downs. They must look forward to the future, and the only way to bear it is to let the days pass and number them by staying busy until they are once again together. After returning Anni back to the Neuman home, Charlie is gone within a day. He will go back to Bayrueth, Germany where he is stationed. There he will prepare for two months to rotate with the Ninth Armored Division out of Europe and back to the United States. It is a bittersweet time for him as he has only a few short visits with his wife.

On October 5, 1945, he leaves for New York, where he will begin making arrangements to have his war bride shipped to him like a reward for all his hard work and sacrifice. The Bronze Stars and the other medals mean nothing to him. His country's victory is reward enough, and being home the same, but his forthcoming bride and wife is a lifetime achievement. Every day in waiting is passed as if he were a five-year-old child waiting out Christmas Eve.

# Love Letters from Charlie

From January 1945 to the culmination of Charlie finding his dream girl, marrying her and returning to America, he continued to express himself through his writings. Reading them, one can fully appreciate who he was through his own words. The following excerpts are from letters to his parents after having met Anni and then letter to her through the waiting of months to finally have his beloved babychen with him never to let go or say good-bye again. At least not in the manner they first endured. Here in his own words Charlie will explain it for himself better than this writer could:

*March 15, 1945*

***"Dear Dad—Received your letter and the dough. Thanks Pa. It doesn't look as though I'll have a chance to use it. We're well inside Hitlerland now…Johnny's air force has done its job well. Thanks for the clippings of the Fourth. We sure are making a name for ourselves…These pictures of you and Mama out at the beach are real good. They do not look posed, and they say that that is the secret to good snapshots. The beach looks nice and clean. Better too. I see the damn dog still chases his stick. Does he still bark as much as always? Well, Dad, this evening we have a special job to do (military secret) so I will close now. I'll be seeing you soon. Love Bub"***

*April 5, 1945*

***"Dear folks—Have received your letter of the 18th. No, no Paris trip as yet. And don't worry about me marrying a girl over here and***

*staying here. I might marry one but all our kids will be strictly American—Republicans!..."*

*July 12, 1945*

*"Dear folks—Just a short one and a post card from Anni. I am going to go back to Esch, as soon as I can, and marry that girl. Yes, as you say—it will be easier for her to come to the States as my wife than if she were only my fiancé'...I want the whole world to know about Anni...The latest dope (and I think it is the real McCoy) is that we are leaving here sometime in October. That means that I'll be home in November sometime. Better not hold off on that vacation Pa. Get the sun while you can..."*

*August 12, 1945*

*"Hello Darling Wife—How is everything Baby? I will beat this letter back to you. The 633's will come in the mail soon...So you started your piano lessons. That's good honey. Every day! Wow—you should learn in no time. Do you like it so far? It will become more and more fun as you learn to play a few songs. We will have a piano in our home as soon as we can afford one. The war news is great. I think it will be over by tomorrow...Do I still love you? Well—what do you think?...I must close now my darling wife...Bye now baby. Be good and I'll be back with you soon. Charlie"*

*August 16, 1945*

*"...So you want me to tell you that I love you in every letter—and am I sure about loving you? You crazy little baby. It will be much nicer when I will be able to tell you these things while holding you in my arms. This letter writing is not so good. I love you more than I ever thought I could love anything or anyone. Other girls just don't seem to exist. You are my sweetheart and my wife, I think of nothing else but getting started on making you the happiest girl in the world."*

*August 17, 1945*

*"Dearest Darling—I don't know about letting you wake me up during thunderstorms. We may have an awful lot of them during the next 50 years. I'll tell you darling. Maybe it will be ok IF you promise to cuddle up in my arms and sing me a song. How's that?*

*September 2, 1945*

*"Anni Darling—Back to camp once again and all is well. Arrived back here about 2:30 and found everything in order. Darling, we are moving from here to Rheims, France on the 5th or 6th of this month. That means that we will be there when you receive this letter. The word is that we will be there for eleven days, then ship home."*

*September 4, 1945*

*"Hello Dearest one—Well, the news is no different. We leave here for Chalon Friday morning and I hope to be with my darling wife around the 13th. Honey, I know I am not doing the right thing in building up your hopes like this. I may not be able to get back. But gosh—I like to talk about it. If I don't, well—you will know that I tried. You will know also that my thoughts are with you every minute from dawn until bedtime. When I get back to the States everything that I do will be for my Brown-eyes."*

*September 5, 1945*

*"...I find myself thinking of you all the day long. Gosh, I hope everything works out well so that I will be able to get lots of nice things. Things are about the same darling. We are leaving here Friday and expect to be in Chalon on the 10th. They moving troops out of Europe very quickly, honey, so even if I do not see you before I go I feel sure that it will not be as much as six months. The time will go very fast, my sweet."*

*October 20, 1945*

*"Dearest Anni—Well darling—I'm beginning to feel more like a civilian now after being in civilian clothes for 48 hours. It's a grand feeling...Everyone asks about you darling. I sure will be glad when I can show you off to my friends."*

*October 23, 1945*

*"Hello Dearest—...Honey, I have good news. I have started in floral design school. The course is for two weeks and then I can stay as long after as I want to gain additional knowledge and experience...I was looking at some rings for my baby over in the city this afternoon. I saw many real nice ones, but I think I'll wait until you get over here and pick out what you like...Goodnight dearest—sleep tight and please don't worry about anything. I love you with all my heart."*

*November 14, 1945*

*"Dearest Anni—...I'm glad that you sound a little more cheerful, honey. It makes me feel better. We want to be together Baby. I know this. And we will not be happy until we are together, but we must be brave and cheerful for a while. It will not be for much longer. I miss you also darling, and would give anything if it would bring you in my arms tonight...Bye bye now—I'll will see you in my dreams. Stay as sweet as you are please, and I will love you forever and ever."*

*November 29, 1945*

*"Dear Baby—...I have good news tonight. We are about to take over a [flower] shop. I was out looking for a location here in Queens Village but found the rents very, very high...I contacted a real estate agent here in the village and he showed me a real nice small shop, no in the main part of town, but sort of in between Queens Village and the next town...Yes, baby, I think we should open up in this little place first, get to 'know the ropes' and then when we are ready, move to a bigger place."*

*December 16, 1945*

*"Dear Baby—Here it is...12:15 Monday morning—and I am once again writing my dearest baby. I've been so gosh darn busy lately that I have not been able to write you as often as I have wanted...in addition to working over in New York, I am making Christmas pieces here at home and selling them. It means very much work and late hours, but if I can make some extra money I want to do it...Yes, Honey, I think it will be February or March when you come over. It will be nice then and we will be able to work together on Easter things...Goodnight now, Brown-eyes, it is one o'clock in the morning and I must go. I love you more than ever tonight."*

*January 2, 1946*

*Letterhead:*

| | |
|---|---|
| Flowers Telegraphed Everywhere | Telephone Missouri 7-5858 |
| Charles D. Adams | 214-41 Jamaica Avenue |
| Flowers | Queens Village, L.I. |
| | New York |

*(Charlie was in full operation of their own flower shop)*

*March 3, 1946*

***"Dearest Anni—. . . Well—how is my pretty baby? You say that you expect to leave March 5th but I cannot believe it until I hear it for sure. So, I will just keep on writing until I know that you are on the way. . . So long now dearest. I hope to see you very soon. Then I will show you that I love you very much. Always, Charlie."***

# An American War Bride: The Adventure Begins

From the day they were first married, July 17, 1945, through the time Charlie rotated back Stateside and then to the day of Anni's departure, nothing came easy. Their personal lives, the efforts to record, identify and legitimize their union in the eyes of two governments and arrangements for the two to reunite in time future was challenging. From the onset of having two weddings, a most unusual honeymoon and only seeing each other an additional two times before Charlie's departure, life for Anni and Charlie was surreal. But their love, determination and perseverance prevailed. For Anni it was a constant battle of paperwork showing who she was and who she married, all the while verifying the legitimate union. Things became complicated almost immediately. In the post-war country of Luxembourg, new identification cards were issued by the local Commissaire de police. Anni first obtained hers February 26, 1945. It had all pertinent information: Name, place of birth, date of birth (November 11, 1926), hair and eye color with a photograph and signature. After her marriage and honeymoon, the first ID card was no longer valid. Five days after her return from the honeymoon, she had to report to the police station to have a new ID card made to show that Luxembourg recognized her as a citizen but also as married, and her husband as a foreigner. In the second identification, August 1, 1945, her name was not only changed but also her birth date (November 12, 1926), and her hair color.

It seemed inconvenient but insignificant at the beginning. It would later launch a cascade of difficulties in obtaining her clearance to leave

Luxembourg and also her freedom to depart for, and enter, America. Charlie had fought a war and Anni had fought to survive. Now, the two of them fought politics, bureaucracy, suspicion and lack of common sense. There was nothing suspect about it; the two were in love, married and wanted to live together in one place for the rest of their natural lives. Anni and Charlie both found themselves traipsing to and fro from one government building and authority to another. Filling out forms was almost a daily routine. Half of them would be found unnecessary or incorrect. It was the "paper war" of immigration.

It took until September 6, 1945 for the first significant order to come through:

> **"Headquarters, Theater Service Forces, European Theater; Subject: Transportation of Dependants. To: Commanding Officer, HQ 9th Armd. Division (Fin. Sec.) APO 259. Tech. Sgt. Charles D. Adams. . . . your dependant Anni J. (Neuman) (Wife) to New York, New York. By command of Lt. General Lee: Sylvia M. Marsili, Captain, AGD."**

The next major document came as follows:

> **"Luxembourg 13 February 1946. Adjutant General's Section, War Bride Transportation Office, Western Base Section, 26, Avenue Kleber, Paris, France. Re: Charles D. Adams…Wife: Anny Adams. Dear Sirs: I am applying for transportation to the United States. My husband applied already in July 1945 but I understand you need additional information. 1. I was married on July 17, 1945 in Esch/Alzette, Gr. D. of Luxembourg. 2. I am not pregnant. 3. I am going to join my husband Charles D. Adams 218-29 94th Drive, Queens-Village, Long Island, N.Y. I would appreciate it if you would notify me of the Status of plans for transportation for me and or the documents needed at this time. Anny Adams, rue de l'Industrie 68, Esch/Alzette, Luxembourg [notice the additional conflict caused by German occupation. Anni v. Anny (letter signed Anni)].**

On February 12, 1946, Anni was finally made a "Priority 1" by order of Headquarters, Western Base Section, Theater Service Forces. On March 5, 1946, she received her *Declartion de Depart* from the

Luxembourg government and her official *Certificat de changement de domicile* from the Esch-sur-Alzette Commissariat De Police. She proceeded immediately to Luxembourg City on March 6, 1946 to meet with the Luxembourg United States Ambassador, George Wallace, along with several other Luxembourg women who were war brides. The parties met and had a celebratory send off with personal handshakes and well-wishes. The train left Luxembourg City bound for Paris, France where the war brides from Belgium, Luxembourg, Netherlands, France, Germany, Czechoslovakia and Poland were processed. The Luxembourg ladies remained for three days, March 7-10, 1946, along with some French War Brides, to be inoculated, indoctrinated and instructed on behavior, etiquette and expectations. They were housed for the classes, shots and examinations and then forwarded like packages to Lahavre, France for boarding and disembarkation aboard the *Vulcania*.

Prior to leaving, Anni received her "Certificate of Vaccination" at Camp Philip Morris on March 10, 1946. It was one of the several "Cigarette Camps" established and maintained by the U.S. Army under the sponsorship of the U.S. tobacco giants. A glaring and poignant advertisement of America's democratic ideal of big business; a clear point of monetary power and effect.

Anni was now well on her way, leaving behind her only-known world, her recently-turned two-year-old sister, soon-to-be twelve-year-old brother, mother and all the family she knew. The two Alberts, one incarcerated and the other flying high in the circus, whereabouts unknown. For that matter, Anni was finding herself in a "whereabouts unknown" situation of sorts. She was boarding, out of great irony, the very same ship that took her American husband home with a thousand other soldiers only months before. Now, the ship had been commissioned by the U.S. Army War Bride Department, along with seven other ships, to transport nearly 350,000 war brides (some with children already) from destinations in Europe and the Pacific to the United States. It was very clear that the American soldier was not always fighting.

On March 11, 1946, the *Vulcania* departed Le Havre harbour with approximately two hundred passengers bound for Southampton, England where it would take on another seven hundred war brides with children in tow. The men had gone first, and now the women were coming to catch up with them, as the saying goes in the wedding vows: for better or worse.

Once the ship had been loaded with women, children and baggage, it lugged out of the Southampton waters. The passengers were check-listed and assigned baggage and bunk numbers with landing cards for the United States. The manifest reflected that, out of some nine hundred plus passengers, No. 509, 2 Brioni, Sheet No. 24, Line No. 1, S.S. *Vulcania* was Anni Jeanne (Anny Neuman) Adams. The cruise ship turned transport was loaded with women, loaded with children, loaded with food and yes, even wine.

It was intoxicating for young Anni just to see it and more to take in than a day would permit. She immediately sheltered herself in the company of seven Luxembourg women of the same circumstances and they became partners for the trip. It was going to be an adventure and it didn't disappoint the daring and tipsy women aboard. They had suffered great hardships through the war and now they were being "driven" across the seas to hope, dreams, fantasy, sadness-unknown, an entire myriad of emotions and thoughts. Most of which would never come true, again for better or worse.

By March 12, 1946, the SS *Vulcania* was fully underway, heading into the deep, dark blue waters of the North Atlantic, destination: New York, New York. The passengers were mostly women ranging in ages from eighteen to twenty-nine, some single, some pregnant, some with children ranging in age from infants to age three, others with children that preceded their newly adopted step-fathers. It was quite a scene for this cruise ship-turned-transport vessel. The crew was under orders to make the passengers as well accommodated as possible. The women passed their time in a wide variety of fashions. Some knitted, some gossiped, some played cards like their GI husbands. Some wrote letters, some tended to the children. Others drank wine and sang without music. The ship's crew provided movies and music for entertainment just as they had done for the American GIs on the previous voyages. Anni mostly took in the movies or listened to the music and chatted with her close group of seven Luxembourg women.

Yes, they were going to be American women, but they were never going to cease being Luxembourgers as well. It wasn't a bad thing, it was a double-blessing. In their hearts, minds and spirits they would always long for home—beautiful, incomparable Luxembourg. On the outside, the industrious side of the women and their common sense, enhanced by wisdom from war sufferings, would be steel-spined women of the future for America. Ready to conquer family life and careers better than the enemy that had once tried to conquer them. They were rare jewels and the "boys" did well to bring them to the States. It was an investment in the future for the world's melting pot. These women had God, grit and determination. They would help their existing families, create new families and join the world of families as one can only know in America. There would be good days and bad, but, the future for America was changed by their presence; these "War Brides" on American soil. In a new land, in a place where it was rumored that freedom rings true.

Halfway across the Atlantic, the transport vehicle for the captured hearts of a thousand men began to roll awash in waves and wind. The ship had ran head-first into a storm of horrendous potential. It wasn't a hurricane nor a storm so severe that the crew felt defeat, but it was strong enough to weaken the stomachs and spirits aboard. The women clung to one another and either prayed or laughed insanely. Just one more episode of terror trying to break the unbreakable. They were veterans as much as their husbands. Some even more so. They had been in battle, fought back with weapons, survived rape, murder and destruction. They had witnessed the loss of countless friends and family. Now, this furious storm sought to shake them. It was foolishness to them. They were unshakable and the storm could blow all it wished. This ship was their ticket to freedom and a future. No storm could outlast the stubbornness of a determined woman. It was futile. For two days the ship rocked in the heavy waves and the roaring sea. For two days, grapefruits rolled around on the mess hall tables and floors. The passengers staggered through the hallways and rolled in their bunks.

They spilt cards, milk and wine. They sang and laughed louder than the wind. The storm was so much that the captain ordered the ship to stay in her position for two whole days to await clear weather and a chance to resume the course. In the meantime, the women made the best of it and knew that another two days was nothing to the time they had already survived. In the United States, nearly a thousand American GIs received word that their wives (and children) would be late. They ship had heaved-to and was waiting out the blow. The men seemed to suffer the most because they lacked the patience. Most had waited six or more months, some even a year or two to see their prize beauties. One day was as excruciating as a thousand. Just like the battles they fought before and survived, it was a "no choice" situation. Just wait.

Once the storm had surrendered and passed, the ship's life took on an added level of festivities. The music returned, the movies reeled away again and the conversations flowed among the women as much as the bountiful feast of foods and bottles of wine. The sight was unimaginable to the women, who had suffered so much desperation over the past years. Ham, chicken, turkey, roast and all with vegetables they hadn't seen in years or in some cases, had never had seen at all. The were fed the best the ship's hold had to offer and it was a warrior's feast for women married to warriors. They were on their way and the two-day delay was no more than a mere bump in the road. But, as the days drew on and the time came close, the apprehensions were palpable and spoiled the air. As the final three days of the eleven-day trip (turned to fourteen by the storm) began to tick away, so did the festivities. The unknowns, uncertainties and anxieties took their place.

The women started to quiet down and began to think to themselves rather than to each other. Once the ship arrived in New York's harbor, they would not be a team of war brides but instead, they would simply be brides. They would all depart in different directions, to various far away places where they would be left alone with one man and a marriage certificate that said they were here to start something. None of them knew what it was they were to start, other than getting to know this man they married, possibly starting a family and staring into the darkest of unknowns. They suddenly realized that they were in charge but out of control as to whether they would have a future or total failure and misery.

Uncertainty was as common for the "cargo" of the *Vulcania* as it was for the ship herself. She had been built in the same year that Anni was born, 1926. This voyage was her last as a transport ship since her commission in 1941 to transport displaced war victims. She served strong and well over her forty-eight years of service. This particular transport ended on March 24, 1946 when the ship arrived in New York. The ship was Italian-made and the man standing in the forefront on the docks to welcome the passengers was the former mayor of New York City, Fiorello Henry LaGuardia. The sixty-three-year-old short but rotund man graciously and warmly welcomed the women and children to his beloved New York and the United States of America. He had only this very month been appointed as Director General of the United Nations Relief and Rehabilitation Administration. There his duties were to secure food, clothing, shelter, medical supplies and other necessities for millions of

Europeans displaced by the war. The whole of it was extraordinarily ironic. Anni and the ship were "born" the same year. One Italian was greeting the other both on the heels of their old jobs and starting new ones. In fact, the *Vulcania* was immediately sent into her new service only five days after this arrival. The ship had carried both Charlie and Anni for the same route.

With eight dollars in her pocket, Anni disembarked the ship, down the gangplank. Charlie was nowhere to be seen in the crowd of nearly three thousand people. It was somewhat chaotic but Former Mayor LaGuardia did what he had always done best—take center stage and organize immediately. The man disarmed the women with a broad and inviting smile backed by a genuine heartfelt appreciation for their ventures and presence. He spoke graciously to them, encouraging them to make New York and the rest of the United States of America their home and to feel free to be free. To rise to whatever challenge awaited them and stand firm in the knowledge that this country would support them as true American women with husbands they could and should be proud of. His jovial speech put the crowd at ease, and the men and women joined even as the welcome ceremony took place.

Anni found Charlie, or maybe the other way around since Charlie recognized the love of his life immediately. However, for Anni it was strangely different. Charlie approached her and went to grab her and hug her in his elation and joy. However, he nearly suffered a slap from the young girl who didn't recognize this brazen stranger attempting to embrace her. "Anni, Anni! It's me, Charlie!" he vented as he recoiled from the shocked figure in front of him. "Charlie?" Anni replied. "You look terrible." These were her first words to her long-awaited husband. It was not what they had expected. Charlie was in civilian clothes and had been back in the States long enough to become more Americanized. Anni didn't even recognize him. There was an eternity of silence as they looked at each other and Anni wondered to herself what she had done. She was thousands of miles from home and there was a strange man standing in front of her declaring to be Charlie Adams and her husband for life, no less.

"Anni, it's me. Babychen!" Charlie protested. "I'm sorry Charlie. I am so sorry!" she replied, nearly in tears as his face and form started to bring back memories and recollection. It had been a long and disorienting journey to say the least. This was obviously going to take some time to settle in her head. She was dizzied by the whole pace of things. She had come from Europe where things were slower. The ride over was slow, but thrust into a crowd of a few thousand people, the noise, sights and sounds of the harbor and the monstrous city in the background was near nauseating to her. This was not what she expected. She had seen America dozens of times and it didn't look anything like this at all. She had come to know America through all the movies she had watched growing up and going to the theater. Where were the quiet main streets where Shirley Temple skipped and sang? Where were the back roads winding down tree-lined dirt roads leading to spectacular Southern homes. And most of all, where were the cowboys and Indians? Anni had truly thought that one of the first things she would see would be one, both or the other, even here in New York. This was not what she had envisioned at all.

Once the thought had settled into their minds that they were with the right person, Charlie gently and gentlemanly took Anni by the arm and grabbed her bags. He led her proudly through the throng of men and women led to parting gates like cattle. Anni presented her identification and was quickly cleared. Outside the front of the terminal, Charlie walked Anni to the family's black sedan. He drove her to a hotel where they could spend some time before having family and friends fawning over her. Charlie had promised this in his letters and felt it would be a good way to ease the transition. Let her have some peace and quiet, time to talk one-on-one before the "inquisition" began at home. Sadly, it wasn't going to work.

They arrived at the hotel and went to their quarters. There the two of them sat silently staring around the room and occasionally at one another. There was not only the language barrier but Anni felt out of place and hurriedly shut herself up in her cocoon. She sat in the corner of the room, slight tears on her cheeks with a heart aching painfully for home. She wanted to go home. This wasn't what she expected and she felt helpless. She just wanted to go home.

Charlie knew this was not going to be easy, but he was not about to have come this far to let things fall to pieces. It was just needing that old-fashioned fix called time. She would eventually come out of her shell and realize the love he had for her and that she could fly free here and seek levels she never could have dreamed of at home. He was determined to make her happy and he patiently waited it out. Frustrating, yes, but he was not a quitter and she was his wife. Charlie had the patience and forgiving understanding of ten men. He coaxed Anni out of her corner, out of the room and they quietly left the hotel. Maybe a change of atmosphere would be better and maybe having some people around would do the trick. He took her for a walk along the streets of New York. He showed her the place where he had studied floral arranging and the flower store where he first worked before opening their shop. It helped but didn't completely bring Anni falling into his arms. More patience and more work was required. He decided to check out of the hotel, call home and head there to have dinner with the folks and let the welcome to the family begin.

Upon arrival at the home of Charlie's parents, it was still evident that Anni was timid and shy. This butterfly may have been strong as iron, resilient and determined but just like any other butterfly, the wrong touch could smudge its wings and it would never be able to fly again. For a butterfly not to fly would be certain death. Charlie was treading very thin ice and had to handle this matter with extreme caution and delicacy. Of course, at the door, Charlie tried to ease Anni in, but it was a full frontal assault of well-intended welcomes. Charlie's mother and father tried to immediately embrace and warm the child and put her at ease. They wanted her to know that she could consider things as if she had been born here and they had been family all her life. Two problems: Anni didn't know them at all and they didn't share a word of mutual language. This was awkward and uncomfortable, and again Anni just wanted to go home. She knew they meant well and they were most certainly kind; however, she was alone in an alien world thousands of miles from all she knew and was accustomed to.

Once inside, the family tried meekly to win Anni's comfort as she was introduced to more members of the family and the smiles and attentions were doled out in excess. No matter how much was tried, she was shell-shocked and would not come out of the cocoon, ever. As they sat down at the table for a fine roast dinner, Charlie placed his young wife safely and securely beside him. The family all gathered to their seats and bowed their heads in a moment of silent prayer. Anni bowed her head also. However, upon lifting it she made the sign of the cross as she had done thousands of times in her life as a Catholic. It drew strange looks. She was in the home of Presbyterians.

As the members of the family began to chatter to cover up the awkward moment, Charlie's mother sliced the steaming roast on the large plate in order to divide the bountiful meal. Unfortunately, as the knife edged its way back and forth along the broad side of the beef, the red center became exposed and the blood of the rare entree' oozed from within and filled the bottom of the platter. Anni's head and stomach took turns reeling and spinning. She got violently nauseated and upped herself from the table without hesitation. Charlie could see it on her face and knew what was happening. He rushed her to the bathroom and there she became violently ill. She sequestered herself in the bathroom for what seemed like hours. She had no appetite and dinner would have to go on without her as she was escorted upstairs to lie down in bed to recover. It was a disaster. The family made the best of it and Charlie assured them that all would be well—it had just been a long journey and soon the family would see that he had made the right choice and that this girl was going to be a great wife. The questions were clearly etched on the faces of the others.

The following morning Anni awoke to find the sunlight broadly filling the room and Charlie nowhere to be found. She dressed herself and meandered downstairs following the faint sounds of voices in the kitchen. "Well, good morning, Anni!" Charlie's mother exclaimed. She was still determined to make the young lass feel at home. Charlie's father had long left for work at his law office and Charlie had left even earlier to tend to the flower shop and meet the pre-dawn arrival of today's flower shipment at the back door. Charlie's mother and his brother Johnny were the only two in the kitchen. They offered breakfast—toast, eggs, bread, bacon, coffee, anything—all to no avail. Anni wasn't hungry yet.

"Where is Charlie?" Anni asked in her now timid English. "Come on, I'll show you," Johnny said. The two of them gathered up and headed out the door and down the street toward the shop that Charlie had purchased and that she was now half owner of. It was far from settled in her mind. As they walked down the street, they passed by the various markets and stores. It was as if she had landed in Oz. So much food, material things and abundance. As they strolled, one thing in particular caught her eyes and they slowed their pace. On the sidewalk in front of the produce store there were big wooden boxes sectioned off, waist-high in front of the windows. Tomatoes, oranges, apples, onions and bananas. Bananas! Anni hadn't seen those in more than four years and Johnny took notice immediately that the girl had an appetite. There wasn't time to waste. He waved at the owner of the store watching from inside behind the counter and grabbed two of them and handed them to Anni.

She looked at Johnny quizzically but assumed he knew what he was doing. She took them and thanked him in her *Lëtzebuergesch* and English. He just laughed and they continued their walk. She ate both the bananas before they arrived at the shop. There they met Charlie busy at work, with not much time to talk. He stopped and showed Anni around, trying his best to explain that this was their store. They owned it and this is where they would work, side by side and madly in love, never leaving each other for a moment. Anni appreciated Charlie's devotion and unbridled passion. She didn't know much else about this place called New York but she did know that this lanky, handsome man in front of her loved her and for that there was no doubt.

Eventually, she and Johnny returned to the house. Shortly thereafter, Helen arrived to take Anni shopping for clothes. Helen was married to George, Charlie's second brother. The two of them made a day of it with hardly a word of English but in the end Anni was comforted, more at ease and now had some fine things to wear. She was becoming Americanized without knowing it.

By the second day, Anni was feeling better and even brisk as she awoke and looked forward to a new day of experiences. However, just like the sudden attacks of sadness after the loss of a loved one, she would think of home and immediately she would fall homesick again. It was a terrible cycle but she made the best of it and was determined to take it one day at a time. Today, she would walk to the shop on her own and see Charlie and maybe even stay a while longer. After all, it was with him that she had the most sense of security. Along the way, she passed the produce stand and there she paused. She looked at the bananas and then inside to the store owner where it appeared he hadn't moved from yesterday. He smiled at her and waved. She half-heartedly lifted her hand with a faint smile, grabbed four bananas and headed for the flower shop. "What a strange country," she thought to herself. "Everything seems to cost money but you can eat all the bananas you want." It wasn't until several days later that Charlie had to explain to Anni that the grocer at the produce stand had known his family a very long time and that the family had credit with him. The bananas she was eating by the handfuls were being charged to their account and Charlie would have to pay for them. Anni felt foolish, but Charlie just did as usual: He laughed it off, hugged her and loved her and told her what a silly girl she was but she would be just fine. "From now on, just try to eat some food at home and ease off on the bananas," was Charlie's advice to his young American/Luxembourg wife.

# Part IV

# Coming of Her Own in America

# For Better or Worse

*Charlie certainly wasn't a man to sit idle. His body and abilities were challenged to keep up with his thoughts and ideas. He had many. He had many conversations in his mind about how to run a successful business, how to look to the future, how to have the greatest marriage he could envision and make his entire family happy. The contemplation made the ideas work nearly every time. The thoughts haggled for days, months and years, depending on the idea. But once the idea had been completely "thought-out," Charlie was on the go and wouldn't rest until the finished idea turned reality. He had more than just a "no guts, no glory," mentality, he had a work ethic that was almost a natural high for him, and he thrived on the challenges. He wouldn't settle for a compromised plan nor would he be settled until it was finished and the next one waited at the door of his mind. Charlie was not just a thinker, he was one very hardworking man that seemed to have a never-ending supply of "go" and that is exactly what he did from sunup to sundown.*

*He was determined to make dreams come true, he was bent on many hopes and he loved to relish in a job finished and well done, a project completed or a happy, smiling face on anyone that was family or friend. He didn't dare make sacrifices at other's expense. He did challenge those around him more than once, but the sacrifices were practically all his and he didn't mind. He grew up in Brooklyn, New York where his father was a hardworking lawyer, not rich and fancy, just paid a decent salary for a state job under the New York Bar Association. Charlie wasn't brought up with a silver spoon in his mouth and he didn't want to raise his own children that way. A strong work ethic was what made America great and it was also what, in his mind, won the war he had just left behind. Plain and simple, you don't stop until the job is done and done right. That's all. He lived up to that philosophy on a daily basis.*

Anni had arrived March 24, 1946. By the first week of May (almost six weeks to the day), Charlie had worked in the store, taught Anni the basics of floral design, put Anni in school to learn English and bought a house of their own on the GI Bill. Six weeks of accomplishments that would have taken some people months and a sluggard a lifetime. Charlie was just getting started, in his own eyes. He had hit the ground running and he was a long way from where his mind had already been. He didn't see endings, only new beginnings or additions. As far as additions went, the store, house and Anni weren't all. On the same week Charlie drove his parents' car, with Anni alongside, to their new and empty home. He had ordered a bedroom set to make his wife comfortable and nothing else. It was a simple start but the ideas in Charlie were as alive as ever and still being thought out. During the same week, he walked Anni from their new home, down the street and pointed it out.

"There it is, Babychen!" He states proudly, with a long, thin finger pointing at the object in front of her. "What?" she asks. "That baby [pointing again], that is our first car!" he exclaims. Anni looks again at the vehicle in front of her and back at Charlie. At first she thinks he is teasing her, as often he does, or is joking most certainly. It is not teasing nor a joke. Charlie is serious. Anni puts on a quick smile before the one on her husband's face fades. In front of her is a 1929 Ford PIN (for Pinto) Model A. It has the juicy little 2.3 liter Ford motor and a four-speed manual shift. Wide running boards link the curvaceous tire wells. The tires are eighteen-inch whitewalls. It has "bug-eyed" headlights at the nose of its snout-like front half, two-tone body paint and a convertible top. "Isn't it a beaut?" Charlie beams to his little Brown-Eyes.

"It's a Model A Ford with all the works and a rumble seat where we can haul the flowers. I got it straight up for $150 cash!" Charlie was very proud of his ideas and dreams coming true. He had his beautiful young bride, a home in his own name with a $45 a month mortgage and a "sporty" car paid for in cash. It was American dreaming at its finest. Done! And on the way. That was how Charlie saw it. Anni, however, was thinking of a house with no furniture, a husband that had the heart of a little boy (obviously head-over-heels in love with her), and now this metal monster. She had no idea how she would ever handle such a beast or drive it. She did smile once about the car. It reminded her of some of the Abbott and Costello movies she had seen. It was an "Abbott and Costello" car. A comedy to Anni and a dreamboat to Charlie. To each his own.

Charlie didn't have much money in his pocket but he was rich. He owned his own business, a house, a paid-for car and had a gorgeous young bride. His life was nearly perfect to him and, although there were some high aspirations waiting in the wings of his mind, he was already at a pinnacle. For Anni, things were different; she had a problem heavy in her heart. It wasn't that she was ungrateful, miserable or disappointed. Not at any of that nor anything to do with Charlie. Anni's problem was one of a different sort that can only be explained from experience. She was homesick. She was with Charlie and she did have a house to live in, even an old-new car to drive, but she wasn't at home. "What good was it all?" she thought to herself. She had more than she could have dreamed of already. A loving and doting husband, a nice house and a vehicle. That was rich, compared to home.

The problem was that she had "it" but no one to share it with. At home, family, friends, neighbors and extended family, from miles away, would be thronging just to see the new husband, not to mention the house and automobile. It made her all the more homesick. She loved Charlie and could see his love for her on his sleeve, in his hands and eyes. But, she couldn't make herself feel as happy as she wanted to be. The things around her were valueless without sharing the joy of having these blessings with family, friends and neighbors. She was of a sharing spirit and yet, she couldn't even share a conversation, to most points, with anyone. The joys were awash in tears of loneliness. Charlie still had some "worse" to deal with before the "better."

After some shrewd negotiations, Charlie managed to work a deal with the men that had delivered the bedroom set. For a trade of business, flowers for their ladies of interest and ten dollars, Mr. Adams would present Mrs. Adams with a couch and a dining room table. The house was being filled already! But Charlie knew he had to keep this woman's heart on him and off her heartbreak for home. So, in addition to the furniture, he added a dog and five living bunny rabbits to warm the place and occupy her. Charlie would stop at nothing to keep her cheered as much as possible. He knew she loved rabbits, and he remembered her story of her uncle that raised them for food. He knew that she had, with the wink from her grandmother, let all the rabbits out of their cages. Yes, she had been mischievous but her act showed her heart. Charlie never forgot the story and brought the good memories back to life for her and made her laugh, even if for a short while. It was okay. He had more new ideas that were being thought out. He was just getting started and he knew in the end that this young girl turned woman would be his forever and totally devoted.

As the year wore on, it was one challenge after the other for Charlie. His diet consisted mostly of cooked noodles or potatoes. Anni was still out of her element and unsure of what to feed her husband. Eventually, with the help of a few experiments with meat and much help from a kind neighbor, Rita, Anni started to feed her husband enough to keep him alive. They worked side by side almost every working hour of seven days per week. The store showed its own potential and the business gradually expanded. With all things considered, the two were a success with unlimited potential. But each night before the lights went out, Charlie knew there was something desperately wrong with his wife and that this was a critical situation. If he couldn't fix this problem, the whole house of cards would collapse. His wife, no matter how hard she tried, no matter how hard he tried, was so deeply rooted to her family and home that she was not going to make it here in New York or in any other state or country. She needed a daily companion, a confidant and a reminder of the sights, sounds and smells of all the seasons of home, of Luxembourg. If Charlie couldn't fix this, it was over and he had met his match only to fail. He set his ideas going and his thoughts chasing hard after them as he began a new plan.

Over the last seven months of the year and into the next, things continued to go well for the two newlyweds. Anni was coming out of her cocoon more often and making friends. The shop was prospering and so were Charlie's ideas on how to keep the ball rolling. His ideas from early on had formulated into one plan, and the thoughts turned into action over the following year. He knew if he wanted to keep his wife, he had to fix this problem. The woman was overwhelmingly Luxembourger and her country called to her in the night. If Charlie didn't fix this, Luxembourg would blow through the window curtains in the night like a vampire and take his Brown-Eyes away.

Charlie knew Anni. Charlie knew Anni's family, friends and neighbors. Charlie knew Luxembourg. Charlie knew Albert, "Bubby." Sometimes alone, he would grin so big that only he and God knew it but it was the answer and it would do the trick. If you can't take her back home, then bring some of her home to her. That was Charlie's idea and plan. In 1948, after much expense of hard work, paperwork and finesse, Charlie brought his bride another gift: her beloved brother and one of her best friends, the clown, the one that made her laugh for years, Albert Neuman (the junior). Bubby was on his way to America and would come live with them and work in the flower shop. It was the only thing that kept Anni from buying a ticket back home. For her, it had been madness and sadness mixed with some happiness. It was just all too bittersweet to have so much love and riches and not have her family to talk to, or anyone that knew where her home country was or that it even existed. Now, Luxembourg was coming to America and Luxembourg was going to live with her. Bubby was on his way. Once again, Charlie pulled off his magic hat.

At the end of 1948, after Anni warmly welcomed Bubby's arrival in the United States, there was another event to add to the swirling emotions. Almost as if Charlie and Anni had exchanged Christmas presents, Anni had received her brother to love, cherish and share their common bonds, memories, language and homeland. But the latest news was a present for Charlie, Anni was pregnant. She would be due in seven months, July 1949. The newlyweds were about to become a rounded-out and complete family. A husband and wife with a child on the way. Anni had an enormous present from home and her gratitude to her husband was expressed in a gift that the two had wrapped together. It wouldn't be opened for Christmas but it was a gift and it was more than Charlie could handle. He had his sweetheart happy. He had a good and close friend and confidant in Bubby, he had the business, the home and the car. Now, he had his first child on the way. His love grew even more, if it were possible. With his, Anni's did also. Dreams were coming true.

If the end of one year had not been eventful enough with joyous news, by the earliest part of 1949, Anni and Charlie found out via mail that Papa (the senior Albert) had not only been released from his confinement, but had received full restoration of his citizenship as a true Luxembourger, and a letter of apology. The man had suffered greatly. Humiliation, loss of family, degradation and imprisonment. He had lost time from his life, and his achievements of the past were tarnished.

Albert Neuman exited the building that had held him for nearly three years and breathed a thirsty breath of air off the wind that blew over his beloved Luxembourg. For all that had happened to him, it was still his home and his country. He could never forget his bitterness for the cruelty of some little minds, but he never questioned his country nor his loyalty to it. He never denied who he was and he was proud just to be back where he belonged. His family was with him and he was with them all, once again restored. The war was the loser. The Neumans won as a family and they won a victory to set an example for all those in the future that keep hope and never give up. If you keep the faith, you just might have a happy ending to each and every challenge, no matter how ugly, bitter or hopeless it may seem. Perseverance, patience and prayer.

In the sweltering heat of a New York summer, in a place where "north" is supposed to be cold, on July 12, 1949, Anni experienced the most pain she had ever felt to date in her life. No matter how much the great was, she couldn't be happier or angrier at the same time. Angry with herself and angry with Charlie—they did this and she was hurting. Happy because she knew she was doing the one thing that is so very special to a woman, something that no man could ever know. She was opening her own cocoon to bring a new life into the glowing lights of life. She had played host to this unborn child for nine long months and enough was enough. The culmination left her exhausted and torn between laughter and tears. She had a baby boy. His name would be George Albert Adams and she would mother him as best she knew how, but her love for the baby, the child, the living human being, was overwhelming to think of. God had blessed her and she was living a life of abundance bought with pain, hard work and struggle. But nevertheless, life was getting better and not worse.

By the close of the year, the new and proud father, Charlie Adams, kept his ideas ahead, his thoughts working and his plans fulfilled. The husband, wife and brother (brother-in-law) trio, along with a slinky pink package, were the occupants of a new location for employment. Even at birth, young George was a part of the workforce. Albeit, he was more of an inconvenient roustabout, but he was in the store and he was minding business. However, the store had now moved to a larger location to meet the new level and standard of business. Things were going quite well for all. Charlie was all smiles from dawn to dusk, Anni had her oldest brother, husband and a baby. Albert was loving America and its women, and George was being spoiled like a baby.

# To Have and to Hold

*Having something doesn't mean that one can always hold it. And, vice versa, holding something or someone doesn't mean you can have it or them permanently. Things come and go. Some are kept and some do last a lifetime. Some things last longer than a lifetime. Likewise, so it goes with people in our lives. They come and go. Some stay for a lifetime and some go beyond that. Some, even though they pass on in the flesh, stay with us a lifetime in memories, thoughts, visions, dreams and memorabilia. Some people last even longer than the lifetime they indwell, our own memories, thoughts and reflections. They go on living in spirit and presence through material things.*

*The things, the little treasures or even someone's accidental trash. There, in the middle of all the coins, papers, pictures, books, etc. In all the "little" things around us, passed by in our daily lives, are the others that have preceded us. Whether it was a year ago or a thousand years ago. One cannot look around without seeing a part of someone else's life. Their names may never be known, but they have most certainly been here and the proof is in the object that presently exists. Sometimes, to have is to hold. Other times to hold is to have. If we do it just right, we can do both, maybe not with our hands, but with our hearts and minds. We can cherish a loved one long gone by holding the memory of their smile in our mind's movie screen. We can lift an old photo album or report card and hold that person again. Likewise, we can take those that are with us as we live in a day and touch the things that no longer exist.*

*One can embrace a mother that is still here with us and still smell the flower you presented to her when you were five. You can hold her in an embrace and feel the thing that brought you both a smile and an everlasting reward, a fond memory. Sometimes, we can dream and there in that dream, both have and hold a thing or person, or both. It was just a dream, yet for that beautiful and wonderful moment, it was to have and to hold. It was a refreshing memory of something stored away in a box somewhere in our mind and gently lifted out by our soul in our sleep. Sometimes we wake and wish to cry for it; missing these things, people and moments hurts. But it is a brave thing to smile and remember: Last night, this morning, today, this evening, in my mind, I did have it. I did hold it. It is still mine, by God's grace, through my mind, will and emotions—to have and to hold for all eternity if I truly wish and believe.*

For Anni, her arms were full. She had her husband to hold at night. She had her baby George to hold, more sometimes than she wanted. She had her brother to hold and, through him, hold the rest of her family, friends and home. She did have a lot and much to be thankful for. Things were getting better and the homesickness was being eased by the business, the baby and the studies. Much was happening and all at a rapid pace. She didn't have to be in New York to experience the fast pace of life. The fast pace of life does not belong solely to those that live in a large city. Anni could be in Luxembourg under these circumstances and have as much to do. It was refreshing to her and she was growing into it. She was also growing in wisdom, age and intellect. She was growing by leaps and bounds in all areas of her life. Of course it was, like a river-course, always changing, and more change was on its way.

The year 1949 gave way to 1950 as the family continued to work together. After exhausting and excruciating trials and errors, Charlie was finally able to teach Anni how to drive the car and she obtained her first driver's license. Charlie and Albert became very close friends and enjoyed each other's company from the shop to a cold beer or home. It was as if they had been friends for life. It warmed Anni's heart toward her husband and altogether. Anni would keep young George in a basket on the floor of the shop or up on a table. All the while, working putting together flower arrangements as the orders continued to grow faster than the baby. However, the business and the baby were running fairly close in growth. It wouldn't be long before a larger store would be needed. By mid 1951, there wasn't enough room for the three adults to rub elbows and work happily. To add to the cluster of confusion, there was a toddler, now two years old, slipping, sliding and laughing on all the loose cuttings lying on the floor. He was an "ankle-biter" and getting to be too much into everything. At times, Anni thought she had given birth to a monster with four hands. He was just too fast for her and Charlie both. Albert would sometimes spend more time entertaining the young George than working, just so the other two could work.

With so much to hold onto, it was only a matter of time before something had to be let go, and it came without anyone in the family's decision. The decision was made by an unknown uncle, "Uncle Sam." Albert, not yet even a naturalized citizen of the United States, was drafted into the Army and sent to serve in Okinawa. Things were heating up on a small peninsula somewhere in Asia, not too distant for the young Luxembourger-turned-American GI, a place called Korea. Albert had never heard of it. But, typical Albert, he looked forward to it with his carnival/gypsy spirit and dreamed of icy drinks and warm island girls. No one could wipe the smile off his face. One more adventure coming up! That was Albert and he was a long way from closing the book on his exploit.

With Albert gone and Anni back home with Charlie, baby George and the shop, it didn't take long for the letters from Mama, Papa, Chuck and Elfie to start stirring the homesickness she had suffered before. It grew steadily in Albert's absence, even with her now close-to-fluent English. She still needed someone from home. Without it, she would go back into her cocoon and close her wings. No one could see the beauty of them—unless she was happy.

Finally, Charlie could stand it no longer and announced some good news to Anni and bad news for himself. He was willing to let go for three months and send both his wife and two-year-old son to Europe, specifically Luxembourg. Charlie was doomed to double labor at the flower shop, to work day and night, come home to an empty house and write letters. He suffered it patiently like the man that he was, but he wasn't going to lie and say he was happy about it either. "Just make the girl happy and she will be a better wife when she gets home," Charlie told himself for the much needed reassurance.

Tickets were purchased with much thought and concern by Charlie. He made the best preparations he could for his wife and son. They had cabin-class tickets on the *Queen Mary*, the same ship that had transported over 760,000 troops during the war and had ferried Winston Churchill as a guest of honor on three separate occasions. Now the ship was back in service as a magnificent giant on the seas, providing the pinnacle of elegance in the cruise ship industry. Anni wasn't going first class according to price, but the ship and the trip were a first-class trip for the girl that had come to America on the bare-boned *Vulcania*. The trip back across the water was in total contrast to the first trip. Now, she was no longer a war bride. She was a wife, mother, sister, daughter-in-law and an upcoming American citizen. Most of all, she was going home for the first time in five years, and the ship couldn't move fast enough to get her there.

For all Charlie's good efforts and best arrangements, there was one thing he couldn't control. Just as she had encountered a storm on her trip headed west, so would Anni face a storm going east. But this one was far worse. The first one, she knew would pass and eventually good weather would appear. This "new" storm was completely unique. It was unpredictable, as most storms are, but worse. It could last longer than winds, rain and high seas. This one could last a very, very long time. Here on this beautiful and ornate ship, things were magnificently wonderful. She and young George were catered to on every level of the twelve-decked ship. The crew was honed in the skills of servitude. All the amenities were laid out before them like a thousand Christmases. Therein lay the trouble, the storm. The storm was two years old, long, far and away from being spent. It was little Georgie, the storm of 1951 and Anni didn't know how long it was going to last but no umbrella, raincoat or shelter could protect her. She had the unenviable task of harnessing the storm that everyone else could either shun or ignore. Anni was a twenty-five-year-old mother with a two-year-old terror on her hands. She had brothers and a sister, but nothing like this. This was her child but she had never been taught how to be a mother. The ship was sure on its course but Anni was totally lost at sea.

Here on the magnificent ship, *Queen Mary*, named after Her living Majesty, there were over two thousand portals and one little George Albert Adams had it in mind to stick his head out each and every one. He once even dared to run to the railing in hopes of diving into the "Peter Pan" water below. Anni was forever chasing, grabbing, chastising and perspiring, keeping this "little Mr. Energy" in her charge. She was not thinking very fondly of Charlie at this time. She refused to recognize her part in it and laid it all at Charlie's feet. It was his son and he caused this to happen. She only wanted a happy husband. Of course, she wanted her children too, she wanted the dream of being a good mother with a fairytale family. But, reality was here and it was running deck by deck, window to window, table to table and Anni was ready to jump overboard herself.

By two days into the trip, Anni was made aware of the fact that one of the glorious programs on the ship was a full-service, around-the-clock day care, so that the adults could enjoy their cruise. Immediately, Anni found the deck and the door where she could deposit her young, handsome, energetic charge. It lasted one day. "Mrs. Adams," said the purser. "We have a small problem, but we also think, with your permission, we can take care of it. The staff in the day-care facilities have indicated that your son is just a little more than they can handle at this time. It isn't that he has been necessarily bad. He has just been a little too active for them to handle. You see, this does happen occasionally and we would like to offer you a one-to-one babysitter when and as you need. Would that be okay with you?" He pleaded with his eyes for a yes answer. "Yes sir," Anni replied. She didn't mind. She knew her son and knew that he was a challenge. In fact, the harder one tried, the better they would have been to have left well enough alone. George wasn't a "bad" child, a little spoiled, maybe even somewhat bratty, but mostly, he just plainly had his father and mother's blood in his mix. A Charles D. Adams and Anni Jeanne Neuman concoction that produced energy levels, curiosity and thirst for adventure that couldn't be harnessed by a dozen mules.

At two years old, give him one hour of your time and he would take away four of your years. That was young Georgie on the rise, and he was just getting started. He was the physical representation and blueprint of his father's mind. One wildly moving on the inside, Charlie. The other moving just as wildly on the outside, young George. It was that very outward excitement and uncontainable George that would help save his mother from a monster and possibly even himself from harm.

Several days into the trip, as things began to steady, Anni and George were ready to retire to their cabin for the night and sleep peacefully. Anni had rang the steward service and requested a night milk for George so that he would fall happily to sleep. When the knock came at the door, it was man, but not the steward. There, within inches of Anni's face was the overwhelming smell of alcohol and a large, burly man. He had been eying the woman traveling alone with the child and figured he had a place to have his way and please himself. He calculated wrong. He used his bulk to press into the room and tried to close the door behind him. However, in the small quarters it wasn't working well for him. Anni began to resist his grabbing and wrestling. She did as she had been taught by her father with the same maneuver she had used years ago on a German soldier. She used her knees to "kick" at a certain target. To make matters worse for the intruder, there in the cramped quarters was a two-year-old child with the lungs of an operatic majesty. Little George let out a scream, well practiced in the past, that would have nearly stopped the entire ship on its course. The man attempted to run away, wounded in the groin and in the ears, only to be taken charge of by the rescue staff.

It began to seem to Anni that whether she was headed for home or away from home, her travels were cursed with challenges of an extraordinary kind. Just once, she would like to go in one or the other direction without an unusual event. Of course, upon her arrival, little George wasn't done with his antics. Throughout the visit, Anni enjoyed seeing her mother, father, Chuck and Elfie for the first time in five years. Young George was introduced and immediately spoiled by the family. It was a nail in the coffin for Anni. "Please, don't spoil him," she begged. All to deaf ears.

It became a daily challenge to enjoy the return home and the breathing of the Luxembourg air, being a new wife, mother and distant member to her family. On one special occasion, the wills of mother and son came to a peak. In a shop, George had found something he wanted. Anni was ready to leave. Outside on the sidewalk, George made his grandest stand and protest. Anni made hers also. As the fitful little Georgie flit, flew and flopped in a furious tantrum on the sidewalk with his whole body like a fish out of water, Anni continued on her path home. "Stay there if you wish, I am going home," she declared. She said he could spend the night there if he wished, but she was not relenting or giving an inch and she meant it. It was time to set some things straight. After an awkward amount of time, an Esch police officer approached the child and set him to standard. He queried as to where the child lived and deduced from the input of the local friends and neighbors, whose child this was and where he was staying. George got an escort home and Anni smiled at the officer for solving a very difficult problem, but ignored any eye contact with George whatsoever. He was commanded to bed and that was that. One battle won, but far from over. He was a lot for the naive mother to have, much more to hold.

Upon their return home to New York, Charlie greeted his wife and son with great joy and elation. He had truly missed them and was ecstatic to have them home. His own little family was back together and now his mind could be at ease over their safety and focus on all the ideas that had been feeding his thoughts through their absence. Charlie didn't like being left alone except for very special occasions. He liked having people around and most of all, family and friends. He had his moments but they were precious and few. They were always kept between him and God and that was good enough.

While the smaller family was together, the extended family remained close regardless of the miles of distance. Both Charlie and Anni wrote letters frequently to all of Anni's family in Luxembourg and to Albert in Okinawa. In turn, the same family members stayed in close contact with the young couple. In fact, Albert, being his industrious self, did more than just stay in touch. He had cornered a market. He was on an island far out in the Pacific Ocean and surrounded by hundreds and hundreds of lonely soldiers. He put his present circumstances to work for his good friend and brother-in-law, Charlie. Albert managed to put a system in place whereby the soldiers could, in their lonely state, place flower orders for their wives, mothers and girlfriends back home. All they had to do was go see Albert and the rest would be taken care of. Albert would forward the orders to Charlie, who then filled them and used FTD's system to reach out to the surrounding states. It was a stroke of genius on Albert's part and showed that he, too, had the American spirit of capitalism and business finesse. The operation continued until Albert's return from his enlistment in 1953, when he finally came back home to Charlie, Anni and little George.

Time waits for no man and Charlie wasn't waiting much for it in return. Nor was Anni. Over the next year Anni, Albert, George and Nina, a friend of Anni's, all returned to Luxembourg for a three-month stay. This time George was a little older and improving on his own. He still had his feistiness, but he did listen to his mother, most of the time. He knew better than to cross his Uncle Albert, it was better to keep him as a fellow clown and troubadour. Once again Charlie was left "defending the fort" so to speak, but he was able to enlist the aid of a young lady to fill in as an assistant. It wasn't much, but it helped. Meanwhile, in Luxembourg, Albert and Anni set about to immediately orchestrate getting the whole family brought to America. Charlie was all for it and encouraged it. He loved the family like his own and wanted to see them take full advantage of the opportunities that were flowing in their hometown. Little George wasn't going to stay "little" long. He celebrated his fourth birthday in his mother's hometown of Esch-sur-Alzette and loved the country and its people. They loved him also.

While in Luxembourg, Albert met a woman that turned his head far enough for the first time to catch him for matrimony. Thus, he set about bringing Jeanny, his bride-to-be, back to the United States with the rest of the family. By the end of 1953, the entire Neuman clan had arrived on American soil and no less than ten people had taken up residence at the small home of Charlie and Anni Adams. It was quite a sight to see and presented a lot of challenges, but everyone did their part and it worked. Papa got a job as a lathe operator in a machine shop without even being able to speak English. Mama went to work babysitting and cleaning houses on the side. Elfie went to school along with George. Of course, for Chuck, things were a little different. He had hardly planted his feet on U.S. soil before, like Albert, he was drafted into the Army and this time, sent into harms way. He went to Korea for a "police action" that took years, if not decades, to be recognized as a war. He served his new country before he even received his citizenship. Though they were Luxembourgers, the Neumans contributed greatly to the United States of America in an untraditional way but with service beyond selfishness. They were willing to show they weren't people to run and hide. They stood up, stood tall and made both Papa and Charlie proud. In the crowded Adams home there wasn't any choice but to have and to hold, if you wanted to eat, sleep, laugh and enjoy life. It was Charlie's only standing rule: No unhappiness, sadness or loneliness aloud. It didn't always work but it stood the test through cooperation and love.

Strange things never ceased to occur for Charlie, Anni and their families. In 1954, when Jeanny arrived to greet her husband Albert, they met at the docks with the rest of the family in tow. Upon arrival, the two lovebirds embraced and kissed. A picture was taken and ended up being published across the wire on the Associated Press. It was called a "cheesecake picture" and was noticed by the producers of the Jack Paar Show. The young couple and the entire family were invited to come play on the trivia show. They accepted the invitation and all arrived for the live show. In the end, after each family member participated by answering their questions, Albert and Jeanny were the winners of more than four thousand dollars to start them off on their marriage. Only in America. The family could never cease finding new ways of making jokes and laughing about it. Good fortune seemed to meet every member of the broad family no matter which way they turned. Their hard work seemed to always payoff. They were truly blessed. After taking in the dough, Albert and Jeanny bought a house and soon his mother, father and sister took the downstairs and he and his new wife took the upstairs quarters.

Almost immediately upon his return from Korea, Chuck landed a job with the Hazeltine Corporation. He went to work hard and fast. He moved to Washington, D.C. for a while and then returned to Long Island to his own apartment. Things were going well, growth was taking place all around and the entire family was prospering. That same year, Charlie decided to make some more steps toward the future. For a mortgage of $150.00 per month, Charlie purchased a half acre of land on the south fork of Long Island, in South Hampton, for the total purchase price of $1,500.00. It was a wise investment. Within a year the land would be paid for, and a house began to rise from the ground as Charlie paid piecemeal for subcontractors to build as the profits came in from the store. Of course, as things were growing for the family on the outside, so was something growing on the inside of the family, not just lots of love, but in Anni another baby was being formed and would be born three days before Charlie's own forty-first birthday.

On March 2, 1956, Jeffrey Charles Adams came into the world and both Charlie and Anni were overjoyed. Even George took great pride in his new baby brother. It was just what he needed, especially at the age of seven years. He had someone to play with and become closer to than just brothers, but real friends. Now there was one more to the family to have and to hold and the bonds were unbreakable. Anni had finally accepted her life here in America—she was American and so were her children. She still held Luxembourg close in her heart and so did the rest of her family. They didn't have to have it in their hands to hold it. It held them and it was a perfect match between love, hope and dreams. There seemed to be no limit to what the future held for all of them. Practically whatever they set their hearts and minds to, they could indeed have and hold.

# In Sickness and in Health

*As long as there is a "mankind," there will be the better and the worse. Also, there will come the times to have and to hold. With it all, it is endured or persevered through sickness and in health. It is a fact of life, a part of life. We all fall victim to sickness at one point or another. Some times it is brief, sometimes it comes and goes, sometimes it lasst a lifetime and eventually, for all, it leads us away from life. This is all the more reason we cherish health. We don't always appreciate it as we should and that is a travesty. Good health is worth more than anything money can buy. In the end, good health is a gift from God. It is to be treasured and adored. Not only the health that we have individually in our mortal bodies but the health of our friends, families and neighbors. It should be that the whole world could experience this precious gift on a daily basis, but it isn't so. It is far too much taken for granted, abused, ignored or disregarded. That is, until the sickness comes to remind us of the true meaning of health.*

*This concept is not just one that concerns our physical bodies. It applies to all areas that make up who we are as "mankind." It applies to our mind, will and emotions (our soul), it applies to our thought life, our purpose for being and it is entrenched in our spirit. If we lose our spirit, we have lost it all. Part of good health has nothing to do with what we eat or how we care for our bodies. It is in our minds. If one dwells upon the negative long enough, that life will become negative and the body with it, and they both will eventually perish. If one focuses on the good things in life—the love, the laughter, songs and joys—it can add years to our life. Focusing on dreams and hopes, even the ones that never came true (at least they were tried), we can learn to laugh and stay healthy in our mind. Our most terminal illness is our own thoughts. The Bible states, "As a man thinketh, so is he," and this truth is evident no matter what one has for philosophy, beliefs, unbelief or desires. It is simple. Our minds, our thoughts, our will and our emotions are something we can control. We have the opportunity to turn bad things to good. No matter how bad it gets, we can find something, some way, to look at it from the other side. Health is not eternal in our body but it can be in our souls. Hope is eternal.*

*We can laugh or we can cry, but we like to laugh. The famous saying, "Laughter is the best medicine," is true. A joyful heart does a soul good. Dwelling on the past will eventually hold a person imprisoned to it. Looking too far to the future and ignoring the present can cause hurtful and painful falls. It is best to focus on the present, enjoy it for its namesake, it is a "present" from God. Again, the Bible states, in the words of Jesus, "Be of good cheer for I have overcome the world." We are made to overcome and the way to good health is living a full and good life on a daily basis. If you have lost someone you love, have never loved, have missed an opportunity to love—anything that causes you to stumble in your peace of mind should be dumped in the wastebasket of the mind. Think of the good things, the good memories. The laughter and the joys. Having done this, by purpose and will, the mind becomes healthy, the body follows and others around will take notice. We can have all the joy in the world even through and in sickness and in health.*

By the year 1958, great things were happening. When it came to health, the word had a very special meaning to Anni, Charlie, the Neuman family and the Adams family. Prosperity was flowing from the fingertips of their collective and individual hard work, labor and ideas. It was a clan of sorts. In a wonderful way. The strangers, once to all, had blended and become an international family with far-reaching, outstretched arms and open hands. Even in the United States both families were impacting family and friends back in Luxembourg. In the United States, friends and family were being literally made by introduction and birth announcements. This strange, happenstance union of one Charlie Adams and one Anny Neuman was growing into its own legacy. It wasn't something that should be kept secret. It was a story to tell and well worth the telling.

The year brought forth new and exciting things for almost everyone. Anni had been elected by FTD to represent the company on the Edward R. Morrow show *Person to Person* during the taped interviews and commercials. The television show was shot on a two-week basis and the commercials along with it. Anni would appear on just about every episode as one of the FTD ladies presenting beautiful flower arrangements which the viewers could order and have shipped almost anywhere in the world. Anni was being seen internationally on television. Her friends and family here in the United States and as far away as Luxembourg would actually use their cameras to take pictures of their television screens to prove that Anni was actually on TV. Several of those pictures still exist as of this writing in both countries. But it didn't end there. She would also do live commercials for FTD presenting flower arrangements during the *Edward R. Morrow News Hour,* and later in the late 60s and early 70s for FTD-sponsored *Sunday Opera* on the NBC television network. Anni was healthy, her family was healthy, business was healthy and the spirit of life the healthiest of all.

Growth seemed to be in everyone's corner of the world. Things were happening fast and fabulous. Life was rich and it was cherished by the family to its very far reaching extensions, including friends and neighbors. Through the year 1959, family times were growing wildly in all directions. There would be cookouts, parties, holidays to celebrate, and times at the beach house in South Hampton. Charlie was 44, Anni was 32, Papa was 60 and Mama was 57. Chuck was 25, Elfie,15, George,10 and Jeffrey was 3 years old. The good times kept rolling even amidst all the hard work and labor this family put together. Challenges arose on a daily basis but they were handled as a family. Nothing, or at least practically nothing, happened without family intervention, study, consternation and resolution. They worked in tandem and with admirable teamwork even when it related to things outside the scope of one part of the family's occupation compared to another in a different field. In the middle, Charlie and Papa stood as the cohesive force—maestros to it all. They didn't do it with pride, they did it because it was in their heart and they were pleased and proud of what other people could do just because they encouraged them rather than discouraged. Two very smart men.

Living arrangements changed almost as much as the seasons. Chuck had met his wife, Mimi, in an ice cream parlor and they ended up dedicating their lives to one another. The senior Albert, his wife Gredy and daughter Elfie came to live in the new home of Charles Neuman and his wife Mimi. Albert had his hands full with his own wife, life and work. Needless to say, Charlie, Anni, George and Jeffrey were experiencing a most unusual life: Charlie working tirelessly in the store, Anni working in the store one day and traveling to a show the next. George continuing to attend school as did the little Jeffrey. George at public school and Jeffrey, where he had started at the age of two years old, at the Catholic school provided by Joachim and Anne. It didn't take long to find out that Jeffrey was a gifted child. His learning abilities were faster than the words from his mouth. He was funny, happy and hard to put down. He and George had their moments. Plenty of push, run and shove. But they had a bond that far too many brothers fail to enjoy. They loved each other and they let it show. That made a world of difference. It formed them into a team rather than a test. They were growing together and George was always quick to push Jeffrey to a new level of understanding in worldly wisdom, even if it was devilish on George's part. It was purely a comedy within the family and it wasn't hampered by their father Charlie. Anni was satisfied if a day could pass that she didn't feel like strangling one, the other or both. Her happiness came when they were both in bed and actually, truly asleep.

Anni forwarded through another couple of years, traveling the globe (literally), meeting famous people. On stage and television she was a star, but at home she was "Ma" to George and "Mama" to Jeffrey. She was their nemesis. Their adversary. Their victim of great pranks and hoaxes. Not because the boys didn't love their mother. It was quite the opposite. She was just so much fun to play upon or play with. They meant her no harm or ill will, it was just that she was always available to their mischievous little minds. She was at times a willing victim and at other times ready to tie the two together and put them in a closet. She was trying to be a good mother but these two boys were more than she expected. Actually, she was a great mother. It was all in her instinct and just her simple way of "forget the fight, give them what they want and they will shut up and love you." For Anni that is how it worked and it did, well, for the most part anyway.

She was smart about it because she knew one certain thing: No matter what the boys did, how they behaved or treated her, there was always Charlie and that set things in order. The boys didn't push him and if they had truly crossed any lines, they would face him and that was no pleasure. He could look at them and they would wish that they could back time up by the days. Charlie was Anni's saving grace when it came to raising the boys. Charlie was the "heavy" and she was the "easy" and they made a good team of it. Later on, much to their surprise, Ma wasn't as naive as they thought, she was just one good mother.

Soon 1960 arrived, and it was a year spectacular for the Adams and Neumans. Life was growing beyond the balance of weight that the scales could hold. Everyone was another year older and their individual endeavors were markedly ahead of schedule. It was a time of summer fun in South Hampton, romping the beach and the city streets. Winters bundled under snow in Long Island and New York, proper. Family and friends growing by leaps and bounds over this year and the next, 1961. Anni was still in high demand, Charlie was also, with the shop and the family, working hard to make a mark on the "American Dream Train" in the land of opportunity. The two families were healthy and enjoying the bounty that was laid before them like a feast. They were blessed beyond their dreams. Yet, for all they had been through, each one of them, it was a gracious reward from above.

Showers of blessings were falling but with them a sorrow would follow. The test for survival of Charles D. Adams and Anni Neuman Adams came to their doorstep. It didn't knock or announce. It entered without notice, welcome or concern. A mental, emotional and spiritual battle had found its way from World War II, long gone, to the year present some nearly twenty years later. Not from politics or governments, countries nor peoples, but from the sheer challenge of human spirit and the burdens of living, trying to have a life and even more, trying to save a life.

The family had weekends in South Hampton that most of America could only dream about. Not because of riches or excess and such, but because of the richness of simplicity and humble circumstances brought upon the wings of hard work and labor. Weekends to rejoice and forget the harsh days that produced a marginal profit for these people. They weren't the elite nor the socialites. They were hardworking men, women and children and family that "back-boned" New York and got to taste from the good life that the wealthy were hand fed.

On a summer weekend, Anni looked out the window of the South Hampton home across from Little Peconic Bay. There, her husband of seventeen years pushed a lawn mower across the rough tundra of Long Island sand and whispering grass that whipped back at you if you didn't cut it the first time. And right alongside or at least a step behind was Jeffrey. All of some six years old with his plastic, but hardy, toy lawn mower, cutting grass alongside his dad. Anni watched from her kitchen window and became weak in body with the love she felt for her family. She was a sincerely blessed woman for all her life of trials, triumphs and tragedies.

From age one through seven, Jeffrey Charles Adams had spent a lifetime gathering in memories as those that gather wheat in the fields of the Midwestern states of America. Jeffrey, or Jeff, if you wish to call him that, was one very special boy and everyone knew it. Jeffrey was good at math, something George hated. Only two people today could tell you the details and they are the very same two that knew him best.

Jeffrey was always coming down with a cold or other minor illness that he just could not shed. It came to the point that he was going to the doctor on monthly visits. His symptoms were always varied but remained constant in that he was sickly. He just could not regain a total sense of well-being. Yet, this was still the beginning of a new year and everyone looked forward to the months of surprises, holidays and happiness that a new year brings.

April 1962 soon arrived and the sun was shining almost as bright as the summer sky. It was time to take young Jeffrey back to the doctor once more for a cold that just would not go away. This cold had lasted nearly a month already. It was getting very frustrating because it interfered with his schooling. On that fateful day, Anni took Jeffrey to the doctor for examination. "Anni, I am concerned about Jeffrey," Doctor Coe started. "He shouldn't be getting sick like this so much and so often. Can you tell me how he got those bruise marks on his legs?" "I don't know. Playing, I guess. He and George are always roughhousing, wrestling and whopping each other. Why, what's wrong?" Anni's stomach began to pinch at her.

"Anni, I want to send Jeffrey to a specialist just for safety's sake and have some tests done. OK? It isn't anything for you to get alarmed about, I just want to do it as a precautionary measure and have him looked at by a hematologist. That is a 'blood doctor' and maybe with his expertise he can find out why Jeffrey gets sick so often and maybe we can get a solution. I don't want you to start worrying. I'll have my office set up the appointment for you and just make sure you take him over there, OK?" he asks. "Yes, I will. How long will it be? Is there something serious?" Anni starts asking and preparing herself for bad answers at the same time. "Anni, I told you, I don't want you to start worrying. It won't do any good for you or Jeffrey. Just go to the specialist and we will go from there. I'm sure it will all be fine, I just want to be clear on this, that's all." Again the doctor tries his best to be comforting but his eyes tell a different story and Anni has become an expert at reading people's eyes. She accepts the finality of the conversation and prepares herself to take her youngest son to the specialist. All she can do now is pray, and that she does, even more so than in the past, if it were possible.

Within hours, Anni and Jeffrey are seen by Dr. Levy, the hematologist. "Mrs. Adams, we ran some blood tests and I have looked Jeffrey over fairly well. I am not going to make any guesses right now, but I would like to do some more tests. I am asking if you will permit us to do what is called a bone marrow test. I am going to tell you right up front that it is a painful procedure. We can give Jeffrey something for the pain and sedate him some before the test, but he is still going to feel it for a short while. I know it isn't anything any mother wants to hear, but I am the one that has to tell you and I prefer to be very frank about it. Do you understand? Is it alright for us to go ahead with the test?" he asks. Anni stares at him blankly for what seems like a month. His eyes are telling all sorts of stories that are worse than Doctor Coe's. His eyes are trying to get away from her examination as if he were about to burst to flames. There is something wrong and this is not good at all. "Yes, of course, Dr. Levy, whatever you need to do, do it. I just want to get Jeffrey well again. Please try to do it without hurting him. He is very sensitive," she pleads.

Within a matter of days, Anni, Jeffrey and Anni's mother all arrive for the bone marrow test to be conducted. Jeffrey is taken back and given a sedative and taken into another room where he must lie on the table face down as they draw fluid from his spine. Outside the door, Anni can hear Jeffrey crying out from the pain. It is heart-wrenching and she wants to rush in and knock them away but she knows she can't. It is a pain that has to be, if she wants him to get better. Gredy holds Anni close and tells her it will be over soon and he will be alright, then they can all go home. It doesn't turn out that way.

After some time passes and the waiting reaches an unbearable level of torment, Dr. Levy confronts Anni and her mother. Jeffrey is kept away and out of sight. He is being tended to and treated by the nurses as they try to ease him from his pain and this experience and get him back to being a happy child again. "Mrs. Adams. Anni, your son has leukemia." He puts it straight out in one line. He isn't about to mince words and play with her emotions. He has done this before and knows it is best to be directly honest and afford people the opportunity to deal with things in their own personal way. It isn't bad bedside manners. It is doing the right thing. "Anni, do understand what I am telling you?" he asks softly.

There is no answer. Anni just looks at those eyes. There seem to be some clear liquid clouding the blue. "Is he about to cry?" she thinks to herself. Then she answers, "Leukemia?" For the first time in her life the word has rolled from her mouth almost as if it were someone else saying it. "It is a blood disease. It is rare and there is no real known reason for it and there is no cure for it either. Jeffrey is going to need a blood transfusion right away. I want to send him over to Long Island Jewish Hospital for it and he will need more blood in the future. I am going to need to check with your family to see if some of them are a match and can donate blood. Whether they do or not, we can do the transfusions and give Jeffrey some time. Do you understand what I am telling you?" he asks as quietly as he can. "No, I don't understand. Jeffrey is going to need blood transfusions. How often? How long? When will he get better? Is it painful?" Her questions start to pour from her mind, which is reeling by now.

"Anni, Jeffrey has about a year." He answers and the room is silent for what seems hours. Anni doesn't say a word at first and Dr. Levy begins to explain the blood disease for her to better grasp. Then she interjects, "He has a year of this? Of blood transfusions? That is a long time. But he will be better after that, right?" "Anni, what I am telling you is that Jeffrey has about a year to live." He puts it out plainly and painfully even to his own heart and soul. She can see it on his face. He is serious and she almost feels sad for the doctor having to tell her. Then she repeats the words in her head. Almost as if a bomb had exploded and she was left numb, deaf, mute and blinded by clouds. She can't think or speak. She goes into shock. Gredy asks to use the phone and calls Charlie. All Anni can hear is her mother's distant voice talking to Charlie and then Charlie is there. She sees him and she sees his eyes. That does it. She comes out of her "fog" and falls to Charlie. Neither one can speak a word. They hold each other and cry. It takes a long time for them to regroup. Charlie starts with his own questions to the doctor and when all is said and done, they clean up, put on their smiles and take Jeffrey home to lie on the couch.

Arrangements were made with the Catholic school, Joachim and Anne, and they overwhelm the family with generosity. Jeffrey would be homeschooled. George was only told that his brother was sickly and that is why he had to stay home. Many, many times both Anni and Charlie battled with that concept. They felt George should know, but, it was advised to them over and over by every doctor, nurse and counselor not to do so. They didn't. It was excruciatingly hard to bottle it inside. Of course, George wasn't naive. Very much the opposite. George showed an especially high level of insight himself. He knew something was up and he wasn't getting all the answers, but he just let it be. He was still going to laugh and have fun with his brother. On practically a daily basis, George found himself as Jeffrey's own personal court jester and clown. Jeffrey had an infectious smile, smiling eyes and laughter that could make an entire room join him and not even know why. It was just that special. On one particular occasion, the laughter at came an unaffordable price to George.

During the months ahead, everyone seemed to be off and about work and school, for George, as normal a life as could be had. Jeffrey had good days and bad days. Sometimes he was completely confined to the couch and on others he could go outside with George. On one particular day, it was getting late and Charlie was still working at the shop. Anni had prepared dinner for everyone and tonight it was hamburgers and french fries. Clearly, the boys got to pick the menu and Anni just served it up. However, the two brothers at the table were getting antsy and conducting their usual taunts and teases. It began to escalate to an annoying level for Anni as she tried to finish the dinner and get it on the table.

They wouldn't quiet for anything and they bickered like chicks. The final straw came when she put the plates in front of the boys. One to Jeffrey and one in front of George. One look at his plate and George started it up, "Why does Jeffrey get a bigger hamburger than me…" He went on and took the discourse a little too far for his mother. Anni got up, picked up George's plate and said, "If you don't like it, then you don't have to eat it" and with that she whacked him on the head with the plate in both her hands. She only meant for it to be a bump to get his attention but instead, the plate broke into pieces. Either it was because of George's hard head, Anni's surprising strength, a weak plate or all the above. One thing was for sure. All three were in total shock.

George sat there stunned that his mother had done such a thing, Anni was stunned at herself and both were looking at the weirdest expression on Jeffrey's face. Suddenly, Jeffrey burst out with laughter and in a split second, George and then his mother followed suit. If it meant his mother doing it a thousand times more, starting right then, George would have begged for it. To see his brother laugh the way he did, how those eyes could shine through darkness it was a curiosity to say the least.

Laughter was always the medicine that worked best and through the ups and downs of days and months, it kept coming. The family stayed strong and played their parts. They were not going to let this be any kind of defeat. Mimi would come over often when Jeffrey was sick and help out. Maybe just by doing some things around the house, fixing something to eat, whatever was of help to ease some of Anni's load. Anni's career was twofold by this time and that part of life was very healthy. She was working practically full time with FTD on various projects and still working side by side with her husband. Add to the mix that both Charlie and Anni were growing large in social circles through different organizations that they belonged to and even headed at times. George continued his schooling and continued also to play clown. On one special occasion it got a little hairy to make an understatement.

The Fourth of July is a special occasion to many people. To the Adams it was an especially wonderful holiday. It meant cookouts and fun times at the beach in South Hampton. This year though, Jeffrey wanted something, and so did George, to make it extraordinary. The challenge was on and George was up to it. He was growing by leaps and bounds in catching up to the industrious mind of his father. George was full of life, energy and always thinking on his feet. This Fourth of July would be special and he was determined to make it so. He deftly left the house without Anni's knowledge. Where he went no one knew but when he came back he was sweating and in one heck of a hurry. He ran over to his younger brother and said, "Quick, put this box under you and sit on it between the cushions. Now place this blanket around you real good. Don't say a word, OK?" He helped tuck the blanket around and just in time. He hustled over to the staircase about the same time the knock came at the door.

Anni came from the kitchen to answer it. There in front of her stood, not one, but two uniformed police officers. "Mind if we come in, ma'am?" they ask as Anni opens the door wider and the two enter. "What's going on officers?" she asks, completely confused. "Well, we have been going door to door here because we got word some boys have gotten a hold of some fireworks and you know that's illegal," they answered. "Yes, I know that," Anni replies. "Well, do you mind if we take a look around?" they press. "No, not at all," she replies.

"Do you have boys?" they continue as they start to move about the living room, glancing up the stairs where George is sitting silently. "Yeah, my youngest over there, he is kind of sickly as you can see," she says, pointing to Jeffrey covered neatly with his blanket and grinning ear to ear with twinkling eyes. "And my oldest, George. He's been home all afternoon," she states to her best knowledge and belief.

"Mind if we take a look in their rooms?" More questions as the cops make a wider search. "Not at all. Help yourself, you won't find anything like that here," she finishes. The cops smile and nod at the innocent looking six-year-old on the couch. They head upstairs past George and peer into the rooms. Back downstairs, after their cursory search, the officers thank Anni, apologize for any inconvenience and head along their way.

With the closing of the door, George bounds down the stairs and Jeffrey breaks out laughing. With that, George starts laughing, too. Anni is in total befuddlement. "What is going on!" she asks. Without saying a word, George goes over to Jeffrey and pulls the blanket back to reveal a huge box of fireworks up under her son's tender bottom. Both the boys are hysterical and so is Anni. Except Anni's isn't from laughter. "You could blow him up!" she shouts at George. "What are you doing? Are you crazy?" she continues but it doesn't diminish the laughter and she knows it is a lost battle. The boys have fireworks and Jeffrey is laughing through his pain. Her heart is torn from being a protective and brooding mother to joyous feelings over the sight of her two boys. She is a very proud mother.

More months ticked away through the end of the year with its holidays and cheer. Anni and Charlie made the very best they could possibly afford of it for their sons. It was a wonderful Thanksgiving and Christmas with friends and family. After the new year had set in, though, Jeffrey was becoming more and more ill. His trips to the hospital occurred with greater frequency and longer stays. In March, Jeffrey turned seven years old and the family celebrated in style. Over all these months Jeffrey had mostly been homebound and passed his time doing his favorite things when he wasn't being schooled. He loved to draw. He would draw picture after picture of clouds, angels, stars, houses and, of course, airplanes.

When he was hardly old enough to speak, he was in Anni's arms as she walked outside somewhere when he looked skyward and said, "Mama, what's that?" His inquisitive look led past his tiny finger up to a long, thin and tight vapor trail with a plane in the lead. "That's an airplane, honey," Anni explained. She explained to him how it works and what it does. "There are people in it and a very special man that flies it with a steering wheel. The man is called a pilot." "That is what I want to be when I grow up!" he said, smiling. "A pilot!" He never gave up on that dream. His pictures often reflected airplanes half the size of the page with a picture of him seated at the big window looking straight at the viewer.

On May 25, 1963, Jeffrey Charles Adams lay in a hospital bed at Long Island Jewish Hospital. It was the weekend and Anni had gone to church and just arrived back to be with her son. The room was full of flowers and "get well" cards. Doctors and nurses were coming and going as Jeffrey sat upright in bed. Anni went into the room and it was just her, Rita (Jeffrey's nurse) and her son. Rita was humming a tune. It was "Goodnight Irene," Jeffrey's favorite song. Doctor Levy had already told her before she went in that he didn't have good news. "Go in right now. I will call Charlie." Those were his words. In a matter of minutes, it seemed, Charlie had taken a cab and arrived at the hospital. He went in and saw his youngest boy. He couldn't handle it and stepped out of the room so that Jeffrey would not see the tears on his cheeks.

Inside the room, Anni talked to Jeffrey until he interrupted her. He was wide awake with his eyes still shining like they always did and looked so happy. "I love you Mama, I have to go. The angels are here. Goodbye." With that, Jeffrey closed his eyes, still smiling and all Anni could see was the peace on his face and a light that radiated all too bright. "See all those lights?" Anni said to Rita. "Yes, Anni I see them. He's gone." Both of them saw the light. It was brighter than being outside in the sun. It permeated the room. Angels had walked in alone and left with a friend. As long as there is a vapor trail in the sky, even today, Anni knows she is not alone. It was and is his gift to his mother. He will forever be there above and will see her again.

There had been sickness and health. It is part of life. There are no words to describe Anni's loss. No one can ever truly describe something so personal when it happens to any one of us. To this very day, Anni is brave enough, strong enough and caring enough to volunteer her time as a "Pink Lady" in her local hospital. Always there to smile, encourage, offer assistance and hope. Likewise, she never ceases to make her annual trips around to her neighbors and collect donations for the Leukemia Society. It is a testament to her willpower but even a greater testament to her faith in God and trust that He will never leave her alone. No matter when, where or what. Someone is always thinking of her and praying for her even today or tonight.

# *T*o Love, Honor and Cherish

***"For I am sure that neither death, nor life, nor angels, nor principalities, nor things present, nor things to come, nor powers, nor height, nor depth, nor anything else in all creation, will be able to separate us from the love of God in Christ Jesus our Lord."***

Romans 8:38-39

*The words "To Love, Honor and Cherish" are probably the second most recognizable words in the wedding vow,s next only to the words "'til death do us part." Most people throughout the world can recite the vows. The words have been heard literally millions of times and are also heard every day that we live here on planet Earth. They have been misquoted, misused, misunderstood and mistaken. Nevertheless, they still exist, they are still used and people quoting them are people with either a sincere heart and intentions or of a devious nature. Along the way they have lost their meaning to many people. Someone hearing them for the first time may find them quite romantic and eloquent. If you deliver the words day after day over people joining in a commitment, supposedly for life, they become rather mundane. That is, unless you do one thing that all these people mentioned should do: Take them seriously. The sad part of it is that it takes two. No one person can recite those vows and keep them without someone else sharing that commitment. If one breaches the vows, they are broken and thus made of no effect. Worthless, useless and meaningless.*

*It seems an almost impossible task. Especially, once the "til death do us part" enters the picture. It sounds like a daunting challenge and it should. It is. It isn't just a choice or a feeling. It is a decision. A decision and a promise. Thus, a vow. Something we commit to and would rather literally die than to go back on our vow. At the given time, under the right circumstances of feelings or emotions, the words are easy and very acceptable. It seems like a sure bet. No problem. Of course, that is, until a problem comes along. In this line, "to love, honor and cherish", seems to be a threefold commitment. It would appear that there is a very serious challenge here and that there is a lot to do. Not just one thing, but three things. I must cherish. How do I do that? Then I must honor, how do I that? And love? Can I cherish but not love? Can I honor and not love? The answer to the last two questions is a resounding yes. But to ask the question, "Can I love and not honor and cherish?" sounds almost absurd. Why? Because if one truly loves, then one will honor and cherish.*

*To honor means simply to hold in high esteem. To equate with goodness and respect. To cherish means simply to hold dear. To keep close to one's thoughts in fondness of memory and heartfelt joy. In order to honor and cherish, all one must do is love. Therein lies the problem. How do we love? How do we love unconditionally to the point that the object of our affection, dare we say love, becomes a point of honor and cherishment. It is a nearly impossible task and yet millions of people have accomplished it in full from the day they first said it to the day the final vow came. Until death parted them physically on earth. But wait. It was accomplished in full but it wasn't ended. No. Because to say it ended at death would be to say that it was a lie and not a vow. It would be a broken vow. A worthless promise. The mistake in the concept of the vows is that "til death do us part" concludes the agreement. That is the worst possible start to a certain disaster. It is all that remains of the vows that are completed at the physical death. However, it is the physical part in the first place that makes love so misunderstood. That is the reason for the thought that physical death means love has died. It is deemed a physical thing. The words "to make love" are immediately associated with a physical act rather than an expression of an eternal feeling through the physical. "Making love" is just that. It is being brought to life and being kept alive by act or acts, thus the physical part. But the life it receives is eternal. It is making something eternal from a commitment, whether physical, ideological or emotional. "To have and to hold," "in sickness and in health," "for richer or poorer" do cease without question upon the death of either committed party. Certainly after death there cannot be a physical holding, nor aiding in sickness nor sharing a meal when poor. But to love, that part of the vow lasts more than a lifetime. It is meant to last for eternity. Why? Because of one simple fact. There is a God. God is love and God is eternal. Therefore, love, genuine love, is an eternal state of being. It cannot be quenched to an end. Or can it? Maybe if we start to fail in honoring, respecting, cherishing or appreciating? Then, yes, love probably could be quenched to an end. Again, it takes two.*

*That is why there are two witnesses. That is why it is said in the eyes and presence of God Almighty. It should not be entered into without thought. To do so, is a death certificate for the thing we call love. It is rendering an eternal state of being into void. No, true love does not last a lifetime. True love lasts. Period. It never ends. It goes on forever. It is an eternal pledge, promise and gift, and most of all, it is real. If you can love. If you can love with a real and true love, then you will honor and cherish, and by doing so, you cut the challenge of trying to do "three" things into just one simple thing. It makes the odds of success much, much better.*

On a very special night, although no one knew it, a man said these words to his wife with a kiss: "I love you. I always have, always will. Take care and sleep tight." Those were the last words spoken in the physical realm from Charlie to Anni, the night of June 12, 1998. Charlie had gone ahead of his young Brown-Eyes, his Babychen, to pave a new road to a new life. An eternal life. A place where they would never part again. Where there would be springs of youth eternal as the days in Luxembourg and the summers at the beach. It had been a good night indeed. Charlie had been diagnosed with prostate cancer more than two years prior. But it wasn't the reason he left. In fact, the physical causation was more one of just plainly being full. His life on earth had been completed far beyond his imagination on the day he said he was "going to marry that girl" in his letter to his parents.

Charlie loved Anni. In the beginning, honestly, Anni thought she was "in love" with Charlie, but she made a prudent decision based on good counsel and advice. Not a bad way to start. It wasn't easy. In fact, it made things harder. Much more difficult. But one thing remained constant: Charlie loved Anni into loving him back. She began first by seeing his integrity. She saw his character and honesty with people. She saw him at his best and at his worst. She saw more of him than any other person on the planet. She grew to respect Charlie. Because of her respect, she grew to honor him. As her honor of him increased, eventually there wasn't a thing he did that she didn't cherish. Even his temper, his anger and his frustration. She cherished it because that was Charlie. Not just Charlie, but her Charlie. And that, she knew, the whole world knew, was Charlie Adams.

If one wishes to meet Charlie Adams today, all they have to do is meet Anni. Talk to George, the spitting image of his father. Speak with Chuck or Elfie and ask about the man. He was a good man, as they say. Today, he still is. He always will be because he loved Anni and that is an eternal thing. They will all pass away. In 1965, Charlie's father passed away. In 1976, Albert Neuman (senior) passed in his sleep, a wonderful seventy-seven years young. In 1977, Charlie's mother passed on. In 1991, Gredy (Boma) Marguerite Neuman passed in her sleep. That same year, several months after having been diagnosed with cancer, the circus clown left the "Big Top" the way he wanted. The senior Albert Neuman succumbed to the disease but went with a smile and a hospice nurse sitting at his bedside playing a guitar and singing his favorite song, "Bridge over Troubled Water." It was a fitting end and Anni was there for every one of them.

On Charlie's night, his grandson Matt was there and his brother-in-law Chuck. They were having such a good time. Anni was tired and said she had to get some sleep. Her husband made a promise, "We won't be loud. I feel good and I'll be in awhile later." The boys had their fun and had their laughs. Charlie finally left after saying good night twice. What a blessing for a man that had seen so much, done so much and achieved so much. Not just in the way of "things" but in the way of family, life in general and how he treated people. Charlie went to sleep that night, but rest assured, he was wide awake the next morning in heaven ready to go to work. That was just Charlie and even now, those houses that we have been promised in heaven are probably being built by the man. One would be hard pressed to find him sitting idle.

Over the years since Jeffrey passed and so many others of the family, Charlie and Anni made quite a mark in their little part of New York. Actually, it extended far beyond that neighborhood. Anni ruled as president of the Chamber of Commerce for Queens Village a total of six consecutive years. She served on many boards of various nature. Charlie was a member of the Veterans of Foreign Wars, the Masons, the American Legion and The Rotary Club. In fact, in the early 70s it was Charlie and Anni who came to a small village in the tiny country of Haiti, and on behalf of the Rotary Club, inaugurated a recently completed freshwater well. There was a cocktail party and a dinner celebration and Anni was the translator once again because of her command of the French language.

Anni has a deep repertoire of languages. She is fluent in English, Luxembourg, German and French. The skills that were forced upon her from the mere fact that she was born in Luxembourg aided her well in life. She learned *Lëtzebuergesch* because that was where she was from and that is who she is. She learned French because it was the most widely used language in Europe and still is today. She learned German because she was forced to, and it was life or death in decades past. She learned English because she met a handsome, young, unrelenting American GI that wouldn't take no for an answer.

Through the years, the two made a special event of this thing called life and did it on a daily basis. One day at a time. They enjoyed the present for what it was, a "present." In 1967, Charlie bought a building, an ice-cream parlor, next to a funeral home. For two years he renovated it and turned it into the much larger flower shop under the same name: Charles D. Adams Flowers. The shops would change hands many times but almost always into the hands of family. Albert was the owner after Charlie retired to South Hampton. Albert kept the shop until his passing. Eventually, the shop was sold to Yardley's. Elfie had her own shop by 1996 and still does to this day. Chuck retired from his lengthy employment working under government contracts and "playing with computers" as he still does to this day in his home. Sometimes he still makes a little room for advising in the field and enjoys getting involved in social activities with his wife, Mimi by his side.

Anni traveled to Holland in 1972 and there she trained with the best floral artists in the world to keep her skills sharp and honed. Thirty years later, she is still practicing a new thing or two. She and Charlie made six consecutive, annual trips to Aruba, their favorite island and hideaway as old newlyweds. Charlie was always trying to make up for that first honeymoon. He did a dozen times over and Anni would tell him so, but Charlie kept trying anyhow. He really must have wanted to get it right and make it perfect. Anni traveled to Vienna in 1996 to study again and became a master in her art. It would be better said that she became a master of what was in her heart. She was indeed the butterfly described throughout this journey, and the lives of so many people were touched. However, if there is one thing, one creature, one person, one entity next to God that knows the most about flowers, it is the butterfly. She saw flowers in the same way that only a pipefitter can appreciate a perfect angle. The way a ship's captain can appreciate the perfect docking. The way Neil Armstrong could appreciate one small step and the way any one of us can appreciate that skip in our heart, that sinking feeling in our stomach and dizziness when we think we are in love.

Anni knows flowers. They are her cocoon. That is where she escapes three days a week even now. She does it because there in that shop, she is surrounded by memories. People she has met, known and knows even now. There in that small flower shop she is surrounded by her past, her present and the future. She is among the little gifts and treasures that people use as tools to express all sorts of wishes. Love, condolences, thankfulness for friendship, holidays, making up for the breakups, wishes for a good day, a great sale and so on. The whole world seems to pass its emotions through such a small portal. Even Jesus said, "Consider the lilies of the field, how they neither toil nor spin, yet, Solomon in all his glory was not clothed as one of them. How much more your father in Heaven cares for you." Flowers are used to convey emotions and meager attempts at love. The love that Anni gave to Charlie was not because of his big dreams and a little flower shop. She loved a man that loved her. The hardest thing on earth to find. More rare than any precious metal. Finding that one person, the one person, the only person that loves you until you love them for loving you. Then, and only then, can they honor and cherish long after the years and tears. Long after the life and death, sickness and health. But all the way into eternity.

Anni moved away from New York after some fifty-three years. She moved to Arizona and lived there for two years. It didn't take long for her to make new friends, and she enjoyed her life there playing golf and being active in her neighborhood. Only the weather didn't agree with her. Her son George was there, but he was looking southeast toward Florida. In 2001, George and his wife Jeanne moved to Florida and Anni followed suit. She was home again. She found new friends quickly in Jean, her neighbor down the street and the ladies at the Brannon Center where she still goes for a morning workout. She works at Six Sisters Flower Shop and stays close to her loving friend and "boss," Tricia. She still does her volunteer work at the hospital as a "Pink Lady," making people smile when she tells them they have a funny accent before they can say the same to her.

She still plays golf and travels amidst it all. She took a hiatus from the golf for nearly three months as we worked on this project. Just this past Sunday, I sent her a gift by permission. My nephew Joshua, my son's girlfriend and a nineteen-year-old boy named Ty all wanted to learn how to play golf and she took them out on the course in the cool weather. She told them how to keep their heads down and she showed them she was no different than they. Age doesn't matter. She brought them home and fed them soup. They left happy and Anni has her own fan club now. She became a part of my family and I became a part of hers. She has introduced me to many people in her life and it has been an honor. I admire and respect so many of them. They are indeed good people. She clings mostly nowadays to her son George, who just moved up the road to be closer. His wife, Jeanne, now has her own little shop and a bright future in business. Anni's grandsons are Brian and Matt and her step-granddaughter, Nicole.

Now that this chapter is about complete and this book nearly finished, I have little to no excuse. Anni has a long list of things she wants to do. She hasn't changed much from that little three-year-old girl at the apex of a human pyramid. She is still reaching for the top and still adding friends and admirers all around. Maybe, just maybe, someday you might have the pleasure of meeting Anni Adams. If you don't, that is okay. There are a million like her but you won't know until you introduce yourself to a person a little older than you and share a harmless conversation. You might actually enjoy the stories to follow. If things go truly well, you might find yourself respecting that person. Maybe even honoring them for their life well-lived or hard won. One thing is for certain, you will cherish the opportunity.

"Love thy neighbor as thyself." With that love comes the honor and cherish. Just ask Anni. She can tell you all about the people that she still loves, honors and cherishes no matter where they are.

# They Met Anni

*In our lives we all meet people. We can hardly go a day without it happening. We don't even have to leave our own cocoon to experience it. We don't necessarily "meet" in person, face to face, but we have meetings. Either by telephone, mail, e-mail, or fax, all the wonderful tools of technology. We don't have the choice, to the greater degree, of who we will meet. We don't always have a choice. We can shelter ourselves or fly wide open into the air of society around us; whichever we choose, we are destined to meet people.*

*The strange thing about it is that we look at it from our viewpoint: "We meet people." Do we ever to stop to think that, just the same, whether by telephone, fax, mail, a bump in a line at the drug store, people meet us? We are the people that people meet. Because we all live in our own evaluation of who we are and what a life we have, the impact we make, wish to make or happen to be attempting to make, people are meeting us. It is truly something to ponder. It is an interesting concept that we look at things from the perspective that "I once me..." or "he/she met..." or "I wish I could meet..." But as you read this, think: Today someone will have met YOU. So much of human life is spent aspiring to "meet people," and yet we seem to not have a clue as to how much more important it is to us that we recognize we have a daily opportunity to be met and make an impact in another person's life, either negative or positive.*

*When we wake in the morning, most of us have an idea of who we will meet through the day's schedule. They are minuscule in comparison, because there are probably tens, maybe dozens, of others we pass by, when we can meet, or ignore and squander an opportunity. Only because we have a list of the people we are scheduled to meet. The person that you passed at the gas station, on the sidewalk, at the mall or in the pawn shop was someone you could have had just a few more words with. If it had happened, if you had taken the present moment as a true gift from God, then you might have found a new friend, a new ally, a person that needed your smile or who might have even made you smile. The sweetest investment afforded: Your precious time, to make them feel special and as if they had* ***"met"*** *someone unique. Maybe that is part of the key. That we should live as if we are unique and have a priceless ability to make someone else's day better, brighter or lighter because we gave them something they didn't deserve, something they didn't earn. Something they couldn't buy or beg. We gave them the most precious gift we have and it is the very thing we guard like misers. To simply let loose of our precious, God-given time.*

*To share a moment of your life with another life. It is better than giving blood. That is something you can do next month. But for one instant, one moment in time, can you give your time? It takes a " hello," a "God bless you," a smile, a help with something heavy, anything that says, "I was here today and I met you, you met me and we won't forget this small meeting, it was a nice moment of human kindness." It is a very, very rich thought, with value and impact. One small second or a multitude of hours. Let us meet each other and know that we are not alone. We don't have to be lonely. The girl behind the counter at the sandwich shop would love for you to say she has nice eyes. The man at the door telling you that you are behind in your payment is doing his job. Can you tell him you understand and make such an impact that he will know he has met you. Not because you were typically hostile, rather than unique. Special? One meeting can lead to a thousand and more. Take a moment and think, just maybe the little meetings mean something after all and shouldn't be wasted or squandered. Much more, they should be treasured and made the best of. After all, you may never know who you have just met.*

"Anni, I want to go over a list I have here of some of the people you've met," I opened the interview. "For the sake of time, I won't go over it in chronological order, we will just address them as they are on my list. Some people, such as Ambassador George Wallace and others have already been mentioned in the book, so we won't address those," I continued. "I know that there are many others that we could add to this list but, again, for the sake of time, I would just like to go through these wonderful stories as a matter of record for the reader. OK?" I finished my interview introduction.

"Whatever you say," was her response. Always so matter-of-fact about these things. Just when I think Anni has told it all, she surprises me with a story about someone and acts as if it were just another day at the mall of life. I don't think anyone will ever truly know how many people Anni has met that were famous in their own way nor do I think we will ever know how many people have had the pleasure of meeting Anni. Even as this book was being written, we were getting introduced to people in high government positions for European countries, especially her beautiful home of Luxembourg. But lest I digress, on with the interview:

"OK, I will just start here with the first name on my list. I know we have talked about this one dozens of times and I know the story pretty well already. I've seen all the pictures and such but let's go over it again. Are you ready?" I inquired, preparing to start down the long, two-hour journey. "Go ahead," she replied.

"Alan Shepard?" as if reading from a list of Who's Who.

"That was the centennial year for Queens Village in New York and I was still the president of the Chamber of Commerce. We wanted to get the best and 'highest up' speaker that we could think of. So I suggested the president [of the United States] first. They said I was crazy, that I was too much. So, I said, 'OK, who else is really big?' and other names were mentioned. Then I said, 'How about Neil Armstrong?' This was in 1972 and he was very popular. The vice-chairman of the Chamber thought I was still asking too much but I didn't think so, and we wouldn't know if we didn't try. So I wrote a letter to Senator Helpern, he was our senator at the time, and I asked if he could help us get a speaker for the centennial celebration. He said that he felt there was no way we could get Neil Armstrong so I said, 'How about Alan Shepard,' he's a famous astronaut. So Senator Helpern said he would see what he could do. We discussed that by phone. So then after I spoke with Senator Helpern I called, on his suggestion, to the public relations department of NASA in Houston [Texas]. I told the woman on the phone who I was and explained the whole thing to her and she was just silent. I think she must have thought I was some kind of nut until she realized I was serious. They said they would look into it. So, we went about making arrangements and kept making these calls.

"Finally I got a call from NASA, and Senator Helpern right after I hung up from NASA, and they both said the same thing. We could have Alan Shepard but it was up to us to put him and his wife, Louise, up for accommodations, make travel arrangements and provide security. So, that is what I set out to do. They also told us we would have to keep things low-key and not have too large of a crowd, so I said OK. This was two weeks after I had made the calls. Well, by that time George was a tall man, he was about six foot two, so I figured he could be security and we would need one other person. I remembered that the lady who owned the shop next to the [our] flower shop was married to a New York police detective, Connie Miller. So, I called her and asked if she thought he would do it. She didn't take long and called me back to say he would. So, we had that taken care of and made the other arrangements.

"The funny part was that on the day that we were to pick him up. Actually, Charlie was supposed to go the airport with George and Connie; well, Charlie had to go out the house in South Hampton to get some papers. When he went he took our dog along, that dog loved to go to the beach. Well, on the way back Charlie was running a little late and to make things worse, the dog threw up in the back seat. At the time, it was all sort of crazy but funny. We had this big green Cadillac and here was Charlie taking a water hose and just pointing it right into the back seat of the car with the doors open washing it all out. It was so funny but Charlie was having to hurry because he still needed to pick up George and Connie. He got it all wiped down and cleaned the best he could. Then when he picked up George and Connie they burned incense in the car to get rid of the smell. They got to the airport and sure enough, they got Mr. Shepard at the airport and picked up his wife, Louise, who was already at the hotel, and brought them back to our house before the dinner. I guess they never told him and nobody talked about it.

"It was very exciting and he was a very, very nice man. He and his wife. We had a cocktail at the house and took some pictures of all of us. My dad was especially proud, he had a commemorative coin of Neil Armstrong made of 24k gold from Luxembourg. So, we all went to the cocktail party, the dinner, and I introduced Mr. Shepard. Boy were my knees shaking. We also presented him with a golf putter because we knew he was an avid golfer and so were George and I. He spoke to the crowd and gave a wonderful speech. He even showed pictures of where he swung a golf club on the moon. We also got his wife, Louise, a necklace, I remember that too. I remember all the way back to the hotel in New York, he [Alan] kept admiring the putter. He really liked it. We had a great time."

Thus she concluded the first query. Of course, I just sat smiling, taking notes, shaking my head and laughing. Thinking to myself, wait until

I write this. Boy is this going get some people laughing. And so I hope it does. Now, it was back to business. Next name on the list.

"Teddy Kollek," I stated outright.

"Oh that was in 1969, I think. It was only ten days after the war. There were eight of us sent by FTD to an Inter Flora International Floral Show at the main auditorium in Tel Aviv [Israel]. He was an especially nice man. He gave a dinner for us all and made us feel very welcomed. He made arrangements for us to tour around the place and just really treated us nice. He was a very good man. He genuinely wanted to add culture from around the world to the people in Jerusalem. The show was a big success. A lot of people showed up and they even paid eight dollars a person for tickets to get in. That was a lot of money in those days. I remember the two people that were supposed to speak, one didn't show up and the other got sick, so I had to speak in front of that whole crowd. I was sick to my stomach. They kept telling me, 'Anni, you've got to do it. We don't have anybody else. You can't back out. You've got to do it!' So, they gave me a double shot of scotch, I think or cognac, and I went out on stage in front of all the cameras and the big screen. It was televised. They had television cameras there and all, it was a really big deal. I will never forget that. I was so scared, but I did it.

"I also remember that when I was giving my speech, my Jewish girlfriend from back in Esch, the one that left before the occupation, heard my voice on the radio. She recognized it and telephoned the radio station. Afterwards, my host took me to her house and we got to spend a few hours together. I never thought I would see or hear from her again. Right there, of all places, we were reunited. She was forty-three years old by that time. Oh my, it was so wonderful. I couldn't believe it. We just hugged and I think we cried. I guess her family made their way out somehow and eventually she moved to Israel. I always had wondered if she lived or not." Anni paused and reflected a moment. I just waited silently and got ready to announce the next name.

"Mrs. Douglas MacArthur," I blurted out.

"Charlie and I were working in the shop one day when we got a call from a man who said he was from a yacht docked at the Sag Harbor Yacht Club. They had just arrived and were going to do some entertaining so they needed a dining table arrangement and arrangements for each of the rooms on the boat. So Charlie and I went down there and met the man. It wasn't a little boat. It was huge. He took us around inside and showed us all the rooms where he wanted the flowers and the long dining table.

We came back later and started working on the arrangements on the dock at the foot of the gangplank. We had flowers scattered all over and boxes with various floral materials. Up walks this lady and she just starts to tell us how beautiful the flowers are and what a wonderful job we are doing. Then Charlie asks, 'Who might we have the pleasure of meeting?' She smiled at us both and said, 'Mrs. Douglas MacArthur.' Charlie looked a little bewildered and we just took it in stride. She continued to rave about the flowers for a minute or so and then she just walked on up the gangplank," Anni completed.

I looked down at my list and with an 'OK,' went on to the next listed person. "Elizabeth Arden," I announced.

"That was another phone call we received in the shop. Someone had called and said they wanted to know if we put flowerbeds in. Charlie took the call and he hardly, if ever, turned down any job. He got the directions and we ended up going to a cottage where Elizabeth Arden kept horses for the Belmont. Actually, she wanted window boxes done and flowers inside the home. Charlie gave her an estimate and we came back in a couple days to do the job. She was so particular. She supervised our every step and watched over each piece of work. She was not mean or anything, but boy was she particular. She was very exacting about the work and also very 'penny-wise.' She was definitely a woman in charge and she was not a wasteful person, at least not when it came to the work we did. She didn't talk much small talk with me. Charlie got her to open up a little more and they kind of hit it off. I guess because they both valued hard work," she ended.

My list is still lengthy and I wonder if I can cut a couple corners, but, I don't. Well, not much. "New York Mayor John V. Lindsay," I presented the name to her.

"Now he was a good man, too. We had a lot of meetings during my six years as president of the Chamber of Commerce for Queens Village. He was there several times but he always listened to what I had to say, even if we didn't agree. The most memorable discussion was during a protest of the 24A Highway-Clearview Expressway project. The plans were drawn up in such a way that a highway was going to basically split Queens Village and we were all very much against it, obviously. Plus it appeared too much like segregation. It was going to divide the town and we had to put a lot of pressure into it or against it, actually. It was a Jamaica to Queens and Nassau border road. We got it stopped at Hillside. I didn't like the segregation stuff. I was very much against it. This was in the late 60s, early 70s."

"OK, on to our next person," I said. "This is kind of a two-in-one here. We've got Charles Boyer and Maurice Chavalier! This has got to be good."

"Yes, that was another funny one. That was in 1951 when I went back to Luxembourg to see my family. I took George with me and he was two at the time. George was all over the place. He wouldn't sit still and was really giving me a fit. So I whopped him one. The man behind me leans over and says, 'It's OK, ma'am, he'll be a good boy, you just have to be patient with him. Right?' he said, looking at George. I recognized right away who he was. It was Charles Boyer, the actor. Toward the end of the train ride, George started up again and the man sitting on the other side just a few seats back came up and leaned over. I guess he couldn't help but notice, too. He looks right at George and says, 'You want me to sing for you, young man?' George looked straight at him and says 'NO!' I mean just like that, and it is Maurice Chavalier. I was a little embarrassed as you can imagine. I think George missed a lifetime opportunity on that one with his own story to tell. But that was just George being George. Mr. Chavalier just laughed and said, 'He will be good, he's going to be important someday." Anni smiled with the look of a thousand memories only a mother could know.

"Here we go, next." I continued the conversation. "Gary Cooper." I can hardly wait for this one.

"Oh, he was quite something. That was in the 60s in South Hampton. He would walk right down Main Street on the weekends. Any time he stayed there, I guess he had a home, he went along Main Street on the weekends for a walk. He would tip his hat every single time he saw a woman. He was quite a character. Very sharply dressed and handsome as ever. I did tell him that I had seen all his movies and we just love them. 'You're a fine actor.' " Anni reminisced with a different kind of smile on her face.

Now, we were making headway, so I went straight to the next name on the list. "Nelson Rockefeller, Mayor of New York," I announced.

"He was kind of like Teddy Kollek. He was just so pleasant and accommodating. We met at the airport in New York. We were all there to greet someone, I don't remember who, but I was there representing the Chamber of Commerce and Mr. Rockefeller was there with his wife Happy. We sat for quite a while and just chatted. He was always asking if we needed anything or wanted anything. A very polite man and his wife was very nice," Anni finished matter-of-factly once again.

"Arnold Palmer." Another name thrown to her memories.

"That was really special. Charlie and I had gone to the Westchester Country Club and while we were there, we saw Mr. Palmer practicing. There was one of the security staff hanging around so I asked if it would be okay if I went over to get an autograph. The guard told me, 'No, he is practicing and doesn't like to be disturbed and he doesn't give autographs.' Well, about that time he looked over and I guess he could pretty well tell what was going on. He just shouted over, 'Come on over, honey,' just like that and the guard let me through. I had a program in my hand so I gave it to him with a pen and he signed it for me. He was very gracious and I know he didn't have to do it or didn't usually do it. It made the day for Charlie and I both and many times after that. It was a kind gesture. That was in the 70s." Anni concluded.

I looked at my list with bated breath for this one. I had already heard it a few times and it was one of my favorites. "Ok, Anni here's a good one," I stated, grinning, "Henry Ford, II."

"Oh boy, that one. I was in East Hampton and my girlfriend Janet and I pulled into a grocery store. It was in 1961 and I think it was a Saturday morning. She had her two children and I had George and Jeffrey with us. So we all went inside and when we got back to the car, it wouldn't start. I got out and started looking all over and under trying to find out how to open the stupid hood. I couldn't figure the darn thing out and was getting really frustrated. The kids were in the back seat and kept getting more restless. I was getting to my wit's end and Janet was just as lost as I was. We didn't know anything about cars but how to drive them. After a short while of looking at all the stuff I didn't know what was what, some man comes over and says, 'Can I help you ladies?' My first response was, 'Do you know anything about cars?' He answered, 'A little, it's probably a minor thing.' Well, he had no problems with the hood, he popped it right open and started to fiddle around, then after a short while he told me to try starting it. I told him he needed to put the hood down first to be safe. Then he said, 'No, just try to start it, I want to see.' After a few tries it finally started and I was ever so grateful. I had already put a quarter in my pocket while he was fiddling with it to thank him for being so kind. The car was running and I just kept telling him thank you and tried to give him the quarter but he absolutely refused it. That was when he told me, 'Actually, my company made this car. I'm Henry Ford.' Janet was so embarrassed she just hid inside. I didn't know what to say. I just told him thank you again. I felt so silly trying to give him that quarter," Anni finished, a smile shining in her eyes.

I looked down at my list and told Anni, "Alright, this next one is a little different but I think it is good to put it in the book." It isn't quite an "Anni meeting," so to speak, but it fits and applies well in this chapter. "Paul Newman," I prompted the story.

"That was in the 80s in Sag Harbor. Every Sunday morning Charlie would drive me to church. He would let me out and then drive over to the Harbor and park along with some of the other men or people along the waterfront. Sometimes they would back their cars in side by side or front first. Charlie was always good about making sure I got to church, but it was his only day to rest and he would go read the newspaper where he parked. It was kind of a man thing in those days. You could see them pull up beside each other and never get out of their cars. They would just chat from their cars door to door. Most of the time Charlie would just go however he got dressed and in those days that was anything laying around. I mean he would go in shorts and a jacket, pajama bottoms, a shirt and sweater, even went with shoes that didn't match. He didn't care, he was comfortable and nobody was going to see him anyhow. Well, he pulled in on a Sunday as sort of usual and he was beside Paul Newman. The two of them just sat there and chatted. This went on several times I guess while Mr. Newman was in New York. Charlie thought I would like to meet him and even tried to get me to skip church and go over one Sunday. I said, 'No thanks, I will see him in his movies,' and left it at that. Charlie always seemed to enjoy that because he said it was just normal guys talking and nobody seemed to make a big deal of it."

"OK," I stated, looked back at the list and readied my pen for notes again. "Joe Lewis," I read off as if it were a roll call.

"Yes, that was in 1963 and it was right after Jeffrey died. I was pretty much out of it at the time, but Inter Flora or FTD had already made arrangements for me to be at a show or presentation in Hamburg, Germany. I was supposed to be a tri-lingual translator and introduce the artists, commentate and describe the arrangements. They said it would do me good to get away and put me in first class. It was on one of those planes where you sit downstairs but with a spiral staircase leading up to a bar. While we were in flight I couldn't just sit there so I went up the stairs to look around. I went up to the bar and sat down. Just really to look. While I sat there, the bartender came over to me and says, 'Do you know who that is sitting behind you?' and before I could even answer, he says, 'Joe Lewis, the boxer.' Before I could get a word out the bartender came around and sort of introduces me. 'Ma'am, this is Mr. Joe Lewis,' he says and then leaves. Mr. Lewis asked me to please have a seat and said, 'And who is it I have the pleasure of meeting?' so I gave him my name. He asked if I would like a drink but I said no, then said a glass of wine. He was very polite and we chatted a little about things and that was it. I went back downstairs."

By this time, even though for months I have known these names and the stories, I find myself still amazed at how nonchalantly Anni takes these things. It would be something special for some of us to meet just one or even two people in her fashion, but the list isn't finished. In fact, there are those that we cannot fit into the project. I press forward.

"Engelbert Humperdinck." I speak after stretching and taking a second to regroup.

"That was in the 70s. We got a call from the 'Englettes Fan Club'. It was a group of ladies that were very devoted fans of Engelbert Humperdinck's music and, of course, to him. They had done business with the shop in the past whenever he [Humperdinck] was in town or doing a show. On this occasion, he was performing at the Lincoln Center in New York. At that time the National Florist Organization had come up with a special kind of rose called 'Cara Mia' and it was sort of dedicated to Engelbert Humperdinck. Especially by the Englettes.

We were asked if we could provide three dozen of the roses in a bouquet and a bottle of brandy for him. We said sure, it would be no problem. So I got the arrangement made up and a couple of the ladies went with me by car to the Lincoln Center. It was about an hour before he was going on stage. We had no problem getting in and we were taken to the backstage dressing room. He just said, 'Come on in girls!' like that. We went in and presented him with the bouquet and the brandy and he was very thankful and kind. He was still in his robe waiting to go out on stage in a short while. He made small talk with us for a nice visit. It came close to time for him to go out, so we left the room. Shortly after that, he went out on stage with the bouquet of roses in his hand and said thank you to all his fans and especially the Englettes for providing him with such a special surprise. He was very gentlemanly and humble. It was a real treat," Anni closed out the story.

I took another look down at my list and, if it was kind of a "save the best for last situation," it wasn't planned. But one of Anni's favorites was indeed the last on the list for tonight. As I mentioned before, there are others but you will have to ask her about those.

"Guy Lombardo," I practically exclaimed, smiling. That made Anni smile and start right in with a fresh look of memory lane on her face.

"That was in 1974. He [Guy Lombardo] owned a restaurant in Freeport Long Island, New York. It was a huge place and very beautiful. Right on the water channel leading out into the ocean. For the past three years, Charlie had been on the organization committee for the New York Long Island FTD Regional Dance. It was for all the florist and business people of FTD in the upper states. That last year, Charlie was the chairman of the dinner dance and he arranged for it to be at Mr. Lombardo's restaurant. Everyone was gathered outside for the dinner and all sorts of arrangements had been made. It was very formal and elegant. A big dance area and white linen tablecloths. After awhile, when everyone was kind of settled in and the cocktail party had started, the orchestra came out on the stage and Mr. Lombardo came out after they were seated. He welcomed everyone to his restaurant and introduced his band, the Royal Canadians, behind him.

"He was very cheerful and told everyone to make themselves comfortable and to have a good time. He was jovial and told everyone not to worry that he was going to be there all night. He complimented everyone on the floral arrangements for the tables and started up the Orchestra. They played a few songs and took their breaks. Eventually, at one point in there, he passed the baton over to someone else and headed straight for the table where Charlie and I were sitting. I guess he knew Charlie was the chairman. He looked at Charlie and asked, 'May I dance with your wife?' Of course Charlie thought it was wonderful and said yes. When we got to the dance floor he asked me if I had a favorite song I would like them to play. All I could say was, just the right thing, 'All of your songs are my favorite.' He just laughed. He danced with several of the other women there that night. He was a very charming and elegant man," she concluded, still beaming over the fact that she could even say that she once danced with Guy Lombardo. But just like that, Anni was back to looking as if it weren't a big deal again. Just keeping it simple but factual and sticking to the truth. It is a very disarming quality that she possesses.

Funny thing about Anni. If you hang around with her long enough, you eventually get to meet some people yourself. It is amazing to watch and see how it happens. It is practically never anticipated, it just happens to her. During the time of our working on this project and my research and writing, we took a three-week trip to Europe. Anni wanted to see home again, I wanted to see Luxembourg with my own eyes and we had a couple of invitations to meet with some interesting people. I don't think I could do justice to this chapter without making note of a very special meeting that I had, and would not have had but for Anni. Of course, she didn't tell me a lot about who I was to meet. In her mind, it was her cousin and her husband. Hary and Elise Diedreich. The names didn't ring a bell to me. Just some nice, distant family members where she would stay while we were in town.

Writing a biography calls for many, many long hours of research and much fact gathering as well as surrounding information elements. During my studies of Luxembourg, World War II and so much history, I felt as though I had earned my master's degree, I came across some men that were very, very special. I am from a very military-oriented family. Most the men in our family have served in one branch or the other and in most conflicts or wars since World War II. Some of us have served with very elite units and know what it takes to get to certain levels in military life and combat. During my studies, I came across a particular group of men called the "Brigade De Piron." It was mostly made up of Belgium men. However, it also included men from Luxembourg who had enormously great national pride and were amazingly brave to say the least. I rank them among the elites of history such as the Normandy Rangers, the Vietnam-era Green Berets and the French Foreign Legionnaires. I was intrigued by their stories and heroics, yet they had very little recognition on an international or world level such as the others mentioned. Out of thirteen hundred Luxembourg men in the Brigade only eight remained alive.

Hary Diedrich was one of those eight. I could not believe my ears as we sat at the table and, through Anni's interpretation, recalled his past. He was such a kind, gentle looking man, approximately eighty-three years young. He still had a distinguishing twinkle in his eyes and a smile that made you think he was going to laugh at any moment. I had met a real hero. At least, he was to me, now. Hary told me how it went for many men like himself in Luxembourg during the occupation by the Nazis. They were told to either serve in the German Army or they and their families could suffer hardship leading to death. Hary was inducted into the German Artillery and sent to Africa to fight the British and American forces. It was there that he displayed and exemplified the spirit and pride that lies in the heart of a true Luxembourger. These are some very amazingly wonderful people.

Hary waited out some time while the fighting was at its worse in the desert battlefield. He defected during the night from his position and, against astronomical odds, avoided being killed by the Germans for escaping or being killed by the British soldiers that he surrendered to. It was a tremendous act of bravery. He could have stayed and fought as he was forced to do and just hope to live through it. But that wasn't Hary and he was Luxembourger not German. After he surrendered to the British, he was taken back to Great Britain, where he would be tried and exonerated. Thus, he went from German soldier to prisoner of war and then became a part of an elite unit with the British Commandos. The small band of men from Belgium and Luxembourg would lead with the first wave of assaults on the beaches at Normandy on D-day, June 6, 1944.

He was used as a guide and translator as land was taken by the Allies. He eventually was branched off into the Luxembourg Artillery units that would fire twenty-five pounders, as they called them. He fought from Africa to Normandy, through France, his homeland of Luxembourg and up to Belgium. He was one of a very few. He lived. He was and is still greeted and honored by his country and its leaders, particularly the Grand Duke of Luxembourg, with whom he served. He is a man that I never would have met had it not been for Anni. He is a man that I will always remember. He showed me his medals, his pictures and his awards. But most of all, he showed me kindness and courtesy. He made me feel as though he were honored by my presence. Thank you Anni for introducing me to one of my lifetime heroes. To meet him person-to-person and talk with him will forever be one of my most memorable moments in life.

# Conclusion: The Butterfly of Luxembourg (Part II)

*"Father God, as I place my hands on this keyboard, let me play it like a piano. Let me write the words you have given me. I put myself aside and ask you to give me the words. This is yours, not mine. Use me to do justice to this work and to write it the way you would have me. Let it be all that you purpose and desire. Let it give hope to those you have predestined. Let it light a fire that burns in the day and night as a beacon to direct those lost in the dark to your Son, Jesus. Show the world, through this writing, that He is King of kings and Lord of lords. I pray that this writing goes forth to a world that needs to know hope and the truth that one faithful servant's life can impact millions. Father, how grateful we are and how thankful I am."*

*The Meeting of Anni Adams: The Butterfly of Luxembourg.* At one moment in time, on April 16, 2003, I walked into a flower shop that I had known for several years. It had been some time since I had been there and what happened can only be explained as inexplicable. For seven months I have prayed the words above or similar. Never the same but basically to the same effect. I never wanted to write anything less than God's best. Maybe not the perfection that He is, but at least the best that I could hope for and that is what this whole project is about: Hope.

On that day of unannounced visit, at a time tied to my schedule as an excuse to "get away" and forget my miserable life, I entered a safe haven. A place where I could pop in and seclude myself from the bad things in life and stand at a counter in a flower shop where everything around represents people thinking of people. Where loves are shared, sympathies expressed and madness amended. There is great solace in a flower shop. I expected to be only a few minutes and wished to gather the arrangement for my sister (who I didn't think deserved it at the time, it was just an excuse), then get back to my car where I could drive slowly for miles and be alone. It didn't work that way. I had been praying. Things were not well with me at all. I had no desire to live and yet knew I had to because of my son, my mother and my family. At the counter, Anni looked up my card in the file and found it. I had presented my card for its monthly punch showing that I had got what I paid for months ago. As she spoke, I noticed the accent, just as everyone else does—and it is the bane of the woman's life. I thought it to be German because of my years in Germany stationed as an American soldier.

For the brief moment, even in my deep and dark melancholy mood, I was pulled from my own dark tunnel to deep-rooted images and memories of a time when I was younger and king of the world. A time when I had brothers-in-arms that were stronger than blood and guts. Young guns willing to die for each other and fight for each other in combat or bars and then laugh about it all. We were giants. We were soldiers of the most elite. We were kind, gentle, loving and caring to the weak and poor. To the right and just, we gave honor; but to those we saw as evil, deceitful, abusive or crude, we had no mercy. It wasn't just our job, it was a time in our lives. If you fell into the second category, we would utterly break, beat, crush and destroy you. We were the ones there for this reason, bought, paid for, owned and trained by our country's government. There for a season.

In a light moment from my own worries and in a vacuum of escape, I took the plunge and spoke the language that had been endeared to me with memories. "Do you speak German?" I asked in the native tongue. What followed was a fast-paced recital that flew over my head and left me nodding and smiling. "What have I done?" I thought to myself. I can hardly speak the language anymore and this woman is fluent. She is no dummy, she is sharp and I underestimated her. I thought she was just another older woman in Florida, most likely retired and living on a small pension. Husband long gone and working for the extra wages.

She smiled at me and took my thoughts away from myself; my interest was piqued. Although she did not care for the German language, she kindly explained to me that she was from Luxembourg. She didn't say she was from Arizona. She didn't say she was from Florida or New York. Not even from the United States. She said she was from Luxembourg. After fifty-seven years, she was still from Luxembourg as if the *Vulcania* were still idling in port at New York harbor waiting for her to close the shop, pack her bags and go home. I was entranced and entwined into the experience. This was no ordinary woman. She seemed so meek and mild, with not much indication of having lived beyond the lower levels of life. The brilliant contrast was hidden behind the facade of the outward appearance. She was a gem, a jewel, a treasure of history and life. She was a living legend and I was talking to her. She was humble in her own protective and secretive way.

She queried me about my life, my job, my experiences and how I had come to know the German language. I found myself sharing my own life's short history and knew immediately that it was absolutely as pale as a bedsheet bleached by the noonday sun on a Georgia summer day. As my inquisitive side took over, and for want of a laugh and a respite from the world outside, I listened, questioned and listened again. This woman was remarkable to say the least. She wasn't sharing the whole story, this much I knew from my legal experience. But she was giving me nuggets of gold for my imagination of what life was like for her and what it was like in her "day."

Nazis, I thought( like most people), were persecutors only of those that were enemies or Jews. I had no concept of what they had done to the countries they occupied. I had heard of French resistance and Belgium underground fighters, but, where in the world was Luxembourg? I never knew that an entire country, small in size, yet large in pride, had been trodden under the boots of tyranny. She was every bit as much a survivor as those that were taken to work camps and worse. I listened and was astonished. "You must have some awesome stories to tell!" I invoked. "Yes, well, my grandson, Brian, keeps telling me, 'Grandma, you should write a book.'"

In that moment, and I still don't know why, I reached to my wallet and pulled out my business card. My paralegal business. I told her I could write the story if she were willing to try. I had no clue as to what I would do but I knew it was worth trying. For several days I heard nothing and forgot about it basically. In fact, when I did think of it, I thought I was crazy for even making such an offer. I wouldn't know where to begin other than with my legal training on gathering information. Several days later, Anni called. "Mr. Story, I decided I would like to take your offer," she said. We made arrangements and met for our first, and most awkward, interview on April 26, 2003. It was the first, last and only time I used a tape recorder. I didn't need it.

We went from formal interview to riveting conversation and I took notes. Her recollection and memory were astounding. She gave me more than I could digest but I would certainly not forget her tales of truth from times past. How could one person have lived such a life, lived through so much and be here in such humble surroundings and appearing so innocuous. She was a fountain of memories, a golden treasure of life and yet she was "just some older woman" to a stranger in a store, or a visitor in a flower shop. She was no "old lady," in fact, my first impression was that she was in her late fifties. Only after delicate inquiry did I discover that she exceeded that by more than twenty years! Remarkable, amazing, boggling is the only way to describe it. I, like many others for decades, had met Anni Jeanne Neuman Adams. It was time for the world to know her and all that she represents.

Having said that, I had to ask myself, "What does she represent?" As I sit here writing this text, it becomes abundantly clear. What makes Anni unique is the fact that she was a seventy-six-year-old "nobody" when I met her. At least, in her own eyes. She was "just average" as she described herself. She repeatedly told me how she was no one special and that this was all crazy, I should be writing about someone famous. Well, I could do that, I could have done that, but it wasn't where I was supposed to be and I knew it. Sometimes I had to ask myself the same question. Now that I have come this far, the answers are finally coming clear.

First of all, Anni certainly isn't a "nobody." In fact, none of us is. Secondly, Anni was "everyone" and that is something most of us aren't. She was the child in us that dared to cross the street to see the gypsies in Marseille. She was the young child in us, charged with many chores that bore soreness into the bone, as she performed family duties that would now violate child labor laws. She was a person, man, woman, child, in utter fear for her life and the life of her family as she raced across a field on a spring day deafened by ringing ears from the blasts and flood of flying dirt as bombers sought out to kill the hunted on the ground like rabbits in front of a dozen shotguns.

Anni has been the "everyone" of us that has aspired to or dreamed of living a full life. Not all in riches and glory or even fame, but a life that says, "This was well-lived and loved, through all the pain, sorrows, joys and hopes," a life lived. The words are a contrast in so many of us that we forget and don't even notice. We can all, as humankind, live; but very few of us have the precious experience of having a "life."

In all of this, Anni constantly asked me what I wanted out of it. My answer then was as it is now: "Anni, I just want to have a life again." By God's grace and the meeting of Anni Adams, I do. Whether it is through this book, this writing, this experience, or all of it, I know that I have another chance with a prayer and hope. Who does Anni represent? She represents all of us, every man, woman, boy and girl on this planet. She had experiences that many of us will never know. She missed things that many of us have experienced. She was a person who loved someone and married that person. She had her questions and doubts but she remained faithful, loyal and true. Because of that, her integrity, she was rewarded. She can look up at the sky and see a vapor trail on any given day and know that Jeffrey is talking to Jesus about her. She can see a ceramic rabbit on a shelf and know that Charlie is watching her, guarding her and protecting her. She can answer the phone and know that her grandsons love her when a voice on the other side says, "Ma, what are you doing?" That would be the voice of George. Still watching his mother and keeping charge as he promised his father he would do.

She leaves the blinds open now when a thunderstorm rolls over her Florida home because someone finally got through to her that it was a silly thing to worry about. Instead, she turns the music up and dances along the tile floor. Is she crazy? Absolutely not. No more than all the people she represents. Those that have been hungry for months and had a feast. Those that have held death in their arms and laughed a year later. Those that have had lavish banquets and dances into the night only to have tears flow the following morning. She represents all the ups and downs of this thing called life. She met people whose names many of us would recognize but the irony is, "Would they know who they met?" They met the whole of mankind wrapped in a steel body and gentle wings. A beautiful creature so elusive that she is indeed the only butterfly that can re-enter the cocoon. Had they been afforded the opportunity to see inside the cocoon, they would have found that she even represented them. It is one thing to be a "somebody"—that is nice at times: rich and full of pride and reward. But for all the "somebodies," this remarkable Butterfly of Luxembourg was, just like her beloved small country, an "everybody." No one taking any great notice, and all the while, the most important impact on others was being made with one solid letter of character: A positive attitude.

Anni is far from done and this story is far from over. This is just the beginning of letting the world see something they may have missed for the past seventy-seven years. A little girl-child born in a distant and small country who literally circled the globe on flight of delicate wings. With a sensitive heart, non-judging opinion and encouragement to all who would accept it, she was and is a lady of honesty and character. From the time she first burst forth into this world in 1926 on Armistice Day, a day dedicated to peace, she became a menagerie of all of us. Our personalities, aspirations, frailties, strengths, dreams and endurance. She represented over 300,000 war brides, as well as men who were veterans of war; she too saw it firsthand. The suffrage as a victim of all sorts of evil and a light in many, many dark rooms. She has wallpapered the planet with more flowers than we could imagine and her art was from her spirit. Charlie was the florist but Anni was the flower and her bloom has not wilted nor faded. She remains an eternal instrument to show what can be done if one never loses the most valuable gift we have, and that is hope. She kept her hope, she kept her faith, she kept her integrity and withstood all the harsh winds and gentle breezes. The most important thing of all, she will tell you is: "I always walked close to God and He never let me down."

# *The Meeting of Anni Adams*
# Order Form

**Postal orders:** 739 Orchard Ave.
Ormond Beach, FL

**Telephone orders:** 386-673-7791

**E-mail orders:** www.lonniestory.com

**Please send *The Meeting of Anni Adams* to:**

Name: ______________________________

Address: ______________________________

City: ____________________ State: __________

Zip: ____________ Telephone: (_____) ____________

**Book Price: $20.95**

**Shipping:** $3.00 for the first book and $1.00 for each additional book to cover shipping and handling within US, Canada, and Mexico. International orders add $6.00 for the first book and $2.00 for each additional book.

**Or order from:**
**ACW Press**
**85334 Lorane Hwy**
**Eugene, OR 97405**

**(800) 931-BOOK**

or contact your local bookstore